AGREEMENTS OF THE PEOPLE'S REPUBLIC OF CHINA

AGREEMENTS OF THE PEOPLE'S REPUBLIC OF CHINA

A Calendar of Events 1966-1980

Hungdah Chiu

PRAEGER

PRAEGER SPECIAL STUDIES • PRAEGER SCIENTIFIC

Library of Congress Cataloging in Publication Data

080619

Chiu, Hungdah, 1936-
   Agreements of the People's Republic of China,
1966-80.

   Includes indexes.
   1. China--Foreign relations--Treaties. I. Title.
JX926 1981.C48   341'.0264'51   81-8686
ISBN 0-03-059443-X   AACR2

Published in 1981 by Praeger Publishers
CBS Educational and Professional Publishing
A Division of CBS, Inc.
521 Fifth Avenue, New York, NY 10175 USA

123456789 145 987654321
Printed in the United States of America

PREFACE AND INTRODUCTION

In 1968, a volume entitled <u>Agreements of the People's Republic of China 1949-1967, A Calendar</u>, compiled jointly by Professor Douglas Johnston and me, was published by Harvard University Press, and was warmly received both inside and outside the academic community. Since then, I have received numerous requests for annual supplements to that volume. Because of the high cost of printing, however, it was not possible to publish such annual supplements. Rather, I decided to wait a number of years and compile a second volume of the Calendar. The present volume is therefore intended to continue the earlier Calendar up to the end of 1980. [1] When the previous Calendar was published in 1968, the official People's Republic of China treaty series for 1966-67 had not yet been published, so it was not possible to consult that source. However, the PRC treaty series for 1966-67 was finally published in 1973, revealing several agreements not included in the earlier Calendar. Thus I have decided to begin this volume with the year 1966.

Although the format of this volume is essentially the same as that employed in the earlier Calendar, I have attempted to take into consideration users' or reviewers' suggestions for ways to improve it. For instance, the date of the <u>Survey of China Mainland Press</u> is now included in the source, and I have used calendar year rather than revolutionary year (i. e. , 1st October to 30th September). This volume includes all official and semiofficial exchanges of commitments involving the PRC, in their widest sense, between 1966 and 1980. Thus, this calendar includes not only every entry in the PRC's official treaty series and every PRC agreement listed in any other national treaty series available to me, but also other classes of documents which seem to meet the test of evidencing an official or semiofficial exchange of commitments involving the PRC. Commitments that are wholly unilateral in function, such as the claim to the continental shelf, are excluded, but not those that are unilateral in substance but bilateral in form, such as gifts. Also, commitments that involve only subnational entities, such as provinces or cities, are generally excluded. The inclusion of some "semiofficial agreements" is the result of a peculiarity of PRC international practice. Because some countries do not have diplomatic relations with the PRC, the latter has at times acted through nominally unofficial organizations, such as the China Fishery Association, to conclude agreements with similar organizations of other countries. Some of these agreements were included in the appendixes of PRC's official treaty series. Now that most countries have established diplomatic relations with the PRC, the resort to semiofficial agreements has become less frequent. When confronted with difficult problems of inclusion, it has been unavoidable that some decisions on inclusion be arbitrary.

To avoid unnecessary duplication I have excluded instruments for ratification of an agreement which is already entered in the calendar at the date of signing. However, such information on ratification is usually noted in the place where the agreement is listed. In the earlier Calendar, agreements to establish diplomatic relations were excluded. In this volume, I have decided to include them in response to suggestions made by users and in view of the fact that the PRC has since 1971 included such documents in its official treaty series.

Until January 1, 1979, all PRC English publications used the Wade-Giles system for transliterating Chinese names, places, and publications. Since then, the Chinese have used the Pinyin (transcription) system. However, for reasons of consistency, this Calendar has used the Wade-Giles system. For the convenience of the user, I have included a table on Wade-Giles-Pinyin conversion.

The format of this Calendar is as follows:

(1) Sequence: All entries, regardless of their nature, are listed chronologically by the date of signing or issue. Where the sources show a discrepancy in the reported date of signing that cannot be resolved by reference to the text, I have decided to accept the date reported in the most authoritative source of information available (for the sequence of available sources in each treaty item, see below). If the date remains doubtful or unavailable, then a question mark (?) is inserted. To facilitate cross-referencing within the Calendar, I have numbered each entry according to the sequence for each calendar year. For example, the cross-reference number of the eighty-fourth entry listed in 1973 is 73-84.

(2) Effective date: The effective date, listed immediately after the date of signing or issue, is the date from which the agreement is reported to be effective. A dash in the text indicates that the effective date is not reported. In the absence of evidence to the contrary, the effective date and the date of entry into force are presumed to be the same. When the listed effective date is earlier than the listed date of signing, this means that the agreement has been made retroactively effective, as in the case of many trade agreements. In most cases where no effective date is listed, because no effective date is reported in the sources available, it may be presumed that both the date of entry into force and the effective date are the same as the date of signature. Some agreements, such as joint communiqués, are never

signed or issued subject to ratification, so it may be presumed that their entry into force is automatic upon signature or issuance.

(3) <u>Ratification</u>: Under the 1954 Constitution of the PRC, the standing Committee of the National People's Congress (NPC) exercises the power "to decide on the ratification or abrogation of treaties concluded with foreign states" (Article 31, paragraph 12). After the decision of the Standing Committee of the NPC, the chairman of the PRC ratifies the treaty (Article 41). In 1968, however, the chairman of the PRC, Liu Shao-ch'i, was purged, and for many years that position remained vacant. In the 1975 PRC Constitution, the position of chairman of the PRC was abolished and the function of ratifying treaties was entrusted to the Standing Committee of the NPC alone (Article 18). The 1978 Constitution provides that, while the Standing Committee of the NPC shall "decide" on the ratification or abrogation of treaties (Article 25, paragraph 9), it is the chairman of the Standing Committee of the NPC who shall "ratify" treaties (Article 26, paragraph 1). Agreements not subject to ratification may be required to be submitted to State Council (Cabinet) for approval; such a requirement is usually provided in the agreement itself.

(4) <u>Place of signature or issuance</u>: Where reported, the place of signature or issuance has been entered immediately before the non-Chinese treaty partner. In some cases, a dash has been inserted to indicate that the place is not known.

(5) <u>Multilateral agreements</u>: In response to users' suggestion, all multilateral agreements in this volume have been separately listed. To facilitate cross-referencing, I have numbered each multilateral entry according to the order of sequence of PRC's accession or ratification to those agreements. The reference number starts with M.

(6) <u>Subject matter</u>: In general, I have described the subject matter of each agreement in accordance with the official Chinese title of the document as given in official treaty series (TYC) or People's Daily (JMJP). Some titles have been abbreviated for economy of space. For the convenience of readers, the contents of joint communiqués have been summarized.

(7) <u>Sources</u>: The sources used are of different kinds. The citations to these sources have been arranged in order, more or less by the degree of authoritativeness of the source from the presumed point of view of the PRC. Based on this criterion, first place is given to untranslated official and semiofficial PRC sources (TYC,[2] JMJP); second place to official PRC sources translated into English by the PRC (NCNA, PR[3]); third place to official PRC sources translated into English outside the PRC (SCMP, FBIS); fourth place to the official international treaty series (UNTS) and to official or unofficial sources other than the PRC (Aust. T. S; JAIL; NYIL; YBCC, etc.). References to NCNA are intended to be supplementary only, since it covers the

same original sources as SCMP. The SCMP is the most useful English language source generally available. (After October 1973, it was renamed as Survey of PRC Press. For purposes of continuity, however, I still use the same abbreviation.) Unfortunately, SCMP ceased to publish in September 1977. For agreement entries appearing after that date, I have used the Foreign Broadcasting Information Service (FBIS). Where the full text is available at the source, an initial, in parentheses, indicates the language in which the text is given. For instance, (C) means the Chinese language text is available in the source cited and (E) means the English text is available in the source cited. If a summary of the text is available, it will be represented by "sum.," following the symbol of the language text. For instance, (E. Sum.) means an English summary is available in the source cited. References not followed by an initial indicate that the information given at the source is limited. In many of these cases there is little to be learned by consulting the source beyond what is already provided in the calendar entry.

In the course of compiling this volume, I was ably assisted by Dr. Jyh-pin Fa, formerly of the University of Virginia Law School, and now with the National Chengchi University in the Republic of China. I am also grateful to Prof. Douglas M. Johnston for providing PRC treaty information he collected between 1968 and 1973, Mr. Nien-tsu Tzou for checking SCMP between 1969 and 1973, Dr. Ying-jeou Ma for checking October-December 1980 People's Daily, Mr. David Salem for checking 1980 FBIS, and Mrs. Sheue-jiau Wang for compiling the drafts of tables. The tedious work of typing and proofreading were ably performed by Lu Ann Young, Shaiw-chei Yin, Julia Fang, and Guey-ching Lee Liaw, to whom I would like to express my sincere thanks.

NOTES

1. The listing of 1979-80 agreements should be considered tentative because of a pressing publication schedule. For that reason Tables 1 to 4 would only cover the period 1966-1978.
2. Only six volumes are now published: Vols. 15 (1966-67), 16 (1968-69), 17 (1970), 18 (1971), 19 (1972), and 20 (1973).
3. Since January 1, 1979, renamed as Beijing Review.

CONTENTS

Page

PREFACE AND INTRODUCTION   v

ABBREVIATIONS   xi

WADE-GILES-PINYIN CONVERSION TABLE   xiii

CALENDAR OF BILATERAL TREATIES   3

CALENDAR OF MULTILATERAL TREATIES   213

TABLE 1—Topical Distribution of PRC Agreements, 1966–78   222

TABLE 2—National Treaty Contacts with PRC: 1966–78   223

TABLE 3—Topical Distribution of Agreements Listed in
      PRC Official Treaty Series (TYC), 1966–73   227

TABLE 4—National Distribution of Agreements Listed in
      PRC Offfcial Treaty Series (TYC), 1966–73   229

APPENDIX: Questionable Agreements   235

INDEX: Bilateral and Trilateral Agreements by Partners   249

      Bilateral Agreements with International Organizations   315

      Agreements by Subject Matter   319

ABOUT THE AUTHOR   331

ABBREVIATIONS

A - Arabic	C - Chinese	E - English
Fr - French	G - German	It - Italian

Note: Following a citation, the abbreviations above mean that the full text of the agreement is available in that source in the language indicated.

Sources

AfD	Africa Diary (New Delhi)
AfR	African Recorder (New Delhi)
AsR	Asian Recorder (New Delhi)
Australian T. S.	Australian Treaty Series (Canberra)
BEVANS	Charles I. Bevans, Treaties and Other International Agreements of the United States of America, 1776-1949
British T. S.	British Treaty Series (London)
Canadian T. S.	Canadian Treaty Series (Ottawa)
CB	Current Background (U. S. Consulate, Hong Kong)
CCD	Communist China Digest (Joint Publications Research Service)
CDSP	Current Digest of Soviet Press (New York)
DSB	Department of State Bulletin
FBIS	Foreign Broadcast Information Service (Washington, D. C.)
FTS (SAS)	Suomen Asetuskokoelman Sopimussarja (Finnish Statute-book and Treaty Series in Finnish; Helsinki)
ICAOCAR	Annual Report of the Council of International Civil Aviation Organization (Montreal)
ICAODOC	International Civil Aviation Organization Document (Montreal)
ILM	International Legal Materials (American Society of International Law, Washington, D. C.)
IYIL	Italian Yearbook of International Law (Rome)
JAIL	Japanese Annual of International Law (Tokyo)
JMJP	Jen-min jih-pao (People's Daily; Peking)
JPRS	Joint Publications Research Service (Washington, D. C.)
JRF	Jounal Officiel de la Republique Francaise (Paris)

KCTYC	Kuo-chi t'iao-yueh-chi (International Treaty Series; Peking)
MTSGPDF	Multilateral Treaties in respect of which the Secretary-General Performs Depositary Functions (United Nations)
NCNA(E)	New China (Hsin-hua) News Agency (English language service), Daily news release (Peking)
NYT	New York Times
NYIL	Netherlands Yearbook of International Law (Amsterdam)
NZ T. S.	New Zealand Treaty Series (Wellington)
PakDS	Pakistan Document Series (Pakistan Embassy, Washington, D. C.)
PYIL	Philippine Yearbook of International Law (Manila)
RFDA	Revue Francaise de Droit Aerien (Paris)
RI	Relazioni Internazionali (Milan)
SCMP	Survey China Mainland Press (U. S. Consulate, Hong Kong)
STAT	United States Statute at Large
TIAS	Treaties and Other International Acts Series (Washington, D. C.)
Trb	Tractatenblad van het Roninkrijk der Nederlanden
T. S.	Treaty Series (U. S.)
TYC	Chung-hua jen-min kung-ho-kuo t'iao-yueh-chi (Compilation of treaties of People's Republic of China; Peking)
UN Reg. N.	United Nations Treaty Registration Number (New York)
UNTS	United Nations Treaty Series
UNYB	United Nations Yearbook
UST	United States Treaties and Other International Acts Series (Washington, D. C.)
YBCC	Yearbook on Chinese Communism (Chung-kung nien pao, Taipei)
ZD	Zbior Dokumentow (Collection of Documents; Polski Instytut Spraw Miedzynarodowych, Warsaw)
ZRGGG	ZHONGHUA RENMIN GONGHEGUO GUOWUYUAN GONGBAO (Gazette of the State Council of the People's Republic of China)

WADE-GILES-PINYIN
CONVERSION TABLE

Wade-Giles	Pinyin	Wade-Giles	Pinyin
a	a	ching	jing
at	ai	ch'ing	qing
an	an	chiu	jiu
ang	ang	ch'iu	qiu
ao	ao	chiung	jiong
		ch'iung	qiong
cha	zha	cho	zhuo
ch'a	cha	ch'o	chuo
chai	zhai	chou	zhou
ch'ai	chai	ch'ou	chou
chan	zhan	chu	zhu
ch'an	chan	ch'u	chu
chang	zhang	chua	zhua
ch'ang	chang	ch'ua	chua
chao	zhao	chuai	zhuai
ch'ao	chao	ch'uai	chuai
che	zhe	chuan	zhuan
ch'e	che	ch'uan	chuan
chci	zhci	chuang	zhuang
chen	zhen	ch'uang	chuang
ch'en	chen	chui	zhiu
cheng	zheng	ch'ui	chui
ch'eng	cheng	chung	zhun
chi	ji	ch'un	chun
ch'i	qi	chung	zhong
chia	jia	ch'ung	chong
ch'ia	qia	chü	ju
chiang	jiang	ch'ü	qu
ch'iang	qiang	chüan	juan
ch'iao	qiao	ch'üan	quan
chich	jie	chüch	jue
ch'ich	qie	ch'üch	que
chien	jian	chün	jun
ch'ien	qian	ch'ün	qun
chih	zhi		
ch'ih	chi	e,o	e
chin	jin	en	en
ch'in	qin	eng	eng

Wade–Giles	Pinyin	Wade–Giles	Pinyin
erh	er	hung	hong
		huo	huo
fa	fa		
fan	fan	i, yi	yi
fang	fang		
fei	fei	jan	ran
fen	fen	jang	rang
feng	feng	jao	rao
fo	fo	je	re
fou	fou	jen	ren
fu	fu	jeng	reng
		jih	ri
ha	ha	jo	ruo
hai	hai	jou	rou
han	han	ju	ru
hang	hang	juan	ruan
hao	hao	jui	rui
hei	hei	jun	run
hen	hen	jung	rong
heng	heng		
ho	he	ka	ga
hou	hou	k'a	ka
hsi	xi	kai	gai
hsia	xia	k'ai	kai
hsiang	xiang	kan	gan
hsiao	xiao	k'an	kan
hsich	xic	kang	gang
hsien	xian	k'ang	kang
hsin	xin	kao	gao
hsing	xing	k'ao	kao
hsiu	xiu	ke, ko	ge
hsiung	xiong	k'e, k'o	ke
hsü	xu	kei	gei
hsüan	xuan	ken	gen
hsüch	xue	k'en	ken
hsün	xun	keng	geng
hu	hu	k'eng	keng
hua	hua	ko, ke	ge
huai	huai	k'o, k'e	ke
huan	huan	kou	gou
huang	huang	k'ou	kou
hui	hiu	ku	gu
hun	hun	k'u	ku

Wade-Giles	Pinyin	Wade-Giles	Pinyin
kua	gua	ma	ma
k'ua	kua	mai	mai
kuai	guai	man	man
k'uai	kuai	mang	mang
kuan	guan	mao	mao
k'uan	kuan	mei	mei
kuang	guang	men	men
k'uang	kuang	meng	meng
kuei	gui	mi	mi
k'uci	kui	miao	miao
kun	gun	mieh	mie
k'un	kun	mien	mian
kung	gong	min	min
k'ung	kong	ming	ming
kuo	guo	miu	miu
k'uo	kuo	mo	mo
		mou	mou
la	la	mu	mu
lai	lai		
lan	lan	na	na
lang	lang	nai	nai
lao	lao	nan	nan
lc	lc	nang	nang
lei	lei	nao	nao
leng	leng	nei	nei
li	li	nen	nen
lia	lia	neng	neng
liang	liang	ni	ni
liao	liao	niang	niang
lieh	lie	niao	niao
lien	lian	nieh	nie
lin	lin	nien	nian
ling	ling	nin	nin
liu	liu	ning	ning
lo	luo	niu	niu
lou	lou	no	no
lu	lu	nou	nou
luan	luan	nu	nu
lun, lün	lun	nuan	nuan
lung	long	nun	nun
lü	lü	nung	nong
lüan	lüan	nü	nü
lüeh	lüe	nüeh	nüe

Wade-Giles	Pinyin	Wade-Giles	Pinyin
o, e	e	se	se
ou	ou	sen	sen
		seng	seng
pa	ba	sha	sha
p'a	pa	shai	shai
pai	bai	shan	shan
p'ai	pai	shang	shang
pan	ban	shao	shao
p'an	pan	she	she
pang	bang	shei	shei
p'ang	pang	shen	shen
pao	bao	sheng	sheng
p'ao	pao	shih	shi
pei	bei	shou	shou
p'ei	pei	shu	shu
pen	ben	shua	shua
p'en	pen	shuai	shuai
peng	beng	shuan	shuan
p'eng	peng	shuang	shuang
pi	bi	shui	shui
p'i	pi	shun	shun
piao	biao	shuo	shuo
p'iao	piao	so	suo
pieh	bie	sou	sou
p'ieh	pie	ssu, szu	si
pien	bian	su	su
p'ien	pian	suan	suan
pin	bin	sui	sui
p'in	pin	sun	sun
ping	bing	sung	song
p'ing	ping	szu, ssu	si
po	bo		
p'o	po	ta	da
pou	bou	t'a	ta
p'ou	pou	tai	dai
pu	bu	t'ai	tai
p'u	pu	tan	dan
		t'an	tan
sa	sa	tang	dang
sai	sai	t'ang	tang
san	san	tao	dao
sang	sang	t'ao	tau
sao	sao	te	de

Wade-Giles	Pinyin	Wade-Giles	Pinyin
t'e	te	tsui	zui
tei	dei	ts'ui	cui
teng	deng	tsun	zun
t'eng	teng	ts'un	cun
ti	di	tsung	zong
t'i	ti	ts'ung	cong
tiao	diao	tu	du
t'iao	tiao	t'u	tu
tieh	die	tuan	duan
t'ieh	tie	t'uan	tuan
tien	dian	tui	dui
t'ien	tian	t'ui	tui
ting	ding	tun	dun
t'ing	ting	t'un	tun
tiu	diu	tung	dong
to	duo	t'ung	tong
t'o	tuo	tzu	zi
tou	dou	tz'u	ci
t'ou	tou		
tsa	za	wa	wa
ts'a	ca	wai	wai
tsai	zai	wan	wan
ts'ai	cai	wang	wang
tsan	zan	wei	wei
ts'an	can	wen	wen
tsang	zang	weng	weng
ts'ang	cang	wo	wo
tsao	zao	wu	wu
ts'ao	cao		
tse	ze	ya	ya
ts'e	ce	yai	yai
tsei	zei	yang	yang
tsen	zen	yao	yao
ts'en	cen	yeh	ye
tseng	zeng	yen	yan
ts'eng	ceng	yi, i	yi
tso	zuo	yin	yin
ts'o	cuo	ying	ying
tsou	zou	yu	you
ts'ou	cou	yung	yong
tsu	zu	yü	yu
ts'u	cu	yüan	yuan
tsuan	zuan	yüeh	yue
ts'uan	cuan	yün	yun

CALENDAR OF BILATERAL TREATIES

66-1   1/6/66 — PEKING   VIETNAM(N)   EXCHANGE OF NOTES
Extension of 1957 Protocol on Exchange of Goods by Local State-
Owned Trading Companies in Border Areas [57-75].
TYC 15:79(C).

66-2   1/6/66 — PEKING   VIETNAM(N)   EXCHANGE OF NOTES
Extension of 1957 Protocol on Small-Scale Trading in Border
Areas [57-76].
TYC 15:80(C).

66-3   1/16/66 — KATMANDU   NEPAL   EXCHANGE OF NOTES
Extension of 1956 Agreement on Maintenance of Friendly Relations
between PRC and Nepal, and Trade and Communication Between
Tibet Region of PRC and Nepal [56-104].
TYC 15:4(C).

66-4   1/22/66 — PEKING   JAPAN   JOINT STATEMENT
Promotion of trade, technical exchanges, exhibitions, maritime,
and other transport. Signed by representatives of China Committee
for Promotion of International Trade and Japan-China Trade Promotion Association.
JMJP 1/23/66; NCNA Peking 1/22/66; SCMP 3624:29 (1/26/66)(E).

66-5   2/1/66   1/1/6   PEKING   GUINEA   PROTOCOL
Trade for 1966.
TYC 15:13(C); JMJP 2/2/66; NCNA Peking 2/1/66; SCMP 3631:26
(2/4/66).

66-6   2/4/66   1/1/66   PEKING   CZECHOSLOVAKIA   AGREE-
MENT
Exchange of goods and payments in 1966.
TYC 15:90(C); JMJP 2/5/66; NCNA Peking 2/4/66; SCMP 3634:28
(2/9/66).

66-7   2/11/66 — PEKING   RUMANIA
1966-67 plan for cultural cooperation.
JMJP 2/12/66; NCNA Peking 2/11/66; SCMP 3639:37 (2/16/66).

66-8   2/20/66   1/1/66   PEKING   HUNGARY   AGREEMENT
Exchange of goods and payments in 1966.
TYC 15:30(C); JMJP 2/21/66; NCNA(E) 2/20/66; SCMP 3645:30
(2/25/66).

66-9   2/20/66 — PEKING   HUNGARY   PROTOCOL
General conditions for delivery of goods.
TYC 15:29(C).

66-10   2/25/66 — PYONGYANG   KOREAN(N)
1966-67 plan for cultural cooperation.
JMJP 2/27/66; NCNA Pyongyang 2/25/66; SCMP 3648:30 (3/2/66).

66-11   3/7/66 — KHARTOUM   SUDAN   PROTOCOL
Trade in 1966.
TYC 15:25(C).

66-12   3/12/66 — RANGOON   BURMA   EXCHANGE OF NOTES
Extension of 1961 Agreements on Trade and Payments [61-3, 61-6].
TYC 15:115(C).

66-13   3/16/66   1/4/66 SOFIA   BULGARIA   AGREEMENT
Exchange of goods and payments in 1966.
TYC 15:69(C); JMJP 3/17/66; NCNA Sofia 3/16/66; SCMP 3661:27
(3/21/66).

66-14   3/21/66 — HANOI   VIETNAM(N)   PROTOCOL
Border railway.
Signed at ninth meeting of Sino-Vietnamese Joint Committee on
Border Railways.
JMJP 3/23/66; NCNA Hanoi 3/22/66; SCMP 3665:41 (3/25/66).

66-15   3/22/66   1/1/66 PEKING   POLAND   AGREEMENT
Exchange of goods and payments in 1966.
TYC 15:60(C); JMJP 3/23/66; NCNA Peking 3/22/66; SCMP 3665:
38 (3/25/66).

66-16   3/22/66 — PEKING   POLAND   PROTOCOL
Extension of 1961 Protocol on General Conditions for Delivery of
Goods [61-95] to 1966.
TYC 15:59(C).

66-17   3/25/66   1/1/66 — BERLIN   GERMANY(E)   AGREEMENT
Exchange of goods and payments in 1966.
TYC 15:138(C); JMJP 3/29/66; NCNA Berlin 3/25/66; SCMP 3668:
25 (3/30/66).

66-18   3/25/66 — BERLIN   GERMANY(E)   PROTOCOL
General conditions for delivery of goods.
TYC 15:122(C).

66-19 3/28/66 1/1/66 PEKING MONGOLIA PROTOCOL
Mutual supply of goods in 1966.
TYC 15:99(C); JMJP 3/29/66; NCNA Peking 3/28/66; SCMP 3670:
34 (4/1/66).

66-20 3/28/66 — PEKING MONGOLIA PROTOCOL
General conditions for delivery of goods.
TYC 15:101(C).

66-21 3/31/66 — PEKING CAMBODIA
1966 plan for cultural and scientific cooperation.
JMJP 4/2/66; NCNA Peking 3/31/66; SCMP 3672:19 (4/5/66).

66-22 3/31/66 — RAWALPINDI PAKISTAN JOINT COMMUNIQUÉ
Talks during visit of Chairman Liu Shao-ch'i and Vice-Premier
Ch'en Yi: Kashmir, PRC representation in UN, etc.
JMJP 4/1/66(C); PR 9. 15:6 (4/8/66)(E); NCNA Peking 3/31/66;
SCMP 3672:27 (4/5/66)(E); CCD 168:101(E); PakDS 3:1:3 (June
1966)(E); RI 1966:15:399(It).

66-23 4/4/66 — MOSCOW USSR AGREEMENT
Civil air transport.
Supersedes 1954 Agreement [54-99].
TYC 15:181(C); JMJP 4/9/66; NCNA Peking 4/8/66; SCMP 3677:
53 (4/14/66); JPRS, Soviet Economic System: Current Developments 133:28; IzV 4/5/66.

66-24 4/4/66 — MOSCOW USSR EXCHANGE OF NOTES
Route problem of Agreement of Civil Air Transportation.
TYC 15:187(C).

66-25 4/8/66 — KABUL AFGHANISTAN JOINT COMMUNIQUÉ
Talks during visit of Chairman Liu Shao-ch'i and Vice Premier
Ch'en Yi: peaceful coexistence, PRC representation in UN, etc.
JMJP 4/9/66(C); PR 9. 16:5 (4/15/66)(E); NCNA Peking 4/8/66;
SCMP 3677:34 (4/14/66)(E); CCD 168:102(E); RI 1966:17:452(It).

66-26 4/8/66 4/8/66 RANGOON BURMA PROTOCOL
Purchase of rice from Burma.
TYC 15:116(C).

66-27 4/14/66 — BRAZZAVILLE CONGO (BRAZZAVILLE)
1966 plan for cultural cooperation.
JMJP 4/16/66; NCNA Brazzaville 4/14/66; SCMP 3681:23 (4/20/66).

66-28 4/19/66 — RANGOON BURMA JOINT COMMUNIQUÉ
Talks during visit of Chairman Liu Shao-ch'i and Vice Premier
Ch'en Yi: anticolonialism, PRC representation in UN, etc.
JMJP 4/20/66(C); PR 9.17:5 (4/22/66)(E); NCNA Peking 4/19/66;
SCMP 3683:27 (4/25/66)(E); CCD 171:61(E).

66-29 4/19/66 1/1/66 PEKING USSR PROTOCOL
Exchange of goods in 1966.
TYC 15:46(C); JMJP 4/20/66; NCNA Peking 4/19/66; SCMP 3683:
34 (4/25/66); JPRS, Soviet Economic System: Current Developments 137:45 Pr 4/20/66.

66-30 4/20/66 — DAMASCUS SYRIA
1966-67 plan for cultural cooperation.
JMJP 4/22/66; NCNA Damascus 4/20/66; SCMP 3684:39 (4/26/66).

66-31 4/22/66 — DAR ES SALAAM TANZANIA MEMORANDUM
Establishment of Sino-Tanzanian Maritime Transport Joint Stock
Company.
JMJP 7/9/66; NCNA Peking 7/7/66; SCMP 3736:31 (7/12/66).

66-32 4/22/66 — PEKING VIETNAM(N) PROTOCOL
Scientific and technical cooperation.
Signed at sixth meeting of Sino-Vietnamese Executive Organ for
Scientific and Technical Cooperation.
JMJP 4/24/66; NCNA Peking 4/22/66; SCMP 3685:37 (4/27/66).

66-33 4/29/66 4/29/66 PHNOM PENH CAMBODIA AGREEMENT
Economic and cultural cooperation.
TYC 15:75(C); JMJP 5/1/66; PR 9.19:5 (5/6/66); NCNA Phnom
Penh 4/29/66; SCMP 3690:26 (5/4/66); CCD 171:59.

66-34 4/30/66 — CONAKRY GUINEA
1966 plan for cultural cooperation.
JMJP 5/2/66; NCNA Conakry 4/30/66; SCMP 3691:36 (5/5/66).

66-35 4/30/66 — PEKING NORWAY
1966-67 plan for cultural exchange.
JMJP 5/2/66; NCNA Peking 4/30/66; SCMP 3690:39 (5/4/66).

66-36 May — SANAA YEMEN(N) PROTOCOL
Extension of 1964 Agreement on Economic and Technical Coopera-
tion [64-79].
AsR 7170.

66-37 5/2/66 5/2/66 PEKING NEPAL AGREEMENT
Trade, intercourse, and related questions between Nepal and the
Tibet autonomous region of PRC.
TYC 15:5(C); JMJP 5/3/66; PR 9. 20:47 (5/13/66); NCNA Peking
5/2/66; SCMP 3691:37 (5/5/66); CCD 171:64; AsR 7124.

66-38 5/4/66 — TIRANA ALBANIA PROTOCOL
Shipping.
Signed at fifth meeting of Administrative Council of Sino-Albanian
Shipping Joint Stock Company.
JMJP 5/6/66; NCNA Tirana 5/4/66; SCMP 3694:20 (5/10/66).

66-39 5/4/66 1/1/66 CAIRO UAR PROTOCOL
Trade in 1966.
TYC 15:41(C); JMJP 5/10/66; NCNA Cairo 5/4/66; SCMP 3694:
35 (5/10/66); AsR 7124.

66-40 5/7/66 — PEKING TANZANIA
1966 plan for cultural cooperation.
JMJP 5/8/66; NCNA Peking 5/7/66; SCMP 3695:50 (5/11/66).

66-41 5/7/66 — CAIRO UAR
1966-67 plan for cultural cooperation.
JMJP 5/10/66; NCNA Cairo 5/7/66; SCMP 3696:44 (5/12/66);
AfD 2920.

66-42 5/11/66 — PEKING ALBANIA JOINT STATEMENT
Talks during Premier Shehu's visit: antirevisionism, national
liberation movements, reorganization of UN, etc.
JMJP 5/15/66; PR 9. 21:5 (5/20/66)(E); NCNA Peking 5/11/66;
SCMP 3698:24 (5/16/66); CCD 171:48(E); ZD 1966:5:540 (P, E);
AsR 7160; CB 788:1(E).

66-43 5/11/66 — PEKING CZECHOSLOVAKIA
1966 plan for cultural cooperation.
JMJP 5/12/66; NCNA Peking 5/11/66; SCMP 3698:28 (5/16/66).

66-44 5/13/66 — BAMAKO MALI
1966 plan for cultural cooperation.
JMJP 5/16/66; NCNA Bamako 5/14/66; SCMP 3700:30 (5/18/66).

66-45 5/19/66 — PEKING JAPAN MINUTES
Trade talks on basis of Liao-Takasaki Memorandum [62-103].
JMJP 5/29/66(C); NCNA Peking 5/19/66; SCMP 3704:29 (5/24/66)
(E).

66-46 5/20/66 5/20/66 RABAT MOROCCO PROTOCOL (supplementary) Trade.
TYC 15:120(C); JMJP 5/22/66; NCNA Rabat 5/20/66; SCMP 3705: 27 (5/25/66); AfR 1370.

66-47 5/23/66 — SANA YEMEN(N)
1966-67 plan for cultural cooperation.
JMJP 5/25/66; NCNA Sana 5/23/66; SCMP 3707:26 (5/27/66).

66-48 5/24/66 — KABUL AFGHANISTAN
1966 plan for cultural cooperation.
JMJP 5/28/66; NCNA Kabul 5/24/66; SCMP 3708:19 (5/31/66).

66-49 5/24/66 — TIRANA ALBANIA
1966-67 plan for cooperation between PRC Academy of Sciences and State University of Tirana.
JMJP 5/28/66; NCNA Tirana 5/25/66; SCMP 3708:19 (5/31/66).

66-50 5/26/66 1/1/66 HAVANA CUBA PROTOCOL
Trade in 1966.
TYC 15:22(C); JMJP 6/2/66; NCNA Havana 5/31/66; SCMP 3712: 25 (6/6/66).

66-51 5/27/66 — HAVANA CUBA
1965-66 plan for cooperation between Academies of Sciences.
JMJP 6/2/66; NCNA Havana 5/31/66; SCMP 3712:26 (6/6/66).

66-52 5/28/66 — HANOI VIETNAM(N)
1966 plan for cultural cooperation.
JMJP 5/29/66; NCNA Hanoi 5/28/66; SCMP 3710:35 (6/2/66).

66-53 5/30/66 — ULAN BATOR MONGOLIA PROTOCOL
Scientific and technical cooperation.
Signed at fourth session of Sino-Mongolian Executive Organ for Scientific and Technical Cooperation.
JMJP 6/2/66; NCNA Ulan Bator 5/31/66; SCMP 3711:34 (6/3/66); CCD 175:50.

66-54 6/1/66 — RANGOON BURMA EXCHANGE OF NOTES
Revision of 1955 Agreement of Civil Air Transportation [55-77].
TYC 15:189(C).

66-55 6/1/66 6/1/66 PARIS FRANCE AGREEMENT
Air communications; a Communiqué was also issued.
TYC 15:173(C); JMJP 6/2/66; NCNA Paris 6/1/66; SCMP 3712:27 (6/6/66); JRF 1966:5324(Fr); AsR 7149; RFDA 20:365 (1966)(Fr).

66-56 6/1/66 — PYONGYANG KOREA(N) AGREEMENT
Mutual assistance and cooperation in prevention and quarantine of animal diseases.
JMJP 6/3/66; NCNA Pyongyang 6/1/66; SCMP 3712:28 (6/6/66).

66-57 6/1/66 — RAWALPINDI PAKISTAN
1966-67 plan for cultural cooperation.
JMJP 6/3/66; NCNA Rawalpindi 6/1/66; SCMP 3713:31 (6/7/66).

66-58 6/2/66 — CONAKRY GUINEA AGREEMENT
Exchange of news between New China News Agency and Guinean Press Agency.
Signed by High Commissioner at Presidency in Charge of Information and Tourism of Guinea and PRC Ambassador to Guinea.
JMJP 6/5/66; NCNA Conakry 6/2/66; SCMP 3714:36 (6/8/66).

66-59 6/2/66 — CONAKRY GUINEA MEMORANDUM
Talks on PRC aid on construction of cinema in Guinea. See note above.
JMJP 6/5/66; NCNA Conakry 6/2/66; SCMP 3714:36 (6/8/66).

66-60 6/4/66 — BAGHDAD IRAQ
1966-67 plan for cultural cooperation.
JMJP 6/9/66; NCNA Baghdad 6/4/66; SCMP 3714:38 (6/8/66).

66-61 6/4/66 — BAGHDAD IRAQ PROTOCOL
Cooperation in radio and television broadcasting.
TYC 15:154(C); JMJP 6/9/66; NCNA Baghdad 6/4/66; SCMP 3714:38 (6/8/66).

66-62 6/8/66 — PEKING TANZANIA AGREEMENT
Economic cooperation.
JMJP 6/9/66; PR 9.25:4 (6/17/66); NCNA Peking 6/8/66; SCMP 3717:29 (6/13/66); AfR 1420.

66-63 6/9/66 — PEKING MALI AGREEMENT
Granting of loans by PRC to Mali.
JMJP 6/10/66; PR 9.25:4 (6/17/66); NCNA Peking 6/9/66; SCMP 3718:31 (6/15/66).

66-64 6/10/66 8/31/66 BELGRADE YUGOSLAVIA PROTOCOL
Exchange of goods in 1966.
TYC 15:77(C); JMJP 6/13/66; NCNA Belgrade 6/10/66; SCMP 3719:38 (6/16/66); WGO 9:20.

66-65 6/11/66 — MOGADISHU SOMALIA
1966 plan for cultural cooperation.
JMJP 6/13/66; NCNA Mogadishu 6/11/66; SCMP 3720:36 (6/17/66).

66-66 6/20/66 — ALGIERS ALGERIA MEMORANDUM
Talks on PRC aid in construction of exhibition hall in Algeria.
JMJP 6/25/66; NCNA Algiers 6/20/66; SCMP 3726:31 (6/27/66).

66-67 6/20/66 — WARSAW POLAND PROTOCOL
Scientific and technical cooperation.
Signed at thirteenth session of Sino-Polish Standing Committee
for Scientific and Technical Cooperation.
JMJP 6/22/66; NCNA Warsaw 6/20/66; SCMP 3725:34 (6/24/66).

66-68 6/23/66 — RAWALPINDI PAKISTAN PROTOCOL
PRC aid in construction of heavy machinery complex in West
Pakistan.
JMJP 6/26/66; NCNA Rawalpindi 6/23/66; SCMP 3729:42 (6/30/66);
AsR 7215.

66-69 6/24/66 — WARSAW POLAND
1966 plan for cultural cooperation.
JMJP 6/26/66; NCNA Warsaw 6/24/66; SCMP 3728:29 (6/29/66).

66-70 6/27/66 — MOSCOW USSR
1966 plan for cultural cooperation.
NCNA Moscow 6/27/66; SCMP 3730:46 (7/1/66); CDSP 18. 26:9;
(7/20/66).

66-71 6/28/66 — TIRANA ALBANIA COMMUNIQUÉ
Talks during visit of Chinese Communist Party and PRC govern-
ment delegation: reaffirmation of Joint Statement of 5/11/66 [66-
42].
TYC 15:11(C); JMJP 6/29/66(C); PR 9. 27:16 (7/1/66)(E); NCNA
Tirana 6/28/66; SCMP 3730:33 (7/1/66)(E); CCD 175:53(E).

66-72 6/30/66 — KATMANDU NEPAL AGREEMENT (supple-
mentary)
Maintenance of Katmandu-Kodari highway.
AsR 7214.

66-73 7/1/66 — SOFIA BULGARIA
1966 plan for cultural cooperation.
NCNA Sofia 7/1/66; SCMP 3733:34 (7/7/66).

66-74 7/2/66 — RANGOON BURMA EXCHANGE OF NOTES
Dispose of unfinished items after termination of 1961.
Agreement of Payments [61-63].
TYC 15:117(C).

66-75 7/2/66 — PEKING VIETNAM(N) AGREEMENT
Agricultural aid by PRC to Vietnam(N).
JMJP 7/3/66; NCNA Peking 7/2/66; SCMP 3733:37 (7/7/66).

66-76 7/4/66 — BERLIN GERMANY(E) PROTOCOL
Scientific and technical cooperation.
Signed at tenth meeting of Sino-German Standing Committee for
Cooperation in Technology and Technical Sciences.
JMJP 7/23/66; NCNA Berlin 7/4/66; SCMP 3735:22 (7/11/66).

66-77 7/4/66 — RAWALPINDI PAKISTAN AGREEMENT
Barter.
AsR 7225.

66-78 7/4/66 1/1/66 RAWALPINDI PAKISTAN PROTOCOL
Trade.
TYC 15:20(C).

66-79 7/5/66 — PEKING KOREA(N) PROTOCOL
Scientific and technical cooperation.
Signed at ninth session of Sino-Korean Committee for Scientific
and Technical Cooperation.
JMJP 7/6/66; NCNA Peking 7/5/66; SCMP 3735:25 (7/11/66).

66-80 7/5/66 — PEKING JAPAN JOINT STATEMENT
Cultural exchange.
Signed by representatives of Chinese People's Association for
Cultural Relations and Friendship with Foreign Countries and
Japan-China Cultural Exchange Association.
JMJP 7/6/66; NCNA Peking 7/5/66; SCMP 3735:24 (7/11/66).

66-81 7/6/66 7/6/66 HAVANA CUBA AGREEMENT
Scientific and technical cooperation.
TYC 15:159(C); JMJP 7/9/66; NCNA Havana 7/7/66; SCMP 3737:
32 (7/13/66).

66-82 7/7/66 — — TANZANIA ACCORD
Establishment of Sino-Tanzanian Maritime Transport Joint Stock
Company.
Implements agreement in Memorandum of 4/22/66 [66-31].

JMJP 7/9/66; NCNA Peking 7/7/66; SCMP 3736:31 (7/12/66); AfR 1432, 1582.

66-83   7/20/66 — BUDAPEST   HUNGARY
1966 plan for cultural cooperation.
JMJP 7/23/66; NCNA Budapest 7/20/66; SCMP 3746:32 (7/26/66).

66-84   7/22/66 — BERLIN   GERMANY(E)
1966 plan for cultural cooperation.
JMJP 7/28/66; NCNA Berlin 7/23/66; SCMP 3748:24 (7/28/66).

66-85   7/25/66 — PEKING   FRANCE   PROTOCOL
Reciprocal grant of technical services in civil aviation.
JMJP 7/28/66; NCNA Peking 7/25/66; SCMP 3749:22 (7/29/66).

66-86   7/27/66   7/27/66   PEKING   SUDAN   PROTOCOL
Trade in 1967.
TYC 15:27(C); JMJP 7/28/66; NCNA Peking 7/27/66; SCMP 3750: 41 (8/1/66).

66-87   7/29/66 — PEKING   AFGHANISTAN   PROTOCOL
Economic and technical cooperation.
JMJP 7/30/66; NCNA Peking 7/29/66; SCMP 3752:26 (8/3/66).

66-88   7/30/66 — PEKING   KOREA(N)
1966-67 plan for cooperation between academies of sciences.
JMJP 7/31/66; NCNA Peking 7/30/66; SCMP 3753:33 (8/4/66).

66-89   7/31/66 — BUCHAREST   RUMANIA   PROTOCOL
Scientific and technical cooperation.
Signed at eleventh meeting of Sino-Rumanian Joint Committee for Scientific and Technical Cooperation.
JMJP 8/1/66; NCNA Bucharest 7/31/66; SCMP 3753:34 (8/4/66).

66-90   8/9/66(?) — BUDAPEST   HUNGARY   PROTOCOL
Scientific and technical cooperation.
Signed at tenth meeting of Sino-Hungarian Committee for Scientific and Technical Cooperation.
JMJP 8/31/66; NCNA Peking 8/10/66; SCMP 3760:17 (8/15/66).

66-91   8/13/66(?) — TANANARIVE   MALAGASY
Technical aid by PRC.
JPRS 37434:21 (Translations on Africa No. 428).

66-92   8/21/66 — PEKING   VIETNAM(N)

1966-67 plan for cooperation between PRC Academy of Sciences and Vietnamese State Commission of Sciences and Technology and Academy of Social Science.
JMJP 8/24/66; NCNA Peking 8/21/66; SCMP 3768:21 (8/25/66).

66-93   8/22/66 — PEKING   ZAMBIA   JOINT PRESS COMMUNIQUÉ
Talks during visit of Vice-President Kamanga; Southern Rhodesia, international situation, etc.
JMJP 8/23/66(C); PR 9. 35:13 (8/26/66)(E); NCNA Peking 8/22/66; SCMP 3768:22 (8/25/66)(E).

66-94   8/22/66 — PEKING   ZAMBIA   AGREEMENT
Cultural cooperation.
JMJP 8/23/66; PR 9. 35:13 (8/26/66); NCNA Peking 8/22/66; SCMP 3768:21 (8/25/66).

66-95   8/29/66 — PEKING   VIETNAM(N)   AGREEMENT
Economic and technical assistance to Vietnam(N).
JMJP 8/30/66; PR 9. 36:3 (9/2/66); NCNA Peking 8/29/66; SCMP 3773:31 (9/2/66).

66-96   8/23/66 — PEKING   GERMANY(E)   EXCHANGE OF NOTES
Revision of 1966 Agreement of Exchange of Goods and Payments [66-17].
TYC 15:141(C).

66-97   9/29/66 — PEKING   MONGOLIA
1966 plan for cultural cooperation.
JMJP 9/30/66; NCNA Peking 9/29/66; SCMP 3793:45 (10/4/66).

66-98   9/30/66 — RABAT   MOROCCO   EXCHANGE OF NOTES
Extension of 1961 Payments Agreement [61-145].
TYC 15:121(C).

66-99   10/10/66 — DAR ES SALAAM   TANZANIA   CONTRACTS(3)
Supply of PRC equipment and technical aid in construction of textile mill in Tanzania.
AfR 1510.

66-100 10/12/66 — PEKING   VIETNAM(N)
1967 plan for cooperation in public health work.
JMJP 10/13/66; NCNA Peking 10/12/66; SCMP 3802:29 (10/18/66).

66-101 10/12/66 — PEKING   JAPAN   JOINT STATEMENT
Further promotion of friendly interchange in all respects.

Signed by representatives of China-Japan Friendship Delegation and Japan-China Friendship Delegation.
JMJP 10/13/66; NCNA Peking 10/20/66; SCMP 3802:20 (10/18/66).

66-102 10/18/66 — KATMANDU NEPAL EXCHANGE OF NOTES(?)
PRC economic aid to Nepal.
PRC agrees to convert total sum of aid due under 1956 and 1960 agreements from Indian rupees to pounds sterling at gold standard value of two currencies prior to devaluation of Indian rupee [56-111; 60-48].
JMJP 10/20/66; NCNA Katmandu 10/18/66; SCMP 3806:35 (10/24/66).

66-103 10/20/66 — PEKING ALBANIA AGREEMENT
PRC loan to Albania for petroleum industry.
JMJP 10/21/66; NCNA Peking 10/20/66; SCMP 3807:29 (10/25/66).

66-104 10/21/66 10/21/66 RAWALPINDI PAKISTAN AGREE-MENT
Maritime transport.
TYC 15:171(C); JMJP 10/22/66; NCNA Rawalpindi 10/21/66; SCMP 3808:36 (10/26/66).

66-105 10/23/66 — MOGADISHU SOMALIA EXCHANGE OF LETTERS
Working conditions for PRC experts in Somalia.
JMJP 10/28/66; NCNA Mogadishu 10/26/66; SCMP 3812:29 (11/1/66); AfD 3207.

66-106 10/23/66 — PEKING VIETNAM(N) MINUTES
Talks on scientific and technical cooperation.
JMJP 10/28/66; NCNA Peking 10/27/66; SCMP 3812:29 (11/1/66).

66-107 10/28/66 — PEKING CZECHOSLOVAKIA PROTOCOL
Scientific and technical cooperation.
Signed at thirteenth meeting of Sino-Czechoslovak Joint Committee for Scientific and Technical Cooperation.
JMJP 11/2/66; NCNA Peking 10/28/66; SCMP 3813:32 (11/2/66).

66-108 11/5/66 11/5/66 — KOREA(N) PROTOCOL
Civil air transportation and mutual service.

66-109 11/6/66 — PEKING USSR PROTOCOL
Scientific and technical cooperation.
Signed at fifteenth session of Sino-Soviet Joint Committee for Sci-

entific and Technical Cooperation.
JMJP 11/7/66; NCNA Peking 11/6/66; SCMP 3819:41 (11/10/66);
AsR 7410; NYT 11/7/66, p. 79.

66-110 11/16/66 — PEKING GUINEA AGREEMENT
Economic and technical cooperation.
JMJP 11/17/66; PR 9.48:5 (11/25/66); NCNA Peking 11/16/66;
SCMP 3824:42 (11/21/66).

66-111 11/16/66 — PEKING GUINEA PROTOCOL
Economic and technical cooperation.
JMJP 11/17/66; PR 9.48:5 (11/25/66); NCNA Peking 11/16/66;
SCMP 3824:42 (11/21/66).

66-112 11/16/66 1/1/67 PEKING GUINEA PROTOCOL
Trade in 1967.
TYC 15:14(C); JMJP 11/17/66; PR 9.48:5 (11/25/66); NCNA
Peking 11/16/66; SCMP 3824:42 (11/21/66).

66-113 11/16/66 — GUINEA AGREEMENT LOAN
TYC 15:15(C); JMJP 11/17/66; PR 9.48:5 (11/25/66); NCNA
Peking 11/16/66; SCMP 3824:42 (11.21.66).

66-114 11/21/66 1/1/67 PEKING ALBANIA PROTOCOL
Exchange of goods and payments in 1967.
TYC 15:37(C); JMJP 11/22/66; NCNA Peking 11/21/66; SCMP
3827:26 (11/25/66).

66-115 11/21/66 — PEKING ALBANIA PROTOCOL
Albania's use of PRC loans in 1967.
JMJP 11/22/66; NCNA Peking 11/21/66; SCMP 3827:26 (11/25/66).

66-116 11/21/66 — PEKING JAPAN
Trade in 1967 in accordance with Liao-Takasaki Memorandum
[62-103].
JMJP 11/22/66; NCNA Peking 11/21/66; SCMP 3827:30 (11/25/66).

66-117 11/23/66 1/1/67 PEKING VIETNAM(N) AGREEMENT
Mutual supply of goods and payments in 1967.
TYC 15:81(C); JMJP 11/24/66; NCNA Peking 11/23/66; SCMP
3828:34 (11/28/66).

66-118 11/23/66 — PEKING VIETNAM(N) EXCHANGE OF NOTES
Extension of 1957 Protocol on Exchange of Goods by Local State-
Owned Trading Companies in Border Areas [57-75].
TYC 15:83 (C).

66-119 11/23/66 — PEKING VIETNAM(N) EXCHANGE OF NOTES
Extension of 1955 Protocol on Small-Scale trading in Border
Areas [55-49].
TYC 15:84(C).

66-120 11/29/66 1/1/67 COLOMBO CEYLON PROTOCOL
Exchange of goods in 1967.
TYC 15:146(C); JMJP 11/30/66; NCNA Colombo 11/29/66;
SCMP 3832:31 (12/2/66).

66-121 11/29/66 — COLOMBO CEYLON CONTRACTS(2)
Exchange of rice and rubber in 1967.
NCNA Colombo 11/29/66; SCMP 3832:31 (12/2/66).

66-122 11/30/66 — TIRANA ALBANIA PROTOCOL
Scientific and technical cooperation.
Signed at eleventh session of Sino-Albanian Joint Committee for
Cooperation in Technology and Technical Science.
JMJP 12/2/66; NCNA Tirana 12/1/66; SCMP 3834:13 (12/6/66).

66-123 12/3/66 1/1/67 PEKING KOREA(N) PROTOCOL
Mutual supply of goods in 1967.
TYC 15:97(C); JMJP 12/4/66; NCNA Peking 12/3/66; SCMP
3835:28 (12/7/66).

66-124 12/20/66 — PEKING GERMANY(E) EXCHANGE OF NOTES
Revision of 1958 Agreement on Noncommercial Payments [58-34].
TYC 15:143(C).

66-125 12/21/66 — KATMANDU NEPAL AGREEMENT
Economic and technical cooperation.
JMJP 12/27/66; NCNA Katmandu 12/22/66; SCMP 3849:37
(12/29/66); AsR 7513.

66-126 12/28/66 12/28/66 KABUL AFGHANISTAN PROTOCOL
Exchange of goods in 1966-67.
TYC 15:45(C); JMJP 12/31/66; NCNA Kabul 12/28/66; SCMP
3852:38 (1/4/67).

66-127 12/30/66 12/30/66 PEKING KOREA(N) AGREEMENT
Cooperation in radio and television broadcasting.
TYC 15:156(C); JMJP 12/31/66; NCNA Peking 12/30/66; SCMP
3852:45 (1/4/67).

66-128 12/31/66 12/31/66 BURMA PROTOCOL
Purchase of rice from Burma.
TYC 15:118(C).

1967

67-1 1/17/67 — RAWALPINDI PAKISTAN
PRC supply of grain.
JMJP 1/19/67; AsR 7577.

67-2 1/26/67 — PEKING FINLAND EXCHANGE OF NOTES
Trademark registration.
FTS (SAS) 1967:22:329(F, E).

67-3 1/31/67 1/1/67 PEKING BULGARIA AGREEMENT
Exchange of goods and payments in 1967.
TYC 15:72(C); JMJP 2/5/67; NCNA Peking 1/31/67; SCMP
3875:27 (2/6/67).

67-4 2/14/67 1/19/67 BUCHAREST RUMANIA AGREEMENT
Exchange of goods and payments in 1967.
TYC 15:50(C); JMJP 2/17/67; NCNA Bucharest 2/14/67; SCMP
3883:29 (2/20/67); Bucharest Domestic Broadcasting 2/14/67
FBIS, Daily Report, 32:JJ. 1 (2/15/67); AsR 7584.

67-5 2/14/67 — BUCHAREST RUMANIA PROTOCOL
Extension of 1961 Protocol on General Conditions for Delivery of
Goods [61-94].
TYC 15:54(C).

67-6 2/16/67 — PEKING MAURITANIA AGREEMENT
Trade.
Ratified by PRC State Council 3/14/67. JMJP 3/19/67, quoting
New China News Agency 3/18/67 news release, reports that
Agreement has formally entered into force.
TYC 15:18(C); JMJP 2/17/67; PR 10. 9:15 (2/24/67); NCNA Peking
2/16/67; SCMP 3883:27 (2/20/67).

67-7 2/16/67 — PEKING MAURITANIA AGREEMENT
Economic and technical cooperation.
See note above.
JMJP 2/17/67; PR 10. 9:15 (2/24/67); NCNA Peking 2/16/67;
SCMP 3883:27 (2/20/67).

67-8   2/16/67 — PEKING   MAURITANIA   AGREEMENT
Cultural cooperation.
See note above.
TYC 15:153(C); JMJP 2/17/67; PR 10. 9:15 (2/24/67); NCNA
Peking 2/16/67; SCMP 3883:27 (2/20/67).

67-9   2/17/67 — PEKING   MAURITANIA   JOINT PRESS COM-
MUNIQUÉ
Talks during visit of Foreign Minister Birane Mamadou Wane:
Vietnam, Palestine Arabs, Rhodesia, PRC representation in UN,
Cultural Revolution, etc.
TYC 15:1(C); JMJP 2/18/67(C); PR 10. 9:14 (2/24/67)(E); NCNA
Peking 2/17/67; SCMP 3884:29 (2/21/67).

67-10 2/25/67 — PEKING   BULGARIA   PROTOCOL
Scientific and technical cooperation.
Signed at tenth session of Sino–Bulgarian Joint Committee for
Scientific and Technical Cooperation.
JMJP 3/1/67; NCNA Peking 2/27/67; SCMP 3890:27 (3/2/67).

67-11 3/14/67 — KATMANDU   NEPAL   CONTRACT
PRC supply of rice to Nepal.
JMJP 3/20/67.

67-12 3/21/67 1/1/67 PEKING   CUBA   PROTOCOL
Trade in 1967.
TYC 15:24(C); JMJP 3/23/67; NCNA Peking 3/21/67; SCMP
3906:26 (3/28/67).

67-13 4/13/67 — DAMASCUS   SYRIA   EXCHANGE OF LETTERS
PRC technical aid in construction of cotton spinning mill in Syria.
JMJP 4/20/67; NCNA Damascus 4/16/67; SCMP 3923:32 (4/20/67);
AsR 7764.

67-14 4/14/67 1/1/67 PEKING   GERMANY(E)   AGREEMENT
Exchange of goods and payments in 1967.
TYC 15:144(C); NCNA Peking 4/14/67; SCMP 3921:32 (4/18/67).

67-15 4/24/67 — TIRANA   ALBANIA
1967-68 plan for cultural cooperation.
JMJP 4/27/67; NCNA Tirana 4/24/67; SCMP 3927:37 (4/27/67).

67-16 4/25/67 1/1/67 HELSINKI   FINLAND   AGREEMENT
Trade in 1967.
TYC 15:44(C); JMJP 4/27/67; NCNA Helsinki 4/25/67; SCMP
3928:30 (4/28/67).

67-17 4/25/67 — PEKING VIETNAM(N)
1967 plan for cultural cooperation.
JMJP 4/27/67; NCNA Peking 4/25/67; SCMP 3927:40 (4/27/67).

67-18 4/25/67 — HELSINKI FINLAND EXCHANGE OF LETTERS
Revision of 1953 Payments Agreement to convert clearing currency
from ruble to Finnish mark [53-32].
FTS (SAS) 1967:46:575(F, E).

67-19 4/28/67 — PEKING ZAMBIA AGREEMENT
Trade.
JMJP 4/29/67; NCNA Peking 4/28/67; SCMP 3931:35 (5/3/67).

67-20 5/25/67 1/1/67 PEKING UAR PROTOCOL
Trade in 1967.
TYC 15:43(C); JMJP 5/27/67; NCNA Peking 5/26/67; SCMP
3949:29 (5/31/67).

67-21 5/25/67 — KATMANDU NEPAL PROTOCOL
PRC aid in construction of power station and transmission line in
Nepal.
Nepalese government Press Communiqué also issued 5/25/67.
JMJP 5/29/67; NCNA Katmandu 5/26/67; SCMP 3950:48 (6/1/67);
AsR 7792.

67-22 5/28/67 — PEKING ALBANIA PROTOCOL
Shipping.
Signed at sixth meeting of Administrative Council of Sino–Albanian
Shipping Joint Stock Company.
JMJP 5/29/67; NCNA Peking 5/28/67; SCMP 3950:31 (6/1/67).

67-23 5/28/67 — KATMANDU NEPAL AGREEMENT(?)
PRC aid in extension of Kodari highway to Katmandu.
AsR 7792.

67-24 5/31/67 — PEKING VIETNAM(N) EXCHANGE OF NOTES
The calculation method of the price of trade is changed from ruble
to people currency.
TYC 15:85(C).

67-25 6/21/67 — BUDAPEST HUNGARY PROTOCOL
General conditions of delivery of goods in 1967.
TYC 15:33(C).

67-26 6/22/67 — BUDAPEST HUNGARY AGREEMENT
Exchange of goods and payments in 1967.

TYC 15:34(C); JMJP 7/2/67; NCNA Budapest 6/29/67; SCMP
3973:42 (7/5/67).

67-27 6/23/67 — PEKING ZAMBIA AGREEMENT
Economic and technical cooperation.
JMJP 6/24/67; NCNA Peking 6/23/67; SCMP 3969:40 (6/28/67);
AfD 3500.

67-28 6/26/67 — PEKING ZAMBIA JOINT COMMUNIQUÉ
Talks during President Kaunda's visit: Rhodesia, PRC representation in UN, national liberation movements, Vietnam, etc.
JMJP 6/27/67(C); PR 10. 27:12 (6/30/67)(E); NCNA Peking
6/25/67; SCMP 3970:45 (6/29/67)(E).

67-29 6/30/67 1/1/67 WARSAW POLAND AGREEMENT
Exchange of goods and payments in 1967.
TYC 15:64(C); JMJP 7/2/67; NCNA Warsaw 7/1/67; SCMP 3973:
43 (7/5/67).

67-30 6/30/67 — WARSAW POLAND PROTOCOL
Extension of 1961 Protocol on General Conditions of Delivery of
Goods [61-95] to 1967.
TYC 15:64(C).

67-31 7/5/67 1/1/67 PRAGUE CZECHOSLOVAKIA AGREE-
MENT
Exchange of goods and payments in 1967.
TYC 15:93(C).

67-32 7/26/67 1/1/67 ULAN BATOR MONGOLIA PROTOCOL
Mutual supply of goods in 1967.
TYC 15:112(C).

67-33 7/27/67 1/1/67 MOSCOW USSR PROTOCOL
Exchange of goods in 1967.
TYC 15:47(C).

67-34 8/3/67 — PEKING VIETNAM(N) PROTOCOL
Scientific and technical cooperation.
Signed at seventh meeting of Sino-Vietnamese Executive Organ
for Scientific and Technical Cooperation.
JMJP 8/4/67; NCNA Peking 8/3/67; SCMP 3997:48 (8/9/67).

67-35 8/5/67 — PEKING VIETNAM(N) AGREEMENT
PRC economic and technical aid.

JMJP 8/6/67; PR 10. 33:28 (8/11/67); NCNA Peking 8/5/67;
SCMP 3997:48 (8/9/67); NYT 8/6/67, p. 2.

67-36 8/14/67 — PEKING MALI AGREEMENT(s)
PRC economic aid to Mali.
JMJP 8/15/67; PR 10. 35:25 (8/25/67).

67-37 8/14/67 8/14/67 PEKING MALI AGREEMENT
PRC grant of commercial loan to Mali.
TYC 15:16(C).

67-38 8/16/67 — MOGADISHU SOMALIA MINUTES
Talks on rice and tobacco experiment station built by PRC experts.
JMJP 8/19/67; NCNA Mogadishu 8/17/67; SCMP 4007:36 (8/23/67).

67-39 8/19/67 — MOGADISHU SOMALIA
1967-68 plan for cultural cooperation.
JMJP 8/20/67; NCNA Mogadishu 8/19/67; SCMP 4007:37 (8/23/67).

67-40 8/31/67 — PEKING YUGOSLAVIA PROTOCOL
Exchange of goods in 1967.
TYC 15:78(C).

67-41 9/5/67 — PEKING TANZANIA & ZAMBIA AGREEMENT
PRC economic and technical aid in construction of Tanzania-
Zambia railway.
TYC 15:199(C); JMJP 9/6/67; NCNA Peking 9/5/67; SCMP 4017:
32 (9/8/67); AsR 7976.

67-42 9/14/67 — PEKING PAKISTAN
1967-68 plan for cultural cooperation.
JMJP 9/15/67; NCNA Peking 9/14/67; SCMP 4024:42 (9/20/67).

67-43 9/18/67 — PYONGYANG KOREA(N) EXCHANGE OF NOTES
Extension of 1957 Agreement on Scientific and Technical Coopera-
tion [57-129].
TYC 15:160(C).

67-44 10/5/67 1/1/68 PEKING VIETNAM(N) AGREEMENT
Mutual Commodity supply and payment in 1968.
TYC 15:86(C); NCNA Peking 10/5/67; SCMP 4038:36 (10/10/67).

67-45 10/5/67 — PEKING VIETNAM(N) EXCHANGE OF NOTES
Extension of 1955 Protocol on Small-Scale Trading in Border
Areas [55-49].
TYC 15:89(C).

67-46 10/5/67 — PEKING VIETNAM(N) EXCHANGE OF NOTES
Extension of 1957 Protocol on Exchange of Goods by Local State-
Owned Trading Companies in Border Areas [57-75].
TYC 15:88(C).

67-47 10/10/67 — PEKING CONGO (BRAZZAVILLE) JOINT
PRESS COMMUNIQUÉ
Talks during visit of Prime Minister Ambroise Noumazalay:
Vietnam, Cultural Revolution, imperialism, etc.
TYC 15:9(C); JMJP 10/11/67(C); PR 10. 42:28 (10/13/67)(E);
NCNA Peking 10/10/67; SCMP 4041:40 (10/13/67)(E).

67-48 10/14/67 — PEKING ALBANIA PRESS COMMUNIQUÉ
Talks during visit of Chairman Mehmet Shehu: imperialism,
revisionism, etc.
JMJP 10/16/67(C); PR 10. 43:5 (10/20/67)(E); NCNA Peking
10/15/67; SCMP 4044:30 (10/19/67)(E).

67-49 10/14/67 — NOUAKCHOTT MAURITANIA PROTOCOL
Supplement to 1967 Agreement of Economic and Technical Co-
operation [67-7].
JMJP 10/17/67; NCNA Peking 10/15/67; SCMP 4044:35 (10/19/67).

67-50 10/17/67 — PEKING POLAND PROTOCOL
Scientific and technical cooperation.
Signed at 14th meeting of Sino-Polish Joint Standing Commission
of Scientific and Technical Cooperation (10/7-10/17/67).
NCNA did not say when the protocol was signed, though it was
presumably on the last day of the meeting.
JMJP 10/20/67; NCNA Peking 10/18/67; SCMP 4046:39 (10/24/67).

67-51 10/21/67 — RAWALPINDI PAKISTAN LETTERS OF
AGREEMENT
To facilitate border trade between territories of Gilgit and Baltis-
tan on Pakistan side and Sinkiang Uighur Autonomous Region on
Chinese side.
JMJP 10/25/67; NCNA Rawalpindi 10/23/67; SCMP 4049:33
(10/27/67).

67-52 10/23/67 — PEKING RUMANIA PROTOCOL
Scientific and technical cooperation.
Signed at twelfth Session of Joint Committee for Sino-Rumania
Scientific and Technical Cooperation.
NCNA did not say when the protocol was signed, presumably on
the last day of the session.
JMJP 10/27/67; NCNA Peking 10/25/67; SCMP 4049:34 (10/27/67).

67-53 10/24/67 — PEKING MAURITANIA JOINT COMMUNIQUÉ
Talks during visit of President Moktar Ould Daddah: Vietnam,
PRC representation in UN, Palestine Arabs, etc.
JMJP 10/26/67; PR 10. 45:8 (11/3/67)(E); NCNA Peking 10/25/67;
SCMP 4049:31 (10/27/67)(E).

67-54 11/6/67 1/1/68 PEKING CEYLON AGREEMENT
Trade and Payments.
TYC 15:148(C); JMJP 11/7/67; NCNA Peking 11/6/67; SCMP
4058:24 (11/9/67).

67-55 11/6/67 1/1/68 PEKING CEYLON PROTOCOL
Exchange of goods for 1968.
TYC 15:151(C); JMJP 11/7/67; NCNA Peking 11/6/67; SCMP
4058:24 (11/9/67).

67-56 11/8/67 — NOUAKCHOTT MAURITANIA PROTOCOL
Dispatch of Chinese medical team to Mauritania.
TYC 15:166(C); JMJP 11/13/67.

67-57 11/10/67 — PEKING JAPAN JOINT STATEMENT
Issued by China Council for Promotion of International Trade and
delegation of friendly trading firms of Kobe branch of Japanese
Association for Promotion of International Trade: U. S. imperialism, cultural revolution, three political principles, three principles for trade, principle of indivisibility of politics and economics,
etc.
JMJP 11/13/67; NCNA Peking 11/10/67; SCMP 4060:32 (11/15/67).

67-58 11/23/67 — PYONGYANG KOREA(N) PROTOCOL
Scientific and technical information.
Signed at tenth meeting of Chinese-Korean Committee for Sci-
entific and Technical Cooperation.
NCNA Pyongyang 11/24/67; SCMP 4068:37 (11/28/67).

67-59 11/25/67 — SHUMCHUN HONG KONG AGREEMENT
Between Hong Kong authorities and Chinese border defense
inspection station.
NCNA Kwangchow 11/29/67; SCMP 4072:24 (12/14/67)(E).

67-60 12/6/67 — KABUL AFGHANISTAN EXCHANGE OF
LETTERS
Technical cooperation in experimental tea planting in Konar
Province with PRC aid.
JMJP 12/16/67; NCNA Kabul 12/14/67; SCMP 4082:28 (12/18/67).

67-61 12/9/67 1/6/68 TIRANA ALBANIA PROTOCOL
Goods Exchange and Payments for 1968.
TYC 15:39(C); JMJP 12/12/67; NCNA Tirana 12/10/67; SCMP
4080:25 (12/14/67).

67-62 12/9/67 — TIRANA ALBANIA PROTOCOL
Albanian government's use of credit granted by PRC.
JMJP 12/12/67; NCNA Tirana 12/10/67; SCMP 4080:25 (12/14/67).

67-63 12/12/67 — PEKING RUMANIA
1967-69 executive plan for scientific cooperation between the
Chinese and Rumanian Academies of Science.
JMJP 12/16/67; NCNA Peking 12/13/67; SCMP 4081:29 (12/15/67).

67-64 12/14/67 — BAMAKO MALI PROTOCOL
Dispatch of Chinese medical team to Mali.
TYC 15:164(C); JMJP 12/18/67.

67-65 12/?/67 — KATMANDU NEPAL EXCHANGE OF NOTES
Maintenance work of Katmandu-Kodari Highway.
NCNA did not say when the notes were exchanged. It only said the
notes were exchanged "recently."
The Chinese side agreed to render assistance in maintenance of
the Katmandu-Kodari Highway for two years from 6/1/67-5/31/68.
NCNA Katmandu 12/16/67; SCMP 4084:16 (12/20/67).

67-66 12/30/67 — CONAKRY GUINEA PROTOCOL
Dispatch of Chinese medical team to Guinea.
TYC 15:162(C); JMJP 1/8/68; NCNA Conakry 1/1/68; SCMP
4093:19 (1/5/68).

67-67 12/30/67 — PEKING KOREA(N)
1967-68 Executive plan of Sino-Korean Agreement on Sanitary
Cooperation.
JMJP 1/1/68; NCNA Peking 12/31/67; SCMP 4092:40 (1/4/68).

67-68 12/30/67 1/1/68 PEKING RUMANIA AGREEMENT
Goods exchange and payments for 1968.
TYC 15:54(C); JMJP 1/1/68; NCNA Peking 12/31/67; SCMP
4092:40 (1/4/68).

1968

68-1 1/11/68 1/11/68 KABUL AFGHANISTAN PROTOCOL
Exchange of goods for 1968.

TYC 16:44(C); JMJP 1/15/68; NCNA Kabul 1/12/68; SCMP 4100: 22 (1/16/68).

68-2   1/20/68   1/1/68   PEKING   FINLAND   AGREEMENT
1968 Trade.
TYC 16:39(C); JMJP 1/21/68; NCNA Kwangchow 1/26/68;
SCMP 4110:16 (2/2/68).

68-3   1/20/68 — PEKING   FINLAND   EXCHANGE OF LETTERS
Amendment of relevant provisions of 1953 Agreement on Pay-
ments [53-32].
TYC 16:40(C).

68-4   1/31/68 — CAIRO   YEMEN(s)   JOINT COMMUNIQUÉ
Establishment of diplomatic relations.
JMJP 2/3/68(C); PR 11. 6:15 (2/9/68)(E).

68-5   2/7/68 — BRAZZAVILLE   CONGO   MINUTES(SUMMARY)
Talks on PRC aid in constructing a shipyard for wooden boats of
small tonnage.
NCNA Brazzaville 2/8/68; SCMP 4117:20 (2/13/68).

68-6   2/26/68 — PEKING   ALBANIA   PROTOCOL
Scientific and Technical Cooperation.
Signed at twelfth session of Joint Committee for Scientific and
Technical Cooperation.
JMJP 2/27/68; NCNA Peking 2/26/68; SCMP 4128:27 (2/29/68).

68-7   3/3/68 — COLOMBO   CEYLON   EXCHANGE OF LETTERS
Extension of 1962 Agreement on Economic and Technical Coopera-
tion [62-94].
TYC 16:101(C).

68-8   3/5/68   1/1/68   PYONGYANG   KOREA(N)   PROTOCOL
Goods exchange for 1968.
TYC 16:87(C); JMJP 3/6/68; NCNA Pyongyang 3/5/68; SCMP
4133:20 (3/7/68).

68-9   3/6/68 — PEKING   JAPAN   COMMUNIQUÉ
Talks between representatives of PRC-Japan Memorandum Trade
Office and Japan-PRC Memorandum Trade Office: three political
principles in Sino-Japanese relations, principle that politics and
economics are inseparable.
TYC 16:115(C); JMJP 3/7/68(C); NCNA Peking 3/6/68; SCMP
4134:26 (3/8/68)(E).

68-10 3/6/68 — PEKING JAPAN AGREEMENT
Memoranda trade for 1968.
JMJP 3/7/68.

68-11 3/6/68 — PEKING JAPAN ACCORD
Amendment of 1964 Minutes on Talks of Mutual Exchange of
Correspondents [64–52].
TYC 16:118(C).

68-12 3/11/68 — COLOMBO CEYLON EXCHANGE OF LETTERS
Amendment of 1967 Agreement on Trade and Payments [67–54].
TYC 16:102(C).

68-13 3/18/68(?) — HANOI VIETNAM(N) PROTOCOL
Border railway transport.
Signed at eleventh meeting of Joint Sino-Vietnamese Boundary
Railway Commission.
JMJP 3/21/68; NCNA Hanoi 3/20/68; SCMP 4145:32 (3/25/68).

68-14 3/19/68 — PEKING JAPAN PROTOCOL
Japanese industrial exhibition at Peking and Shanghai.
JMJP 3/20/68; NCNA Peking 3/19/68; SCMP 4144:24 (3/22/68).

68-15 3/19/68 — PEKING JAPAN MINUTES
Talks between China Council for Promotion of International Trade
and six organizations belonging to Japanese.
Association for Promotion of International Trade.
JMJP 3/20/68; PR 11.13:9 (3/29/68); NCNA Peking 3/19/68;
SCMP 4144:24 (3/22/68)(E).

68-16 3/20/68 — KATMANDU NEPAL EXCHANGE OF LETTERS
Extension of 1960 Agreement on Economic Aid [60–48].
TYC 16:13(C).

68-17 3/24/68(?) — KATMANDU NEPAL
1968 plan for cultural and scientific exchange.
JMJP 3/30/68.

68-18 3/26/68 1/1/68 PEKING CZECHOSLOVAKIA AGREE-
MENT
Goods exchange and payments for 1969.
TYC 16:80(C); JMJP 3/28/68.

68-19 3/30/68 — PHNOM PENH CAMBODIA DOCUMENT
Turn-over of PRC-aided Ma-Te-Wang textile factory to Cambodia.
JMJP 4/4/68; NCNA Phnom Penh 4/2/68; SCMP 4154:27 (4/8/68).

68-20 4/2/68 1/1/68 SOFIA BULGARIA AGREEMENT
Goods exchange and payments for 1968.
TYC 16:63(C); JMJP 4/4/68; NCNA Sofia 4/2/68; SCMP 4154:27
(4/8/68).

68-21 4/6/68 — DAMASCUS SYRIA AGREEMENT
News cooperation between NCNA and Syria Arab News Agency.
NCNA Damascus 4/6/68; SCMP 4156:31 (4/10/68).

68-22 4/8/68 — DAR ES SALAAM TANZANIA & ZAMBIA PRO-
TOCOL
Survey and design work.
It implemented the 1967 Agreement on PRC Economic and Techni-
cal Aid in construction of Tanzania-Zambia railway [67-41].
JMJP 4/12/68; PR 11.16:26 (4/19/68); NCNA Dar es Salaam
4/9/68; SCMP 4159:39 (4/17/68).

68-23 4/8/68 — DAR ES SALAAM TANZANIA & ZAMBIA PRO-
TOCOL
Remuneration and working conditions for Chinese technical per-
sonnel.
It implemented the 1967 Agreement on PRC Economic and Tech-
nical Aid in construction of Tanzania-Zambia railway [67-41].
JMJP 4/12/68; PR 11.16:26 (4/19/68); NCNA Dar es Salaam
4/9/68); SCMP 4159:39 (4/17/68).

68-24 4/8/68 — DAR ES SALAAM TANZANIA & ZAMBIA PRO-
TOCOL
Method of supplying loan.
It implemented the 1967 Agreement on PRC Economic and Tech-
nical Aid in Construction of Tanzania-Zambia railway [67-41].
JMJP 4/12/68; PR 11.16:26 (4/19/68); NCNA Dar es Salaam
4/9/68; SCMP 4159:39 (4/17/68).

68-25 4/9/68 1/1/68 PEKING POLAND AGREEMENT
Goods exchange and payments.
TYC 16:52(C); JMJP 4/11/68; NCNA Peking 4/10/68; SCMP
4158:29 (4/16/68).

68-26 4/9/68 — PEKING POLAND PROTOCOL
Extension of 1961 Protocol on General Conditions for Delivery
of Goods [61-95].
TYC 16:52(C).

68-27 4/10/68 — PEKING JAPAN MINUTES

Talks between representatives of China-Japan Friendship Association and representatives of Headquarters of Japan-China Friendship Association (Orthodox): cultural revolution, U. S. imperialism, Soviet revisionism, etc.
JMJP 4/11/68(C); PR 11.16:26 (4/19/68)(E); NCNA Peking 4/10/68; SCMP 4158:27 (4/16/68)(E).

68-28   4/27/68   4/27/68   RAWALPINDI   PAKISTAN   PROTOCOL
Trade.
TYC 16:4(C); JMJP 4/29/68; NCNA Rawalpindi 4/27/68; SCMP 4168:31 (5/1/68).

68-29   4/27/68   —   DAR ES SALAAM   TANZANIA & ZAMBIA AGREEMENT
Accounting procedures for loans for railway.
JMJP 4/29/68; NCNA Dar es Salaam 4/27/68; SCMP 4168:31 (5/1/68).

68-30   4/27/68   —   DAR ES SALAAM   TANZANIA & ZAMBIA   PROTOCOL
Basic technical principles for construction of Tanzania-Zambia railway.
JMJP 4/29/68; NCNA Dar es Salaam 4/27/68; SCMP 4168:31 (5/1/68).

68-31   5/3/68   1/1/68   BERLIN   GERMANY(E)   AGREEMENT
Goods exchange and payments for 1968.
TYC 16:96(C); JMJP 5/5/68; NCNA Berlin 5/4/68; SCMP 4173:22 (5/8/68).

68-32   5/3/68   —   PEKING   HUNGARY   PROTOCOL
General conditions for delivery of goods for 1968.
TYC 16:18(C).

68-33   5/4/68   1/1/68   PEKING   HUNGARY   AGREEMENT
Goods exchange and payments in 1968.
TYC 16:19(C); JMJP 5/5/68; NCNA Peking 5/4/68; SCMP 4173:22 (5/8/68).

68-34   5/6/68   —   DAR ES SALAAM   TANZANIA   PROTOCOL
PRC dispatching a medical team to Tanzania.
TYC 16:110(C); JMJP 5/8/68; NCNA Dar es Salaam 5/6/68; SCMP 4176:34 (5/13/68).

68-35   5/13/68   —   BAMAKO   MALI   EXCHANGE OF NOTES

Extension of 1963 Agreement on Cooperation in Radio Broadcasting [63-103].
TYC 16:108(C).

68-36 5/13/68 1/1/68 PEKING MONGOLIA PROTOCOL
Mutual supply of goods for 1968.
TYC 16:91(C); JMJP 5/14/68; NCNA Peking 5/13/68; SCMP 4181:
26 (5/20/68).

68-37 5/14/68 1/1/68 CONAKRY GUINEA PROTOCOL
1968 Trade.
TYC 16:1(C); JMJP 5/18/68; NCNA Conakry 5/15/68; SCMP 4183:
31 (5/22/68).

68-38 5/24/68 — PEKING GUINEA & MALI AGREEMENT
Construction of Guinea-Mali railway.
JMJP 5/26/68; PR 11. 22:8 (5/31/68); NCNA Peking 5/31/68;
SCMP 4192:29 (6/6/68).

68-39 5/25/68 — PEKING GUINEA & MALI JOINT COMMUNIQUÉ
Talks during visit of Foreign Ministers Ousman Ba and Lansana
Beavogui: Vietnam, anti-imperialism, Africa, etc.
JMJP 6/1/68(C); NCNA Peking 5/31/68; SCMP 4192:28 (6/6/68)(E).

68-40 5/28/68 5/19/68 PEKING NEPAL AGREEMENT
Trade.
TYC 16:14(C); JMJP 5/29/68; NCNA Peking 5/28/68; SCMP 4191:
34 (6/5/68).

68-41 5/28/68 5/19/68 PEKING NEPAL PROTOCOL
Trade.
TYC 16:16(C); JMJP 5/29/68; NCNA Peking 5/28/68; SCMP 4191:
34 (6/5/68).

68-42 6/1/68 — PEKING NEPAL JOINT COMMUNIQUÉ
Talks during visit of Deputy Prime Minister Kirti Nidhi Bista:
economic cooperation, PRC continuing assistance, etc.
JMJP 6/2/68(C); NCNA Peking 6/1/68; SCMP 4193:29 (6/7/68)(E).

68-43 6/11/68 — TIRANA ALBANIA PROTOCOL
Signed at seventh meeting of Administrative Council of Sino-
Albanian Shipping Joint Stock Company.
JMJP 6/13/68; NCNA Tirana 6/11/68 /12/68; SCMP 4200:23
(6/18/68).

68-44 6/13/68 — KATMANDU NEPAL AGREEMENT
Exchange of news between NCNA of PRC and Rastriya Sambad
Samiti (national news agency of Nepal).
JMJP 6/15/68; NCNA Katmandu 6/13/68; SCMP 4201:30 (6/19/68).

68-45 6/16/68 1/1/69 PRAGUE CZECHOSLOVAKIA AGREE-
MENT
Exchange of goods and payments.
TYC 16:83(C).

68-46 6/20/68 — KHARTOUM SUDAN PROTOCOL
1968 trade.
TYC 16:28(C); JMJP 6/22/68; NCNA Khartoum 6/20/68; SCMP
4206:23 (6/26/68).

68-47 7/4/69 1/1/68 CAIRO UAR PROTOCOL
1968 trade.
TYC 16:31(C); JMJP 7/6/68; NCNA Cairo 7/4/68; SCMP 4215:30
(7/11/68).

68-48 7/4/68 — CAIRO UAR EXCHANGE OF LETTERS
Extension 1962 Agreements on Trade and Payments to another
three years [62-24, 62-25].
TYC 16:33(C); JMJP 7/6/68; NCNA Cairo 7/4/68; SCMP 4215:
3- (7/11/68).

68-49 7/4/68 — CAIRO UAR EXCHANGE OF LETTERS
Amendment of provision seven of 1962 Agreement on Payments
[62-25].
TYC 16:34(C).

68-50 7/4/68 — CAIRO UAR EXCHANGE OF LETTERS
Amendment of provision four of 1962 Agreement on Payments
[62-25].
TYC 16:36(C).

68-51 7/9/68 — SANAA YEMEN(N) SETTLEMENT(FINAL)
Building expenditure account of Sanaa cotton textile, printing, and
dyeing mill.
JMJP 7/12/68; NCNA Sanaa 7/9/68; SCMP 4219:27 (7/17/68).

68-52 7/19/68 1/1/68 HAVANA CUBA PROTOCOL
1968 trade.
TYC 16:8(C); JMJP 7/24/68.

68-53 7/19/68 — HAVANA CUBA EXCHANGE OF LETTERS
Revision of some provisions of 1964 Protocol of General Conditions
for Delivery of Goods between Foreign Trade Organizations of Two
Countries [64-193].
TYC 16:9(C).

68-54 7/23/68 — PEKING VIETNAM(N) AGREEMENT
Economic and technical aid.
Some protocols were also signed.
JMJP 7/25/68; PR 11. 31:30 (8/2/68); NCNA Peking 7/24/68;
SCMP 4229:25 (7/31/68).

68-55 8/12/68 — BRAZZAVILLE CONGO SUMMARY
Talks on establishment of state farm in Kombe with PRC assist-
ance.
JMJP 8/16/68; NCNA Brazzaville 8/13/68; SCMP 4243:22 (8/21/68).

68-56 8/26/68 — CONAKRY GUINEA AGREEMENT
PRC providing items of cultural construction.
TYC 16:106(C).

68-57 9/13/68 — BELGRADE YUGOSLAVIA EXCHANGE OF
LETTERS
Extension of 1967 Protocol on Exchange of Goods [67-40].
TYC 16:70(C).

68-58 9/24/68 — PEKING SOUTHERN YEMEN JOINT PRESS
COMMUNIQUÉ
Talks during visit of Foreign Minister Saif Ahmad Dhalai.
JMJP 9/26/68(C); PR 11. 40:41 (10/4/68)(E); NCNA Peking 9/25/68;
SCMP 4269:36 (10/1/68)(E).

68-59 9/24/68 — PEKING SOUTHERN YEMEN AGREEMENT
Economic and technical cooperation.
JMJP 9/25/68; PR 11. 39:30 (9/27/68); NCNA Peking 9/24/68;
SCMP 4268:34 (9/30/68).

68-60 9/24/68 — PEKING SOUTHERN YEMEN AGREEMENT
Trade.
TYC 16:62(C); JMJP 9/25/68; PR 11. 39:30 (9/27/68); NCNA
Peking 9/24/68; SCMP 4268:34 (9/30/68).

68-61 9/27/68 — KATMANDU NEPAL AGREEMENT
Construction of Katmandu-Bhaktapur highway.
JMJP 10/4/68; NCNA Katmandu 9/29/68; SCMP 4272:39 (10/4/68).

68-62 9/30/68 1/1/69 PEKING VIETNAM(N) AGREEMENT
Mutual supply of goods and payments for 1969.
TYC 16:73(C); JMJP 10/6/68; NCNA Peking 9/30/68; SCMP 4273:
37 (10/8/68).

68-63 9/30/68 — PEKING VIETNAM(N) EXCHANGE OF LETTERS
Extension of 1955 Protocol on Exchange of Goods between Local
State Trading Companies in Border Areas [55-48].
TYC 16:76(C).

68-64 9/30/68 — PEKING VIETNAM(N) EXCHANGE OF LETTERS
Extension of 1955 Protocol on Small-Scale Trading in Border Areas
[55-49].
TYC 16:75(C).

68-65 10/5/68 — PHNOM PENH CAMBODIA DOCUMENT
Turnover of PRC-aided Siem Reap airport.
JMJP 10/11/68; NCNA Phnom Penh 10/7/68; SCMP 4278:30
(10/15/68).

68-66 11/7/68 — KASHGAR (SINKIANG UIGHUR AUTONOMOUS
REGION) PAKISTAN EXCHANGE OF LETTERS
Border trade.
NCNA Urumchi 11/17/68; SCMP 4302:37 (11/20/68).

68-67 11/14/68 — KWANGCHOW JAPAN AGREEMENT
Japan importing meat from PRC.
NCNA Kwangchow 5/15/69; SCMP 4420:22 (5/21/69).

68-68 11/20/68 — PEKING ALBANIA AGREEMENT
PRC grants a loan to Albania.
JMJP 11/23/68; NCNA Peking 11/20/68; SCMP 4306:22 (11/26/68).

68-69 11/20/68 — PEKING ALBANIA PRESS COMMUNIQUÉ
Trade talks.
JMJP 11/23/68(C); NCNA Peking 11/22/68; SCMP 4308:15
(11/29/68)(E).

68-70 11/20/68 — PEKING ALBANIA PROTOCOL
PRC providing technical aid and complete sets of equipment to
Albania.
JMJP 11/23/68; NCNA Peking 11/20/68; SCMP 4306:22 (11/26/68).

68-71 11/20/68 — PEKING ALBANIA PROTOCOL
PRC providing machines, equipment, materials, and ships to
Albania.

JMJP 11/23/68; NCNA Peking 11/20/68; SCMP 4306:22
(11/26/68).

68-72 11/20/68 1/1/69 PEKING ALBANIA PROTOCOL
Goods exchange and payments.
TYC 16:26(C); JMJP 11/23/68; NCNA Peking 11/20/68; SCMP
4306:22 (11/26/68).

68-73 11/29/68 — PEKING ALBANIA PROTOCOL
Albania's use of PRC loan in 1969.
JMJP 11/23/68; NCNA Peking 11/20/68; SCMP 4306:22 (11/26/68).

68-74 12/26/68 — RAWALPINDI PAKISTAN AGREEMENT
Economic and technical cooperation.
JMJP 12/28/68; NCNA Rawalpindi 12/26/68; SCMP 4330:35
(1/3/69).

1969

69-1 1/7/69 1/1/69 COLOMBO CEYLON PROTOCOL
Exchange of goods for 1969.
TYC 16:103(C); JMJP 1/9/69; NCNA Colombo 1/8/69; SCMP 4337:
20 (1/14/69).

69-2 1/22/69 — PHNOM PENH CAMBODIA DOCUMENT
Turn-over PRC-aided glass factory to Cambodia.
JMJP 1/25/69.

69-3 1/24/69 1/1/69 PEKING KOREA(N) PROTOCOL
Goods exchange for 1969.
TYC 16:89(C); JMJP 1/25/69; NCNA Peking 1/24/69; SCMP 4349:
24 (1/30/69).

69-4 1/26/69 1/26/69 KABUL AFGHANISTAN PROTOCOL
Goods exchange for 1969.
TYC 16:45(C); NCNA Kabul 1/27/69; SCMP 4351:17 (2/3/69).

69-5 2/14/69 1/1/69 PEKING CUBA PROTOCOL
1969 trade.
TYC 16:12(C); NCNA Peking 2/14/69; SCMP 4363:19 (2/25/69).

69-6 2/14/69 — LUSAKA ZAMBIA EXCHANGE OF LETTERS
Construction of Lusaka-Mankoya road with PRC aid.
JMJP 2/16/69; NCNA Peking 2/15/69; SCMP 4363:27 (2/25/69).

69-7   2/28/69   2/28/69   PEKING   GUINEA   AGREEMENT
PRC providing loan to Guinea in form of commodities.
TYC 16:2(C); JMJP 3/1/69; PR 12. 10:4 (3/7/69); NCNA Peking
2/28/69; SCMP 4370:22 (3/6/69).

69-8   2/28/69   1/1/69   PEKING   GUINEA   PROTOCOL
1969 trade.
TYC 16:3(C); JMJP 3/1/68; PR 12. 10:4 (3/7/69); NCNA Peking
2/28/69; SCMP 4370:22 (3/6/69).

69-9   3/5/69   1/1/69   PEKING   UAR   PROTOCOL
1969 trade.
TYC 16:37(C); JMJP 3/6/69; NCNA Peking 3/5/69; SCMP 4374:16
(3/12/69).

69-10   3/8/69   —   KABUL   AFGHANISTAN   NOTES
Talks on PRC providing assistance in artificial breeding of fish
fry at Darunta experimental fish-breeding center.
JMJP 3/13/69; NCNA Kabul 3/9/69; SCMP 4377:17 (3/17/69).

69-11   3/17/69   —   PEKING   YUGOSLAVIA   AGREEMENT
Trade and payments.
TYC 16:71(C); JMJP 3/19/69; NCNA Peking 3/18/69; SCMP 4383:
30 (3/25/69).

69-12   3/18/69   —   MOGADISHU   SOMALIA   MINUTES
Talks on drilling of wells in Belet Uen and hydrogeological
prospecting and survey in Hargeisa with PRC assistance.
JMJP 3/30/69; NCNA Mogadishu 3/18/69; SCMP 4384:27 (3/26/69).

69-13   3/26/69   —   PEKING   FRANCE   AGREEMENT
Trade.
Yearbook on Chinese Communism 2:XI-89 (1970).

69-14   3/26/69   —   PEKING   FRANCE   AGREEMENT
Technical question concerning PRC export of frozen pork to France.
Yearbook on Chinese Communism 2:XI-89 (1970).

69-15   4/1/69   —   KHARTOUM   SUDAN   PROTOCOL
1969 trade.
TYC 16:30(C); JMJP 4/3/69; NCNA Khartoum 4/1/69; SCMP 4392:
24 (4/10/69).

69-16   4/4/69   —   PEKING   JAPAN   COMMUNIQUÉ
Talks between representatives of PRC-Japan Memorandum Trade

Office and Japan-PRC Memorandum Trade office: Taiwan, Japan-U.S. "security treaty," normalization of diplomatic relations, etc.
TYC 16:116(C); JMJP 4/5/69; NCNA Peking 4/4/69; SCMP 4393:
35 (4/11/69)(E).

69-17 4/4/69 — PEKING JAPAN AGREEMENT
1969 memorandum trade extension.
JMJP 4/5/69; NCNA Peking 4/4/69; SCMP 4393:37 (4/11/69);
JAIL 14:191 (1970).

69-18 4/22/69 1/1/69 HELSINKI FINLAND AGREEMENT
1969 trade.
TYC 16:42(C); JMJP 4/24/69; NCNA Peking 4/23/69; SCMP 4405:
27 (4/30/69).

69-19 5/15/69 — KWANGCHOW JAPAN MINUTES
Talks on Japan importing meat from PRC.
NCNA Kwangchow 5/15/69; SCMP 4420:22 (5/21/69).

69-20 5/21/69 — PHNOM PENH CAMBODIA DOCUMENT
Turnover of PRC-aided in construction of works on Chuang-Lung
Cambodia-Chinese people paper mill.
JMJP 5/24/69.

69-21 5/28/69 — KWANGCHOW JAPAN PROTOCOL
Special steel project under memorandum trade.
Yearbook on Chinese Communism 2:XI-86 (1970).

69-22 6/3/69 1/1/69 BUDHAREST RUMANIA AGREEMENT
1969 trade.
TYC 16:47(C); JMJP 6/5/69; NCNA Bucharest 6/3/69; SCMP 4434:
25 (6/11/69).

69-23 6/3/69 — BUCHAREST RUMANIA PROTOCOL
Extension of 1961 Protocol on General Conditions for Delivery of
Goods [61-94].
TYC 16:51(C).

69-24 6/16/69 1/1/69 PRAGUE CZECHOSLOVAKIA AGREE-
MENT
1969 trade.
TYC 16:83(C); JMJP 6/19/69; NCNA Peking 6/18/69; SCMP 4443:
28 (6/25/69).

69-25 6/24/69 — DAR ES SALAAM TANZANIA MINUTES

Talks concerning expansion of national stadium in Dar Es Salaam
with PRC assistance.
JMJP 6/25/69; NCNA Dar es Salaam 6/24/69; SCMP 4447:24
(7/2/69).

69-26 6/25/69 — PEKING JAPAN AGREEMENT
PRC purchasing chemical fertilizer from Japan.
Central News Agency Tokyo 6/26/69 cited in Yearbook on Chinese
Communism 2:XI-86 (1970).

69-27 7/4/69 1/1/69 PEKING BULGARIA AGREEMENT
1969 trade.
TYC 16:66(C); JMJP 7/6/69; NCNA Peking 7/5/69; SCMP 4453:19
(7/11/69).

69-28 7/7/69 1/1/69 PEKING GERMANY(E) AGREEMENT
Goods exchange and payments for 1969.
TYC 16:98(C); JMJP 7/8/69; NCNA Peking 7/7/69; SCMP 4454:22
(7/14/69).

69-29 7/12/69 — DAR ES SALAAM TANZANIA PROTOCOL
Signed at third meeting of directors of PRC-Tanzania Joint Ocean
Shipping Company.
JMJP 7/19/69; NCNA Dar es Salaam 7/17/69; SCMP 4461:29
(7/24/69).

69-30 7/14/69 — SANNA SOUTHERN YEMEN MINUTES
PRC grants gratuitous assistance in building a secondary technical
school for Yemen.
JMJP 7/17/69; NCNA Sanna 7/14/69; SCMP 4460:25 (7/23/69).

69-31 7/24/69 1/1/69 ULAN BATOR MONGOLIA PROTOCOL
Mutual delivery of goods for 1969.
TYC 16:94(C); JMJP 7/27/69; NCNA Ulan Bator 7/26/69; SCMP
4466:23.

69-32 8/2/69 — BUDAPEST HUNGARY PROTOCOL
Extension of 1962 protocol on General Conditions for Delivery of
Goods (62-34).
TYC 16:22(C).

69-33 8/5/69 1/1/69 BUDAPEST HUNGARY AGREEMENT
Goods exchange and payments for 1969.
TYC 16:23(C); JMJP 8/7/69; NCNA Budapest 8/6/69; SCMP 4474:
22 (8/13/69).

69-34 8/7/69 1/1/69 WARSAW POLAND AGREEMENT
Goods exchange and payments for 1969.
TYC 16:57(C); JMJP 8/9/69; NCNA Warsaw 8/8/69; SCMP 4475:
25 (8/14/69).

69-35 8/7/69 — WARSAW POLAND PROTOCOL
Extension of 1961 Protocol on General Conditions for Delivery of
Goods [61-95].
TYC 16:57(C).

69-36 8/8/69 — POLI (SOVIET UNION) USSR MINUTES
Navigation on boundary rivers.
Signed at sixteenth regular meeting of Sino-Soviet Joint Commis-
sion for Navigation on Boundary Rivers.
NCNA Harbin 8/11/69; SCMP 4477:22 (8/18/69).

69-37 9/6/69 — BRAZZAVILLE CONGO AGREEMENT
Plan of construction of a small-size wooden boat building yard in
Congo with PRC assistance.
JMJP 9/8/69; NCNA Brazzaville 9/7/69; SCMP 4494:14 (9/12/69).

69-38 9/26/69 — PEKING VIETNAM(N) AGREEMENT
1970 economic aid to Vietnam.
JMJP 9/27/69; PR 12. 40:40 (10/3/69); NCNA Peking 9/26/69;
SCMP 4508:26 (10/2/69).

69-39 9/28/69 — KWANGCHOW JAPAN CONTRACT
Export of machines to PRC.
Central News Agency Tokyo 11/18/69 cited in Yearbook on Chinese
Communism 2:XI-86 (1970).

69-40 10/9/69 — PEKING GUINEA AGREEMENT
Economic and technical cooperation.
JMJP 10/10/69; NCNA Peking 10/9/69; SCMP 4518:18 (10/16/69).

69-41 10/10/69 — PEKING CONGO(B) AGREEMENT
Economic and technical cooperation.
JMJP 10/11/69; PR 12. 42:10 (10/17/69); NCNA Peking 10/10/69;
SCMP 4519:23 (10/17/69).

69-42 10/15/69 — PEKING VIETNAM(S) (NATIONAL FRONT
LIBERATION) JOINT COMMUNIQUÉ
Talks during visit of President Hguyen Huu Tho: U. S. imperial-
ism in Vietnam.
JMJP 10/17/69(C); PR 12. 43:6 (10/24/69)(E); NCNA Peking
10/16/69; SCMP 4522:36 (10/23/69).

69-43 10/18/69 — PEKING(?) USSR COMMUNIQUÉ
Negotiation to be held on Sino-Soviet boundary question at the
level of vice-minister of Foreign Affairs in Peking on 10/20/69.
JMJP 10/19/69(C); NCNA Peking 10/18/69; SCMP 4523:30
(10/24/69)(E).

69-44 10/22/69 1/1/70 PEKING CEYLON PROTOCOL
Exchange of goods for 1970.
TYC 16:104(C); JMJP 10/23/69; NCNA Peking 10/22/69; SCMP
4526:21 (10/29/69).

69-45 10/23/69 — PEKING VIETNAM(N) AGREEMENT
Exchange of goods and payments in 1970.
TYC 16:77(C).

69-46 10/25/69 — PEKING VIETNAM(N) COMMUNIQUÉ
Talks during visit of Premier Pham Van Dong: cultural revolution,
U. S. imperialism in Vietnam, etc.
JMJP 10/26/69(C); PR 12. 44:6 (10/31/69)(E); NCNA Peking
10/25/68; SCMP 4527:19 (10/30/69)(E).

69-47 11/7/69 — PEKING IRAQ AGREEMENT
Civil air transportation.
JMJP 11/8/69; PR 12. 46:31 (11/14/69); NCNA Peking 11/7/69;
SCMP 4537:25 (11/14/69).

69-48 11/13/69 — KWANGCHOW JAPAN CONTRACT
Export papers.
Central News Agency Tokyo 11/18/69 cited in Yearbook on Chinese
Communism 2:XI-86 (1970).

69-49 11/14/69 — LUSAKA TANZANIA & ZAMBIA AGREE-
MENT (SUPPLEMENTARY)
Construction of Tanzania-Zambia railway.
JMJP 11/18/69; NCNA Lusaka 11/16/69; SCMP 4543:21 (11/24/69).

69-50 11/14/69 — LUSAKA TANZANIA & ZAMBIA PROPOSAL
(SUPPLEMENTARY)
Certain technical principles concerning construction of railway.
JMJP 11/18/69; NCNA Lusaka 11/16/69; SCMP 4543:21 (11/24/69).

69-51 11/14/69 — LUSAKA TANZANIA & ZAMBIA MINUTES
Talks on preparatory works concerning Tanzania-Zambia railway.
JMJP 11/18/69; NCNA Lusaka 11/16/69; SCMP 4543:21 (11/24/69).

69-52   11/23/69 — PEKING   VIETNAM(N)   AGREEMENT
Mutual goods supply and payments in 1970.
JMJP 11/24/69; NCNA Peking 11/23/69; SCMP 4547:28 (12/1/69).

69-53   11/26/69 — PEKING   VIETNAM(N)   EXCHANGE OF
LETTERS
Extension of 1955 Protocol on Small-Scale Trading in Border
Areas [55-49].
TYC 16:79(C).

69-54   11/27/69 — NOUAKCHOTT   MAURITANIA   CONTRACT
Project of sinking wells in Mauritania with PRC assistance.
JMJP 12/3/68; NCNA Nouakchott 11/29/69; SCMP 4552:28 (12/8/69).

69-55   12/4/69 — ADEN   SOUTHERN YEMEN   PROTOCOL
Dispatch of a medical team to Southern Yemen.
TYC 16:112(C); JMJP 12/8/69; NCNA Aden 12/6/69; SCMP 4556:
23 (12/12/69).

69-56   12/20/69(?) — KABUL   AFGHANISTAN   MINUTES
Talks on experimental tea planting in Afghanistan with PRC
assistance.
JMJP 12/25/69; NCNA Kabul 12/23/69; SCMP 4568:27 (1/2/70).

69-57   12/31/69 — LUSAKA   ZAMBIA   EXCHANGE OF LETTERS
PRC's provision gratis of broadcast transmitters and other
auxiliary equipment for Zambia.
JMJP 1/7/70; NCNA Peking 1/5/70; SCMP 4574:43 (1/12/70).

1970

70-1   1/3/70 — TIRANA   ALBANIA   PROTOCOL
Scientific and technical cooperation.
Signed at thirteenth session of the Joint China-Albania Committee
for Cooperation in Technology and Technical Science.
JMJP 1/5/70; NCNA Tirana 1/3/70; SCMP 4573:183 (1/9/70).

70-2   1/19/70   1/1/70   TIRANA   ALBANIA   PROTOCOL
Barter and Payments for 1970.
TYC 17:9(C); JMJP 1/21/70; NCNA Tirana 1/20/70; SCMP 4585:
49 (1/27/70).

70-3   1/19/70 — TIRANA   ALBANIA   PROTOCOL
Albania's use in 1970 of credits granted by PRC.
JMJP 1/21/70; NCNA Tirana 1/20/70; SCMP 4585:49 (1/27/70).

70-4   1/29/70 — SHENYANG   KOREA(N)   ACCORD
Border river navigation.
Signed at ninth meeting of Cooperation Commission for Navigation
in Yalu and Tumen Rivers.
JMJP 1/31/70; NCNA Shenyang 1/30/70; SCMP 4592:121 (2/5/70).

70-5   1/30/70 — LUSAKA   ZAMBIA   SUMMARY   MINUTES
Talks on construction of Lusaka–Kaoma highway.
JMJP 2/1/70; NCNA Peking 1/31/70; SCMP 4593:26 (2/10/70).

70-6   1/30/70 — LUSAKA   ZAMBIA   EXCHANGE OF NOTES
Treatment and working conditions for the Chinese technical
personnel.
JMJP 2/1/70; NCNA Peking 1/31/70; SCMP 4593:26 (2/10/70).

70-7   1/30/70 — CONAKRY   GUINEA   PROTOCOL
Trade for 1970.
JMJP 2/3/70; NCNA Conakry 2/1/70; SCMP 4594:55 (2/11/70).

70-8   1/31/70 1/1/70 PEKING   FINLAND   AGREEMENT
Trade.
TYC 17:19(C); JMJP 2/1/70; NCNA Peking 1/31/70; SCMP 4593:
17 (2/10/70).

70-9   2/8/70 — COLOMBO   CEYLON   EXCHANGE OF LETTERS
Building of cotton spinning and weaving mill at Minneriya with
PRC assistance.
JMJP 2/12/70; NCNA Colombo 2/9/70; SCMP 4599:134 (2/18/70).

70-10   3/2/70 1/1/70 PYONGYANG   KOREA(N)   PROTOCOL
Mutual delivery of goods for 1970.
TYC 17:45(C); JMJP 3/3/70; NCNA Pyongyang 3/2/70; SCMP
4612:52 (3/10/70).

70-11   3/10/70 — CONAKRY   GUINEA   PROTOCOL
Medical cooperation (dispatch of Chinese medical team to Guinea).
JMJP 3/13/70; NCNA Conakry 3/11/70; SCMP 4618:110 (3/18/70).

70-12   3/14/70 — HANOI   VIETNAM(N)   PROTOCOL
Agreement on scientific and technical cooperation for 1970.
JMJP 3/16/70; NCNA Hanoi 3/15/70; SCMP 4619:143 (3/19/70).

70-13   3/17/70 8/?/70 ALGIERS   ALGERIA   PROTOCOL
Medical cooperation (dispatch of Chinese medical team to Algeria).
TYC 17:62(C); JMJP 3/20/70; NCNA Algiers 3/17/70; SCMP
4623:76 (3/25/70).

70-14 3/19/70 — CAIRO UAR PROTOCOL
Trade for 1970.
JMJP 3/21/70; NCNA 3/19/70; SCMP 4625:36 (3/30/70).

70-15 3/23/70 — LUSAKA ZAMBIA MINUTES
Talks concerning construction of Zambia broadcast transmitter.
JMJP 3/29/70; NCNA Peking 3/26/70; SCMP 4628:185 (4/2/70).

70-16 3/23/70 — LUSAKA ZAMBIA
Technical plan for construction of Zambia broadcast transmitter.
JMJP 3/29/70; NCNA Peking 3/26/70; SCMP 4628:185 (4/2/70).

70-17 3/23/70 — KABUL AFGHANISTAN CERTIFICATE
Transferring documents concerning soil construction, equipment,
and production technique.
NCNA 3/27/70, cited in Yearbook on Chinese Communism: 11-93
(1971).

70-18 3/28/70 1/1/70 PEKING RUMANIA AGREEMENT
Trade and payments for 1970.
TYC 17:30(C); JMJP 3/29/70; NCNA Peking 3/28/70; SCMP 4630:
54 (4/7/70).

70-19 3/28/70 — PEKING RUMANIA PROTOCOL
Extension of 1961 Protocol on General Conditions for Delivery of
Goods [61-94].
TYC 17:34(C).

70-20 4/5/70 — MOGADISHU SOMALIA DOCUMENT
Transferring PRC-aided rice and tobacco experimental station to
Somalia.
JMJP 4/8/70; NCNA Mogadishu 4/5/70; SCMP 4635:82 (4/14/70).

70-21 4/7/70 — PYONGYANG KOREA(N) JOINT COMMUNIQUÉ
Talks during Premier Chou En-lai's visit: Vietnam, U. S.-Japan
Security Treaty, Korea, etc.
JMJP 4/9/70 C); PR 13. 15:3 (4/10/70)(E); NCNA Peking 4/7/70;
SCMP 4637:154 (4/16/70)(E).

70-22 4/9/70 — PEKING ALBANIA PROTOCOL
Shipping.
Signed at eighth session of Administration Commission for Sino-
Albanian Shipping Joint Stock Company.
JMJP 4/10/70; NCNA Peking 4/9/70; SCMP 4637:147 (4/16/70).

70-23 4/9/70 — RAWALPINDI PAKISTAN PROTOCOL
Economic and technical cooperation agreement.
JMJP 4/11/70; NCNA Rawalpindi 4/9/70; SCMP 4638:196 (4/17/70).

70-24 4/14/70 — PEKING JAPAN JOINT STATEMENT
Signed by PRC Council for Promotion of International Trade and
Japanese Association for Promotion of International Trade and
six other Japanese trading organizations: Japan-U. S. security
treaty, Okinawa, Taiwan, etc.
JMJP 4/15/70(C); PR 13. 17:29 (4/24/70)(E); NCNA Peking 4/14/70;
SCMP 4641:90 (4/23/70)(E).

70-25 4/19/70 — PEKING JAPAN COMMUNIQUÉ
Talks between representatives of PRC-Japan Memorandum Trade
Office and Japan-PRC Memorandum Trade Office: Okinawa, Japan-
U. S. Security Treaty, Taiwan, etc.
TYC 17:65(C); JMJP 4/20/70(C); PR 13. 17:31 (4/24/70)(E); NCNA
Peking 4/19/70; SCMP 4645:120 (4/29/70)(E); JAIL 15:206 (1971).

70-26 4/19/70 — PEKING JAPAN AGREEMENT
Memorandum trade for 1970.
JMJP 4/20/70; PR 13. 17:33 (4/24/70); NCNA Peking 4/19/70;
SCMP 4645:122 (4/29/70); JAIL 15:106 (1971).

70-27 5/5/70 — PEKING PAKISTAN PROTOCOL
Trade.
JMJP 5/6/70; NCNA Peking 5/5/70; SCMP 4656:167 (5/14/70).

70-28 5/8/70 — DAR ES SALAAM TANZANIA MINUTES
Talks on construction of Tanzanian Mbarali state farm with PRC
assistance.
JMJP 5/14/70; NCNA Dar es Salaam 5/10/70; SCMP 4660:103
(5/20/70).

70-29 5/21/70 — RAWALPINDI PAKISTAN LETTERS
Further development of border trade between PRC and Pakistan.
JMJP 5/24/70; NCNA Rawalpindi 5/21/70; SCMP 4668:80 (6/2/70).

70-30 5/21/70 — KHARTOUM SUDAN PROTOCOL
Trade for 1970.
JMJP 5/24/70; NCNA Khartoum 5/22/70; SCMP 4668:80 (6/2/70).

70-31 5/25/70 — PEKING VIETNAM(N) PROTOCOL (SUPPLE-
MENTARY)
Economic and military materials as gratuitous aid to Vietnam by
PRC.

JMJP 5/27/70; PR 13. 23:38 (6/5/70); NCNA Peking 5/26/70; SCMP 4670:171 (6/4/70).

70-32 5/ ?/70 — KARACHI PAKISTAN CONTRACT
Purchasing passenger plane from Pakistan.
Yearbook on Chinese Communism: 11-83 (1971).

70-33 5/ ?/70 — PEKING CAMBODIA AGREEMENT
Loan.
Ta Kung Pao Hong Kong 8/19/70; SCMP 4723:195 (8/21/70).

70-34 6/3/70 — PYONGYANG KOREA(N) EXCHANGE OF NOTES
Extension of Protocol and Supplementary Protocol on transporting wood in Yalu and Tumen Rivers.
These two protocols were said to be concluded on 1/14/61 and 1/14/65 respectively.
TYC 17:7(C).

70-35 6/4/70 — DAR ES SALAAM TANZANIA CERTIFICATE
Transferring PRC aided agricultural instruments factory to Tanzania.
JMJP 6/14/70; NCNA Dar es Salaam 6/6/70; SCMP 4678:106 (6/17/70).

70-36 6/16/70 1/1/70 PEKING CZECHOSLOVAKIA AGREE-MENT
Exchange of goods and payment for 1970.
TYC 17:39(C); JMJP 6/18/70; NCNA Peking 6/17/70; SCMP 4684: 120 (6/25/70).

70-37 6/16/70 — PEKING CZECHOSLOVAKIA EXCHANGE OF NOTES
Changing ruble account into Swiss franc account.
TYC 17:42(C).

70-38 6/19/70 — PEKING SOMALIA PROTOCOL
Economic and technical cooperation.
JMJP 6/20/70; PR 13. 26:6 (6/26/70); NCNA Peking 6/19/70; SCMP 4685:153 (6/26/70).

70-39 6/20/70 — PEKING JAPAN COMMUNIQUÉ
Talks between delegation of China Fishery Association and Japan-China Fishery Association: extension of validity of Sino-Japanese Fishery Agreement [65-156] for another two years, supplementary provisions for Fishery Agreement, etc.

TYC 17:68(C); JMJP 6/21/70(C); NCNA Peking 6/20/70; SCMP 4686:19 (6/29/70)(E); JAIL 15:208 (1971).

70-40 6/29/70 6/29/70 PEKING RUMANIA PROTOCOL
Gratuitous material aid to Rumania by PRC.
TYC 17:35(C); JMJP 6/30/70; PR 13. 28:40 (7/10/70); NCNA Peking 6/29/70; SCMP 4693:208 (7/9/70).

70-41 6/29/70 — HAVANA CUBA PROTOCOL
Trade in 1970.
JMJP 7/3/70; NCNA Havana 6/30/70; SCMP 4695:33 (7/13/70).

70-42 6/30/70 1/1/70 BERLIN GERMANY(E) AGREEMENT
Exchange of goods and payments for 1970.
TYC 17:55(C); JMJP 7/2/70; NCNA Berlin 6/30/70; SCMP 4695: 34 (7/13/70).

70-43 7/2/70 1/1/70 PEKING POLAND AGREEMENT
Exchange of goods and payments for 1970.
TYC 17:21(C); JMJP 7/3/70; NCNA Peking 7/2/70; SCMP 4695:35 (7/13/70).

70-44 7/2/70 — PEKING POLAND PROTOCOL
Extension of 1961 Protocol on General Conditions for Delivery of Goods [61-95].
TYC 17:25(C).

70-45 7/2/70 — PEKING POLAND EXCHANGE OF NOTES
Opening Swiss franc account and scheme of calculation.
TYC 17:26(C).

70-46 7/8/70 — PEKING JAPAN CONTRACT
Sale of soybeans under 1970 Memorandum Trade Agreement [70-26]. Concluded between China Food, Oil, and Cereal Export Co. and the Soybean Delegation of Japan-PRC Memorandum Trade Office.
Yearbook on Chinese Communism: 11-94 (1971).

70-47 7/9/70 — BRAZZAVILLE CONGO PROTOCOL
Supplement to Agreement on Sending Chinese Medical Team to Congo.
Time and date of Agreement was not released.
JMJP 7/11/70; NCNA Brazzaville 7/9/70; SCMP 4701:99 (7/22/70).

70-48 7/10/70 HEIHO (HEILUNGKIANG, CHINA) USSR AGREE-MENT

Border river navigation.
Signed at sixteenth regular meeting of Sino-Soviet Joint Commission for Navigation on Boundary Rivers.
NCNA Peking 6/30/70; SCMP 4694:237 (7/10/70).

70-49   7/12/70 — PEKING   TANZANIA & ZAMBIA   PROTOCOL
Concerning amount of loan for construction of Tanzania-Zambia railway and method of its payment.
JMJP 7/13/70; PR 13. 29:16 (7/17/70); NCNA Peking 7/12/70; SCMP 4701:116 (7/22/70).

70-50   7/12/70 — PEKING   TANZANIA & ZAMBIA   PROTOCOL
Concerning "Report on Survey and Design for Tan-Zan Railway. "
JMJP 7/13/70; PR 13. 29:16 (7/17/70); NCNA Peking 7/12/70; SCMP 4701:116 (7/22/70).

70-51   7/12/70 — PEKING   TANZANIA & ZAMBIA   MINUTES
Talks on construction of Tan-Zan railway.
JMJP 7/13/70; PR 13. 29:16 (7/17/70); NCNA Peking 7/12/70; SCMP 4701:116 (7/22/70).

70-52   7/14/70   1/1/70   PEKING   MONGOLIA   PROTOCOL
Mutual supply of goods for 1970.
TYC 17:51(C); JMJP 7/15/70; NCNA Peking 7/14/70; SCMP 4702: 146 (7/23/70).

70-53   7/24/70   1/1/70   PEKING   HUNGARY   AGREEMENT
Exchange of goods and payment.
TYC 17:15(C); JMJP 7/25/70; NCNA Peking 7/24/70; SCMP 4709: 45 (8/3/70).

70-54   7/24/70 — PEKING   HUNGARY   PROTOCOL
General conditions for delivery of goods.
TYC 17:18(C).

70-55   7/30/70 — ADEN   SOUTHERN YEMEN   PROTOCOL
Supplement to 1970 Agreement on Economic and Technical Co-operation [70-58].
JMJP 8/2/70; NCNA Aden 7/31/70; SCMP 4715:74 (8/11/70).

70-56   7/30/70 — ADEN   SOUTHERN YEMEN   EXCHANGE OF LETTERS
Dispatch of PRC engineering and technical personnel to Southern Yemen.
JMJP 8/2/70; NCNA Aden 7/31/70; SCMP 4715:75 (8/11/70).

70-57 7/31/70 — ZANZIBAR TANZANIA MINUTES
Talks on PRC aid to Tanzania for constructing a mill factory at
Zanzibar.
JMJP 8/6/70.

70-58 8/7/70 — PEKING SOUTHERN YEMEN AGREEMENT
Economic and technical cooperation.
JMJP 8/8/70; NCNA Peking 8/7/70; SCMP 4719:60 (8/17/70).

70-59 8/12/70 — PEKING SUDAN AGREEMENT
Economic and technical cooperation.
JMJP 8/13/70; PR 13. 34:31 (8/21/70); NCNA Peking 8/12/70;
SCMP 4722:153 (8/20/70).

70-60 8/12/70 — PEKING SUDAN AGREEMENT
Cultural, scientific, and technical cooperation.
JMJP 8/13/70; PR 13. 34:31 (8/21/70); NCNA Peking 8/12/70;
SCMP 4722:153 (8/20/70).

70-61 8/14/70 — PEKING SOUTHERN YEMEN JOINT COM-
MUNIQUÉ
Talks during visit of Chairman Salem Robaya Ali: Indochina,
Palestinian Arabs, Arabian Gulf, etc.
JMJP 8/15/70(C); PR 13. 34:6 (8/21/70)(E); NCNA Peking 8/14/70;
SCMP 4724:29 (8/24/70)(E).

70-62 8/17/70 — PEKING JAPAN AGREEMENT
Purchase of chemical fertilizers from Japan.
Yearbook on Chinese Communism: 11-94 (1971).

70-63 8/17/70 — PEKING CAMBODIA AGREEMENT
PRC providing gratuitous military aid to Cambodia.
JMJP 8/18/70; PR 13. 35:22 (8/28/70); NCNA Peking 8/17/70;
SCMP 4724:79 (8/24/70).

70-64 8/25/70 — PEKING JAPAN CONTRACT
Japanese export of urea to PRC for 1970.
Concluded between China Chemical Engineering Co. and Mitsui
Toatsu Chemical Company.
Yearbook on Chinese Communism: 11-94 (1971).

70-65 8/31/70 1/1/70 SOFIA BULGARIA AGREEMENT
Exchange of goods and payments for 1970.
TYC 17:36(C); JMJP 9/2/70; NCNA Sofia 9/1/70; SCMP 4735:80
(9/9/70).

70-66 9/5/70 — ENTEBBE UGANDA PROTOCOL
Supplement to 1965 Agreement on Sino-Uganda Economic-Technical Cooperation [65-55].
JMJP 9/8/70; NCNA Dar es Salaam 9/6/70; SCMP 4740:134 (9/18/70).

70-67 9/12/70 — PEKING CEYLON AGREEMENT
Loan.
JMJP 9/13/70; PR 13. 38:29 (9/18/70); NCNA Peking 9/12/70; SCMP 4743:124 (9/23/70).

70-68 10/6/70 — PEKING VIETNAM(N) AGREEMENT
Economic and technical aid.
JMJP 10/7/70; NCNA Peking 10/6/70; SCMP 4759:309 (10/16/70).

70-69 10/6/70 — PEKING VIETNAM(N) PROTOCOL
Military aid.
JMJP 10/7/70; NCNA Peking 10/6/70; SCMP 4759:309 (10/16/70).

70-70 10/13/70 10/13/70 PEKING CANADA JOINT COMMUNIQUÉ
Establishment of diplomatic relations.
TYC 17:1(C); JMJP 10/14/70(C); PR 13. 42:12 (10/16/70)(E); NCNA Peking 10/13/70; SCMP 4764:235 (10/23/70)(E).

70-71 10/15/70 — SANTA ISABEL EQUATORIAL GUINEA JOINT COMMUNIQUÉ
Establishment of diplomatic relations.
TYC 17:1(C); JMJP 10/21/70(C); PR 13. 43:10 (10/23/70)(E); NCNA Peking 10/20/70; SCMP 4768:165 (10/29/70)(E).

70-72 10/15/70 — COLOMBO CEYLON EXCHANGE OF NOTES
Extension of 1957 Agreement on Economic Aid [57-87].
TYC 17:54(C).

70-73 10/16/70 — PEKING ALBANIA AGREEMENT
Long-term interest-free PRC loan to Albania.
JMJP 10/17/70; PR 13. 43:3 (10/23/70); NCNA Peking 10/16/70; SCMP 4766:65 (10/27/70).

70-74 10/16/70 1/1/71 PEKING ALBANIA AGREEMENT
Goods exchange and payments from 1971 to 1975.
TYC 17:1(C); JMJP 10/17/70; PR 13. 43:3 (10/23/70); NCNA Peking 10/16/70; SCMP 4766:65 (10/27/70).

70-75 10/16/70 — PEKING ALBANIA PROTOCOL
PRC provide Albania with complete sets of equipment for projects.
JMJP 10/17/70; PR 13. 43:3 (10/23/70); NCNA Peking 10/16/70;
SCMP 4766:65 (10/27/70).

70-76 10/16/70 — PEKING ALBANIA PROTOCOL
PRC supply Albania with general materials.
JMJP 10/17/70; PR 13. 43:3 (10/23/70); NCNA Peking 10/16/70;
SCMP 4766:65 (10/27/70).

70-77 10/16/70 — PEKING ALBANIA PROTOCOL
Use of PRC loan by Albania for 1971.
JMJP 10/17/70; PR 13. 23:3 (10/23/70); NCNA Peking 10/16/70;
SCMP 4766:66 (10/27/70).

70-78 10/16/70 1/1/71 PEKING ALBANIA PROTOCOL
Delivery of goods and payments for 1971.
TYC 17:13(C); JMJP 10/17/70; PR 13. 43:3 (10/23/70); NCNA
Peking 10/16/70; SCMP 4766:66 (10/27/70).

70-79 10/17/70 — TIRANA ALBANIA
Plan for scientific cooperation between Chinese Academy of
Sciences and Tirana State University for 1970-1971.
JMJP 10/26/70; NCNA Tirana 10/18/70; SCMP 4767:115 (10/28/70).

70-80 10/17/70 — PEKING KOREA(N) AGREEMENT
Economic and technical aid to Korea.
JMJP 10/18/70; PR 13. 43:3 (10/23/70); NCNA Peking 10/17/70;
SCMP 4766:74 (10/27/70).

70-81 10/17/70 1/1/71 PEKING KOREA(N) AGREEMENT
Mutual supply of main items of goods between 1971 to 1976.
TYC 17:48(C); JMJP 10/18/70; PR 13. 43:3 (10/23/70); NCNA
Peking 10/17/70; SCMP 4766:74 (10/27/70).

70-82 10/17/70 1/1/71 PEKING KOREA(N) PROTOCOL
Mutual supply of goods for 1971.
TYC 17:49(C); JMJP 10/18/70; PR 13. 43:3 (10/23/70); NCNA
Peking 10/17/70; SCMP 4766:74 (10/27/70).

70-83 10/20/70 — BUCHAREST RUMANIA PROTOCOL
Scientific and technical cooperation.
Signed at thirteenth session of Sino-Rumania Joint Commission
on Scientific and Technical Cooperation.
JMJP 10/23/70; NCNA Bucharest 10/21/70; SCMP 4769:204
(10/30/70).

70-84 10/31/70 — SINEJU KOREA(N) PROTOCOL
Border railway transport.
Signed at regular meeting of Sino-Korean Border Railway Joint
Committee.
JMJP 11/1/70; NCNA Pyongyang 10/31/70; SCMP 4776:74
(11/10/70).

70-85 10/31/70 1/1/71 PEKING VIETNAM(N) AGREEMENT
Mutual supply of goods and payments for 1971.
TYC 17:43(C); JMJP 11/1/70; PR 13.45:29 (11/6/70); NCNA
Peking 10/31/70; SCMP 4776:75 (11/10/70).

70-86 10/31/70 — PEKING VIETNAM(N) PROTOCOL
Supply of material to Vietnam for 1971.
JMJP 11/1/70; PR 13.45:29 (11/6/70); NCNA Peking 10/31/70;
SCMP 4776:75 (11/10/70).

70-87 10/31/70 — PEKING VIETNAM(N) PROTOCOL
PRC aid to Vietnam in form of complete projects.
JMJP 11/1/70; PR 13.45:29 (11/6/70); NCNA Peking 10/31/70;
SCMP 4776:75 (11/10/70).

70-88 10/31/70 — PEKING VIETNAM(N) PROTOCOL
Living standard and working conditions of PRC technical person-
nel sent to Vietnam.
JMJP 11/1/70; PR 13.45:29 (11/6/70); NCNA Peking 10/31/70;
SCMP 4776:75 (11/10/70).

70-89 10/31/70 — PEKING VIETNAM(N) PROTOCOL
Delivery of equipment and materials for complete projects to
Vietnam.
JMJP 11/1/70; PR 13.45:29 (11/6/70); NCNA Peking 10/31/70;
SCMP 4776:75 (11/10/70).

70-90 11/1/70 — PEKING JAPAN JOINT STATEMENT
Talks during visit of Tomomi Narita, Chairman of Central
Executive Committee of Japanese Socialist Party: nuclear
weapons, Korea, Indo-China, U.S. imperialism, etc.
JMJP 11/2/70(C); PR 13.45:14 (11/6/70)(E); NCNA Peking
11/1/70; SCMP 4776:64 (11/10/70)(E).

70-91 11/2/70 — PEKING GUINEA PROTOCOL
Supplement to 1969 Agreement on Economic and Technical Co-
operation (69-40).
JMJP 11/3/70; PR 13.47:21 (11/20/70); NCNA Peking 11/2/70;
SCMP 4777:17 (11/12/70).

70-92 11/6/70 11/6/70 PEKING ITALY JOINT COMMUNIQUÉ
Establishment of diplomatic relations.
TYC 17:2(C); JMJP 11/7/70(C); PR 13.46:6 (11/13/70)(E); NCNA
Peking 11/6/70; SCMP 4779:26 (11/16/70)(E).

70-93 11/14/70 — PEKING PAKISTAN JOINT COMMUNIQUÉ
Talks during visit of President Agha Muhammad Yahya Khan:
Indo-China, Middle East, nuclear weapons, etc.
JMJP 11/15/70(C); PR 13.47:8 (11/20/70)(E); NCNA Peking
11/14/70; SCMP 4785:67 (11/24/70)(E).

70-94 11/14/70 — PEKING PAKISTAN AGREEMENT
Economic and technical cooperation.
JMJP 11/15/70; NCNA Peking 11/14/70; SCMP 4785:66 (11/24/70).

70-95 11/14/70 — KABUL AFGHANISTAN EXCHANGE OF
LETTERS
Supply of commodities by PRC to Afghanistan from loan.
JMJP 11/18/70; NCNA Kabul 11/17/70; SCMP 4787:149 (11/27/70).

70-96 11/22/70 — PEKING USSR AGREEMENT
Exchange of goods and payments.
TYC 17:27(C); JMJP 11/23/70; PR 13.48:23 (11/27/70); NCNA
Peking 11/22/70; SCMP 4790:126 (12/2/70).

70-97 11/23/70 11/23/70 PEKING USSR PROTOCOL
Revision of Article 20 of 1957 Protocol on General Conditions for
Delivery of Goods [57-39].
TYC 17:29(C).

70-98 11/24/70 — ADDIS ABABA ETHIOPIA JOINT COMMUNI-
QUÉ
Establishment of diplomatic relations.
TYC 17:3(C); JMJP 12/2/70(C); PR 13.50:7 (12/11/70)(E); NCNA
Peking 12/1/70; SCMP 4794:71 (12/8/70)(E).

70-99 11/25/70 — PEKING RUMANIA AGREEMENT
Long-term interest-free loan provided by PRC to Rumania.
JMJP 11/26/70; PR 13.50:21 (12/11/70); NCNA Peking 11/25/70;
SCMP 4791:171 (12/3/70).

70-100 11/27/70 — NOUAKCHOTT MAURITANIA CERTIFICATE
Transfer of a PRC gift of "youth home" constructed at Nouakchott
to Mauritania.
JMJP 12/10/70; NCNA Nouakchott 11/28/70; SCMP 4794:75
(12/8/70).

70-101 12/9/70 — PEKING   KOREA(N)   PROTOCOL
Scientific and technical cooperation.
Signed at eleventh session of Sino-Korean Standing Committee for
Cooperation in Technology and Technical Services.
JMJP 12/10/70; PR 13. 51:23 (12/18/70); NCNA Peking 12/9/70;
SCMP 4800:93 (12/16/70).

70-102 12/14/70 — KHARTOUM   SUDAN   PROTOCOL
Dispatch of PRC medical teams to Sudan.
It was signed in accordance with Agreement on Cultural, Scientific, and Technological Cooperation which was signed in August
this year [70-60].
TYC 17:60(C); JMJP 12/18/70; NCNA Khartoum 12/14/70; SCMP
4804:69 (12/22/70).

70-103 12/15/70   12/15/70 — PARIS   CHILE   JOINT COMMUNIQUÉ
Establishment of diplomatic relations.
JMJP 1/6/71(C); PR 14. 2:3 (1/8/71)(E); NCNA Peking 1/5/71;
SCMP 4817:55(E) (1/12/71)(E).

70-104 12/19/70 — HEIHO (HEILUNGKIANG, CHINA)   USSR   SUM-
MARY
Border river navigation.
Signed at sixteenth regular meeting of Sino-Soviet Joint Commis-
sion for Navigation on Border Rivers.
JMJP 12/24/70; PR 14. 1:7 (1/1/71); NCNA Peking 12/23/70;
SCMP 4810:175 (12/31/70).

70-105 12/21/70 — PEKING   MALI   AGREEMENT
Economic and technical cooperation.
JMJP 12/22/70; PR 13. 52:4 (12/25/70).

70-106 12/24/70 — KATMANDU   NEPAL   LETTER OF EXCHANGE
Construction of a power transmission and transformation project
in Nepal with PRC assistance.
JMJP 12/26/70; NCNA Katmandu 12/24/70; SCMP 4812:91 (1/5/71).

70-107 12/26/70 — PEKING   AFGHANISTAN   AGREEMENT
Trade and payments.
JMJP 12/27/70; PR 14. 1:7 (1/1/71); NCNA Peking 12/26/70;
SCMP 4812:87 (1/5/71).

70-108 12/26/70 — PEKING   AFGHANISTAN   PROTOCOL
Exchange of goods.
JMJP 12/27/70; PR 14. 1:7 (1/1/71); NCNA Peking 12/26/70;
SCMP 4812:87 (1/5/71).

70-109 12/31/70 — PEKING JAPAN COMMUNIQUÉ
Talks between Fishery Association of PRC and Japan-PRC Fishery Association: concluding Regulations concerning Purse-Seining
with Lighting Ship.
TYC 17:70(C); JMJP 1/1/71(C); NCNA Peking 12/31/70; SCMP
4815:238 (1/8/71)(E).

70-110 12/31/70 — PEKING JAPAN REGULATION
Purse-Seining with lighting ships.
TYC 17:72(C); JMJP 1/1/71; NCNA Peking 12/31/70; SCMP 4815:
234 (1/8/71)(E).

<u>1971</u>

71-1   1/21/71 1/1/71 COLOMBO CEYLON (SRI LANKA)
PROTOCOL
Exchange of goods in 1971.
TYC 18:97(C); JMJP 1/23/71; PR 14. 6:4 (2/5/71); NCNA
Colombo 1/22/71; SCMP 4830:106 (2/3/71).

71-2   1/21/71 — COLOMBO CEYLON (SRI LANKA) CONTRACT
Sale of 41,000 tons of rubber to PRC.
JMJP 1/23/71; PR 14. 6:4 (2/5/71); NCNA Colombo 1/22/71;
SCMP 4830:106 (2/3/71).

71-3   1/21/71 — COLOMBO CEYLON (SRI LANKA) CONTRACT
Sale of 200,000 tons of rice to Ceylon.
JMJP 1/23/71; PR 14. 6:4 (2/5/71); NCNA Colombo 1/22/71;
SCMP 4830:106 (2/3/71).

71-4   1/22/71 — PEKING EQUATORIAL GUINEA AGREEMENT
Economic and technical cooperation.
JMJP 1/23/71; PR 14. 5:4 (1/29/71); NCNA Peking 1/22/71);
SCMP 4830:109 (2/3/71).

71-5   1/22/71 1/22/71 PEKING EQUATORIAL GUINEA AGREE-
MENT
Trade.
TYC 19:75(C); JMJP 1/23/71; PR 14. 5:4 (1/29/71); NCNA Peking
1/22/71; SCMP 4830:109 (2/3/71).

71-6   1/27/71 — BRAZZAVILLE CONGO(B) MINUTES
Talks for construction of Congolese hospital with PRC assistance.
JMJP 2/1/71; NCNA Brazzaville 1/30/71; SCMP 4835:129 (2/10/71).

71-7   2/1/71 — PEKING JAPAN SUMMARY
Talks between Table Tennis Association of PRC, Chinese People's Association for Friendship with Foreign Countries and Japanese Table Tennis Association, Japan-China Cultural Exchange Association: PRC participation in thirty-first World Table Tennis Championships, friendly exchanges between two countries under three political principles, etc.
JMJP 2/2/71(C); NCNA Peking 2/1/71; SCMP 4835:130 (2/10/71) (E).

71-8   2/8/71 1/1/71 HELSINKI FINLAND AGREEMENT
Trade for 1971.
TYC 18:46(C); JMJP 2/11/71; PR 14.10:16 (3/5/71); NCNA Peking 2/10/71; SCMP 4841:148 (2/19/71).

71-9   2/8/71 1/1/71 CONAKRY GUINEA PROTOCOL
Trade for 1971.
TYC 19:36(C); JMJP 2/12/71; NCNA Conakry 2/9/71; SCMP 4843:85 (2/23/71).

71-10 2/10/71 — CAIRO NIGERIA JOINT COMMUNIQUÉ
Establishment of diplomatic relations.
TYC 18:1(C); JMJP 2/11/71(C); PR 14.8:5 (2/19/71)(E); NCNA Peking 2/10/71; SCMP 4841:148 (2/19/71)(E).

71-11 2/15/71 — PEKING VIETNAM(N) AGREEMENT
Supplementary economic and military aid to Vietnam in 1971.
JMJP 2/16/71; NCNA Peking 2/15/71; SCMP 4845:188 (2/25/71).

71-12 2/18/71 1/1/72 BUCHAREST RUMANIA AGREEMENT
Long-term trade for mutual supply of main goods during 1972-75.
TYC 18:51(C); JMJP 2/20/71; PR 14.9:5 (2/26/71); NCNA Bucharest 2/19/71; SCMP 4848:80 (3/2/71).

71-13 2/18/71 1/1/71 BUCHAREST RUMANIA AGREEMENT
Trade and payments for 1971.
TYC 18:52(C); JMJP 2/20/71; PR 14.9:5 (2/26/71); NCNA Bucharest 2/19/71; SCMP 4848:80 (3/2/71).

71-14 2/18/71 — BUCHAREST RUMANIA PROTOCOL
Extension of 1961 Protocol on General Conditions for delivery of goods [61-94].
TYC 18:56(C).

71-15 2/22/71 — PEKING VIETNAM(N) PROTOCOL
Agreement on PRC Supplementary Economic and Military Aid to
Vietnam in 1971 [71-11].
JMJP 2/23/71; PR 14. 9:5 (2/26/71); NCNA Peking 2/22/71;
SCMP 4850:160 (3/4/71).

71-16 3/1/71 — PEKING JAPAN COMMUNIQUÉ
Talks between representatives of China-Japan Memorandum Trade
Offices of China and representatives of Japan-China Memorandum
Trade Offices of Japan. PRC will not have trade exchange with
factories, firms, and enterprises which are U. S. -Japan enter-
prises or subsidiaries of U. S. company in Japan, or have large
investment in Taiwan or Korea(S), etc.
TYC 18:125(C); JMJP 3/2/71(C); PR 14. 10:4 (3/5/71); NCNA
Peking 3/1/71; SCMP 4855:156 (3/11/71)(E).

71-17 3/1/71 — PEKING JAPAN AGREEMENT
Memorandum trade for 1971.
JMJP 3/2/71; NCNA Peking 3/1/71; SCMP 4855:158 (3/11/71)
JAIL 16:168 (1972).

71-18 3/3/71 — KATMANDU NEPAL EXCHANGE OF LETTERS
Repair of work of the Asaniko Highway (Katmandu-Kodan highway).
JMJP 3/8/71; NCNA Katmandu 3/7/71; SCMP 4859:105 (3/17/71).

71-19 3/8/71 — HANOI VIETNAM(N) JOINT COMMUNIQUÉ
Talks during Premier Chou En-lai's visit: U. S. imperialism,
Indochina, Taiwan, etc.
JMJP 3/11/71(C); PR 14. 11:18 (3/12/71)(E); NCNA Peking
3/10/71; SCMP 4861:191 (3/19/71)(E).

71-20 3/9/71 — KHARTOUM SUDAN PROTOCOL
Trade for 1971.
TYC 18:39(C); JMJP 3/12/71; PR 14. 12:26 (3/19/71); NCNA
Khartoum 3/10/71; SCMP 4862:46 (3/22/71).

71-21 3/17/71 — PEKING KOREA(N) DECISION
Signed at meeting of Boards of Directors and Supervisors of
China-Korea Yalu River Hydro-Electric Power Co.
JMJP 3/18/71; NCNA Peking 3/17/71; SCMP 4866:226 (3/26/71).

71-22 3/22/71 — KUWAIT KUWAIT JOINT COMMUNIQUÉ
Establishment of diplomatic relations.
TYC 18:2(C); JMJP 3/30/71(C); PR 14. 14:16 (4/2/71)(E); NCNA
Peking 3/29/71; SCMP 4874:147 (4/8/71)(E).

71-23   3/22/71 — PEKING   RUMANIA   PROTOCOL
Supply Rumania with whole plants and technical aid by PRC.
JMJP 3/23/71; PR 14.14:20 (4/2/71); NCNA Peking 3/22/71;
SCMP 4870:211 (4/1/71).

71-24   3/22/71 — PEKING   RUMANIA   PROTOCOL
Conditions of delivering complete sets of equipment and material
supplied by PRC.
JMJP 3/23/71; PR 14.14:20 (4/2/71); NCNA Peking 3/22/71;
SCMP 4870:211 (4/1/71).

71-25   3/22/71 — PEKING   RUMANIA   PROTOCOL
Treatment and work of technical personnel in Rumania.
JMJP 3/23/71; PR 14.14:20 (4/2/71); NCNA Peking 3/22/71;
SCMP 4870:211 (4/1/71).

71-26   3/26/71 — YAOUNDE   CAMEROON   JOINT COMMUNIQUÉ
Establishment of diplomatic relations.
TYC 18:2(C); JMJP 4/3/71(C); PR 14.15:9 (4/9/71)(E); NCNA
Peking 4/2/71; SCMP 4876:87 (4/13/71)(E).

71-27   4/1/71 — PEKING   MAURITANIA   AGREEMENT
Economic and technical cooperation.
JMJP 4/2/71; PR 14.15:22 (4/9/71); NCNA Peking 4/1/71; SCMP
4876:89 (4/13/71).

71-28   4/9/71   1/1/71   PEKING   BULGARIA   AGREEMENT
Exchange of goods and payment for 1971.
TYC 18:66(C); JMJP 4/11/71; PR 14.16:18 (4/16/71); NCNA
Peking 4/10/71; SCMP 4881:59 (4/20/71).

71-29   4/20/71 — SANTIAGO   CHILE   AGREEMENT
Trade.
TYC 19:109(C); JMJP 4/22/71; PR 14.18:22 (4/30/71); NCNA
Peking 4/21/71; SCMP 4888:192 (4/30/71).

71-30   4/20/71   PEKING   KOREA(N)   EXCHANGE OF NOTES
Change currency used in trade between PRC and Korea.
TYC 18:82(C).

71-31   4/22/71 — PYONGYANG   KOREA(N)
1971-72 executive plan for scientific cooperation between PRC
Academy of Sciences and Academy of Sciences of Korea(N).
JMJP 4/24/71; PR 14.18:23 (4/30/71); NCNA Pyongyang 4/23/71;
SCMP 4890:71 (5/4/71).

71-32 4/26/71 4/26/71 RABAT MOROCCO PROTOCOL
Trade for 1971.
TYC 18:93(C); JMJP 4/28/71; PR 14.19:31 (5/7/71); NCNA
Peking 4/27/71; SCMP 4893:230 (5/7/71).

71-33 4/28/71 1/1/71 PEKING HUNGARY AGREEMENT
Exchange of goods and payments for 1971.
TYC 18:30(C); JMJP 4/29/71; PR 14.19:30 (5/7/71); NCNA
Peking 4/28/71; SCMP 4894:41 (5/10/71).

71-34 4/28/71 — PEKING HUNGARY PROTOCOL
General conditions for delivery of goods in 1971.
TYC 18:33(C).

71-35 4/28/71 — KARACHI PAKISTAN MINUTES
Talks on building a sugar mill for Pakistan.
This sugar mill will be built with PRC aid in accordance with
protocol signed on 4/9/70 [70-23].
JMJP 5/3/71; NCNA Rawalpindi 5/1/71; SCMP 4896:158 (5/12/71).

71-36 4/28/71 — LIMA PERU MINUTES
Trade talks between PRC vice-minister of Foreign Trade and
Peruvian secretary-general of Foreign Ministry.
TYC 18:70(C); JMJP 5/14/71(C); PR 14.21:23 (5/21/71)(E);
NCNA Peking 5/14/71; SCMP 4904:48 (5/24/71)(E).

71-37 5/6/71 5/6/71 PARIS SAN MARINO PROTOCOL
Establishment of official relations at consular level.
TYC 18:4(C); JMJP 5/8/71(C); PR 14.20:7 (5/14/71)(E); NCNA
Peking 5/7/71; SCMP 4900:96 (5/18/71)(E).

71-38 5/8/71 — PARIS TURKEY PRESS COMMUNIQUÉ
Starting of talks for establishment of diplomatic relations.
JMJP 5/9/71; NCNA Peking 5/8/71; SCMP 4901:146(E) (5/19/71).

71-39 5/11/71 1/1/71 PEKING CUBA AGREEMENT
New five-year trade.
TYC 19:56(C); JMJP 5/12/71; PR 14.21:28 (5/21/71); NCNA
Peking 5/11/71; SCMP 4902:180 (5/20/71).

71-40 5/11/71 1/1/71 PEKING CUBA AGREEMENT
New five-year payments.
TYC 19:59(C); JMJP 5/12/71; PR 14.21:28 (5/21/71); NCNA
Peking 5/11/71; SCMP 4902:180 (5/20/71).

71-41 5/11/71 — PEKING CUBA PROTOCOL
1971 trade.
JMJP 5/12/71; PR 14. 21:28 (5/21/71); NCNA Peking 5/11/71;
SCMP 4902:180 (5/20/71).

71-42 5/13/71 — PEKING YUGOSLAVIA CONTRACT
Purchase of freighters.
Signed by PRC National Machinery Import and Export Corporation
and Yugoslav May-Third Shipyard and Marine Diesel Engine Works.
JMJP 5/14/71; NCNA Peking 5/13/71; SCMP 4904:52 (5/24/71).

71-43 5/18/71 1/1/71 PRAGUE CZECHOSLOVAKIA AGREE-
MENT
Exchange of goods and payments for 1971.
TYC 18:77(C); JMJP 5/20/71; PR 14. 22:22 (5/28/71); NCNA
Peking 5/19/71; SCMP 4907:185 (5/27/71).

71-44 5/18/71 — PRAGUE CZECHOSLOVAKIA EXCHANGE OF
NOTES
Related questions concerning the change of Swiss franc.
TYC 18:80(C).

71-45 5/18/71 1/1/71 PEKING GERMANY(E) AGREEMENT
Exchange of goods and payments for 1971.
TYC 18:94(C); JMJP 5/19/71; PR 14. 22:22 (5/28/71); NCNA
Peking 5/18/71; SCMP 4907:186 (5/27/71).

71-46 5/25/71 — PEKING ITALY JOINT PRESS COMMUNIQUÉ
Trade talks.
JMJP 5/26/71(C); PR 14. 23:22 (6/4/71)(E); NCNA Peking 5/25/71;
SCMP 4912:39 (6/7/71)(E).

71-47 5/26/71 5/28/71 BUCHAREST AUSTRIA JOINT COM-
MUNIQUÉ
Establishment of diplomatic relations.
TYC 18:4(C); JMJP 5/28/71(C); PR 14. 23:11 (6/4/71)(E); NCNA
Peking 5/27/71; SCMP 4913:83 (6/8/71)(E).

71-48 5/27/71 — COLOMBO CEYLON AGREEMENT
Provision of exchangeable currency loan by PRC to Ceylon.
JMJP 5/28/71; PR 14. 23:22 (6/4/71); NCNA Colombo 5/27/71;
SCMP 4913:92 (6/8/71).

71-49 5/29/71 — URUMCHI (SINKIANG) PAKISTAN EXCHANGE
OF NOTES

China-Pakistan border trade.
JMJP 5/30/71; PR 14.23:22 (6/4/71); NCNA Urumchi 5/29/71;
SCMP 4914:147 (6/9/71).

71-50 5/30/71 — PEKING VIETNAM(N) AGREEMENT
Civil air transport (re-signed).
JMJP 5/31/71; NCNA Peking 5/30/71; SCMP 4914:146 (6/9/71).

71-51 5/31/71 1/1/71 WARSAW POLAND AGREEMENT
Goods exchange and payments for 1971.
TYC 18:60(C); JMJP 6/2/71; NCNA Warsaw 5/31/71; SCMP 4916:
225 (6/11/71).

71-52 5/31/71 — WARSAW POLAND PROTOCOL
Extension of 1961 Protocol on General Conditions for Delivery of
Goods to 1971 [61-75].
TYC 18:64(C).

71-53 5/31/71 — WARSAW POLAND EXCHANGE OF NOTES
Calculating problem of mutual obligation resulting from change
of Swiss franc.
TYC 18:65(C).

71-54 6/5/71 1/1/71 ULAN BATOR MONGOLIA PROTOCOL
Goods exchange for 1971.
TYC 18:90(C); JMJP 6/7/71; NCNA Peking 6/6/71; SCMP 4919:
127 (6/16/71).

71-55 6/7/71 — PEKING SOMALIA AGREEMENT
Economic and technical cooperation.
JMJP 6/8/71; PR 14.26:18 (6/25/71); NCNA Peking 6/7/71;
SCMP 4920:191 (6/17/71).

71-56 6/9/71 — PEKING RUMANIA JOINT COMMUNIQUÉ
Talks during visit of President Nicolae Ceausescu: Indochina,
territorial integrity, anti-imperialism, etc.
JMJP 6/10/71(C); PR 14.24:8 (6/11/71)(E); NCNA Peking 6/9/71;
SCMP 4920:180 (6/17/71)(E).

71-57 6/15/71 — PEKING PERU MINUTES
Fishery talks.
TYC 18:72(C); JMJP 6/17/71(C); PR 14.26:4 (6/25/71)(E);
NCNA Peking 6/16/71; SCMP 4924:184 (6/25/71)(E).

71-58 6/15/71 — PEKING YUGOSLAVIA COMMUNIQUÉ
Talks during visit of Yugoslav Government Delegation: sovereignty
and territorial integrity, promotion of development of relations,
etc.
JMJP 6/16/71(C); PR 14. 25:17 (6/18/71)(E); NCNA Peking 6/15/71;
SCMP 4924:190 (6/25/71)(E).

71-59 6/16/71 — PEKING PERU MINUTES
Trade talks.
TYC 18:73(C); JMJP 6/17/71(C); PR 14. 26:4 (6/25/71)(E); NCNA
Peking 6/16/71; SCMP 4924:182 (6/25/71)(E).

71-60 6/21/71 — PEKING IRAQ AGREEMENT
Economic and technical cooperation.
JMJP 6/22/71; PR 14. 27:38 (7/2/71); NCNA Peking 6/21/71;
SCMP 4927:142 (6/30/71).

71-61 6/23/71 — PEKING FRANCE CONTRACT
Buying diesel locomotives from France.
Signed by PRC National Machinery Import and Export Cooperation
and the Alsthom Group and M. T. E. Group of France.
JMJP 6/27/71; NCNA Peking 6/23/71; SCMP 4928:179 (7/1/71).

71-62 7/2/71 — PEKING CANADA PRESS COMMUNIQUÉ
Trade talks.
JMJP 7/3/71(C); NCNA Peking 7/2/71; SCMP 4935:92 (7/13/71)
(E).

71-63 7/2/71 — PEKING JAPAN JOINT STATEMENT
Signed by Delegation of China-Japan Friendship Association and
Delegation of Japanese Komeido (Komei Party): Okinawa, nuclear
weapons, 1969 Sato-Nixon Joint Communiqué, Korea, Taiwan, etc.
TYC 18:128(C); JMJP 7/3/71(C); NCNA Peking 7/2/71; SCMP 4935:
99 (7/13/71)(E); JAIL 16:173 (1972).

71-64 7/3/71 10/1/71 PEKING KOREA(N) AGREEMENT
Cooperation in rescue at sea.
TYC 18:120(C); JMJP 7/4/71; NCNA Peking 7/3/71; SCMP 4936:
171 (7/14/71).

71-65 7/4/71 — PEKING VIETNAM(N) PROTOCOL
Supplementary gratuitous supply of military equipment and materials to Vietnam in 1971.
JMJP 7/5/71; PR 14. 28:22 (7/9/71); NCNA Peking 7/4/71; SCMP
4937:223 (7/15/71).

71-66   7/6/71 — ADEN   YEMEN(S)   MINUTES
Talks on reconstruction of Khormakasar salt works.
JMJP 7/9/71; NCNA Aden 7/7/71; SCMP 4939:46 (7/19/71).

71-67   7/6/71 — ADEN   YEMEN(S)   MINUTES
Talks on establishment of Yemen cotton textile printing–dyeing
combined enterprise.
JMJP 7/9/71; NCNA Aden 7/7/71; SCMP 4939:46 (7/19/71).

71-68   7/16/71 — KATMANDU   NEPAL   EXCHANGE OF NOTES
Dispatch of a cotton planting survey team for survey of experi-
mental cotton growth in Nepal.
JMJP 7/20/71; NCNA Katmandu 7/17/71; SCMP 4945:175 (7/28/71).

71-69   7/16/71 — KATMANDU   NEPAL   EXCHANGE OF NOTES
PRC aid in construction of bitumen infiltration payment for
Katmandu-Pokhara Highway.
JMJP 7/20/71; NCNA Katmandu 7/17/71; SCMP 4945:175 (7/28/71).

71-70   7/27/71 — PEKING   ALGERIA   AGREEMENT
Economic and technical cooperation.
JMJP 7/28/71; PR 14. 34:23 (8/20/71); NCNA Peking 7/27/71;
SCMP 4951:156 (8/6/71).

71-71   7/29/71   7/29/71   PEKING   SIERRA LEONE   COMMUNI-
QUÉ
Establishment of diplomatic relations.
TYC 18:5(C); JMJP 7/31/71(C); PR 14. 32:22 (8/6/71)(E); NCNA
Peking 7/30/71; SCMP 4953:84 (8/10/71)(E).

71-72   7/29/71   7/29/71   PEKING   SIERRA LEONE   AGREEMENT
Economic and technical cooperation.
TYC 18:88(C); JMJP 7/31/71; NCNA Peking 7/30/71; SCMP 4953:
83 (8/10/71).

71-73   7/29/71 — PEKING   SIERRA LEONE   AGREEMENT
Trade and payments.
JMJP 7/31/71; NCNA Peking 7/30/71; SCMP 4953:83 (8/10/71).

71-74   7/30/71 — PEKING   SIERRA LEONE   COMMUNIQUÉ
Talks during visit of government delegation of Sierra Leone: PRC
representation in UN, anti–imperialism, 200–nautical mile terri-
torial sea, etc.
TYC 18:6(C); JMJP 7/31/71(C); PR 14. 32:23 (8/6/71)(E); NCNA
Peking 7/30/71; SCMP 4953:85 (8/10/71)(E).

71-75 7/31/71 — PEKING VIETNAM(N) PROTOCOL
Scientific and technical cooperation plan for 1971.
JMJP 8/1/71; NCNA Peking 7/31/71; SCMP 4954:138 (8/11/71).

71-76 7/31/71 — PEKING VIETNAM(N)
1971-72 executive plan for scientific cooperation.
JMJP 8/1/71; NCNA Peking 7/31/71; SCMP 4954:138 (8/11/71).

71-77 8/1/71 — PEKING ALGERIA JOINT COMMUNIQUÉ
Talks during visit of government delegation of Algeria: Palestinian
Arabs, Vietnam, foreign military base, etc.
TYC 18:8(C); JMJP 8/3/71(C); PR 14. 32:24 (8/6/71)(E); NCNA
Peking 8/2/71; SCMP 4955:179 (8/12/71)(E).

71-78 8/2/71 1/1/71 PEKING UAR PROTOCOL
Trade for 1971.
TYC 18:40(C); JMJP 8/3/71; PR 14. 33:29 (8/13/71); NCNA
Peking 8/2/71; SCMP 4956:239 (8/13/71).

71-79 8/2/71 — PEKING UAR EXCHANGE OF NOTES
Extension and revision of Article 4 of 1962 Agreement on Pay-
ments [62-25].
TYC 18:43(C).

71-80 8/2/71 — PEKING UAR EXCHANGE OF NOTES
Revision of Article 7 of 1962 Agreement on Payments [62-25].
TYC 18:45(C).

71-81 8/2/71 — PEKING UAR EXCHANGE OF NOTES
Extension of 1962 Agreement on Trade and Payments [62-24;
62-25].
TYC 18:42(C); JMJP 8/3/71; PR 14. 33:29 (8/13/71); NCNA
Peking 8/2/71; SCMP 4956:239 (8/13/71).

71-82 8/4/71 8/4/71 PARIS TURKEY JOINT COMMUNIQUÉ
Establishment of diplomatic relations.
TYC 18:12(C); JMJP 8/6/71(C); PR 14. 33:6 (8/13/71)(E); NCNA
Peking 8/5/71; SCMP 4957:47 (8/18/71)(E).

71-83 8/5/71 — ISLAMABAD PAKISTAN EXCHANGE OF NOTES
Giving Karachi and Gwadar branches of Bank of China to Pakistan.
JMJP 8/8/71; NCNA Rawalpindi 8/5/71; SCMP 4959:129 (8/20/71).

71-84 8/5/71 8/5/71 MOSCOW USSR AGREEMENT
Goods exchange and payments.

TYC 18:49(C); JMJP 8/7/71; PR 14. 33:29 (8/13/71); NCNA
Moscow 8/5/71; SCMP 4958:93 (8/19/71).

71-85 8/14/71 — ADEN YEMEN (PDRY) MINUTES
Talks on construction of a road from Ain to Manfid.
JMJP 8/18/71; PR 14. 35:31 (8/27/71); NCNA Aden 8/15/71;
SCMP 4964:204 (8/27/71).

71-86 8/14/71 — ADEN YEMEN (PDRY) MINUTES
Talks on construction of Zingiban bridge.
JMJP 8/18/71; PR 14. 35:31 (8/27/71); NCNA Aden 8/15/71;
SCMP 4964:204 (8/27/71).

71-87 8/14/71 — ADEN YEMEN (PDRY) MINUTES
Talks on drilling wells.
JMJP 8/18/71; PR 14. 35:31 (8/27/71); NCNA Aden 8/15/71;
SCMP 4964:204 (8/27/71).

71-88 8/15/71 — PEKING KOREA(N) AGREEMENT
Economic cooperation.
JMJP 8/16/71; PR 14. 34:22 (8/20/71); NCNA Peking 8/15/71;
SCMP 4963:165 (8/26/71).

71-89 8/16/71 — ISLAMABAD IRAN JOINT COMMUNIQUÉ
Establishment of diplomatic relations.
TYC 18:12(C); JMJP 8/18/71(C); PR 14. 34:4 (8/20/71)(E); NCNA
Peking 8/17/71; SCMP 5011:141 (11/10/71)(E).

71-90 8/19/71 — SANTIAGO CHILE AGREEMENT
Telecommunication service.
JMJP 8/21/71; PR 14. 35:31 (8/27/71); NCNA Santiago 8/19/71;
SCMP 4967:108 (9/2/71).

71-91 8/25/71 8/25/71 PEKING KOREA(N) PROTOCOL
Mutual supply of goods.
TYC 18:83(C).

71-92 8/28/71 — KUALA LUMPUR MALAYSIA JOINT COM-
MUNIQUÉ
Trade talks.
JMJP 8/30/71(C); NCNA Peking 8/29/71; SCMP 4972:211
(9/10/71)(E).

71-93 9/6/71 — PEKING KOREA(N) AGREEMENT
Providing gratis military aid to Korea.

JMJP 9/8/71; PR 14. 38:22 (9/17/71); NCNA Peking 9/7/71;
SCMP 4977:241 (9/17/71).

71-94 9/27/71 — HANOI VIETNAM(N) AGREEMENT
Economic, military, and material assistance to Vietnam in 1972.
JMJP 9/28/71; PR 14. 40:22 (9/30/71); NCNA Hanoi 9/27/71;
SCMP 4990:142 (10/7/71).

71-95 9/29/71 — CONAKRY GUINEA EXCHANGE OF NOTES
Extension of 1960 Agreement on Long-Term Trade and Payments
[60-95].
TYC 18:29(C).

71-96 10/2/71 — PEKING JAPAN JOINT STATEMENT
Talks during visit of delegation to China of Japanese Dietmen's
League for Promoting Restoration of Japan-China Diplomatic
Relations: Japan-PRC diplomatic relations, foreign troops with-
drawal, Japanese militarism, etc.
JMJP 10/3/71(C); NCNA Peking 10/2/71; SCMP 4993:133
(10/13/71)(E).

71-97 10/7/71 — RANGOON BURMA EXCHANGE OF LETTERS
Extension of 1961 Agreement on Economic, Technical Cooperation,
and Time of Repayment [61-2].
JMJP 10/9/71; NCNA Peking 10/8/71; SCMP 4997:92 (10/19/71).

71-98 10/8/71 — COLOMBO CEYLON (SRI LANKA) AGREEMENT
An interest-free loan from PRC in the form of supplies of 100,000
metric tons of rice to Ceylon.
JMJP 10/10/71; PR 14. 42:19 (10/15/71; NCNA Colombo 10/8/71;
SCMP 4998:150 (10/20/71).

71-99 10/9/71 10/9/71 PEKING ETHIOPIA AGREEMENT
Trade.
TYC 18:68(C); JMJP 10/10/71; PR 14. 42:7 (10/15/71); NCNA
Peking 10/9/76; SCMP 4998:153 (10/20/71).

71-100 10/9/71 — PEKING ETHIOPIA AGREEMENT
Economic and technical cooperation.
JMJP 10/10/71; PR 14. 42:7 (10/15/71); NCNA Peking 10/9/71;
SCMP 4998:153 (10/20/71).

71-101 10/13/71 10/13/71 DAR ES SALAAM BURUNDI JOINT
COMMUNIQUÉ
Restoration of diplomatic relations.

JMJP 10/15/71(C); PR 14.43:4 (10/22/71)(E); NCNA Peking 10/14/71; SCMP 5000:266 (10/22/71)(E).

71-102 10/15/71 10/15/71 PYONGYANG KOREA(N) AGREE-
MENT
Broadcast and television cooperation.
TYC 18:99(C); JMJP 10/16/71; NCNA Pyongyang 10/15/71;
SCMP 5001:40 (10/26/71).

71-103 10/16/71 — PEKING JAPAN JOINT STATEMENT
Talks during visit of Delegation of Japan–China Friendship Association (Orthodox): Japanese militarism, U. S. imperialism, PRC
representation in UN, Taiwan, etc.
JMJP 10/17/71(C); NCNA Peking 10/16/71; SCMP 5001:35
(10/26/71)(E).

71-104 10/16/71 — PEKING RUMANIA PROTOCOL
PRC supply of complete projects and technical assistance to
Rumania.
JMJP 10/17/71; PR 14.44:22 (10/29/71); NCNA Peking 10/16/71;
SCMP 5001:45 (10/26/71).

71-105 10/19/71 — PEKING ALBANIA PROTOCOL
Scientific and technical cooperation.
Signed at fourteenth meeting of Joint Committee for Cooperation
in Technology and Technical Science.
JMJP 10/20/71; PR 14.44:23 (10/29/71); NCNA Peking 10/19/71;
SCMP 5003:120 (10/29/71).

71-106 10/25/71 10/25/71 PARIS BELGIUM JOINT COMMUNI-
QUÉ
Establishment of diplomatic relations.
TYC 18:13(C); JMJP 10/27/71(C); PR 14.44:4 (10/29/71)(E);
NCNA Peking 10/26/71; SCMP 5007:165 (11/4/71)(E).

71-107 10/27/71 1/1/72 ALGIERS ALGERIA AGREEMENT
Long-term trade.
TYC 18:36(C); JMJP 10/29/71; NCNA Algiers 10/27/71; SCMP
5009:31 (11/8/71).

71-108 10/27/71 — KATMANDU NEPAL EXCHANGE OF
LETTERS
Surveys on mineral deposits in Nepal.
JMJP 10/29/71; NCNA Katmandu 10/28/71; SCMP 5008:220
(11/5/71).

71-109 10/28/71 — ALGIERS   ALGERIA   JOINT PRESS COM-
MUNIQUÉ
Visit of PRC government trade delegation.
JMJP 10/30/71(C); NCNA Algiers 10/28/71; SCMP 5010:83
(11/9/71)(E).

71-110 10/28/71 — PEKING   RUMANIA   AGREEMENT
Long-term interest-free loan to Rumania.
JMJP 10/30/71; PR 14. 45:23 (11/5/71); NCNA Peking 10/29/71;
SCMP 5009:44 (11/8/71).

71-111 10/29/71 — PEKING   AFRO-ASIAN TABLE TENNIS
TOURNAMENT   PRESS COMMUNIQUÉ
Meeting of sponsoring nations of Afro-Asian Table Tennis Friend-
ship Invitational Tournament.
Issued by the Information Committee of Afro-Asian Table Tennis
Friendship Invitational Tournament.
JMJP 10/30/71(C); NCNA Peking 10/29/71; SCMP 5009:28
(11/8/71)(E).

71-112 10/29/71   1/1/72   ROME   ITALY   AGREEMENT
Trade and payments.
TYC 18:86(C); JMJP 10/31/71; NCNA Rome 10/29/71; SCMP
5010:85 (11/9/71).

71-113 11/1/71 — PEKING   AFRO-ASIAN TABLE TENNIS
TOURNAMENT PRESS COMMUNIQUÉ
First meeting of heads of table tennis delegations: method of
competition, technical consultation committee.
Issued by the Information Committee of Afro-Asian Table Tennis
Friendship Invitational Tournament.
JMJP 11/2/71(C); NCNA Peking 11/1/71; SCMP 5011:123
(11/10/71)(E).

71-114 11/2/71   11/2/71   PEKING   PERU   JOINT COMMUNIQUÉ
Establishment of diplomatic relations.
TYC 18:14(C); JMJP 11/3/71(C); PR 14. 45:5 (11/5/71)(E); NCNA
Peking 11/2/71; SCMP 5012:224 (11/11/71)(E).

71-115 11/9/71   11/9/71   PARIS   LEBANON   JOINT COMMUNIQUÉ
Establishment of diplomatic relations.
TYC 18:14(C); JMJP 11/11/71(C); PR 14. 47:3 (11/19/71)(E); NCNA
Peking 11/10/71; SCMP 5018:221 (11/19/71)(E).

71-116 11/12/71 11/12/71 KIGALI RWANDA JOINT COM-
MUNIQUÉ
Establishment of diplomatic relations.
TYC 18:15(C); JMJP 11/15/71(C); PR 14. 47:4 (11/19/71)(E);
NCNA Peking 11/14/71; SCMP 5021:114 (11/24/71)(E).

71-117 11/13/71 — PEKING AFRO-ASIAN TABLE TENNIS
TOURNAMENT COMMUNIQUÉ
Meeting of heads of delegation to Afro-Asian Table Tennis Friendship Invitational Tournament: entrusting preparatory committee
to decide upon date and place of next tournament.
JMJP 11/14/71(C); NCNA Peking 11/13/71; SCMP 5021:102
(11/24/71)(E).

71-118 11/14/71 — PEKING GUYANA AGREEMENT
Import and export commodities.
JMJP 11/15/71; PR 14. 47:4 (11/19/71); NCNA Peking 11/14/71;
SCMP 5021:108 (11/24/71).

71-119 11/14/71 — PEKING GUYANA AGREEMENT
Developing trade and reciprocal establishment of trade offices,
import and export commodities.
JMJP 11/15/71; PR 14. 47:4 (11/19/71); NCNA Peking 11/14/71;
SCMP 5021:108 (11/24/71).

71-120 11/16/71 — PEKING GUYANA PRESS COMMUNIQUÉ
Trade talks.
JMJP 11/17/71(C); NCNA Peking 11/16/71; SCMP 5023:40
(11/29/71)(E).

71-121 11/17/71 11/17/71 PYONGYANG KOREA(N) AGREE-
MENT
Cooperation in ship overhaul.
TYC 18:122(C); JMJP 11/20/71; NCNA Pyongyang 11/19/71;
SCMP 5024:103 (11/30/76).

71-122 11/18/71 1/1/72 PEKING FINLAND AGREEMENT
Trade.
TYC 18:48(C); JMJP 11/19/71; NCNA Peking 11/18/71; SCMP
5024:98 (11/30/71).

71-123 11/18/71(?) — PEKING KOREAN(N) PROTOCOL
Border river transport.
Signed at eleventh meeting of PRC-Korean Committee for Co-
operation in Border River Transport.

JMJP 11/25/71; NCNA Peking 11/22/71; SCMP 5026:216
(12/2/71).

71-124 11/19/71 11/19/71 PEKING BURMA AGREEMENT
Trade.
TYC 18:92(C); JMJP 11/20/71; NCNA Peking 11/19/71; SCMP
5024:94 (11/30/71).

71-125 11/19/71 — PEKING BURMA AGREEMENT
Commodity loan.
JMJP 11/20/71; NCNA Peking 11/19/71; SCMP 5024:94 (11/30/71).

71-126 11/20/71 — PEKING JAPAN JOINT STATEMENT
Talks during visit of Japanese delegation of National Council for
Restoration of Japan-China Diplomatic Relations: PRC-Japan
diplomatic relations, Okinawa, U. S. imperialism, etc.
JMJP 11/21/71(C); NCNA Peking 11/20/71; SCMP 5025:148
(12/1/71)(E).

71-127 11/25/71 — PEKING VIETNAM(N) JOINT COMMUNIQUÉ
Talks during visit of Premier Pham Van Dong: U. S. imperialism,
Laos, Vietnam, Cambodia, etc.
TYC 18:16(C); JMJP 11/27/71(C); PR 14.49:8 (12/3/71)(E); NCNA
Peking 11/26/71; SCMP 5029:93 (12/8/71)(E).

71-128 11/26/71 1/1/72 PEKING RUMANIA PROTOCOL
Exchange of goods and payments for 1972.
TYC 18:57(C); JMJP 11/27/71; PR 14.50:24 (12/10/71); NCNA
Peking 11/26/71; SCMP 5029:125 (12/8/71).

71-129 11/28/71 — PEKING PERU AGREEMENT
Economic and technical cooperation.
JMJP 11/29/71; PR 14.50:3 (12/10/71); NCNA Peking 11/28/71;
SCMP 5030:171 (12/9/71).

71-130 11/30/71 — HUHEHOT MONGOLIA PROTOCOL
Boundary railway traffic.
Signed at regular meeting of Boundary Railway Joint Service
Committee.
JMJP 12/1/71; NCNA Huhehot 11/30/71; SCMP 5032:38 (12/13/71).

71-131 12/2/71 — KARACHI PAKISTAN MINUTES
Talks on PRC aid to design and construction of a refractory factory.
Signed in accordance with stipulation of Protocol to 1970 Agree-
ment on Economic and Technical Cooperation [70-23].
JMJP 12/4/71; NCNA Karachi 12/2/71; SCMP 5033:91 (12/14/71).

71-132 12/5/71 — TIRANA ALBANIA PROTOCOL
Albania's use of PRC loan for 1972.
JMJP 12/7/71; PR 14. 52:4 (12/24/71); NCNA Tirana 12/6/71;
SCMP 5035:155 (12/16/71).

71-133 12/5/71 1/1/72 TIRANA ALBANIA PROTOCOL
Goods exchange and payments.
TYC 18:34(C); JMJP 12/7/71; PR 14. 52:4 (12/24/71); NCNA
Tirana 12/6/71; SCMP 5035:155 (12/16/71).

71-134 12/5/71 1/1/72 PEKING VIETNAM(N) PROTOCOL
Mutual supply of goods and payments for 1972.
JMJP 12/6/71; NCNA Peking 12/5/71; SCMP 5034:128 (12/15/71).

71-135 12/5/71 — PEKING VIETNAM(N) PROTOCOL
PRC supplying Vietnam with general goods in 1972.
JMJP 12/6/71; NCNA Peking 12/5/71; SCMP 5034:128 (12/15/71).

71-136 12/5/71 — PEKING VIETNAM(N) PROTOCOL
PRC supplying Vietnam with complete projects.
JMJP 12/6/71; NCNA Peking 12/5/71; SCMP 5034:128 (12/15/71).

71-137 12/5/71 12/5/71 PEKING VIETNAM(N) PROTOCOL
PRC providing gratis relief material to Vietnam.
TYC 18:74(C).

71-138 12/7/71 — DAKAR SENEGAL JOINT COMMUNIQUÉ
Establishment of diplomatic relations.
TYC 18:26(C); JMJP 12/11/71(C); PR 14. 51:4 (12/17/71)(E);
NCNA Peking 12/10/71; SCMP 5038:80 (12/21/71)(E).

71-139 12/8/71 12/8/71 COPENHAGEN ICELAND JOINT COM-
MUNIQUÉ
Establishment of diplomatic relations.
TYC 18:27(C); JMJP 12/15/71(C); PR 14. 51:4 (12/17/71)(E);
NCNA Peking 12/14/71; SCMP 5041:29 (12/27/71)(E).

71-140 12/13/71 — DAMASCUS SYRIA AGREEMENT
PRC's assistance to Syria in construction of spinning mill.
JMJP 12/21/71; NCNA Damascus 12/14/71; SCMP 5041:42
(12/27/71).

71-141 12/14/71 12/14/71 NEW YORK CYPRUS COMMUNIQUÉ
Establishment of diplomatic relations.
TYC 18:28(C); JMJP 1/13/72(C); PR 15. 3:3 (1/21/72)(E); NCNA
Peking 1/12/72; SCMP 5060:33 (1/24/72)(E).

71-142 12/20/71 — PEKING SUDAN AGREEMENT
Economic and technical cooperation.
JMJP 12/21/71; PR 14. 52:4 (12/24/71); NCNA Peking 12/20/71;
SCMP 5044:194 (12/30/71).

71-143 12/21/71 — PEKING JAPAN COMMUNIQUÉ
Talks during visit of representatives of Japan-China Memorandum
Trade Office: Taiwan, PRC representation in UN, etc.
TYC 18:132(C); JMJP 12/22/71(C); PR 14. 53:4 (12/31/71)(E);
NCNA Peking 12/21/71; SCMP 5045:23 (1/3/72)(E).

71-144 12/22/71 — DAR ES SALAAM TANZANIA & ZAMBIA
SUMMARY
Signed at fifth round of talks on Tanzania-Zambia railway.
JMJP 12/24/71; PR 15. 1:21 (1/7/72); NCNA Dar es Salaam
12/23/71; SCMP 5047:112 (1/5/72).

71-145 12/27/71 — PYONGYANG KOREA(N) PROTOCOL
Scientific and technical cooperation.
Signed at twelfth session of PRC-Korea Committee for Scientific
and Technical Cooperation.
JMJP 12/29/71; NCNA Pyongyang 12/28/71; SCMP 5049:201
(1/7/72).

71-146 12/28/71 12/28/71 COLOMBO CEYLON AGREEMENT
Parcel post service.
TYC 18:101(C); JMJP 12/30/71; NCNA Colombo 12/28/71;
SCMP 5050:35 (1/10/72).

71-147 12/28/71 — COLOMBO CEYLON EXCHANGE OF NOTES
Nullification of 12/21/31 Agreement on Mutual Exchange Parcels.
TYC 18:118(C).

71-148 12/30/71 1/1/72 PYONGYANG KOREA(N) PROTOCOL
Goods exchange for 1972.
TYC 18:84(C); JMJP 12/31/71; PR 15. 1:7 (1/7/72); NCNA
Pyongyang 12/30/71; SCMP 5051:106 (1/11/72).

1972

72-1 1/6/72 1/6/72 PEKING BURUNDI AGREEMENT
Economic and technical cooperation.
TYC 19:127(C); JMJP 1/7/72; PR 15. 2:21 (1/14/72); NCNA
Peking 1/6/72; SCMP 5055:36 (1/17/72).

72-2   1/6/72   1/6/72   PEKING   BURUNDI   AGREEMENT
Trade.
TYC 19:55(C); JMJP 1/7/72; PR 15. 2:21 (1/14/72); NCNA Peking
1/6/72; SCMP 5055:36 (1/17/72).

72-3   1/13/72 — ADEN   YEMEN(PDRY)   MINUTES
Talks on building agricultural implements and hardware factory
with PRC's assistance.
JMJP 1/17/72; PR 15. 4:4 (1/28/72); NCNA Aden 1/15/72; SCMP
5063:164 (1/27/72).

72-4   1/14/72 — KATMANDU   NEPAL   EXCHANGE OF LETTERS
PRC providing 1, 200 tons of iron bars and 3, 750 tons of cement
for building Katmandu sports stadium and some other sports
equipment.
JMJP 1/18/72; PR 15. 4:4 (1/28/72); NCNA Katmandu 1/15/72;
SCMP 5063:161 (1/27/72).

72-5   1/22/72 — PEKING   VIETNAM(N)   PROTOCOL
Supplementary gratuitous supply of military equipment and eco-
nomic materials by PRC to Vietnam.
JMJP 1/23/72; PR 15. 4:4 (1/28/72); NCNA Peking 1/22/72;
SCMP 5067:131 (2/2/72).

72-6   1/31/72   1/31/72   ROME   MALTA   JOINT COMMUNIQUÉ
Establishment of diplomatic relations.
TYC 19:4(C); JMJP 2/26/72(C); PR 15. 9:3 (3/3/72)(E); NCNA
Peking 2/25/72; SCMP 5088:133 (3/8/72)(E).

72-7   2/2/72 — PEKING   PAKISTAN   JOINT COMMUNIQUÉ
Talks during visit of President Butto: peaceful coexistence,
repatriate prisoners of war, withdrawal of Indian forces from
Eastern Pakistan, etc.
TYC 19:9(C); JMJP 2/3/72(C); PR 15. 5:7 (2/4/72)(E); NCNA
Peking 2/2/72; SCMP 5075:44 (2/14/72)(E).

72-8   2/5/72   2/5/72   PEKING   GUINEA   AGREEMENT
Commodity loan by PRC to Guinea.
TYC 19:38(C).

72-9   2/5/72   1/1/72   PEKING   GUINEA   PROTOCOL
Trade for 1972.
TYC 19:37(C); JMJP 2/6/72; NCNA Peking 2/5/72; SCMP 5077:
31 (2/22/72).

72-10 2/10/72 1/1/72 PEKING CZECHOSLOVAKIA AGREEMENT
Exchange of goods and payments for 1972.
TYC 19:95(C); JMJP 2/11/72; PR 15. 10:4 (3/10/72); NCNA Peking
2/10/72; SCMP 5079:121 (2/24/72).

72-11 2/11/72 — PEKING CAMBODIA AGREEMENT
Economic and military supplies in 1972.
JMJP 2/12/72; PR 15. 8:26 (2/25/72); NCNA Peking 2/11/72;
SCMP 5080:156 (2/25/72).

72-12 2/14/72 2/14/72 NEW YORK MEXICO JOINT COM-
MUNIQUÉ
Establishment of diplomatic relations.
TYC 19:32(C); JMJP 2/16/72(C); PR 15. 8:26 (2/25/72)(E); NCNA
Peking 2/15/72; SCMP 5081:64 (2/28/72)(E).

72-13 2/16/72 2/19/72 BUCHAREST ARGENTINA JOINT
COMMUNIQUÉ
Establishment of diplomatic relations.
TYC 19:18(C); JMJP 2/20/72(C); PR 15. 8:26 (2/25/72)(E); NCNA
Peking 2/19/72; SCMP 5083:165 (3/1/72)(E).

72-14 2/18/72 — COLOMBO CEYLON PROTOCOL
Trade for 1972 (exchange of goods).
JMJP 2/21/72; PR 15. 10:4 (3/10/72); NCNA Colombo 2/18/72;
SCMP 5084:206 (3/2/72).

72-15 2/28/72 — SHANGHAI U. S. A. JOINT COMMUNIQUÉ
Talks during visit of President Nixon: normalization, Indochina,
antihegemonism in Asia-Pacific region, Taiwan, promote con-
tacts and exchanges, etc.
TYC 19:20(C); JMJP 2/28/72(C); PR 15. 9:4 (3/3/72)(E); NCNA
Shanghai 2/27/72; SCMP 5089:185 (3/9/72)(E); ILM 11. 2:443-445
(March 1972)(E).

72-16 2/29/72 2/29/72 LAGOS GHANA PRESS COMMUNIQUÉ
Resumption of diplomatic relations.
TYC 19:13(C); JMJP 3/1/72(C); PR 15. 9:3 (3/3/72)(E); NCNA
Peking 2/29/72; SCMP 5090:226 (3/10/72)(E).

72-17 3/2/72 3/2/72 BUCHAREST RUMANIA AGREEMENT
Radio and television cooperation.
TYC 19:136(C); JMJP 3/3/72; PR 15. 10:4 (3/10/72); NCNA
Bucharest 3/2/72; SCMP 5092:73 (3/14/72).

72-18 3/4/72 3/4/72 HAVANA CUBA AGREEMENT
Loan by PRC.
TYC 19:64(C).

72-19 3/4/72 1/1/72 HAVANA CUBA PROTOCOL
Trade for 1972.
TYC 19:62(C); JMJP 3/72/72; PR 15. 11:3 (3/17/72); NCNA
Havana 3/6/72; SCMP 5095:191 (3/17/72).

72-20 3/13/72 3/13/72 PEKING UK JOINT COMMUNIQUÉ
Exchange of ambassadors.
TYC 19:19(C); JMJP 3/14/72(C); PR 15. 11:3 (3/17/72)(E); NCNA
Peking 3/13/72; SCMP 5100:175 (3/24/72)(E).

72-21 3/14/72 1/1/72 PEKING HUNGARY AGREEMENT
Goods exchange and payments for 1972.
TYC 19:68(C); JMJP 3/15/72; NCNA Peking 3/14/72; SCMP 5101:
33 (3/27/72).

72-22 3/14/72 — PEKING HUNGARY PROTOCOL
General conditions for delivery of goods in 1972.
TYC 19:70(C).

72-23 3/14/72 — KATMANDU NEPAL EXCHANGE OF NOTES
Economic cooperation items.
JMJP 3/16/72; NCNA Katmandu 3/15/72; SCMP 5101:38 (3/27/72).

72-24 3/14/72 — PEKING RUMANIA PROTOCOL
Scientific and technical cooperation.
Signed at fourteenth session of Sino-Rumanian Joint Commission
on Scientific and Technical Cooperation.
JMJP 3/15/72; NCNA Peking 3/14/72; SCMP 5100:182 (3/24/72).

72-25 3/15/72 — PEKING KOREA(N) & JAPAN COMMUNIQUÉ
Talks during visit of representatives of Table Tennis Association
of Korea(N) and Japan denunciation of "Asian Table Tennis Fed-
eration."
JMJP 3/16/72(C); NCNA Peking 3/15/72; SCMP 5101:36 (3/27/72)
(E).

72-26 3/15/72 — PEKING JAPAN COMMUNIQUÉ
Talks during visit of Japanese Table Tennis Association and
Japan-China Cultural Exchange Association: exchange activities
in 1972.
JMJP 3/16/72(C); NCNA Peking 3/15/72; SCMP 5101:34 (3/27/72)(E).

72-27 3/16/72 1/1/72 PEKING POLAND AGREEMENT
Exchange of goods and payments for 1972.
TYC 19:86(C); JMJP 3/17/72; NCNA Peking 3/16/72; SCMP 5102:
85 (3/28/72).

72-28 3/16/72 — PEKING POLAND PROTOCOL
Extension validity of 1961 Protocol on General Conditions for
Delivery of Goods [61-95] to 1972.
TYC 19:90(C).

72-29 3/16/72 — SANAA YEMEN(N) MINUTES
Talks on building Taiz Hospital for Yemen.
JMJP 3/24/72; PR 15.13:20 (3/31/72); NCNA Sanaa 3/21/72;
SCMP 5106:97 (4/4/72).

72-30 3/18/72 1/1/72 CAIRO EGYPT PROTOCOL
Trade for 1972.
TYC 16:94(C); JMJP 3/20/72; PR 15.13:20 (3/31/72); NCNA
Cairo 3/18/72; SCMP 5103:119 (3/29/72).

72-31 3/24/72 — PEKING JAPAN SUMMARY
Talks during visit of Japanese Volleyball Association and Japan-
China Cultural Exchange Association: expanding friendly exchanges.
JMJP 3/25/72(C); NCNA Peking 3/24/72; SCMP 5108:177 (4/7/72)
(E).

72-32 3/24/72 — PEKING PAKISTAN EXCHANGE OF LETTERS
Supply of general commodities by PRC under loan.
JMJP 3/25/72; NCNA Peking 3/24/72; SCMP 5108:182 (4/7/72).

72-33 3/28/72 3/28/72 TIRANA ALBANIA AGREEMENT
Civil air transport.
TYC 16:177(C); JMJP 3/30/72; PR 15.15:17 (4/14/72); NCNA
Tirana 3/29/72; SCMP 5111:127 (4/12/72).

72-34 4/4/72 4/4/72 KABUL AFGHANISTAN PROTOCOL
Exchange of goods for 1972.
TYC 19:71(C); JMJP 4/5/72; NCNA Kabul 4/4/72; SCMP 5115:75
(4/18/72).

72-35 4/5/72 — PEKING KOREA(N) AGREEMENT
Mutual aid and cooperation on fisheries.
JMJP 4/6/72; PR 15.15:17 (4/14/72); NCNA Peking 4/5/72;
SCMP 5115:90 (4/18/72).

72-36 4/6/72 7/31/72 BUCHAREST RUMANIA AGREEMENT
Civil air transport.
TYC 16:182(C); JMJP 4/8/72; PR 15.15:17 (4/14/72); NCNA
Bucharest 4/7/72; SCMP 5116:138 (4/19/72); UN Reg. N:12510.

72-37 4/8/72 — TIRANA ALBANIA PROTOCOL
Signed at ninth meeting of Administrative Council of Sino-Albania
Joint Stock Shipping Company.
JMJP 4/10/72; NCNA Tirana 4/9/72; SCMP 5118:32 (4/24/72).

72-38 4/8/72 — KWANGCHOW (CANTON) MALTA AGREEMENT
Long-term interest-free loan to Malta.
JMJP 4/28/72; PR 15.18:22 (5/5/72); NCNA Peking 4/27/72;
SCMP 5129:87 (5/9/72).

72-39 4/9/72 4/9/72 GEORGETOWN GUYANA AGREEMENT
Economic and technical cooperation.
TYC 19:130(C); JMJP 4/16/72; NCNA Peking 4/13/72; SCMP
5120:118 (4/26/72).

72-40 4/11/72 — PEKING ALBANIA AGREEMENT
Loan for farm machinery to Albania by PRC.
JMJP 4/12/72; PR 15.16:4 (4/21/72); NCNA Peking 4/11/72;
SCMP 5119:74 (4/25/72).

72-41 4/13/72 — PEKING JAPAN JOINT STATEMENT
Talks during visit of Ikko Kasuga, Chairman of Central Executive
Committee of Japanese Democratic Socialist Party: Taiwan,
Japanese militarism, nuclear weapons, etc.
JMJP 4/14/72(C); NCNA Peking 4/13/72; SCMP 5120:120
(4/26/72)(E).

72-42 4/14/72 4/14/72 BELGRADE YUGOSLAVIA AGREEMENT
Civil air transport.
TYC 19:188(C); JMJP 4/16/72; NCNA Belgrade 4/14/72; SCMP
5122:248 (4/28/72).

72-43 4/15/72 — PEKING MAURITIUS JOINT COMMUNIQUÉ
Establishment of diplomatic relations.
TYC 19:11(C); JMJP 4/16/72(C); PR 15.16:9 (4/21/72)(E); NCNA
Peking 4/15/72; SCMP 5121:178 (4/27/72)(E).

72-44 4/18/72 1/1/72 SOFIA BULGARIA AGREEMENT
Goods exchange and payments for 1972.
TYC 19:91(C); JMJP 4/20/72; NCNA Sofia 4/19/72; SCMP 5125:
112 (5/3/72).

72-45 4/19/72 — PYONGYANG KOREA(N) AGREEMENT
Exchange of newsreel materials.
JMJP 4/25/72; NCNA Pyongyang 4/20/72; SCMP 5125:120 (5/3/72).

72-46 4/20/72 — COLOMBO CEYLON AGREEMENT
Joint shipping service.
JMJP 4/24/72; PR 15. 20:20 (5/19/72); NCNA Colombo 4/22/72;
SCMP 5126:156 (5/4/72).

72-47 4/24/72 1/1/72 BERLIN GERMANY(E) AGREEMENT
Goods exchange and payments for 1972.
TYC 19:123(C); JMJP 4/28/72; NCNA Berlin 4/26/72; SCMP
5129:75 (5/9/72).

72-48 5/5/72 — WARSAW POLAND PROTOCOL
Shipping.
Signed at twenth-second meeting of Joint Standing Commission of
Sino-Polish Shipbrokers Company.
JMJP 5/9/72; NCNA Warsaw 5/7/72; SCMP 5136:188 (5/18/72).

72-49 5/7/72 — PEKING   ATTU (ASIAN TABLE TENNIS UNION)
COMMUNIQUÉ
ATTU Inauguration meeting.
JMJP 5/8/72(C); NCNA Peking 5/7/72; SCMP 5136:174 (5/18/72)(E).

72-50 5/7/72 — GILGIT (PAKISTAN) PAKISTAN EXCHANGE OF
LETTERS
Border trade in 1972 between Sinkiang Uighur Autonomous Region
of PRC and Gilgit Agency of Pakistan.
JMJP 5/9/72; NCNA Gilgit 5/7/72; SCMP 5136:187 (5/18/72).

72-51 5/12/72 1/1/72 PEKING MONGOLIA PROTOCOL
Mutual supply of goods for 1972.
TYC 19:118(C); JMJP 5/13/72; PR 15. 20:20 (5/19/72); NCNA
Peking 5/12/72; SCMP 5139:90 (5/23/72).

72-52 5/13/72 — KIGALI (IN RWANDA) RWANDA AGREEMENT
Economic and technical cooperation.
JMJP 5/20/72; NCNA Peking 5/19/72; SCMP 5144:94 (5/31/72).

72-53 5/16/72 — PEKING HUNGARY PROTOCOL
Scientific and technical cooperation.
Signed at eleventh meeting of Sino-Hungarian Commission for
Scientific and Technical Cooperation.
JMJP 5/17/72; PR 15. 21:20 (5/26/72); NCNA Peking 5/16/72;
SCMP 5142:210 (5/26/72).

72-54 5/16/72 — PEKING MAURITANIA PROTOCOL (SUPPLE-
MENTARY)
To the 1967 Trade Agreement [67-6].
TYC 19:42(C); JMJP 5/17/72; PR 15. 21:20 (5/21/72); NCNA
Peking 5/16/72; SCMP 5142:214 (5/26/72).

72-55 5/16/72 5/18/72 PEKING NETHERLANDS JOINT COM-
MUNIQUÉ
Raising level of diplomatic relations from offices of chargés
d'affaires to embassies as from 5/18/72.
TYC 19:24(C); JMJP 5/17/72(C); PR 15. 21:20 (5/26/72)(E);
NCNA Peking 5/17/72; SCMP 5142:217 (5/26/72)(E).

72-56 5/19/72 — RANGOON BURMA AGREEMENT
Mutual cooperation between Hsinhua News Agency and News
Agency of Burma (NAB).
NCNA Rangoon 5/22/72; SCMP 5146:178 (6/2/72).

72-57 5/19/72 — COLOMBO CEYLON EXCHANGE OF NOTES
Extension of 1957 Agreement on Economic Aid [57-87].
TYC 19:134(C).

72-58 5/19/72 — COLOMBO CEYLON EXCHANGE OF NOTES
Sending teachers to Ceylon.
TYC 19:137(C).

72-59 5/19/72 — PEKING TUNISIA PROTOCOL
Trade.
It does not say when the trade agreement was signed.
JMJP 5/20/72; NCNA Peking 5/19/72; SCMP 5144:102 (5/31/72).

72-60 5/20/72(?) — PEKING CANADA DRAFT (INITIAL)
Technical matters relating to air traffic.
JMJP 5/22/72; PR 15. 22:4 (6/2/72); NCNA Peking 5/20/72;
SCMP 5144:87 (5/31/72).

72-61 5/24/72 — PEKING SYRIA AGREEMENT
Economic and technical cooperation.
JMJP 5/25/72; PR 15. 22:4 (6/2/72); NCNA Peking 5/24/72;
SCMP 5147:43 (6/5/72).

72-62 5/27/72 — KHARTOUM SUDAN PROTOCOL
Trade for 1972.
TYC 19:72(C); JMJP 5/29/72; NCNA Khartoum 5/27/72; SCMP
5150:161 (6/8/72).

72-63 6/5/72 6/5/72 TIRANA GREECE JOINT COMMUNIQUÉ
Establishment of diplomatic relations.
TYC 19:18(C); JMJP 6/6/72(C); PR 15. 23:3 (6/9/72)(E); NCNA
Peking 6/5/72; SCMP 5155:146 (6/16/72)(E).

72-64 6/8/72 6/8/72 PEKING CHILE AGREEMENT
Economic and technical cooperation.
JMJP 6/9/72; PR 15. 24:4 (6/16/72); NCNA Peking 6/8/72; SCMP
5157:74 (6/20/72).

72-65 6/8/72 — PEKING CHILE AGREEMENT
Exchange of commodities.
JMJP 6/9/72; PR 15. 24:4 (6/16/72); NCNA Peking 6/8/72; SCMP
5157:74 (6/20/72).

72-66 6/8/72 — PEKING CHILE AGREEMENT
Trade and payments.
TYC 19:113(C); JMJP 6/9/72; PR 15. 24:4 (6/16/72); NCNA Peking
6/8/72; SCMP 5157:74 (6/20/72).

72-67 6/8/72 6/8/72 PEKING CHILE AGREEMENT
Long-term trade.
TYC 19:112(C); JMJP 6/9/72; PR 15. 24:4 (6/16/72); NCNA Peking
6/8/72; SCMP 5157:74 (6/20/72).

72-68 6/13/72 6/13/72 PEKING U. S. S. R. AGREEMENT
Goods exchange and payments for 1972.
TYC 19:80(C); JMJP 6/14/72; PR 15. 25:19 (6/23/72); NCNA
Peking 6/13/72; SCMP 5161:39 (6/26/72).

72-69 6/23/72 6/23/72 ISLAMABAD PAKISTAN PROTOCOL
Trade for 1972-73.
TYC 19:39(C); JMJP 6/24/72; PR 15. 27:19 (7/7/72); NCNA
Rawalpindi 6/23/72; SCMP 5167:82 (7/5/72).

72-70 6/23/72 7/6/72 PEKING RWANDA AGREEMENT
Trade.
TYC 19:53(C); JMJP 6/24/72; PR 15. 26:17 (6/30/72); NCNA
Rawalpindi 6/23/72; SCMP 5167:83 (7/5/72).

72-71 6/27/72 6/27/72 LONDON GUYANA JOINT COMMUNI-
QUÉ
Establishment of diplomatic relations.
TYC 19:17(C); JMJP 6/29/72(C); PR 15. 27:5 (7/7/72)(E); NCNA
Peking 6/28/72; SCMP 5170:32 (7/10/72)(E).

72-72   6/28/72 — PEKING   VIETNAM(N)   AGREEMENT
Supplementary economic and military material aid to Vietnam for
1972.
JMJP 6/29/72; PR 15. 27:19 (7/7/72); NCNA Peking 6/28/72;
SCMP 5171:76 (7/11/72).

72-73   6/28/72 — PEKING   VIETNAM(N)   PROTOCOL
1972 supplementary supply of general materials to Vietnam.
JMJP 6/29/72; PR 15. 27:19 (7/7/72); NCNA Peking 6/28/72;
SCMP 5171:76 (7/11/72).

72-74   6/28/72 — PEKING   VIETNAM(N)   PROTOCOL
1972 supplementary gratuitous supply of military equipment and
material to Vietnam.
JMJP 6/29/72; PR 15. 27:19 (7/7/72); NCNA Peking 6/28/72;
SCMP 5171:76 (7/11/72).

72-75   6/29/72 — PEKING   CEYLON (SRI LANKA)   AGREEMENT
Economic and technical cooperation.
JMJP 6/30/72; PR 15. 27:4 (7/7/72); NCNA Peking 6/29/72;
SCMP 5171:71 (7/11/72).

72-76   6/29/72 — PEKING   CEYLON (SRI LANKA)   AGREEMENT
Construction of a cotton, spinning, weaving, printing, and dying
mill.
JMJP 6/30/72; PR 15. 27:4 (7/7/72); NCNA Peking 6/29/72;
SCMP 5171:71 (7/11/72).

72-77   7/5/72 — SHANGHAI   SRI LANKA (CEYLON)   JOINT COM-
MUNIQUÉ
Talks during visit of Prime Minister Mrs. Sirimavo Bandaranaike:
peaceful coexistence, developing countries, Indian Ocean as a zone
of peace, etc.
TYC 19:25(C); JMJP 7/7/72(C); PR 15. 28:11 (7/14/72)(E); NCNA
Peking 7/6/72; SCMP 5176:72 (7/18/72)(E).

72-78   7/12/72 — PEKING   YEMEN (PDRY)   AGREEMENT
Economic and technical cooperation.
JMJP 7/13/72; NCNA Peking 7/12/72; SCMP 5180:32 (7/24/72).

72-79   7/17/72 — PEKING   YEMEN (PDRY)(S)   COMMUNIQUÉ
Talks during visit of President Abdul Fattah Ismail: Palestinian,
Korea, anti-imperialism, etc.
TYC 19:1(C); JMJP 7/19/72(C); PR 15. 29:12 (7/21/72)(E); NCNA
Peking 7/18/72; SCMP 5184:196 (7/28/72)(E).

72-80   7/21/72 — PEKING   YEMEN (YAR)(N)   AGREEMENT
Economic and technical cooperation.
JMJP 7/22/72; NCNA Peking 7/21/72; SCMP 5186:72 (8/1/72).

72-81   7/25/72 — KABUL   AFGHANISTAN   EXCHANGE OF IN-
STRUMENTS
Gratuitous construction of a hospital of 200-250 beds by PRC for
Afghanistan.
JMJP 7/26/72; NCNA Kabul 7/25/72; SCMP 5189:208 (8/4/72).

72-82   7/26/72   7/3/73   KABUL   AFGHANISTAN   AGREEMENT
Civil air transportation.
TYC 19:170(C); JMJP 7/28/72; PR 15. 31:19 (8/4/72); NCNA
Kabul 7/26/72; SCMP 5190:22 (8/8/72).

72-83   7/27/72 — PYONGYANG   KOREA(N)   RESOLUTION
Signed at meeting of Board of Directors and Supervisors of Yalu
River Hydroelectric Co.
JMJP 7/28/72; NCNA Pyongyang 7/27/72; SCMP 5190:36 (8/8/72).

72-84   7/27/72 — PEKING   YEMEN (YAR)   COMMUNIQUÉ
Talks during visit of Prime Minister Mohsin Ahmed Al Aini:
Palestinian, anti-imperialism, peaceful coexistence, etc.
TYC 19:2(C); JMJP 7/29/72; PR 15. 31:17 (8/4/72)(E); NCNA
Peking 7/28/72; SCMP 5191:71 (8/9/72)(E).

72-85   7/30/72 — PEKING   ETHIOPIA   AGREEMENT
Civil air transport.
JMJP 7/31/72; NCNA Peking 7/30/72; SCMP 5192:128 (8/10/72).

72-86   8/9/72 — PORT LOUIS (MAURITIUS CAPITAL)   MAURITIUS
AGREEMENT
Economic and technical cooperation.
A protocol was also signed.
JMJP 8/16/72; NCNA Peking 8/15/72; SCMP 5203:207 (8/25/72).

72-87   8/9/72 — LIMA   PERU   AGREEMENT
Trade.
JMJP 8/11/72; NCNA Lima 8/9/72; SCMP 5200:75 (8/22/72).

72-88   8/16/72 — ULAN BATOR   MONGOLIA   EXCHANGE OF
NOTES
Extension of 1952 Agreement on Economic and Cultural Coopera-
tion [52-54].
TYC 19:28(C); JMJP 8/18/72; NCNA Ulan Bator 8/16/72; SCMP
5205:88 (8/30/72).

72-89 8/17/72 11/6/72 PEKING CAMEROON AGREEMENT
Economic and technical cooperation.
TYC 19:132(C); JMJP 8/18/72; PR 15. 34:4 (8/25/72); NCNA
Peking 8/17/72; SCMP 5205:73 (8/30/72).

72-90 8/17/72 11/6/72 PEKING CAMEROON AGREEMENT
Trade.
TYC 19:107(C); JMJP 8/18/72; PR 15. 34:4 (8/25/72); NCNA
Peking 8/17/72; SCMP 5205:73 (8/30/72).

72-91 8/17/72 8/17/72 NOUAKCHOTT MAURITANIA PRO-
TOCOL
Dispatch of medical teams to Mauritania.
TYC 19:142(C); JMJP 8/23/72; NCNA Nouakchott 8/21/72;
SCMP 5208:32 (9/5/72).

72-92 8/27/72 — PEKING TUNISIA AGREEMENT
Economic and technical cooperation.
JMJP 8/28/72; PR 15. 35:23 (9/1/72); NCNA Peking 8/27/72;
SCMP 5211:163 (9/8/72).

72-93 9/7/72 9/7/72 — MONGOLIA PROTOCOL
Reconstruction of landmark 548-I in boundary.
TYC 19:34(C).

72-94 9/11/72 — PEKING ATT UNION COMMUNIQUÉ
Issued by Preparatory Committee of Asian-Afro-Latin American
Table Tennis Friendship Tournament.
JMJP 9/12/72.

72-95 9/13/72 — PEKING ATT UNION COMMUNIQUÉ
Adopted at closing session of first Congress of Asian Table Tennis
Union: first Asian-African-Latin American Table Tennis Friend-
ship Invitational Tournament to be held in Peking from 8/25/73 to
9/7/73; second Asian Table Tennis Championship to be held in
Japan in 1973 spring, etc.
JMJP 9/14/72(C); NCNA Peking 9/13/72; SCMP 5223:74 (9/26/72)
(E).

72-96 9/14/72 3/26/73 PEKING GHANA AGREEMENT
Long-term trade and payments.
TYC 19:44(C); JMJP 9/15/72; NCNA Peking 9/14/72; SCMP 5223:
84 (9/26/72).

72-97 9/14/72 3/26/73 PEKING GHANA PROTOCOL
Trade.
TYC 19:49(C); JMJP 9/15/72; NCNA Peking 9/14/72; SCMP 5223:
84 (9/26/72).

72-98 9/14/72 — PEKING GHANA EXCHANGE OF LETTERS
Economic and technical cooperation.
JMJP 9/15/72; NCNA Peking 9/14/72; SCMP 5223:84 (9/26/72).

72-99 9/14/72 1/9/73 ANKARA TURKEY AGREEMENT
Civil air transportation.
TYC 19:150(C); JMJP 9/17/72; NCNA Peking 9/16/72; SCMP
5225:159 (9/28/72).

72-100 9/16/72 — PEKING CEYLON (SRI LANKA) AGREEMENT
Loan on providing a cargo ship by PRC to Sri Lanka.
JMJP 9/17/72; NCNA Peking 9/16/72; SCMP 5224:111 (9/27/72).

72-101 9/18/72 — CONAKRY GUINEA PROTOCOL
Sending third medical team to Guinea.
TYC 19:140(C).

72-102 9/19/72 — PEKING TOGO JOINT COMMUNIQUÉ
Establishment of diplomatic relations.
TYC 19:15(C); JMJP 9/27/72(C); PR 15. 39:4 (9/29/72)(E);
NCNA Peking 9/26/72; SCMP 5231:215 (10/6/72)(E).

72-103 9/19/72 — PEKING TOGO AGREEMENT
Economic and technical cooperation.
JMJP 9/28/72; PR 15. 40:30 (10/6/72); NCNA Peking 9/27/72;
SCMP 5232:52 (10/10/72).

72-104 9/23/72 — ULAN BATOR MONGOLIA PROTOCOL
Border railway traffic.
Signed at 1972 regular meeting of Sino-Mongolian through Rail-
way Traffic.
JMJP 9/28/72; NCNA Ulan Bator 9/27/72; SCMP 5232:42 (10/10/72).

72-105 9/?/72 — CHENGJIN CITY KOREA(N) PROTOCOL
Border railway.
Signed at meeting of Sino-Korean Border Railway Joint Committee.
JMJP 9/28/72; NCNA Pyongyang 9/27/72; SCMP 5232:43 (10/10/72).

72-106 9/29/72 9/29/72 PEKING JAPAN JOINT STATEMENT
Establishment of diplomatic relations.

TYC 19:6(C); JMJP 9/30/72(C); PR 15.40:12 (10/6/72)(E); NCNA Peking 9/29/72; SCMP 5232:31 (10/10/72)(E); JAIL 17:81(E)(1973).

72-107 10/5/72 — PEKING   ALBANIA
1972-73 executive plan for scientific cooperation between PRC Academy of Science and State University of Tirana of Albania.
JMJP 10/6/72; NCNA Peking 10/5/72; SCMP 5237:71 (10/18/72).

72-108 10/6/72 10/6/72 FREETOWN SIERRA LEONE   PROTOCOL
Dispatch of medical teams to Sierra Leone.
TYC 19:144(C); JMJP 10/8/72; NCNA Freetown 10/6/72; SCMP 5239:208 (10/20/72).

72-109 10/8/72 2/13/75 PEKING ITALY AGREEMENT
Maritime transport.
TYC 19:195(C); JMJP 10/9/72; NCNA Peking 10/8/72; SCMP 5239:194 (10/20/72); IYIL 2:445(E) (1976).

72-110 10/9/72 — PEKING KOREA(N) AGREEMENT
Economic and technical cooperation in geology.
JMJP 10/10/72; NCNA Peking 10/9/72; SCMP 5240:43 (10/24/72).

72-111 10/9/72 — FREETOWN SIERRA LEONE   PROTOCOL
To the 1971 Agreement on Economic and Technical Cooperation [71-72].
JMJP 10/11/72; NCNA Freetown 10/9/72; SCMP 5240:48 (10/24/72).

72-112 10/11/72 10/11/72 PEKING GERMANY(W) JOINT COM-MUNIQUÉ
Establishment of diplomatic relations and agreement to exchange ambassadors.
TYC 19:31(C); JMJP 10/12/72(C); PR 15.42:4 (10/20/72)(E); NCNA Peking 10/11/72; SCMP 5241:108 (10/25/72)(E).

72-113 10/11/72 — KIGALI RWANDA PROTOCOL
To 1972 Agreement of Economic and Technical Cooperation [72-52].
JMJP 10/13/72; NCNA Peking 10/12/72; SCMP 5242:153 (10/26/72).

72-114 10/12/72 — PEKING ALBANIA PROTOCOL
Economic and technical cooperation in civil aviation.
JMJP 10/14/72; NCNA Peking 10/13/72; SCMP 5242:142 (10/26/72).

72-115 10/13/72 — OTTAWA CANADA AGREEMENT
Civil air transport.
JMJP 10/15/72; PR 15.42:18 (10/20/72); NCNA Ottawa 10/13/72; SCMP 5243:196 (10/27/72).

72-116 10/14/72 ˍ 10/14/72 COLOMBO(?) MALDIVES JOINT
COMMUNIQUÉ
Establishment of diplomatic relations.
TYC 19:5(C); JMJP 10/15/72(C); PR 15.42:5 (10/20/72)(E); NCNA
Peking 10/14/72; SCMP 5243:204 (10/27/72)(E).

72-117 10/16/72 — WARSAW POLAND PROTOCOL
Signed at eleventh session of Shareholders' Meeting of Chinese-
Polish Shipbrokers' Company.
JMJP 10/19/72; NCNA Warsaw 10/17/72; SCMP 5245:84 (10/31/72).

72-118 10/19/72 10/19/72 BRAZZAVILLE CONGO(B) AGREE-
MENT
Economic and technical cooperation.
TYC 19:129(C); JMJP 10/21/72; NCNA Brazzaville 10/19/72;
SCMP 5246:122 (11/1/72).

72-119 10/24/72 — BATA EQUATORIAL GUINEA PROTOCOL
(SUPPLEMENTARY)
To 1971 Agreement of Economic and Technical Cooperation [71-4].
JMJP 10/28/72; NCNA Peking 10/26/72; SCMP 5250:85 (11/7/72).

72-120 10/27/72 — PEKING MEXICO PRESS COMMUNIQUÉ
Trade talks.
JMJP 10/28/72(C); NCNA Peking 10/27/72; SCMP 5250:88
(11/7/72)(E).

72-121 10/29/72 — PEKING JAPAN AGREEMENT
China-Japan Memorandum Trade for 1973.
Signed by representatives of PRC-Japan Memorandum Trade
Office of PRC and Japan-PRC Memorandum Trade Office of Japan.
JMJP 10/30/72; PR 15.44:31 (11/3/72); NCNA Peking 10/29/72;
SCMP 5252:194 (11/9/72); JAIL 17:223 (1973).

72-122 11/2/72 6/1/73 PEKING AUSTRIA AGREEMENT
Trade and payments.
TYC 19:116(C); JMJP 11/3/72; NCNA Peking 11/2/72; SCMP
5254:37 (11/13/72); UN Reg. N:12675.

72-123 11/3/72 LAGOS NIGERIA AGREEMENT
Economic and technical cooperation.
JMJP 11/5/72; NCNA Lagos 11/3/72; SCMP 5256:131 (11/15/72).

72-124 11/3/72 7/11/73 LAGOS NIGERIA AGREEMENT
Trade.

TYC 19:50(C); JMJP 11/5/72; NCNA Lagos 11/3/72; SCMP 5256: 131 (11/15/72).

72-125 11/6/72 — PEKING ALGERIA JOINT PRESS COMMUNIQUÉ
Trade talks.
JMJP 11/7/72(C); NCNA Peking 11/6/72; SCMP 5257:183 (11/16/72)
(E).

72-126 11/6/72 1/1/73 PEKING ALGERIA PROTOCOL
Trade for 1973.
TYC 19:74(C); JMJP 11/7/72; PR 15. 46:17 (11/17/72); NCNA
Peking 11/6/72; SCMP 5257:182 (11/16/72).

72-127 11/6/72 — PEKING ALGERIA DOCUMENTS
Implementation of 1971 Agreement on Economic and Technical
Cooperation [71-70].
JMJP 11/7/72; PR 15. 46:17 (11/17/72); NCNA Peking 11/6/72);
SCMP 5257:182 (11/16/72).

72-128 11/6/72 11/6/72 PEKING MALAGASY JOINT COM-
MUNIQUÉ
Establishment of diplomatic relations.
TYC 19:4(C); JMJP 11/7/72(C); PR 15. 45:4 (11/10/72)(E); NCNA
Peking 11/6/72; SCMP 5257:189 (11/16/72)(E).

72-129 11/8/72 — PEKING GUYANA AGREEMENT
Import and export of commodities.
JMJP 11/9/72; NCNA Peking 11/8/72; SCMP 5259:37 (11/20/72).

72-130 11/8/72 — PEKING GUYANA PROTOCOL
To 1972 Agreement of Economic and Technical Cooperation [72-39].
JMJP 11/9/72; NCNA Peking 11/8/72; SCMP 5259:37 (11/20/72).

72-131 11/9/72 1/1/73 PEKING ALBANIA PROTOCOL
Exchange of goods and payments for 1973.
TYC 19:77(C); JMJP 11/10/72; PR 15. 48:23 (12/1/72); NCNA
Peking 11/9/72; SCMP 5259:29 (11/20/72).

72-132 11/9/72 — PEKING ALBANIA PROTOCOL
Automatic extension of 1957 Protocol on General Conditions for
Delivery of Goods [57-27].
TYC 19:79(C).

72-133 11/13/72 11/16/72 MOSCOW LUXEMBOURG JOINT
COMMUNIQUÉ

Establishment of diplomatic relations.
TYC 19:15(C); JMJP 11/17/72(C); PR 15. 47:4 (11/24/72)(E);
NCNA Peking 11/16/72; SCMP 5264:85 (11/28/72)(E).

72-134 11/14/72 — PEKING KOREA(N)
1973-74 plan for scientific cooperation between Academy of
Science of PRC and Academy of Science of Korea.
JMJP 11/15/72; NCNA Peking 11/14/72; SCMP 5262:195 (11/24/72).

72-135 11/16/72 — VALLETTA MALTA PROTOCOL
Development projects and technical assistance.
JMJP 11/18/72; NCNA Peking 11/17/72; SCMP 5265:140 (11/29/72).

72-136 11/17/72 — PEKING VENEZUELA MINUTES
Talks between Ministry of Foreign Trade of PRC and Venezuela
Institute of Foreign Trade.
JMJP 11/20/72(C); NCNA Peking 11/19/72; SCMP 5265:153
(11/29/72)(E).

72-137 11/18/72 6/24/73 PEKING IRAN AGREEMENT
Civil air transport.
TYC 19:162(C); JMJP 11/19/72; PR 15. 48:23 (12/1/72); NCNA
Peking 11/18/72; SCMP 5265:137 (11/29/72).

72-138 11/18/72 — PEKING NEPAL AGREEMENT
Economic and technical cooperation.
JMJP 11/19/72; NCNA Peking 11/18/72; SCMP 5265:146 (11/29/72).

72-139 11/19/72 11/24/72 PARIS ZAIRE JOINT COMMUNIQUÉ
Normalization of relations.
TYC 19:12(C); JMJP 11/26/72(C); PR 15. 48:4 (12/1/72)(E); NCNA
Peking 11/25/72; SCMP 5270:137 (12/6/72)(E).

72-140 11/21/72 — COLOMBO CEYLON (SRI LANKA) AGREE-
MENT
Loan on providing a cargo ship by PRC to Sri Lanka.
JMJP 11/23/72; NCNA Colombo 11/21/72; SCMP 5269:68 (12/5/72).

72-141 11/21/72 11/21/72 OTTAWA JAMAICA JOINT COM-
MUNIQUÉ
Establishment of diplomatic relations.
TYC 19:12(C); JMJP 11/24/72(C); PR 15. 48:4 (12/1/72)(E); NCNA
Peking 11/23/72; SCMP 5268:31 (12/4/72)(E).

72-142 11/26/72 — PEKING VIETNAM(N) AGREEMENT
PRC gratuitous economic and military materials assistance to
Vietnam in 1972.
JMJP 11/27/72; PR 15.48:3 (12/1/72); NCNA Peking 11/26/72;
SCMP 5271:169 (12/7/72).

72-143 11/26/72 — PEKING VIETNAM(N) PROTOCOL
Gratuitous supply of military equipment and materials to Vietnam
by PRC in 1973.
JMJP 11/27/72; PR 15.48:3 (12/1/72); NCNA Peking 11/26/72;
SCMP 5271:169 (12/7/72).

72-144 11/27/72 1/1/73 BUCHAREST RUMANIA PROTOCOL
Goods exchange and payments for 1973.
TYC 19:82(C); JMJP 11/29/72; NCNA Bucharest 11/28/72; SCMP
5272:229 (12/8/72).

72-145 11/27/72 — BUCHAREST RUMANIA PROTOCOL
Extension of 1961 Protocol on General Conditions for Delivery of
Goods [61-94].
TYC 19:85(C).

72-146 11/28/72 — PEKING(?) CHAD JOINT COMMUNIQUÉ
Establishment of diplomatic relations.
TYC 19:14(C); JMJP 11/29/72(C); PR 15.49:3 (12/8/72)(E);
NCNA Peking 11/29/72; SCMP 5272:221 (12/8/72)(E).

72-147 11/29/72 12/20/74 PEKING LEBANON AGREEMENT
Trade.
TYC 19:120(C); JMJP 11/30/72; NCNA Peking 11/29/72; SCMP
5273:30 (12/11/72).

72-148 11/29/72 — PEKING LEBANON EXCHANGE OF NOTES
Mutual purchasing more commodities.
TYC 19:122(C).

72-149 12/5/72 12/5/72 PYONGYANG KOREA(N) AGREEMENT
Plant inspection and combat against insect pests.
TYC 19:146(C); JMJP 12/7/72; NCNA Pyongyang 12/6/72; SCMP
5277:173 (12/15/72).

72-150 12/7/72 — PYONGYANG KOREA(N)
1972-73 executive plan for cooperation in public health.
JMJP 12/8/72; NCNA Pyongyang 12/7/72; SCMP 5278:42
(12/18/72).

72-151 12/13/72 — PEKING GUINEA AGREEMENT
Providing financial credit to Guinea.
JMJP 12/14/72; PR 15. 51:4 (12/22/72); NCNA Peking 12/13/72;
SCMP 5282:195 (12/22/72).

72-152 12/13/72 — PEKING GUINEA AGREEMENT
Providing credit in commodities to Guinea.
JMJP 12/14/72; PR 15. 51:4 (12/22/72); NCNA Peking 12/13/72;
SCMP 5282:195 (12/22/72).

72-153 12/13/72 1/1/73 PEKING KOREA(N) PROTOCOL
Mutual supply of goods for 1973.
TYC 19:98(C); JMJP 12/20/72; NCNA Peking 12/13/72; SCMP
5282:198 (12/14/72).

72-154 12/18/72 1/1/73 COLOMBO CEYLON (SRI LANKA)
AGREEMENT
Trade and payments.
TYC 19:102(C); JMJP 12/21/72; PR 15. 52:4 (12/29/72); NCNA
Colombo 12/19/72; SCMP 5286:22 (1/2/73).

72-155 12/19/72 — PEKING KOREA(N) AGREEMENT
Joint breeding protection and utilization of fish resources in
Shuifeng Reservoir.
JMJP 12/20/72; NCNA Peking 12/19/72; SCMP 5286:26 (1/2/73).

72-156 12/20/72 — BAGHDAD IRAQ PROTOCOL
Development of economic and technical cooperation.
JMJP 12/24/72; NCNA Baghdad 12/21/72; SCMP 5288:86 (1/4/73).

72-157 12/21/72 12/21/72 PARIS AUSTRALIA JOINT COM-
MUNIQUÉ
Establishment of diplomatic relations.
TYC 19:31(C); JMJP 12/23/72(C); PR 15. 52:3 (12/29/72)(E);
NCNA Peking 12/22/72; SCMP 5288:83 (1/4/73)(E).

72-158 12/21/72 12/21/72 NEW YORK NEW ZEALAND JOINT
COMMUNIQUÉ
Establishment of diplomatic relations.
TYC 19:30(C); JMJP 12/23/72(C); PR 15. 52:3 (12/29/72)(E);
NCNA Peking 12/22/72; SCMP 5288:88 (1/4/73)(E).

72-159 12/22/72 1/1/73 COLOMBO CEYLON (SRI LANKA)
PROTOCOL
Exchange of commodities for 1973.

TYC 19:106(C); JMJP 12/24/72; NCNA Colombo 12/22/72;
SCMP 5288:107 (1/4/73).

72-160 12/23/72 — PEKING KOREA(N) PROTOCOL
Scientific and technical cooperation.
Signed at thirteenth session of Committee for Scientific and
Technical Cooperation.
JMJP 12/24/72; PR 15. 52:4 (12/29/72); NCNA Peking 12/23/72;
SCMP 5288:89 (1/4/73).

72-161 12/23/72 — HANOI VIETNAM(N) PROTOCOL
1972 Scientific and technical cooperation.
JMJP 12/25/72; NCNA Hanoi 12/23/72; SCMP 5289:146 (1/5/73).

72-162 12/25/72 — PYONGYANG KOREA(N) PRESS COMMUNIQUÉ
Talks during visit of Foreign Minister Chi Peng-fei: Vietnam,
Korea, U. S. imperialism, etc.
JMJP 12/26/72(C); PR 15. 52:9 (12/29/72)(E); NCNA Pyongyang
12/25/72; SCMP 5290:22 (1/8/73)(E).

72-163 12/27/72 — PEKING VIETNAM(N) PROTOCOL
Supply with complete projects to Vietnam for 1973.
JMJP 12/28/72; PR 16. 3:5 (1/19/73); NCNA Peking 12/27/72;
SCMP 5291:66 (1/9/73).

72-164 12/27/72 — PEKING VIETNAM(N) PROTOCOL
Supply with general goods to Vietnam for 1973.
JMJP 12/28/72; PR 16. 3:5 (1/19/72); NCNA Peking 12/27/72;
SCMP 5291:66 (1/9/73).

72-165 12/27/72 1/1/73 PEKING VIETNAM(N) AGREEMENT
Mutual supply of goods and payments for 1973.
TYC 19:100(C); JMJP 12/28/72; PR 16. 3:5 (1/19/73); NCNA
Peking 12/27/72; SCMP 5291:66 (1/9/73).

72-166 12/29/72 12/29/72 PEKING DAHOMEY JOINT COM-
MUNIQUÉ
Resumption of diplomatic relations.
TYC 19:16(C); JMJP 12/30/72(C); PR 16. 1:8 (1/5/73)(E); NCNA
Peking 12/29/72; SCMP 5292:105 (1/10/73)(E).

72-167 12/29/72 PEKING DAHOMEY AGREEMENT
Economic and technical cooperation.
JMJP 12/30/72; NCNA Peking 12/29/72; SCMP 5292:104
(1/10/73).

72-168 12/29/72 12/29/72 PEKING DAHOMEY AGREEMENT
Trade and payments.
TYC 19:66(C); JMJP 12/30/72; NCNA Peking 12/29/72; SCMP
5292:104 (1/10/73).

1973

73-1 1/1/73 — PEKING VIETNAM(S) REPUBLIC OF SOUTH
VIETNAM (R. S. V. N.) JOINT COMMUNIQUÉ
Talks during visit of Foreign Affairs Minister Nguyen Thi Binh:
Vietnam war, U. S. aggression against Vietnam, etc.
JMJP 1/2/73(C); PR 16. 1:14 (1/5/73)(E); NCNA Peking 1/1/73;
SCMP 5294:205 (1/12/73)(E).

73-2 1/8/73 1/29/75 PEKING ITALY AGREEMENT
Civil air transport.
TYC 20:241(C); JMJP 1/9/73; NCNA Peking 1/8/73; SCMP 5299:
170 (1/19/73); IYIL 2:457(E) (1976).

73-3 1/8/73 — PEKING ITALY EXCHANGE OF NOTES
Concluding a reciprocal agreement for trademark registration.
TYC 20:110(C); JMJP 1/11/73; NCNA Peking 1/10/73; SCMP
5300:30 (1/22/73).

73-4 1/13/73 — PEKING CAMBODIA AGREEMENT
Gratuitous supply of military equipment and material to Cambodia
in 1973 by PRC.
JMJP 1/14/73; PR 16. 3:5 (1/19/73); NCNA Peking 1/13/73;
SCMP 5302:107 (1/24/73).

73-5 1/13/73 — PEKING CAMBODIA AGREEMENT
PRC economic aid in 1973.
JMJP 1/14/73; PR 16. 3:5 (1/19/73); NCNA Peking 1/13/73;
SCMP 5302:107 (1/24/73).

73-6 1/13/73 — PEKING JAPAN MINUTES
Talks on Ice-Hockey Exchange between PRC and Japan sports
organizations.
JMJP 1/14/73; NCNA Peking 1/13/73; SCMP 5302:113 (1/24/73).

73-7 1/13/73 — PEKING JAPAN MINUTES
Talks on energetic exchange in the field of badminton and on
questions of common interest.
JMJP 1/14/73; NCNA Peking 1/13/73; SCMP 5302:112 (1/24/73).

73-8   1/14/73   1/14/73   PEKING   ZAIRE   AGREEMENT
Economic and technical cooperation.
TYC 20:100(C); JMJP 1/15/73; NCNA Peking 1/14/73; SCMP
5303:161 (1/26/73).

73-9   1/14/73   1/14/73   PEKING   ZAIRE   AGREEMENT
Trade.
TYC 20:28(C); JMJP 1/15/73; NCNA Peking 1/14/73; SCMP
5303:161 (1/26/73).

73-10   1/19/73   —   PYONGYANG   KOREA(N)   PROTOCOL
Cooperation in border river transport.
Signed at twelfth meeting of China-Korea Committee for Co-
operation in Border River Transport.
JMJP 1/21/73; NCNA Pyongyang 1/19/73; SCMP 5307:161 (2/1/73).

73-11   1/19/73   —   PEKING   RUMANIA   PROTOCOL
PRC provide complete plants and technical assistance to Rumania.
JMJP 1/20/73; NCNA Peking 1/19/73; SCMP 5306:116 (1/31/73).

73-12   1/20/73   —   PEKING   ZAIRE   PRESS COMMUNIQUÉ
Talks during visit of President Mobutu Sense Seko Kuku Ngbendu
Wa Za Banga: anti-imperialism, colonialism and neocolonialism,
self-determination, Third World, etc.
JMJP 1/21/73(C); PR 16. 4:8 (1/26/73)(E); NCNA Peking 1/20/73;
SCMP 5307:165 (2/1/73)(E).

73-13   1/25/73   1/25/73   KABUL   AFGHANISTAN   PROTOCOL
Goods exchange for 1973.
TYC 20:42(C); JMJP 1/28/73; NCNA Kabul 1/25/73; SCMP 5311:
125 (2/9/73).

73-14   1/25/73   —   KHARTOUM   SUDAN   NOTE
Talks on construction of factories in Sudan.
JMJP 1/28/73; NCNA Khartoum 1/25/73; SCMP 5312:38 (2/12/73).

73-15   1/26/73   —   SANTIAGO   CHILE   AGREEMENT
Maritime transport.
JMJP 1/28/73; PR 16. 5:13 (2/2/73); NCNA Santiago 1/26/73;
SCMP 5312:33 (2/12/73).

73-16   2/2/73   —   PEKING   CZECHOSLOVAKIA   PROTOCOL
Banking formalities for settling accounts of goods exchange and
payments.
JMJP 2/3/73; NCNA Peking 2/2/73; SCMP 5316:182 (2/16/73).

73-17 2/14/73 — PEKING KOREA(N) PRESS COMMUNIQUÉ
Talks during Foreign Minister Ho Dam's visit: Vietnam peace
treaty, U. S. intervention in Laos and Cambodia, anti-imperial-
ism, etc.
JMJP 2/15/73(C); NCNA Peking 2/15/73; SCMP 5323:113 (2/28/73)
(E).

73-18 2/16/73 1/1/73 CONAKRY GUINEA AGREEMENT
Trade for 1973.
TYC 20:26(C); JMJP 2/18/73; NCNA Conakry 2/17/73; SCMP
5324:148 (3/1/73).

73-19 2/19/73 1/1/73 PEKING BULGARIA AGREEMENT
Exchange of goods and payments in 1973.
TYC 20:64(C); JMJP 2/20/73; NCNA Peking 2/19/73; SCMP
5326:28 (3/5/73).

73-20 2/20/73 — ADDIS ABABA ETHIOPIA PROTOCOL
Supplementary to 1971 Agreement on Economic and Technical
Cooperation [71-100].
JMJP 2/22/73; NCNA Addis Ababa 2/20/73; SCMP 5327:69 (3/6/73).

73-21 2/22/73 — PEKING U. S. A. COMMUNIQUÉ
Talks during visit of Dr. Henry A. Kissinger: Shanghai Communi-
qué, establishment of liaison office, trade, scientific, and cul-
tural exchanges, etc.
TYC 20:7(C); JMJP 2/23/73(C); PR 16. 8:4 (2/23/73)(E); NCNA
Peking 2/22/73; SCMP 5328:123 (3/7/73)(E).

73-22 2/26/73 — KATMANDU NEPAL EXCHANGE OF LETTERS
PRC technical assistance in sending technicians working at Sunkosi
hydroelectric station.
JMJP 2/28/73; NCNA Katmandu 2/27/73; SCMP 5331:22 (3/12/73).

73-23 2/ /73 — KABUL AFGHANISTAN NOTES
Talks on PRC aid in expansion of Bagrami textile mill.
JMJP 3/2/73; NCNA Kabul 3/1/73; SCMP 5333:95 (3/14/73).

73-24 3/1/73 1/1/73 ULAN BATOR MONGOLIA PROTOCOL
Goods exchange for 1973.
TYC 20:75(C); JMJP 3/3/73; NCNA Ulan Bator 3/1/73; SCMP
5333:100 (3/14/73).

73-25 3/3/73 1/1/73 HELSINKI FINLAND AGREEMENT
Trade for 1973.

TYC 20:52(C); JMJP 3/4/73; NCNA Peking 3/3/73; SCMP 5334: 148 (3/15/73).

73-26 3/5/73 1/1/73 PEKING GERMANY(E) AGREEMENT
Exchange of goods and payments for 1973.
TYC 20:86(C); JMJP 3/6/73; NCNA Peking 3/5/73; SCMP 5335: 181 (3/16/73).

73-27 3/5/73 — HEIHO (PRC'S HEILUNGKIANG) U. S. S. R. SUMMARY
Navigation and work concerning navigational channels.
Signed at eighteenth regular meeting of Sino-Soviet Commission for Navigation on Boundary Rivers.
JMJP 3/9/73; NCNA Peking 3/8/73; SCMP 5337:81 (3/20/73).

73-28 3/7/73 1/1/73 BUDAPEST HUNGARY AGREEMENT
Goods exchange and payments for 1973.
TYC 20:40(C); JMJP 3/10/73; NCNA Budapest 3/7/73; SCMP 5337:73 (3/20/73).

73-29 3/9/73 3/9/73 PARIS SPAIN JOINT COMMUNIQUÉ
TYC 20:4(C); JMJP 3/11/73(C); PR 16. 11:3 (3/16/73)(E); NCNA Peking 3/10/73; SCMP 5338:115 (3/21/73)(E).

73-30 3/20/73 1/1/73 PRAGUE CZECHOSLOVAKIA AGREEMENT
Goods exchange and payments in 1973.
TYC 20:66(C); JMJP 3/21/73; NCNA Prague 3/20/73; SCMP 5345:180 (3/30/73).

73-31 3/20/73 — KATMANDU NEPAL SUMMARY
Talks on PRC aid in construction of ring road in Katmandu.
JMJP 3/24/73; NCNA Katmandu 3/21/73; SCMP 5347:78 (4/3/73).

73-32 3/23/73 1/1/73 PEKING CUBA PROTOCOL
Trade for 1973.
TYC 20:31(C); JMJP 3/24/73; NCNA Peking 3/23/73; SCMP 5347: 74 (4/3/73).

73-33 3/23/73 — ULAN BATOR MONGOLIA MINUTES
Handing over seven incomplete projects to Mongolia which PRC helped Mongolia build according to 1958 and 1960 Agreements on Economic and Technical Aid [58-115, 60-73].
Also exchange of notes were signed.
JMJP 3/28/73; NCNA Peking 3/27/73; SCMP 5350:38 (4/9/73).

73-34   3/23/73   1/1/73   WARSAW   POLAND   AGREEMENT
Goods exchange and payments.
TYC 20:58(C); JMJP 3/25/73; NCNA Warsaw 3/23/73; SCMP
5348:124 (4/4/73).

73-35   3/23/73 — WARSAW   POLAND   PROTOCOL
Extension of 1961 Protocol of General Conditions for Delivery
Goods (61-95).
TYC 20:63(C).

73-36   3/23/73   3/23/73   PARIS   FRANCE   AGREEMENT
Exhibition of PRC archaeological finds in Paris from 5/4/73 to
9/3/73.
TYC 20:114(C).

73-37   3/24/73 — ADEN   YEMEN(PDRY)(S)   MINUTES
Talks on construction of Mahfid-Mukalla Road.
JMJP 3/30/73; NCNA Aden 3/25/73; SCMP 5349:180 (4/6/73).

73-38   3/26/73 — KATMANDU   NEPAL   MINUTES
Talks on construction of Katmandu-Bhaktapur trolley bus service
project.
JMJP 4/3/73; NCNA Katmandu 3/28/73; SCMP 5351:84 (4/10/73).

73-39   3/28/73   3/28/73   PEKING   CAMEROON   AGREEMENT
Economic and technical cooperation.
TYC 20:105(C); JMJP 3/29/73; NCNA Peking 3/28/73; SCMP
5351:76 (4/10/73).

73-40   3/31/73 — BUCHAREST   RUMANIA
1973-74 plan for scientific cooperation.
JMJP 4/2/73; NCNA Bucharest 4/1/73; SCMP 5353:150 (4/12/73).

73-41   4/2/73 — VIENNA   AUSTRIA   EXCHANGE OF NOTES
Related to 1972 Trade and Payments Agreement [72-122].
JMJP 4/4/73; NCNA Vienna 4/2/73; SCMP 5355:23 (4/17/73).

73-42   4/2/73 — PEKING   CAMEROON   PRESS COMMUNIQUÉ
Talks during President El Hadj Ahmadou Ahidjo's visit: Africa,
self-determination, anti-imperialism, hegemonism, racism, etc.
JMJP 4/3/73(C); PR 16. 14:7 (4/6/73)(E); NCNA Peking 4/2/73;
SCMP 5354:177 (4/13/73)(E).

73-43   4/3/73 — PEKING   JAPAN   MINUTES
Talks between PRC and Japan football organizations.
JMJP 4/4/73; NCNA Peking 4/3/73; SCMP 5355:35 (4/17/73)(E).

73-44 4/3/73 — PEKING NEW ZEALAND PRESS COMMUNIQUÉ
Talks during visit of Associate Minister of Foreign Affairs and
Minister of Overseas Trade J. A. Walding: disarmament and
nuclear testing, anti-imperialism in Asian-Pacific region, etc.
JMJP 4/4/73(C); NCNA Peking 4/3/73; SCMP 5354:182 (4/13/73)
(E).

73-45 4/4/73 — BAMAKO MALI PROTOCOL
PRC's sending of medical teams to Mali.
TYC 20:127(C); JMJP 4/6/73; NCNA Bamako 4/4/73; SCMP 5356:
75 (4/18/73).

73-46 4/8/73 6/16/73 PEKING IRAN AGREEMENT
Trade.
TYC 20:34(C); JMJP 4/10/73; NCNA Peking 4/8/73; SCMP 5358:
26 (4/23/73).

73-47 4/8/73 6/16/73 PEKING IRAN AGREEMENT
Payments.
TYC 20:37(C); JMJP 4/10/73; NCNA Peking 4/8/73; SCMP 5358:
26 (4/23/73).

73-48 4/20/73 — PEKING BULGARIA EXCHANGE OF NOTES
Extension of 1955 Agreement on Scientific and Technical Cooperation [55-18].
TYC 20:124(C); JMJP 4/22/73; NCNA Peking 4/21/73; SCMP 5366:
169 (5/3/73).

73-49 4/20/73 — PEKING CZECHOSLOVAKIA PROTOCOL
Scientific and technical cooperation.
Signed at fifteenth session of Sino-Czechoslovak Joint Commission
for Scientific and Technical Cooperation.
JMJP 4/21/73; NCNA Peking 4/20/73; SCMP 5365:119 (5/2/73).

73-50 4/22/73 — PEKING BELGIUM PRESS COMMUNIQUÉ
Establishment of a Sino-Belgium Trade Joint Committee Meeting
once a year.
JMJP 4/2/73(C); PR 16.18:17 (5/4/73)(E); NCNA Peking 4/23/73;
SCMP 5367:220 (5/4/73)(E).

73-51 4/22/73 11/26/75 PEKING MEXICO AGREEMENT
Trade.
TYC 20:91(C); JMJP 4/23/73; NCNA Peking 4/22/73; SCMP 5367:
227 (5/4/73).

73-52 4/22/73 — PEKING MEXICO EXCHANGE OF NOTES
Cultural, scientific, and technical exchanges for 1973-74.
JMJP 4/23/73; NCNA Peking 4/22/73; SCMP 5367:227 (5/4/73).

73-53 4/24/73 — SHANGHAI MEXICO JOINT COMMUNIQUÉ
Talks during visit of President Luis Echeverria: anti-imperialism, Vietnam peace treaty, complete prohibition and thorough
destruction of nuclear weapons, international economic relations,
200-nautical mile sea rights, etc.
TYC 20:16(C); JMJP 4/25/73(C); PR 16. 17:6 (4/27/73)(E); NCNA
Shanghai 4/24/73; SCMP 5368:41 (5/7/73)(E).

73-54 5/4/73 — ALGIERS ALGERIA AGREEMENT
Insurance.
JMJP 5/7/73; NCNA Algiers 5/5/73; SCMP 5375:119 (5/16/73).

73-55 5/4/73 5/4/73 PEKING JAPAN AGREEMENT
Seabed cable.
TYC 20:136(C); JMJP 5/5/73; PR 16. 19:23 (5/11/73); NCNA
Peking 5/4/73; SCMP 5374:83 (5/15/73); JAIL 18:218 (1974).

73-56 5/12/73 — PEKING NORWAY AGREEMENT
Air transport.
JMJP 5/13/73; NCNA Peking 5/12/73; SCMP 5380:132 (5/23/73).

73-57 5/18/73 5/18/73 PEKING DENMARK AGREEMENT
Civil air transport.
JMJP 5/19/73; NCNA Peking 5/18/73; SCMP 5384:79 (5/30/73);
UN Reg. N:12915; ICAO DOC. 2438(E).

73-58 5/19/73 — PEKING AUSTRALIA PRESS COMMUNIQUÉ
Trade talks.
JMJP 5/20/73(C); PR 16. 21:3 (5/25/73); NCNA Peking 5/19/73;
SCMP 5384:76 (5/30/73)(E).

73-59 5/20/73 — URUMCHI PAKISTAN EXCHANGE OF INSTRU-
MENT
1973 border trade.
JMJP 5/24/73; NCNA Peking 5/23/73; SCMP 5387:40 (6/4/73).

73-60 5/22/73 5/22/73 PEKING RUMANIA AGREEMENT
Cooperation in technical survey of ships.
TYC 20:258(C); JMJP 5/24/73; NCNA Peking 5/23/73; SCMP
5387:41 (6/4/73).

73-61 5/23/73 5/23/73 PEKING GREECE AGREEMENT
Trade and payments.
TYC 20:48(C); JMJP 5/24/73; NCNA Peking 5/23/73; SCMP
5387:35 (6/4/73).

73-62 5/23/73 5/23/73 PEKING GREECE AGREEMENT
Maritime transport.
TYC 20:254(C); JMJP 5/24/73; NCNA Peking 5/23/73; SCMP
5387:35 (6/4/73).

73-63 5/23/73 1/14/75 PEKING GREECE AGREEMENT
Civil air transport.
TYC 20:216(C); JMJP 5/24/73; NCNA Peking 5/23/73; SCMP
5387:35 (6/4/73).

73-64 5/24/73 — BRAZZAVILLE CONGO PROTOCOL
Economic and technical cooperation.
JMJP 5/29/73; NCNA Brazzaville 5/24/73; SCMP 5388:78 (6/6/73).

73-65 5/27/73 — PEKING GREECE COMMUNIQUÉ
Talks during visit of Deputy Prime Minister Nikolaos Macarezos:
further develop mutual relations.
JMJP 5/27/73(C); PR 16. 22:3 (6/1/73)(E); NCNA Peking 5/27/73;
SCMP 5389:133 (6/7/73)(E).

73-66 5/28/73 — LUSAKA ZAMBIA CERTIFICATE
Transferring of a PRC-aid medium and short-wave broadcasting
transmitting station to Zambia which was built in accordance with
exchange letters [69-57] and 1970 Minutes of 1969 talks [70-15].
JMJP 6/3/73; NCNA Lusaka 5/29/73; SCMP 5391:42 (6/11/73).

73-67 5/29/73 5/29/73 SANTA ISABEL EQUATORIAL GUINEA
PROTOCOL
Sending a PRC medical team to work in Equatorial Guinea.
TYC 20:129(C); JMJP 6/4/73; NCNA Peking 5/31/73; SCMP 5392:
72 (6/12/73).

73-68 5/31/73 — BUCHAREST RUMANIA PROTOCOL
Scientific and technical cooperation.
Signed at fifteenth session of Sino-Rumanian Joint Commission
on Scientific and Technical Cooperation.
JMJP 6/3/73; NCNA Bucharest 5/31/73; SCMP 5393:132 (6/13/73).

73-69 6/1/73 6/1/73 PEKING SWEDEN AGREEMENT
Civil air transportation.

JMJP 6/2/73; NCNA Peking 6/1/73; SCMP 5393:134 (6/13/73).
UN Reg. N:13137(E); ICAO DOC. 2439(E).

73-70   6/2/73 — BUDAPEST   HUNGARY   PROTOCOL
Scientific and technical cooperation.
Signed at twelfth meeting of Sino-Hungarian Commission for
Scientific and Technical Cooperation.
JMJP 6/6/73; NCNA Budapest 6/3/73; SCMP 5395:215 (6/15/73).

73-71   6/4/73 — PEKING   CANADA   EXCHANGE OF NOTES
Settling and Terminating the loan contracted by Ming Sung Indus-
trial Co. , Ltd. from Canadian Bank on October 30, 1946.
Canadian T. S. , 1973, No. 19(E); ILM 13. 4:870-871 (July 1974)(E).

73-72   6/5/73 — TUNIS   TUNISIA   PROTOCOL
Dispatch of a PRC medical team to Tunisia.
TYC 20:131(C); JMJP 6/11/73; NCNA Peking 6/6/73; SCMP 5396:
52 (6/18/73).

73-73   6/5/73 — PEKING   VIETNAM(N)
1973-74 executive plan of public health cooperation.
JMJP 6/6/73; NCNA Peking 6/5/73; SCMP 5396:40 (6/18/73).

73-74   6/6/73 — KIGALI   RWANDA   MINUTES
Talks on road, sugar refinery, rice cultivation.
JMJP 6/9/73; NCNA Peking 6/8/73; SCMP 5398:173 (6/20/73).

73-75   6/8/73 — PEKING   VIETNAM(N)   AGREEMENT
PRC's gratuitous economic and military assistance to Vietnam in
1974.
JMJP 6/9/73; PR 16. 24:3 (6/15/73); NCNA Peking 6/8/73; SCMP
5398:164 (6/20/73).

73-76   6/11/73   6/11/73   OTTAWA   CANADA   AGREEMENT
Civil air transport.
TYC 20:203(C); JMJP 6/13/73; NCNA Ottawa 6/11/73; SCMP
5401:28 (6/25/73); ICAO DOC. 2400; UN Reg. N:13109; Canadian
T. S. , 1973, No. 21(E).

73-77   6/11/73   6/11/73   OTTAWA   CANADA   PROTOCOL
Technical requirements and Procedure in civil transport.
TYC 20:213(C); JMJP 6/13/73; NCNA Ottawa 6/11/73; SCMP
5401:28 (6/25/73).

73-78 6/11/73 — PEKING VIETNAM(N) JOINT COMMUNIQUÉ
Talks during visit of First Secretary LeDuan and Premier Pham
Van Dong: anti-imperialism, anti-colonialism, U. S. aggression
in Indochina countries, etc.
TYC 20:10(C); JMJP 6/12/73(C); PR 16.24:6 (6/15/73)(E); NCNA
Peking 6/12/73; SCMP 5400:245 (6/22/73)(E).

73-79 6/18/73 — PEKING KOREA(N) AGREEMENT
Economic and technical cooperation.
A protocol was also signed.
JMJP 6/19/73; PR 16.25:3 (6/22/73); NCNA Peking 6/18/73;
SCMP 5404:190 (6/28/73).

73-80 6/18/73 — PEKING KOREA(N) PROTOCOL
Economic and technical cooperation.
JMJP 6/19/73; PR 16.25:3 (6/22/73); NCNA Peking 6/18/73;
SCMP 5404:190 (6/28/73).

73-81 6/21/73 — PEKING(?) JAPAN EXCHANGE OF NOTES
Extension of 1965 Sino-Japanese non-governmental Fishery Agree-
ment [65-156] to another year.
JMJP 6/22/73; NCNA Peking 6/21/73; SCMP 5406:33 (7/2/73).

73-82 6/24/73 6/24/73 PEKING MALI AGREEMENT
Economic and technical cooperation.
TYC 20:98(C); JMJP 6/25/73; PR 16.26:4 (6/29/73); NCNA Peking
6/24/73; SCMP 5409:194 (7/6/73).

73-83 6/26/73 — CAIRO EGYPT MINUTES
Talks on PRC aid in building a sand brick factory in Egypt.
JMJP 6/29/73; NCNA Cairo 6/27/73; SCMP 5411:75 (7/10/73).

73-84 7/2/73 7/2/73 LONDON U.K. AGREEMENT
Exhibition of PRC archaeological finds in London from 9/28/73 to
1/23/74.
TYC 20:115(C); NCNA London 7/2/73; SCMP 5414:206 (7/13/73);
UN Reg. N:13283; British T.S., 1973, No. 102(E).

73-85 7/4/73 — PEKING SUDAN PROTOCOL
Trade for 1973.
TYC 20:44(C); JMJP 7/5/73; NCNA Peking 7/4/73; SCMP 5415:45
(7/16/73).

73-86 7/5/73 7/5/73 BONN GERMANY(W) AGREEMENT
Trade and payments.

TYC 20:89(C); JMJP 7/7/73; NCNA Bonn 7/5/73; SCMP 5417:155 (7/19/73).

73-87 7/16/73 — PEKING CANADA EXCHANGE OF NOTES
Confirming reached an Agreement on Registration of Trademarks.
TYC 20:109(C); JMJP 7/17/73; NCNA Peking 7/16/73; SCMP
5423:188 (7/27/73); Canadian T. S. , 1973, no. 29(E).

73-88 7/19/73 — PEKING VIETNAM(S) (R. S. V. N.) AGREE-
MENT
PRC providing emergency supplementary free economic aid to
Vietnam.
JMJP 7/20/73; PR 16. 30:3 (7/27/73); NCNA Peking 7/19/73;
SCMP 5425:70 (7/31/73).

73-89 7/24/73 7/24/73 CANBERRA AUSTRALIA AGREEMENT
Trade.
TYC 20:93(C); JMJP 7/26/73; PR 16. 32:4 (8/10/73); NCNA Can-
berra 7/24/73; SCMP 5429:23 (8/6/73); Australian T. S. , 1973,
No. 21(E).

73-90 7/30/73 7/30/73 PEKING CONGO(B) AGREEMENT
Loan.
TYC 20:104(C); JMJP 7/31/73; NCNA Peking 7/30/73; SCMP
5432:170 (8/9/73).

73-91 7/31/73 — PEKING KOREA(N) RESOLUTION
Signed at twenth-sixth session of Sino-Korean Council of Yalu
River Hydroelectric Power Corporation.
JMJP 8/3/73; NCNA Peking 8/2/73; SCMP 5434:40 (8/13/73).

73-92 8/1/73 8/1/73 MOSCOW USSR AGREEMENT
Goods exchange and payments for 1973.
TYC 20:46(C); JMJP 8/3/73; NCNA Moscow 8/1/73; SCMP 5434:
55 (8/13/73).

73-93 8/1/73 — MOSCOW USSR EXCHANGE OF NOTES
Same conditions for mutual supply of goods in 1974 before signing
1974 agreement.
TYC 20:48(C).

73-94 8/3/73 — FREETOWN SIERRA LEONE MINUTES
Talks on construction of a national stadium in Sierra Leone with
PRC aid.
JMJP 8/7/73; NCNA Freetown 8/3/73; SCMP 5435:98 (8/14/73).

73-95 8/12/73 — PEKING GREECE MINUTES
Talks on establishing Peking–Athens direct satellite communications service.
JMJP 8/14/73; NCNA Peking 8/13/75; SCMP 5441:99 (8/22/73).

73-96 8/16/73 — DAR ES SALAAM TANZANIA PROTOCOL
Shipping.
Signed at seventh meeting of board of directors of PRC-Tanzanian Joint Shipping Company.
NCNA Dar es Salaam 8/17/73; SCMP 5445:78 (8/29/73).

73-97 9/10/73 — KISIN KOREA(N) PROTOCOL
Border railway transportation.
Signed at a meeting on Sino-Korean border railway transportation.
JMJP 9/22/73; NCNA Peking 9/21/73; SCMP 5467:100 (10/2/73).

73-98 9/14/73 — PEKING FRANCE COMMUNIQUÉ
Talks during visit of President Georges Pompidou: Indochina situation, European security disarmament, international trade, etc.
TYC 20:5(C); JMJP 9/18/73(C); PR 16. 38:4 (9/21/73)(E); NCNA Peking 9/17/73; SCMP 5464:215 (9/27/73)(E).

73-99 9/15/73 — PEKING UPPER VOLTA JOINT COMMUNIQUÉ
Establishment of diplomatic relations.
TYC 20:1(C); JMJP 9/16/73(C); PR 16. 38:3 (9/21/73)(E); NCNA Peking 9/15/73; SCMP 5463:172 (9/26/73)(E).

73-100 9/15/73 — PEKING UPPER VOLTA AGREEMENT
Economic and technical cooperation.
JMJP 9/16/73; NCNA Peking 9/15/73; SCMP 5463:173 (9/26/73).

73-101 9/15/73(?) — PEKING UGANDA CONTRACT
Trade.
NCNA Peking 9/16/73; SCMP 5464:227 (9/27/73).

73-102 9/19/73 9/19/73 PEKING CYPRUS AGREEMENT
Trade and payments.
TYC 20:77(C); JMJP 9/20/73; NCNA Peking 9/19/73; SCMP 5466:25 (10/1/73).

73-103 9/19/73 — VALLETTA MALTA PROTOCOL
PRC aid in development projects and technical assistance to Malta.
JMJP 9/21/73; NCNA Peking 9/20/73; SCMP 5467:101 (10/2/73).

73-104 9/20/73 9/20/73 PEKING CHAD AGREEMENT
Trade.
TYC 20:29(C); JMJP 9/21/73; NCNA Peking 9/20/73; SCMP 5467:
78 (10/2/73).

73-105 9/20/73 9/20/73 PEKING CHAD AGREEMENT
Economic and technical cooperation.
TYC 20:102(C); JMJP 9/21/73; NCNA Peking 9/20/73; SCMP 5467:
78 (10/2/73).

73-106 9/22/73 — SOFIA BULGARIA PROTOCOL
Signed at eleventh session of Sino-Bulgarian Scientific and Tech-
nical Commission.
JMJP 9/24/73; NCNA Sofia 9/22/73; SCMP 5468:133 (10/3/73).

73-107 9/27/73 9/27/73 PEKING YUGOSLAVIA AGREEMENT
Technical cooperation of shipping registration.
TYC 20:262(C); JMJP 9/29/73; NCNA Peking 9/28/73; SCMP
5472:127 (10/11/73).

73-108 10/5/73 — PEKING VIETNAM(N) PROTOCOL
Gratuitous supply of military equipment and materials to Vietnam
in 1974 by PRC.
JMJP 10/6/73; NCNA Peking 10/5/73; SCMP 5477:322 (10/8/73).

73-109 10/9/73 — PEKING KOREA(N) AGREEMENT
Border railway transportation.
JMJP 10/10/73; NCNA Peking 10/9/73; SCMP 5479:41 (10/23/73).

73-110 10/9/73 10/9/73 PEKING NEW ZEALAND AGREEMENT
Trade.
TYC 20:83(C); JMJP 10/10/73; NCNA Peking 10/9/73; SCMP 5479:
44 (10/23/73); New Zealand T.S., 1973, no. 12(E).

73-111 10/13/73 10/13/73 PEKING CANADA AGREEMENT
Trade.
TYC 20:33(C); JMJP 10/14/73; NCNA Peking 10/13/73; SCMP
5482:186 (10/26/73); Canadian T.S., 1973, no. 31(E).

73-112 10/16/73 10/16/73 ADEN YEMEN(PDRY) PROTOCOL
Sending medical team to Yemen by PRC.
TYC 20:125(C).

73-113 10/19/73 1/1/74 PEKING VIETNAM(N) AGREEMENT
Mutual supply of goods and payments for 1974.

TYC 20:73(C); JMJP 10/20/73; NCNA Peking 10/19/73; SCMP
5486:171 (11/1/73).

73-114 10/19/73 — PEKING VIETNAM(N) PROTOCOL
PRC aid in form of complete projects to Vietnam.
JMJP 10/20/73; NCNA Peking 10/19/73; SCMP 5486:171 (11/1/73).

73-115 10/19/73 — PEKING VIETNAM(N) PROTOCOL
Supply with general goods in 1974 by PRC.
JMJP 10/20/73; NCNA Peking 10/19/73; SCMP 5486:171 (11/1/73).

73-116 10/25/73(?) — PEKING GUYANA AGREEMENT
Import and export commodities for 1974.
NCNA Peking 10/25/73; SCMP 5489:66 (11/6/73).

73-117 10/30/73 1/31/74 VIENNA AUSTRIA AGREEMENT
Exhibition of PRC archaeological finds in Vienna from 2/14/74 to
4/20/74.
TYC 20:118(C).

73-118 11/4/73 — PEKING AUSTRALIA JOINT PRESS COMMUNI-
QUÉ
Talks during visit of Prime Minister E. G. Whitlam: antihegem-
onism in Asian-Pacific region, mutual respect for sovereignty and
territorial integrity, peaceful co-existence, etc.
TYC 20:19(C); JMJP 11/5/73(C); PR 16.45:12 (11/9/73)(E); NCNA
Peking 11/4/73; SCMP 5495:121 (11/14/73)(E).

73-119 11/4/73 — HUHEHOT MONGOLIA PROTOCOL
Border railway traffic.
Signed at regular meeting of Sino-Mongolian Boundary through
Railway Traffic.
JMJP 11/5/73; NCNA Huhehot 11/4/73; SCMP 5496:169 (11/15/73).

73-120 11/6/73 — PYONGYANG KOREA(N) PROTOCOL
Scientific and technical cooperation.
Signed at fourteenth session of China-Korea Committee for Sci-
entific and Technical Cooperation.
JMJP 11/7/73; NCNA Pyongyang 11/6/73; SCMP 5496:166 (11/15/73).

73-121 11/9/73 12/10/73 PEKING SWEDEN AGREEMENT
Exhibition of PRC archaeological finds in Stockholm from 5/12/74
to 7/16/74.
TYC 20:119(C).

73-122 11/10/73 — PEKING SIERRA LEONE PROTOCOL
Supplement to Agreement on Economic and Technical Cooperation
[71-72].
JMJP 11/11/73; NCNA Peking 11/10/73; SCMP 5499:78 (11/20/73).

73-123 11/10/73 — PEKING SIERRA LEONE SUMMARY
Talks on further development of trade relations.
JMJP 11/11/73; NCNA Peking 11/10/73; SCMP 5499:78 (11/20/73).

73-124 11/12/73 2/3/75 BERN SWITZERLAND AGREEMENT
Civil air transport.
TYC 20:227(C); JMJP 11/14/73; NCNA Geneva 11/12/73; SCMP
5501:163 (11/23/73); ICAO DOC: 2561(E).

73-125 11/12/73 — BERN SWITZERLAND AGREEMENT(2)
Concerning air transport.
JMJP 11/14/73; NCNA Geneva 11. 12. 73; SCMP 5501:163 (11/23/73).

73-126 11/12/73 — BERN SWITZERLAND MINUTES
Talks on designation of airlines and landing places.
TYC 20:239(C).

73-127 11/14/73 — PEKING U. S. A. COMMUNIQUÉ
Talks during visit of Dr. Henry A. Kissinger: Shanghai Communi-
qué, antihegemonism, respect for sovereignty and territorial in-
tegrity, peaceful coexistence, etc.
TYC 20:8(C); JMJP 11/15/73(C); PR 16. 46:10 (11/16/73)(E); NCNA
Peking 11/14/73; SCMP 5501:166 (11/23/73)(E).

73-128 11/20/73 — PEKING VIETNAM(S) (R. S. V. N.) AGREEMENT
PRC's gratuitous economic assistance to Vietnam for 1974.
JMJP 11/21/73; NCNA Peking 11/20/73; SCMP 5505:184 (11/29/73).

73-129 11/21/73 — KABUL AFGHANISTAN NOTES
Talks on PRC's gratuitous construction of a 250-bed hospital for
Afghanistan.
JMJP 11/24/73; NCNA Kabul 11/21/73; SCMP 5507:24 (12/3/73).

73-130 11/21/73 — PEKING VIETNAM(S) (R. S. V. N.) JOINT COM-
MUNIQUÉ
Talks during visit of President Nguyen Huu Tho: Paris Agreement,
Cambodia, Laos, etc.
JMJP 11/24/73(C); PR 16. 48:7 (11/30/73)(E); NCNA Peking
11/24/73; SCMP 5507:54 (12/3/73)(E).

73-131 11/21/73 11/21/73 PEKING ALBANIA AGREEMENT
Scientific cooperation.
TYC 20:122(C); JMJP 11/22/73; NCNA Peking 11/21/73; SCMP
5506:218 (11/30/73).

73-132 11/21/73 — PEKING ALBANIA
1974 executive plan of scientific cooperation.
JMJP 11/22/73; NCNA Peking 11/21/73; SCMP 5506:218 (11/30/73).

73-133 11/22/73 — PEKING RUMANIA PROTOCOL
Extension of 1961 Protocol of General Conditions for Delivery of
Goods.
TYC 20:54(C).

73-134 11/22/73 — ADDIS ABABA ETHIOPIA EXCHANGE OF
NOTES
Sending medical team to Ethiopia by PRC.
TYC 20:133(C).

73-135 11/23/73 1/1/74 PEKING RUMANIA PROTOCOL
Goods exchange and payments for 1974.
TYC 20:55(C); JMJP 11/24/73; PR 16. 48:3 (11/30/73); NCNA
Peking 11/23/73; SCMP 5508:101 (12/4/73).

73-136 11/23/73 7/20/76 PEKING SENEGAL AGREEMENT
Trade.
TYC 20:81(C); JMJP 11/24/73; NCNA Peking 11/23/73; SCMP
5508:103 (12/4/73).

73-137 11/23/73 — PEKING SENEGAL AGREEMENT
Economic and technical cooperation.
JMJP 11/24/73; NCNA Peking 11/23/73; SCMP 5508:103 (12/4/73).

73-138 11/24/73 11/24/73 PEKING RUMANIA AGREEMENT
Exhibition of PRC archaeological finds in Bucharest from 12/28/73
to 2/28/74.
TYC 20:112(C).

73-139 11/25/73 — BAGHDAD IRAQ MINUTES
Talks on building Mosul bridge with PRC aid.
JMJP 12/1/73; NCNA Baghdad 11/27/73; SCMP 5511:232 (12/7/73).

73-140 11/30/73 — HANOI VIETNAM(N)
1973-74 executive plan for cooperation in science between Academy

of Science of China and State Commission for Science and Technology and Commission of Social Science of Vietnam.
JMJP 12/1/73; NCNA Hanoi 11/30/73; SCMP 5512:39 (12/10/73).

73-141 12/3/73 12/3/73 OUAGADOUGOU UPPER VOLTA
AGREEMENT
Economic and technical cooperation.
TYC 20:97(C); JMJP 12/7/73; NCNA Peking 12/5/73; SCMP
5516:183 (12/14/73).

73-142 12/11/73 — TIRANA ALBANIA PROTOCOL
Scientific and technical cooperation.
Signed at fifteenth session of China-Albania Joint Committee for
Scientific and Technical Cooperation.
JMJP 12/13/73; NCNA Tirana 12/12/73; SCMP 5520:159
(12/20/73).

73-143 12/14/73 — PEKING NEPAL JOINT COMMUNIQUÉ
Talks during visit of King Birendra Bir Bikram Shah Dev: self-
existence, spheres of influence, peaceful coexistence, etc.
TYC 20:2(C); JMJP 12/15/73(C); PR 16. 51:6 (12/21/73)(E);
NCNA Peking 12/14/73; SCMP 5522:25 (12/26/73)(E).

73-144 12/17/73 1/1/74 PEKING CZECHOSLOVAKIA AGREE-
MENT
Goods exchange and payments in 1974.
TYC 20:69(C); JMJP 12/18/73; NCNA Peking 12/17/73; SCMP
5524:92 (12/28/73).

73-145 12/20/73 1/1/74 PEKING SRI LANKA PROTOCOL
Exchange of goods in 1974.
TYC 20:72(C); JMJP 12/21/73; PR 16. 52:20 (12/28/73); NCNA
Peking 12/20/73; SCMP 5526:60 (1/3/74).

73-146 12/28/73 — PEKING VIETNAM(S) (R. S. V. N.) AGREE-
MENT
Mutual exemption of visa.
JMJP 12/29/73; NCNA Peking 12/28/73; SCMP 5530:107 (1/9/74).

73-147 12/31/73 — PEKING KOREA(N) PROTOCOL
Border river transport.
Signed at thirteenth session of Sino-Korean Committee for Co-
operation in Border River Transport.
JMJP 1/1/74; NCNA Peking 12/31/73; SCMP 5532:182 (1/11/74).

1974

74-1   1/5/74   6/22/74   PEKING   JAPAN   AGREEMENT
Trade.
JMJP 1/6/74; PR 17. 2:4 (1/11/74); NCNA Peking 1/5/74; SCMP
5535:100 (1/16/74); ILM 13. 4:872-876 (July 1974)(E); JAIL 19:243
(C) (1975).

74-2   1/5/74 — PEKING   JAPAN   MEMORANDUM
Expansion of exchange of journalists.
JAIL 19:232 (1975).

74-3   1/5/74 — PYONGYANG   KOREA(N)   PROTOCOL
Mutual supply of goods in 1974.
JMJP 1/6/74; NCNA Pyongyang 1/5/74; SCMP 5536:130 (1/17/74).

74-4   1/15/74 — TIRANA   ALBANIA   PROTOCOL
Albania's use of PRC loan in 1974.
JMJP 1/17/74; NCNA Tirana 1/16/74; SCMP 5542:94 (1/30/74).

74-5   1/15/74 — TIRANA   ALBANIA   PROTOCOL
Exchange of goods and payments in 1974.
JMJP 1/17/74; NCNA Tirana 1/16/74; SCMP 5542:94 (1/30/74).

74-6   1/18/74 — PEKING   MALAGASY   AGREEMENT
Economic and technical cooperation.
JMJP 1/19/74; NCNA Peking 1/18/74; SCMP 5543:135 (1/31/74).

74-7   1/18/74 — PEKING   MALAGASY   AGREEMENT
Trade.
JMJP 1/19/74; NCNA Peking 1/18/74; SCMP 5543:135 (1/31/74).

74-8   2/7/74 — TUNIS   TUNISIA   PROTOCOL (ADDITIONAL)
Relating to Trade Agreement.
JMJP 2/10/74; NCNA Tunis 2/8/74; SCMP 5556:74 (2/20/74).

74-9   2/8/74 — BUCHAREST   RUMANIA   AGREEMENT
Health cooperation.
JMJP 2/10/74; NCNA Bucharest 2/9/74; SCMP 5556:70 (2/20/74).

74-10   2/12/74 — PEKING   FINLAND   AGREEMENT
Trade in 1974.
NCNA Peking 2/12/74; SCMP 5558:148 (2/22/74).

74-11 2/12/74 — KINGSTON JAMAICA AGREEMENT
Economic and technical cooperation.
JMJP 2/14/74; NCNA Peking 2/13/74; SCMP 5559:31 (2/25/74).

74-12 2/15/74 — SOFIA BULGARIA AGREEMENT
Exchange of goods and payments in 1974.
JMJP 2/17/74; NCNA Sofia 2/15/74; SCMP 5561:105 (2/27/74).

74-13 2/15/74 — PEKING GUINEA AGREEMENT
PRC grant of commercial loan to Guinea.
JMJP 2/16/74; PR 17. 8:3 (2/22/74); NCNA Peking 2/15/74;
SCMP 5560:66 (2/26/74).

74-14 2/15/74 — PEKING GUINEA PROTOCOL
1974 trade.
JMJP 2/16/74; PR 17. 8:3 (2/22/74); NCNA Peking 2/15/74;
SCMP 5560:66 (2/26/74).

74-15 2/16/74 — PEKING IRAQ MINUTES
Trade talks.
JMJP 2/18/74; NCNA Peking 2/17/74; SCMP 5561:107 (2/27/74).

74-16 2/21/74 — BERLIN GERMANY(E) AGREEMENT
Exchange of goods and payments in 1974.
JMJP 2/25/74; NCNA Berlin 2/21/74; SCMP 5565:79 (3/5/74).

74-17 2/23/74 — ALGIERS ALGERIA PROTOCOL
1974 trade.
JMJP 2/25/74; NCNA Algiers 2/23/74; SCMP 5566:114 (3/6/74).

74-18 2/24/74 — PEKING ZAMBIA AGREEMENT
Economic and technical cooperation.
JMJP 2/25/74; PR 17. 9:5 (3/1/74); NCNA Peking 2/24/74; SCMP
5566:127 (3/6/74).

74-19 3/2/74 — PEKING ALGERIA JOINT COMMUNIQUÉ
Talks during visit of President Houari Boumediene: Middle East,
Africa, fourth Summit Conference of Nonaligned Countries, Indo-
china, etc.
JMJP 3/4/74(C); PR 17. 10:10 (3/8/74)(E); NCNA Peking 3/3/74;
SCMP 5571:119 (3/13/74)(E).

74-20 3/11/74 — PEKING POLAND AGREEMENT
Exchange of goods and payments in 1974.
JMJP 3/12/74; NCNA Peking 3/11/74; SCMP 5577:138 (3/21/77).

74-21 3/15/74 — CONAKRY GUINEA-BISSAU JOINT COMMUNI-
QUÉ
Establishment of diplomatic relations.
JMJP 3/21/74(C); PR 17.13:6 (3/29/74)(E); NCNA Peking 3/20/74;
SCMP 5583:171 (3/29/74)(E).

74-22 3/15/74 — PEKING CANADA AGREEMENT
Exhibition of Archaeological finds of the PRC.
Canadian T.S., 1974, no. 10(E).

74-23 3/21/74 — BLAGOVESHCHENSK (HALANPAO CHINA)
U.S.S.R. MINUTES
Border river transport.
Signed at nineteenth regular session of Sino-Soviet Joint Commis-
sion for Navigation on Border Rivers.
JMJP 3/23/74; NCNA Peking 3/22/74; SCMP 5584:38 (4/1/74).

74-24 3/23/74 — PEKING VIETNAM(N) PROTOCOL
Scientific and technical cooperation in 1973-74.
JMJP 3/24/74; NCNA Peking 3/23/74; SCMP 5585:69 (4/2/74).

74-25 3/25/74 — PEKING HUNGARY AGREEMENT
Exchange of goods and payments in 1974.
JMJP 3/26/74; NCNA Peking 3/25/74; SCMP 5587:138 (4/4/74).

74-26 3/29/74 — PEKING TANZANIA AGREEMENT
Economic and technical cooperation.
JMJP 3/30/74; NCNA Peking 3/29/74; SCMP 5590:109 (4/10/74).

74-27 4/10/74 — KINSHASA ZAIRE AGREEMENT
Maritime transport.
JMJP 4/14/74.

74-28 4/20/74 — LIBREVILLE GABON JOINT COMMUNIQUÉ
Establishment of diplomatic relations.
JMJP 4/30/74(C); PR 17.18:7 (5/3/74)(E); NCNA Peking 4/29/74;
SCMP 5611:211 (5/10/74)(E).

74-29 4/20/74 5/24/74 PEKING JAPAN AGREEMENT
Civil air transport.
JMJP 4/21/73; PR 17.17:3 (4/26/74); NCNA Peking 4/20/74;
SCMP 5605:172 (5/2/74); JAIL 19:245(C) (1975).

74-30 4/21/74 — KABUL AFGHANISTAN PROTOCOL
Exchange of goods in 1974.
JMJP 4/23/74; NCNA Kabul 4/22/74; SCMP 5606:211 (5/3/74).

74-31 4/21/74 — KABUL AFGHANISTAN AGREEMENT
Trade and payments in 1974.
JMJP 4/23/74; NCNA Kabul 4/22/74; SCMP 5606:211 (5/3/74).

74-32 4/21/74 — NANMING VIETNAM(N) PROTOCOL
Border railway transport.
Signed at sixteenth session of Sino-Vietnamese Border Railway
Commission.
JMJP 4/23/74; NCNA Nanming 4/22/74; SCMP 5606:222 (5/3/74).

74-33 4/26/74 — PEKING MONGOLIA PROTOCOL
Mutual supply of goods in 1974.
JMJP 4/27/74; NCNA Peking 4/26/74; SCMP 5609:132 (5/8/74).

74-34 4/30/74 — GHANA PROTOCOL
1974 trade.
JMJP 5/1/74; NCNA Peking 4/30/74; SCMP 5612:39 (5/13/74).

74-35 5/4/74 — WARSAW POLAND PROTOCOL
Signed at twenty-fourth session of Joint Standing Commission of
Sino-Polish Shipping Joint Stock Company.
JMJP 5/9/74; NCNA Warsaw 5/7/74; SCMP 5616:245 (5/17/74).

74-36 5/7/74 10/17/74 — NETHERLANDS EXCHANGE OF
LETTERS
Establishment of Mixed Netherlands-Chinese Commission for
Economy & Trade.
Treaty Series of the Kingdom of the Netherlands (Trb).
Trb 1974, 99 & 209; NYIL 6:323 (1975).

74-37 5/14/74 — PEKING PAKISTAN JOINT COMMUNIQUÉ
Talks during Prime Minister Zulfikar Ali Bhutto's visit: interna-
tional economic order, second Islamic Summit Conference, Third
World, etc.
JMJP 5/15/74(C); PR 17. 20:10 (5/17/74)(E); NCNA Peking 5/14/74;
SCMP 5621:222 (5/24/74)(E).

74-38 5/15/74 — PEKING U.S.S.R. AGREEMENT
Exchange of goods and payments for 1974.
JMJP 5/16/74; NCNA Peking 5/15/74; SCMP 5622:44 (5/28/74).

74-39 5/18/74 — PEKING SENEGAL JOINT COMMUNIQUÉ
Talks during visit of President Leopold Sedar Senghor: Africa,
Indochina, international economic relations, etc.
JMJP 5/19/74(C); PR 17. 21:8 (5/24/74)(E); NCNA Peking 5/18/74;
SCMP 5624:140 (5/30/74)(E).

74-40 5/26/74 — PEKING CAMBODIA AGREEMENT
PRC grant gratis provision of military equipment and supplies to
Cambodia for 1974.
JMJP 5/27/74; NCNA Peking 5/26/74; SCMP 5629:193 (6/6/74).

74-41 5/27/74 — PEKING CAMBODIA JOINT COMMUNIQUÉ
Talks during visit of Deputy Prime Minister Khieu Samphan:
Indochina, Africa, Third World, etc.
JMJP 5/28/74(C); PR 17. 22:10 (5/31/74)(E); NCNA Peking 5/27/74;
SCMP 5630:229 (6/7/74)(E).

74-42 5/31/74 5/31/74 PEKING MALAYSIA JOINT COMMUNI-
QUÉ
Establishment of diplomatic relations.
JMJP 6/1/74(C); PR 17. 23:8 (6/7/74)(E); NCNA Peking 5/31/74;
SCMP 5633:127 (6/12/74)(E); ILM 13. 4:877 (July 1974)(E).

74-43 5/31/74 — KATMANDU NEPAL AGREEMENT
Trade and payments.
JMJP 6/2/74; NCNA Katmandu 6/1/74; SCMP 5634:179 (6/13/74).

74-44 5/31/74 — PEKING ZAIRE AGREEMENT
Civil air transport.
JMJP 6/1/73; PR 17. 23:7 (6/7/74); NCNA Peking 5/31/74;
SCMP 5633:141 (6/12/74).

74-45 6/4/74 — SOFIA BULGARIA AGREEMENT
Maritime transport.
JMJP 6/7/74; NCNA Sofia 6/4/74; SCMP 5636:33 (6/17/74).

74-46 6/20/74 6/20/74 NEW YORK TRINIDAD & TOBAGO
JOINT COMMUNIQUÉ
Establishment of diplomatic relations.
JMJP 6/22/74(C); PR 17. 26:3 (6/28/74)(E); NCNA Peking 6/21/74;
SCMP 5646:78 (7/3/74)(E).

74-47 6/28/74 6/28/74 CARACAS VENEZUELA JOINT COM-
MUNIQUÉ
Establishment of diplomatic relations.
JMJP 6/29/74(C); PR 17. 27:5 (7/5/74)(E); NCNA Peking 6/28/74;
SCMP 5650:145 (7/10/74)(E).

74-48 7/10/74 — HAVANA CUBA PROTOCOL
1974 trade.
JMJP 7/15/74; NCNA Havana 7/11/74; SCMP 5660:116 (7/24/74).

74-49 7/12/74 — COLOMBO SRI LANKA PROTOCOL
Construction of Gin Ganga (River) controlling project.
Some related documents were also signed.
JMJP 7/17/74; NCNA Colombo 7/12/74; SCMP 5661:176 (7/25/74).

74-50 7/14/74 — PEKING TUNISIA ACCORD
Implementation of 1972 Agreement on Economic and Technical
Cooperation [72-92].
JMJP 7/15/74; NCNA Peking 7/14/74; SCMP 5661:179 (7/25/74).

74-51 7/16/74 — PEKING TURKEY AGREEMENT
Trade.
JMJP 7/17/74; NCNA Peking 7/16/74; SCMP 5662:227 (7/26/74).

74-52 7/20/74 7/20/74 PEKING NIGER JOINT COMMUNIQUÉ
Establishment of diplomatic relations.
JMJP 7/21/74(C); PR 17. 30:4 (7/26/74)(E); NCNA Peking 7/20/74;
SCMP 5665:107 (7/31/74)(E).

74-53 7/20/74 — PEKING NIGER AGREEMENT
Economic and technical cooperation.
JMJP 7/21/74; NCNA Peking 7/20/74; SCMP 5665:108 (7/31/74).

74-54 7/27/74 — PEKING PAKISTAN PROTOCOL
Trade.
JMJP 7/28/74; NCNA Peking 7/27/74; SCMP 5669:61 (8/6/74).

74-55 8/2/74 — PEKING NORWAY AGREEMENT
Maritime transport.
JMJP 8/3/74; NCNA Peking 8/2/74; SCMP 5674:96 (8/13/74).

74-56 8/15/74 8/15/74 BRASILIA BRAZIL JOINT COMMUNIQUÉ
Establishment of diplomatic relations.
JMJP 8/16/74(C); PR 17. 34:4 (8/23/74)(E); NCNA Peking 8/?/74;
SCMP 5683:22 (8/27/74)(E).

74-57 8/27/74 — PEKING LAOS AGREEMENT
Civil air transport.
JMJP 8/28/74; PR 17. 37:29 (9/13/74); NCNA Peking 8/27/74;
SCMP 5692:67 (9/10/74).

74-58 8/27/74 — TOKYO JAPAN AGREEMENT
Operation with Japan Air Lines Company—opening regular air
services.
JMJP 9/5/74; NCNA Tokyo 9/1/74; SCMP 5695:207 (9/13/74);
JAIL 19:236 (1975).

74-59 8/27/74 — TOKYO JAPAN AGREEMENT
Technical problems of aviation.
JMJP 9/5/74; NCNA Tokyo 9/1/74; SCMP 5695:207 (9/13/74).

74-60 9/5/74 — PEKING TOGO PROTOCOL
Economic and technical cooperation.
JMJP 9/6/74; PR 17. 37:6 (9/13/74); NCNA Peking 9/5/74;
SCMP 5697:77 (9/17/74).

74-61 9/15/74 — PEKING NIGERIA PRESS COMMUNIQUÉ
Talks during visit of General Yakubu Gowon: Third World, Africa,
Palestinian, anti-imperialism, colonialism and hegemonism, etc.
JMJP 9/17/74(C); PR 17. 38:11 (9/20/74)(E); NCNA Peking 9/16/74;
SCMP 5705:256 (9/27/74)(E).

74-62 9/19/74 — PEKING MAURITANIA AGREEMENT
Economic and technical cooperation.
JMJP 9/20/74; NCNA Peking 9/19/74; SCMP 5707:86 (10/2/74).

74-63 9/21/74 — PEKING BULGARIA PROTOCOL
Scientific and technical cooperation.
Signed at twelfth session of Sino-Bulgarian Commission for Sci-
entific and Technical Cooperation.
JMJP 9/22/74; NCNA Peking 9/21/74; SCMP 5709:187 (10/4/74).

74-64 9/23/74 — PEKING PHILIPPINES EXCHANGE OF LETTERS
Further development of PRC-Philippines trade.
JMJP 9/24/74; PR 17. 39:5 (9/27/74); NCNA Peking 9/23/74;
SCMP 5710:51 (10/7/74).

74-65 9/24/74 — PRAGUE CZECHOSLOVAKIA PROTOCOL
Scientific and technical cooperation.
Signed at sixteenth session of Sino-Czechoslovak Joint Committee
for Scientific and Technical Cooperation.
JMJP 9/26/74; NCNA Prague 9/24/74; SCMP 5712:160 (10/9/74).

74-66 9/30/74 — PEKING ALBANIA PROTOCOL
Exchange of goods and payments for 1975.
JMJP 10/1/74; PR 17. 41:5 (10/11/74); NCNA Peking 9/30/74;
SCMP 5715:48 (10/15/74).

74-67 9/30/74 — PEKING RUMANIA PROTOCOL
PRC providing complete plants and technical assistance.
JMJP 10/1/74; NCNA Peking 9/30/74; SCMP 5715:68 (10/15/74).

74-68   10/3/74 — PEKING   LAOS   AGREEMENT
Economic and technical cooperation.
JMJP 10/4/74; NCNA Peking 10/3/74; SCMP 5718:300 (10/18/74).

74-69   10/6/74 — PEKING   GABON   AGREEMENT
Trade.
JMJP 10/7/74; PR 17.41:5 (10/11/74); NCNA Peking 10/6/74;
SCMP 5720:117 (10/24/74).

74-70   10/6/74 — PEKING   GABON   AGREEMENT
Economic and technical cooperation.
JMJP 10/7/74; PR 17.41:5 (10/11/74); NCNA Peking 10/6/74;
SCMP 5720:117 (10/24/74).

74-71   10/9/74 — PEKING   GABON   PRESS COMMUNIQUÉ
Talks during visit of President El Hadj Omar Bongo: Africa,
Arab countries, Indochina situation, etc.
JMJP 10/10/74(C); PR 17.42:17 (10/18/74)(E); NCNA Peking
10/9/74; SCMP 5722:41 (10/29/74)(E).

74-72   10/12/74   10/12/74   PEKING   AUSTRALIA   EXCHANGE
OF NOTES
Registration of Trade Marks.
NCNA Peking 10/12/74; SCMP 5724:143 (11/1/74); Australian
T.S., 1974, no. 24(E).

74-73   10/19/74 — PEKING   NORWAY   EXCHANGE OF NOTES
Establishment of a Joint PRC-Norway Trade Committee.
JMJP 10/26/74; NCNA 10/25/74; SCMP 5731:102 (11/12/74).

74-74   10/20/74 — PEKING   LAOS   AGREEMENT
Postal and telecommunications.
JMJP 10/21/74; PR 17.44:5 (11/1/74); NCNA Peking 10/20/74;
SCMP 5728:226 (11/7/74).

74-75   10/21/74 — PEKING   DENMARK   AGREEMENT
Maritime transport.
JMJP 10/22/74.

74-76   10/21/74 — PEKING   DENMARK   EXCHANGE OF LETTERS
Establishment of a Joint Sino-Danish Committee for purpose of
trade promotion and development of economic relations.
JMJP 10/22/74; PR 17.43:4 (10/25/74); NCNA Peking 10/21/74;
SCMP 5729:263 (11/8/74).

74-77 10/22/74 — SARIWON CITY KOREA(N) PROTOCOL
Border railway transport.
Signed at a regular meeting on Sino-Korean Border Railway
Transport.
JMJP 10/30/74; NCNA Pyongyang 10/26/74; SCMP 5731:101
(11/12/74).

74-78 10/24/74 — HANOI VIETNAM(N)
1975-76 plan for public health cooperation.
JMJP 10/26/74; NCNA Hanoi 10/25/74; SCMP 5731:108 (11/12/74).

74-79 10/26/74 — PEKING VIETNAM(N) AGREEMENT
Exchange of goods and payments in 1975.
JMJP 10/27/74; PR 17.44:3 (11/1/74); NCNA Peking 10/26/74;
SCMP 5731:112 (11/12/74).

74-80 10/26/74 PEKING VIETNAM(N) AGREEMENT
Economic and military aid to Vietnam in 1975.
JMJP 10/27/74; PR 17.44:3 (11/1/74); NCNA Peking 10/26/74;
SCMP 5731:112 (11/12/74).

74-81 10/26/74 PEKING VIETNAM(N) PROTOCOL
Supply of general goods by PRC to Vietnam.
JMJP 10/27/74; PR 17.44:3 (11/1/74); NCNA Peking 10/26/74;
SCMP 5731:112 (11/12/74).

74-82 10/26/74 — PEKING VIETNAM(N) PROTOCOL
Gratuitous supply of military equipment and materials by PRC in
1975.
JMJP 10/27/74; PR 17.44:3 (11/1/74); NCNA Peking 10/26/74;
SCMP 5731:112 (11/12/74).

74-83 10/26/74 — PEKING HUNGARY PROTOCOL
Scientific and technical cooperation.
Signed at thirteenth meeting of Sino-Hungarian Commission for
Scientific and Technical Cooperation.
JMJP 10/27/74; PR 17.44:5 (11/1/74); NCNA Peking 10/26/74;
SCMP 5731:91 (11/12/74).

74-84 10/26/74(?) — ULAN BATOR MONGOLIA PROTOCOL
Border railway.
Signed at 1974 regular meeting of Sino-Mongolian Boundary-
Through Railway Traffic.
NCNA Ulan Bator 10/27/74; SCMP 5732:150 (11/13/74).

74-85 10/27/74(?) — PEKING TURKEY AGREEMENT
Cooperation between Hsinhua News Agency and Anatolian News
Agency of Turkey.
JMJP 10/30/74; NCNA Peking 10/28/74; SCMP 5732:158 (11/13/74).

74-86 10/28/74 10/28/74 — NETHERLANDS AGREEMENT
Exhibition of archaeological discoveries of PRC.
Trb 1974:239; NYIL 6:335 (1975).

74-87 11/4/74 — PYONGYANG KOREA(N)
1975-76 plan for scientific cooperation between Korean and China
Academy of Sciences.
JMJP 11/6/74; NCNA Pyongyang 11/5/74; SCMP 5736:98 (11/19/74).

74-88 11/5/74 — PEKING VIETNAM(N) AGREEMENT
Broadcast and television cooperation.
Signed by Central Broadcasting Administration of PRC and "Voice
of Vietnam" Radio of Vietnam.
JMJP 11/6/74; NCNA Peking 11/5/74; SCMP 5736:119 (11/19/74).

74-89 11/6/74 — PEKING KOREA(N) PROTOCOL
Scientific and technical cooperation.
Signed at fifteenth session of Sino-Korean Committee for Scientific
and Technical Cooperation.
JMJP 11/7/74; NCNA Peking 11/6/74; SCMP 5737:150 (11/20/74).

74-90 11/8/74 — PEKING NORWAY EXCHANGE OF LETTERS
Agreement on reciprocal registration of trademarks.
JMJP 11/9/74; NCNA Peking 11/8/74; SCMP 5739:242 (11/22/74).

74-91 11/11/74 — PEKING TRINIDAD & TOBAGO PRESS COM-
MUNIQUÉ
Talks during visit of Prime Minister Dr. Eric Williams: student
exchange, mutual respect for sovereignty and territorial integrity,
peaceful coexistence, etc.
JMJP 11/12/74(C); PR 17.46:8 (11/15/74)(E); NCNA Peking
11/11/74; SCMP 5740:33 (11/25/74)(E).

74-92 11/12/74 — PEKING YUGOSLAVIA AGREEMENT
Scientific and technical cooperation.
JMJP 11/13/74; PR 17.47:5 (11/22/74); NCNA Peking 11/12/74;
SCMP 5741:90 (11/26/74).

74-93 11/13/74 — 6/4/74 TOKYO JAPAN AGREEMENT
Maritime transport.

JMJP 11/14/74; PR 17. 47:4 (11/22/74); NCNA Tokyo 11/13/74;
SCMP 5742:121 (11/27/74); JAIL 20:171(C) (1976).

74-94 11/13/74 — PEKING YEMEN (PDRY) AGREEMENT
Economic and technical cooperation.
JMJP 11/14/74; NCNA Peking 11/13/74; SCMP 5742:136 (11/27/74).

74-95 11/20/74 — PEKING YEMEN (PDRY) PRESS COMMUNIQUÉ
Talks during visit of Chairman Salem Robaya Ali: antiimperialism,
colonialism and power politics, Arab and Palestinian, Africa,
Third World, etc.
JMJP 11/21/74(C); PR 17. 48:10 (11/29/74)(E); NCNA Peking
11/20/74; SCMP 5746:145 (12/4/74)(E).

74-96 11/22/74 — OUAGADOUGOU UPPER VOLTA PROTOCOL
Agricultural cooperation projects.
NCNA Peking 11/25/74; SCMP 5749:52 (12/9/74).

74-97 11/29/74 — PEKING ALGERIA PROTOCOL
Trade for 1975.
JMJP 11/30/74; NCNA Peking 11/29/74; SCMP 5751:153 (12/11/74).

74-98 11/29/74 — PEKING U. S. A. COMMUNIQUÉ
Talks during visit of Dr. Henry A. Kissinger: Shanghai Communiqué and President Ford's visit.
JMJP 11/30/74(C); PR 17. 49:4 (12/6/74)(E); NCNA Peking
11/29/74; SCMP 5751:164 (12/11/74)(E).

74-99 12/7/74 — TUNIS TUNISIA EXCHANGE OF NOTES
Local expenditure of 1972 Agreement on Economic and Technical
Cooperation [72-92].
JMJP 12/10/74; NCNA Tunis 12/8/74; SCMP 5757:172 (12/19/74).

74-100 12/8/74 — KINSHASA ZAIRE JOINT COMMUNIQUÉ
News exchange.
JMJP 12/10/74; NCNA Kinshasa 12/8/74; SCMP 5757:176 (12/19/74).

74-101 12/8/74 — PEKING AFGHANISTAN AGREEMENT
Economic and technical cooperation.
JMJP 12/9/74; PR 17. 50:4 (12/13/74); NCNA Peking 12/8/74;
SCMP 5757:157 (12/19/74).

74-102 12/9/74 — TANANARIVE MADAGASCAR
Dispatch of medical teams to Madagasy by PRC.
JMJP 12/13/74; NCNA Peking 12/10/74; SCMP 5758:214 (12/20/74).

74-103 12/11/74 — CONAKRY GUINEA PROTOCOL
Dispatch of medical teams to Guinea.
JMJP 12/15/74; NCNA Conakry 12/11/74; SCMP 5760:72 (12/24/74).

74-104 12/14/74 — BUCHAREST RUMANIA PROTOCOL
Exchange of goods and payments for 1975.
JMJP 12/16/74; NCNA Bucharest 12/14/74; SCMP 5761:120
(12/27/74).

74-105 12/17/74 — PEKING FINLAND DRAFT
Civil air transport.
JMJP 12/18/74; NCNA Peking 12/17/74; SCMP 5763:78 (12/31/74).

74-106 12/17/74 12/14/74 NOUAKCHOTT(?) GAMBIA JOINT
COMMUNIQUÉ
Establishment of diplomatic relations.
JMJP 12/18/74; PR 17. 51:5 (12/20/74)(E); NCNA Peking 12/17/74;
SCMP 5763:79 (12/31/74)(E).

74-107 12/20/74 — PRAGUE CZECHOSLOVAKIA AGREEMENT
Exchange of goods and payments in 1975.
JMJP 12/23/74; NCNA Prague 12/20/74; SCMP 5765:171 (1/3/75).

74-108 12/20/74 — HELSINKI FINLAND AGREEMENT
Trade for 1975.
JMJP 12/23/74; NCNA Helsinki 12/20/74; SCMP 5765:171 (1/3/75).

74-109 12/20/74 — BERN SWITZERLAND AGREEMENT
Trade.
JMJP 12/23/74; NCNA Geneva 12/20/74; SCMP 5765:179 (1/3/75).

74-110 12/21/74 — PEKING KOREA(N) PROTOCOL
Mutual supply of goods in 1975.
JMJP 12/22/74; NCNA Peking 12/21/74; SCMP 5765:172 (1/3/75).

74-111 12/21/74 — PEKING RUMANIA PROTOCOL
Scientific and technical cooperation.
Signed at sixteenth session of Sino-Rumanian Joint Commission
on Scientific and Technical Cooperation.
JMJP 12/22/74; NCNA Peking 12/21/74; SCMP 5765:174 (1/3/75).

74-112 12/23/74 — DAKAR SENEGAL PROTOCOL
Dispatch of medical teams to Senegal by PRC.
JMJP 12/25/74; NCNA Dakar 12/23/74; SCMP 5767:72 (1/7/75).

74-113 12/24/74 — SINUIJU KOREA(N) AGREEMENT
Border river transport.
Signed at fourteenth meeting of the China-Korea Committee
for Cooperation in Border River Transport.
JMJP 12/28/74; NCNA Pyongyang 12/26/74; SCMP 5769:165
(1/9/75).

74-114 12/26/74 — PYONGYANG KOREA(N) PROTOCOL
Hydroelectric power corporation in Yalu River.
Signed at twenth-seventh meeting of Council of Sino-Korean Yalu
River Hydroelectric Power Corporation.
JMJP 12/28/74; NCNA Pyongyang 12/27/74; SCMP 5769:164
(1/9/75).

74-115 12/28/74 — PEKING VIETNAM(S)(R.S.V.N.) AGREEMENT
PRC providing gratuitous economic aid to Vietnam in 1975.
JMJP 12/29/74; NCNA Peking 12/28/74; SCMP 5769:169 (1/9/75).

74-116 12/30/74 — COTONOU DAHOMEY PROTOCOL
Agricultural project.
JMJP 1/3/75; NCNA Peking 1/2/75; SCMP 5772:90 (1/14/75).

74-117 12/30/74 — COTONOU DAHOMEY EXCHANGE OF LET-
TERS
Legal expenses related to Protocol of Agricultural Project (74-113).
JMJP 1/3/75; NCNA Peking 1/2/75; SCMP 5772:90 (1/14/75).

1975

75-1 1/6/75 1/6/75 NEW YORK BOTSWANA JOINT COMMUNI-
QUÉ
Establishment of diplomatic relations.
JMJP 1/8/75(C); PR 18.2:4 (1/10/75)(E); NCNA Peking 1/7/75;
SCMP 5776:35 (1/20/75)(E).

75-2 1/10/75 — PEKING LAOS PROTOCOL
Mutual supply of technical service on aviation.
JMJP 1/12/75; NCNA Peking 1/11/75; SCMP 5778:97 (1/22/75).

75-3 1/10/75 — PEKING LAOS AGREEMENT(2)
Civil air transport.
NCNA Peking 1/11/75; SCMP 5778:97 (1/22/75).

75-4   1/17/75 — VIENTIANE   LAOS   MINUTES
Talks on building of dwellings for 500 people in Luang Probang City.
JMJP 1/20/75; NCNA Vientiane 1/18/75; SCMP 5784:149 (1/30/75).

75-5   1/17/75 — VIENTIANE   LAOS   MINUTES
Talks on building of a highway from upper Laos to city of Luang Probang.
JMJP 1/20/75; NCNA Vientiane 1/18/75; SCMP 5784:149 (1/30/75).

75-6   1/17/75 — VIENTIANE   LAOS   PROTOCOL
Working conditions and living standards of Chinese engineering and technical personnel in Laos.
JMJP 1/20/75; NCNA Vientiane 1/18/75; SCMP 5784:149 (1/30/75).

75-7   1/18/75 — PEKING   SWEDEN   AGREEMENT
Maritime transport.
JMJP 1/19/75; NCNA Peking 1/18/75; SCMP 5783:116 (1/29/75).

75-8   1/25/75 — PEKING   GERMANY(E)   AGREEMENT
Exchange of goods and payment for 1975.
JMJP 1/26/75; NCNA Peking 1/25/75; SCMP 5787:85 (2/4/75).

75-9   1/29/75 — PEKING   ITALY   EXCHANGE OF LETTERS
Confirmation of establishment of Sino-Italian Amalgamated Committee to promote trade and economic relations.
JMJP 1/30/75; NCNA Peking 1/29/75; SCMP 5790:221 (2/7/75).

75-10   2/2/75 — PEKING   GAMBIA   AGREEMENT
Economic and technical cooperation.
JMJP 2/3/75; PR 18.6:5 (2/7/75); NCNA Peking 2/2/75; SCMP 5793:29 (2/18/75).

75-11   2/2/75 — KATMANDU   NEPAL   AGREEMENT
Construction of Pokhara-Surkhet highway.
JMJP 2/4/75; NCNA Katmandu 2/2/75; SCMP 5793:32 (2/18/75).

75-12   2/3/75 — PEKING   TRINIDAD & TOBAGO   AGREEMENT
Establishment of embassies.
JMJP 2/4/75; PR 18.6:4 (2/7/75); NCNA Peking 2/3/75; SCMP 5793:37 (2/18/75).

75-13   2/4/75 — COLOMBO   SRI LANKA   PROTOCOL
1975 trade.
JMJP 2/10/75; NCNA Colombo 2/4/75; SCMP 5794:74 (2/19/75).

75-14 2/6/75 — PEKING   TRINIDAD & TOBAGO   PRESS COM-
MUNIQUÉ
Talks during visit of Prime Minister Dr. Eric Williams: seventh
special session of U. N. General Assembly, question of petroleum
and transfer of technology, etc.
JMJP 2/7/75(C); PR 18. 7:10 (2/14/75); NCNA Peking 2/6/75;
SCMP 5795:112 (2/20/75)(E).

75-15 2/7/75 — KATMANDU   NEPAL   JOINT PRESS COMMUNIQUÉ
Economic and technical cooperation.
JMJP 2/10/75(C); NCNA Katmandu 2/8/75; SCMP 5797:33 (2/24/75).

75-16 3/2/75 — PEKING   CONGO   EXCHANGE OF LETTERS
Items of economic and technical cooperation.
JMJP 3/3/75; PR 18. 10:3 (3/7/75); NCNA Peking 3/2/75; SCMP
5810:175 (3/13/75).

75-17 3/2/75 — PEKING   MOZAMBIQUE   PRESS COMMUNIQUÉ
Talks during visit of President Samora Moises Machel: Africa,
Indochina countries, Korea, Arab and Palestinian, etc.
JMJP 3/3/75(C); PR 18. 10:13 (3/7/75)(E); NCNA Peking 3/2/75;
SCMP 5811:224 (3/14/75)(E).

75-18 3/3/75 — BUDAPEST   HUNGARY   AGREEMENT
Exchange of goods and payments for 1975.
JMJP 3/5/75; NCNA Budapest 3/4/75; SCMP 5812:35 (3/17/75).

75-19 3/11/75 — PEKING   BULGARIA   AGREEMENT
Exchange of goods and payments for 1975.
JMJP 3/12/75; NCNA Peking 3/11/75; SCMP 5816:183 (3/21/75).

75-20 3/11/75 — CONAKRY   GUINEA   AGREEMENT
Provision of commodity loan.
JMJP 3/13/75; NCNA Conakry 3/11/75; SCMP 5817:33 (3/24/75).

75-21 3/11/75 — CONAKRY   GUINEA   PROTOCOL
Trade for 1975.
JMJP 3/13/75; NCNA Conakry 3/11/75; SCMP 5817:33 (3/24/75).

75-22 3/11/75 — WARSAW   POLAND   AGREEMENT
Exchange of goods and payments for 1975.
JMJP 3/15/75; NCNA Warsaw 3/13/75; SCMP 5818:97 (3/25/75).

75-23 3/14/75 — PEKING   GUYANA   AGREEMENT
Economic and technical cooperation.
JMJP 3/15/75; NCNA Peking 3/14/75; SCMP 5818:89 (3/25/75).

75-24 3/17/75 — PEKING GUYANA PRESS COMMUNIQUÉ
Talks during visit of Prime Minister Linden Forbes S. Burnham:
Third World, international economy, etc.
JMJP 3/18/75(C); PR 18. 12:10 (3/21/75)(E); NCNA Peking
3/17/75; SCMP 5820:187 (3/27/75)(E).

75-25 3/19/75 — PEKING MOROCCO AGREEMENT
Cooperation in constructing a sports complex in Morocco.
JMJP 3/20/75; PR 18. 13:3 (3/28/75); NCNA Peking 3/19/75;
SCMP 5822:71 (4/1/75).

75-26 3/19/75 — PEKING MOROCCO AGREEMENT
Long-term trade.
JMJP 3/20/75; PR 18. 13:3 (3/28/75); NCNA Peking 3/19/75;
SCMP 5822:71 (4/1/75).

75-27 3/19/75 — PEKING MOROCCO PROTOCOL
Dispatch of medical teams to Morocco by PRC.
JMJP 3/20/75; PR 18. 13:3 (3/28/75); NCNA Peking 3/19/75;
SCMP 5822:71 (4/1/75).

75-28 3/28/75 — TIRANA ALBANIA
1975 executive plan for scientific cooperation.
JMJP 3/31/75; NCNA English 3/29/75; SCMP 5828:107 (4/9/75).

75-29 4/10/75 1/22/75 PEKING BELGIUM EXCHANGE OF
NOTES
Agreement on reciprocal trademark registration.
JMJP 4/11/75; NCNA Peking 4/10/75; SCMP 5836:65 (4/22/75);
Agreement on entering into force JMJP 1/23/77; NCNA Peking
1/22/77; SCMP 6271:74 (2/1/77).

75-30 4/10/75 1/22/77 PEKING LUXEMBOURG EXCHANGE
OF NOTES
Agreement on reciprocal trademark registration.
JMJP 4/11/75; NCNA Peking 4/10/75; SCMP 5836:65 (4/22/75);
Agreement on entering into force JMJP 1/23/77; NCNA Peking
1/22/77; SCMP 6271:74 (2/1/77).

75-31 4/10/75 1/22/77 PEKING NETHERLANDS EXCHANGE
OF NOTES
Agreement on reciprocal trademark registration.
JMJP 4/11/75; NCNA Peking 4/10/75; SCMP 5836:65 (4/22/75);
Agreement on entering into force JMJP 1/23/77; NCNA Peking
1/22/77; SCMP 6271:74 (2/1/77).

75-32 4/18/75 — COLOMBO SRI LANKA EXCHANGE OF
LETTERS
Mutual exemption from income and other taxes on freight earnings
by vessels.
JMJP 4/21/75; NCNA Colombo 4/18/75; SCMP 5843:195 (5/1/75).

75-33 4/19/75 — PEKING GREECE EXCHANGE OF NOTES
Agreement on reciprocal trademark registration.
JMJP 4/20/75; NCNA Peking 4/19/75; SCMP 5843:188 (5/1/75).

75-34 4/19/75 — ULAN BATOR MONGOLIA PROTOCOL
Mutual supply of goods for 1975.
JMJP 4/23/75; NCNA Ulan Bator 4/20/75; SCMP 5844:236 (5/2/75).

75-35 4/19/75 — HANOI VIETNAM(N) PROTOCOL
Border railway.
Signed at seventeenth meeting of Sino-Vietnam Border Railway.
JMJP 4/21/75; NCNA Hanoi 4/20/75; SCMP 5844:246 (5/2/75).

75-36 4/20/75 — PEKING BELGIUM AGREEMENT
Maritime transport.
JMJP 4/21/75; NCNA Peking 4/20/75; SCMP 5844:229 (5/2/75).

75-37 4/20/75 — PEKING BELGIUM AGREEMENT
Civil air transport.
JMJP 4/21/75; NCNA Peking 4/20/75; SCMP 5844:229 (5/2/75).

75-38 4/26/75 — PEKING KOREA(N) JOINT COMMUNIQUÉ
Talks during visit of President Kim Il Sung: anti-imperialism,
Third World, Indochina, Africa, Middle East, etc.
JMJP 4/28/75(C); PR 18.18:8 (5/2/75)(E); NCNA Peking 4/28/75;
SCMP 5849:251 (5/9/75)(E).

75-39 5/7/75 — YAOUNDE CAMEROON PROTOCOL
Dispatch of PRC medical teams to Cameroon.
JMJP 5/10/75; NCNA Yaounde 5/8/75; SCMP 5857:123 (5/21/75).

75-40 5/8/75 — PEKING CUBA PROTOCOL
Trade for 1975.
JMJP 5/9/75; NCNA Peking 5/8/75; SCMP 5856:82 (5/20/75).

75-41 5/8/75 — ADEN YEMEN(PDRY) EXCHANGE OF NOTES
PRC aid in the construction of Shihr-Sayhut road.
JMJP 5/10/75; NCNA Aden 5/8/75; SCMP 5857:140 (5/21/75).

75-42   5/11/75 — KABUL   AFGHANISTAN   PROTOCOL
Exchange of goods for 1975.
JMJP 5/12/75; NCNA Kabul 5/11/75; SCMP 5858:166 (5/22/75).

75-43   5/12/75 — PEKING   JAPAN   JOINT STATEMENT
Talks during visit of Tomomi Narita, Chairman of Central Executive Committee of Japanese Socialist Party: Korea, abrogation of Japan-U. S. "security treaty," recovery of northern territories, peace treaty, etc.
JMJP 5/13/75; NCNA Peking 5/12/75; SCMP 5859:219 (5/23/75).

75-44   5/20/75 — ACCRA   GHANA   PROTOCOL
Trade for 1975.
JMJP 5/24/75; NCNA Accra 5/20/75; SCMP 5866:118 (6/4/75).

75-45   5/31/75 — PEKING   EGYPT   PROTOCOL
Trade for 1975.
JMJP 6/1/75; NCNA Peking 5/31/75; SCMP 5872:142 (6/12/75).

75-46   5/31/75 — PEKING   EGYPT   EXCHANGE OF LETTERS
Extension of Trade Agreement and Payments Agreement from 1/1/74 to 12/31/76.
JMJP 6/1/75; NCNA Peking 5/31/75; SCMP 5872:142 (6/12/75).

75-47   5/31/75 — BUCHAREST   RUMANIA   AGREEMENT
Postal and telecommunications.
JMJP 6/2/75; NCNA Bucharest 5/31/75; SCMP 5873:189 (6/13/75).

75-48   6/9/75   6/9/75   PEKING   PHILIPPINES   JOINT COMMUNI-
QUÉ
Establishment of diplomatic relations.
JMJP 6/10/75; PR 18. 24:7 (6/13/75)(E); NCNA Peking 6/9/75;
SCMP 5878:211 (6/20/75)(E), PYIL 4:159(E) (1975).

75-49   6/9/75 — PEKING   PHILIPPINES   AGREEMENT
Trade.
JMJP 6/10/75; PR 18. 24:5 (6/13/75); NCNA Peking 6/9/75;
SCMP 5878:214 (6/20/75).

75-50   6/16/75 — URUMCHI   PAKISTAN   EXCHANGE OF LETTERS
Border trade in 1975.
NCNA Peking 6/21/75; SCMP 5886:124 (7/2/75).

75-51   6/18/75 — PEKING   NEW ZEALAND   EXCHANGE OF
LETTERS

Agreement on reciprocal registration of trademarks.
JMJP 6/19/75; NCNA Peking 6/18/75; SCMP 5884:36 (6/30/75).

75-52   6/23/75 — PEKING   BRAZIL   AGREEMENT
Representation on pharmaceuticals.
Signed by Orpheu Santos Salles, Chairman of Board of Directors
of Brazilian Cibrascex Foreign Trade Company and PRC National
Chemical Import and Export Corporation.
JMJP 6/24/75; NCNA Peking 6/23/75; SCMP 5887:160 (7/3/75).

75-53   7/1/75   7/1/75   PEKING   THAILAND   JOINT COMMUNIQUÉ
Establishment of diplomatic relations.
JMJP 7/2/75(C); PR 18. 27:8 (7/4/75)(E); NCNA Peking 7/1/75;
SCMP 5893:43 (7/14/75)(E).

75-54   7/2/75 — MAPUTO (Lourenco Marques)   MOZAMBIQUE
AGREEMENT
Economic and scientific cooperation.
JMJP 7/4/75; NCNA Lourenco Marques 7/3/75; SCMP 5894:97
(7/15/75).

75-55   7/3/75 — PEKING   ALBANIA   AGREEMENT
Long-term interest-free loan to Albania.
JMJP 7/4/75; PR 18. 28:7 (7/11/75); NCNA Peking 7/3/75;
SCMP 5894:88 (7/15/75).

75-56   7/3/75 — PEKING   ALBANIA   AGREEMENT
Exchange of goods and payments between 1976-80.
JMJP 7/4/75; PR 18. 28:7 (7/11/75); NCNA Peking 7/3/75;
SCMP 5894:88 (7/15/75).

75-57   7/3/75 — PEKING   ALBANIA   PROTOCOL
PRC providing complete project equipments to Albania.
JMJP 7/4/75; PR 18. 28:7 (7/11/75); NCNA Peking 7/3/75;
SCMP 5894:88 (7/15/75).

75-58   7/3/75 — PEKING   ALBANIA   PROTOCOL
PRC providing general materials to Albania.
JMJP 7/4/75; PR 18. 28:7 (7/11/75); NCNA Peking 7/3/75;
SCMP 5894:88 (7/15/75).

75-59   7/6/75 — PEKING   IRAQ   DOCUMENT
Development of trade.
JMJP 7/7/75; NCNA Peking 7/6/75; SCMP 5896:196 (7/17/75).

75-60   7/6/75 — PEKING   IRAQ   DOCUMENT
Economic and technical cooperation.
JMJP 7/7/75; NCNA Peking 7/6/75; SCMP 5896:196 (7/17/75).

75-61   7/7/75 — PEKING   IRAQ   PRESS COMMUNIQUÉ
Further developing friendly relations and cooperation.
JMJP 7/9/75(C); NCNA Peking 7/8/75; SCMP 5897:246 (7/18/75)(E).

75-62   7/9/75 — PEKING   GUINEA-BISSAU   AGREEMENT
Economic and technical cooperation.
JMJP 7/10/75; NCNA Peking 7/9/75; SCMP 5898:32 (7/21/75).

75-63   7/10/75 — PEKING   ECUADOR   AGREEMENT
Trade.
JMJP 7/11/75; NCNA Peking 7/10/75; SCMP 5899:76 (7/22/75).

75-64   7/10/75 — PEKING   ECUADOR   AGREEMENT
Establishment of commercial offices.
JMJP 7/11/75; NCNA Peking 7/10/75; SCMP 5899:76 (7/22/75).

75-65   7/12/75 — SAO TOME   SAO TOME & PRINCIPE   JOINT
COMMUNIQUÉ
Establishment of diplomatic relations.
JMJP 7/17/75(C); PR 18. 30:3 (7/25/75)(E); NCNA Peking 7/16/75;
SCMP 5903:30 (7/28/75)(E).

75-66   7/15/75 — PEKING   FRANCE   EXCHANGE OF NOTES
Agreement on trademark registration.
JMJP 7/16/75; NCNA Peking 7/15/75; SCMP 5902:194 (7/25/75).

75-67   7/18/75 — BUCHAREST   RUMANIA   DRAFT
Maritime transport agreement.
JMJP 7/22/75; NCNA Bucharest 7/19/75; SCMP 5905:103 (7/30/75).

75-68   7/23/75 — PEKING   MADAGASCAR   AGREEMENT
Economic and technical cooperation.
JMJP 7/29/75; PR 18. 31:4 (8/1/75); NCNA Peking 7/28/75;
SCMP 5910:114 (8/7/75).

75-69   7/24/75 — MOSCOW   U. S. S. R.   AGREEMENT
Exchange of goods and payments for 1975.
JMJP 7/26/75; NCNA Moscow 7/24/75; SCMP 5908:35 (8/5/75).

75-70   8/8/75 — PEKING   GERMANY(W)   EXCHANGE OF LETTER
Agreement for trademark registration.
JMJP 8/10/75; NCNA Peking 8/8/75; SCMP 5918:81 (8/19/75).

75-71 8/14/75 — PEKING NETHERLANDS AGREEMENT
Maritime transport.
JMJP 8/15/75; NCNA Peking 8/14/75; SCMP 5922:46 (8/26/75);
NYIL 7:296 (1976).

75-72 8/15/75 12/22/75 TOKYO JAPAN AGREEMENT
Fishery.
JMJP 8/16/75; NCNA Tokyo 8/15/75; SCMP 5922:42 (8/26/75);
JAIL 20:173(C) (1976).

75-73 8/15/75 — PEKING JAPAN EXCHANGE OF NOTES
Establishment of consulates-general in Shanghai and Osaka.
JMJP 8/16/75; PR 18. 34:5 (8/22/75); NCNA Peking 8/15/75;
SCMP 5922:42 (8/26/75); JAIL 20:163 (1976).

75-74 8/18/75 — PEKING CAMBODIA JOINT COMMUNIQUÉ
Talks during visit of Deputy Prime Minister Khieu Samphan:
Third World, anti-imperialism, Vietnam, Laos, Korea, etc.
JMJP 8/20/75(C); PR 18. 34:6 (8/22/75)(E); NCNA Peking 8/19/75;
SCMP 5925:159 (8/29/75)(E).

75-75 8/18/75 — PEKING CAMBODIA AGREEMENT
Economic and technical cooperation.
JMJP 8/19/75; NCNA Peking 8/18/75; SCMP 5924:120 (8/28/75).

75-76 8/28/75 — COSTONOU DAHOMEY MINUTES
Talks on PRC aid in construction of tobacco factory.
JMJP 9/12/75.

75-77 8/30/75 — PEKING GERMANY(W) DRAFT
Maritime transport agreement.
JMJP 9/2/75; NCNA Peking 8/31/75; SCMP 5933:159 (9/11/75).

75-78 9/3/75(?) — PORT MORESBY PAPUA NEW GUINEA
CONTRACT
Trade on cocoa, copper ores, and other products.
JMJP 9/6/75; NCNA Peking 9/4/75; SCMP 5936:98 (9/16/75).

75-79 9/5/75 — NIAMEY NIGER PROTOCOL
Dispatch of medical teams to Niger by PRC.
JMJP 9/8/75; NCNA Peking 9/6/76; SCMP 5937:156 (9/17/75).

75-80 9/5/75 — NIAMEY NIGER PROTOCOL
Agricultural cooperation.
JMJP 9/8/75; NCNA Peking 9/6/75; SCMP 5937:156 (9/17/75).

75-81   9/9/75 — MEXICO CITY   MEXICO   AGREEMENT
Scientific and technical cooperation.
JMJP 9/11/75; NCNA Mexico City 9/9/75; SCMP 5940:35 (9/23/75).

75-82   9/9/75 — MEXICO CITY   MEXICO   EXCHANGE OF NOTES
Programme of cultural exchange for 1975.
JMJP 9/11/75; NCNA Mexico City 9/9/75; SCMP 5940:35 (9/23/75).

75-83   9/10/75 — PORT LOUIS   MAURITIUS   EXCHANGE OF LET-
TERS
Agricultural technical cooperation.
JMJP 9/12/75; NCNA Peking 9/11/75; SCMP 5941:84 (9/24/75).

75-84   9/18/75 — PEKING   TANZANIA & ZAMBIA   MINUTES
Talks on seventh Round of Tanzania-Zambia Railway.
Three protocols were also signed.
JMJP 9/19/75; PR 18. 39:9 (9/26/75); NCNA Peking 9/18/75;
SCMP 5946:131 (10/1/75).

75-85   9/22/75 — PEKING   JAPAN   PROTOCOL
Safety in fishing operation.
JMJP 9/23/75; NCNA Peking 9/22/75; SCMP 5948:217 (10/3/75).

75-86   9/22/75 — PEKING   SYRIA   AGREEMENT
Broadcasting and television cooperation.
NCNA Peking 9/22/75; SCMP 5848:232 (10/3/75).

75-87   9/24/75 — SANAA   YEMEN (YAR)   CREDENTIALS
Handing over of Sanaa industrial technical school to Yemen.
JMJP 9/26/75; NCNA Sanaa 9/24/75; SCMP 5951:178 (10/8/75).

75-88   9/25/75 — PEKING   VIETNAM(N)   AGREEMENT
PRC granting an interest-free loan to Vietnam.
JMJP 9/26/75; PR 18. 40:9 (10/3/75); NCNA Peking 9/25/75;
SCMP 5950:100 (10/7/75).

75-89   9/25/75 — PEKING   VIETNAM(N)   PROTOCOL
Supply of general goods by PRC.
JMJP 9/26/75; PR 18. 40:9 (10/3/75); NCNA Peking 9/25/75;
SCMP 5950:100 (10/7/75).

75-90   9/28/75 — PEKING   FRANCE   AGREEMENT
Maritime transport.
JMJP 10/1/75; NCNA Peking 9/29/75; SCMP 5953:274 (10/10/75).

75-91 10/2/75 — PEKING FINLAND AGREEMENT
Civil air transport.
JMJP 10/3/75; NCNA Peking 10/2/75; SCMP 5956:206 (10/17/75).

75-92 10/4/75 10/4/75 NEW YORK BANGLADESH JOINT
COMMUNIQUÉ
Establishment of diplomatic relations.
JMJP 10/7/75(C); PR 18. 41:5 (10/10/75)(E); NCNA Peking
10/6/75; SCMP 5959:156 (10/22/75)(E).

75-93 10/12/75 — PEKING YUGOSLAVIA PRESS COMMUNIQUÉ
Talks during visit of President Dzemal Bijedic: further developing
multiform cooperation and establish a mixed Sino-Yugoslav Trade
Committee.
JMJP 10/13/77(C); PR 18. 42:7 (10/17/75)(E); NCNA Peking
10/12/75; SCMP 5962:47 (10/28/75)(E).

75-94 10/14/75 — HUHEHOT MONGOLIA PROTOCOL
Border railway traffic.
Signed at 1975 regular meeting of Sino-Mongolian Boundary-
Through Railway Traffic.
JMJP 10/16/75; NCNA Huhehot 10/15/75; SCMP 5964:145
(10/30/75).

75-95 10/16/75 — PEKING ALBANIA PROTOCOL
Technology and science cooperation.
Signed at sixteenth meeting of Sino-Albanian Committee for Co-
operation in Technology and Technical Service.
JMJP 10/17/75; NCNA Peking 10/16/75; SCMP 5964:132 (10/30/75).

75-96 10/18/75 — PEKING CZECHOSLOVAKIA PROTOCOL
Scientific and technical cooperation.
Signed at seventeenth session of Sino-Czechoslovak Joint Commis-
sion for Scientific and Technical Cooperation.
JMJP 10/19/75; NCNA Peking 10/18/75; SCMP 5966:39 (11/3/75).

75-97 10/18/75 — PEKING GUINEA PROTOCOL
Trade for 1976.
JMJP 10/19/75; NCNA Peking 10/18/75; SCMP 5966:41 (11/3/75).

75-98 10/20/75 — ALGIERS ALGERIA DRAFT
Shipping.
JMJP 10/26/75; NCNA Algiers 10/21/75; SCMP 5968:151 (7/5/75).

75-99 10/20/75 — BELGRADE YUGOSLAVIA PROTOCOL
Scientific and technical cooperation from 1975 to 1976.
JMJP 10/23/75; NCNA Belgrade 10/20/75; SCMP 5967:126
(11/4/75).

75-100 10/21/75(?) — PEKING CAMEROON AGREEMENT
Cooperation between Hsinhua News Agency and Cameroon Press
Agency.
JMJP 10/26/75; NCNA Peking 10/22/75; SCMP 5968:153 (11/5/75).

75-101 10/23/75 — PEKING GUYANA AGREEMENT
Imports and exports commodities.
JMJP 10/24/75; NCNA Peking 10/23/75; SCMP 5968:155 (11/5/75).

75-102 10/25/75 — RAWALPINDI PAKISTAN PROTOCOL
Trade for 1976.
JMJP 10/27/75; NCNA Rawalpindi 10/25/75; SCMP 5970:290
(11/7/75).

75-103 10/25/75 — PEKING VIETNAM(N) AGREEMENT
Exchange of goods and payments.
JMJP 10/26/75; NCNA Peking 10/25/75; SCMP 5970:296 (11/7/75).

75-104 10/27/75 — COLOMBO SRI LANKA MINUTES
Talks on third regular session of Sino-Sri Lanka Joint Commission
for Joint Shipping Services.
An agreement was also signed.
JMJP 11/1/75(C); NCNA Colombo 10/30/75; SCMP 5973:148
(11/12/75).

75-105 10/31/75 — PEKING GERMANY(W) AGREEMENT
Maritime transport.
JMJP 11/1/75; NCNA Peking 10/31/75; SCMP 5973:156 (11/12/75).

75-106 10/31/75 — PEKING GERMANY(W) AGREEMENT
Civil air transport.
JMJP 11/1/75; NCNA Peking 10/31/75; SCMP 5973:156 (11/12/75).

75-107 10/31/75 — PEKING GERMANY(W) EXCHANGE OF NOTES
Establishment of a joint committee for promotion of economic and
trade relations.
JMJP 11/1/75; NCNA Peking 10/31/75; SCMP 5973:156 (11/12/75).

75-108 11/3/75 — SHENYANG KOREA(N) PROTOCOL
Border railway transport.
JMJP 11/4/75; NCNA Shenyang 11/3/75; SCMP 5975:239 (11/14/75).

75-109 11/4/75 — SOFIA BULGARIA PROTOCOL
Scientific and technical cooperation.
Signed at thirteenth meeting of Sino-Bulgarian Joint Commission
for Scientific and Technical Cooperation.
JMJP 11/8/75; NCNA Sofia 11/4/75; SCMP 5977:63 (11/18/75).

75-110 11/5/75 11/5/75 CANBERRA FIJI JOINT COMMUNIQUÉ
Establishment of diplomatic relations.
JMJP 11/6/76(C); PR 18.46:3 (11/14/75)(E); NCNA Peking 11/5/75;
SCMP 5977:65 (11/18/75)(E).

75-111 11/5/75 — PEKING GAMBIA AGREEMENT
Trade.
JMJP 11/6/75; NCNA Peking 11/5/75; SCMP 5977:67 (11/18/75).

75-112 11/5/75 — BUDAPEST HUNGARY PROTOCOL
Scientific and technical cooperation.
Signed at fourteenth meeting of Sino-Hungarian Joint Commission
for Scientific and Technical Cooperation.
JMJP 11/8/75; NCNA Budapest 11/5/75; SCMP 5977:67 (11/18/75).

75-113 11/6/75 11/6/75 APIA WEST SAMOA JOINT COMMUNI-
QUÉ
Establishment of diplomatic relations.
JMJP 11/15/75(C); PR 18.47:5 (11/21/75)(E); NCNA Peking
11/14/75; SCMP 5982:92 (11/25/75)(E).

75-114 11/8/75 — PEKING FINLAND DRAFT
Maritime transport.
JMJP 11/9/75; NCNA Peking 11/7/75; SCMP 5978:110 (11/19/75).

75-115 11/8/75 — PEKING MEXICO PROTOCOL
Scientific and technical cooperation.
Signed at first session of Sino-Mexican Commission of Scientific
and Technical Cooperation.
JMJP 11/9/75; NCNA Peking 11/8/75; SCMP 5978:111 (11/19/75).

75-116 11/10/75 — DAMASCUS SYRIA AGREEMENT
Civil air transport.
JMJP 11/13/75; NCNA Damascus 11/11/75; SCMP 5981:28
(11/24/75).

75-117 11/12/75 — PEKING PAPUA-NEW GUINEA CONTRACT
Exporting timber to PRC.
JMJP 11/13/75; NCNA Peking 11/12/75; SCMP 5981:26 (11/24/74).

75-118 11/13/75 — NEW YORK COMOROS JOINT COMMUNIQUÉ
Establishment of diplomatic relations.
JMJP 11/19/75(C); PR 18. 48:4 (11/28/75)(E); NCNA Peking
11/18/75; SCMP 5985:26 (12/1/75)(E).

75-119 11/14/75 — MANILA PHILIPPINES AGREEMENT
Petroleum trade.
JMJP 11/17/75; NCNA Peking 11/15/75; SCMP 5984:180 (11/28/75).

75-120 11/15/75 — PEKING BURMA JOINT COMMUNIQUÉ
Talks during visit of President U Ne Win: five principles of peaceful coexistence, Southeast Asia, etc.
JMJP 11/16/75(C); PR 18. 47:6 (11/21/75)(E); NCNA Peking
11/15/75; SCMP 5983:128 (11/26/75)(E).

75-121 11/30/75 — PEKING SRI LANKA PROTOCOL
Exchange of goods in 1976.
JMJP 12/1/75; NCNA Peking 11/30/75; SCMP 5993:170 (12/11/75).

75-122 11/30/75 — BAGHDAD IRAQ PROTOCOL
Amending 1960 trade agreement [60-69].
JMJP 12/2/75; NCNA Baghdad 11/39/75; SCMP 5994:211 (12/12/75).

75-123 12/1/75 — HANOI VIETNAM PROTOCOL
Scientific and technical cooperation from 1975-76.
JMJP 12/4/75; NCNA Hanoi 12/1/75; SCMP 5994:223 (12/12/75).

75-124 12/2/75 — PYONGYANG KOREA(N) PROTOCOL
Scientific and technical cooperation.
Signed at sixteenth session of China-Korea Committee for Sci-
entific and Technical Cooperation.
JMJP 12/4/75; NCNA Pyongyang 12/2/75; SCMP 5994:215 (12/12/75).

75-125 12/5/75 — PEKING FINLAND AGREEMENT
Trade for 1976.
JMJP 12/6/76; NCNA Peking 12/5/75; SCMP 5996:69 (12/16/75).

75-126 12/9/75 — PEKING CZECHOSLOVAKIA AGREEMENT
Exchange of goods and payments for 1976.
JMJP 12/10/75; NCNA Peking 12/9/75; SCMP 5999:182 (12/19/75).

75-127 12/15/75 — PEKING IRAN EXCHANGE OF NOTES
Agreement on reciprocal trademark registration.
JMJP 12/16/75; NCNA Peking 12/15/75; SCMP 6002:104 (12/24/75).

75-128 12/15/75 — MPIKA TANZANIA & ZAMBIA CERTIFICATES
PRC hand over of Tanzania-Zambia railway training school at
Mpika and customs and immigration office building on Zambian-
Tanzanian border to Tanzania and Zambia.
JMJP 12/31/75; NCNA Lusaka 12/16/75; SCMP 6004:74 (12/30/75).

75-129 12/18/75 — PEKING RUMANIA AGREEMENT
Scientific and technical cooperation.
JMJP 12/19/75; NCNA Peking 12/18/75; SCMP 6003:70 (12/29/75).

75-130 12/18/75 — PEKING RUMANIA
1975-76 plan for scientific cooperation.
JMJP 12/19/75; NCNA Peking 12/18/75; SCMP 6003:70 (12/29/75).

75-131 12/19/75 — YAOUNDE CAMEROON DOCUMENT
PRC aid in construction of a culture palace.
JMJP 12/21/75; NCNA Yaounde 12/19/75; SCMP 6006:165 (1/2/76).

75-132 12/19/75 — YAOUNDE CAMEROON DOCUMENTS
PRC aid in construction of Lagdo hydroelectric power station.
JMJP 12/21/75; NCNA Yaounde 12/19/75; SCMP 6006:165 (1/2/76).

75-133 12/20/75 — BERLIN GERMANY(E) AGREEMENT
Exchange of goods and payments for 1976.
JMJP 12/22/75; NCNA Berlin 12/20/75; SCMP 6006:166 (1/2/76).

75-134 12/21/75 — MOGADISHU SOMALI MINUTES
Talks on well drilling and water supply works in Baidoa.
NCNA Mogadishu 12/23/75; SCMP 6009:172 (1/7/76).

75-135 12/25/75 — PEKING SAO TOME & PRINCIPE AGREEMENT
Trade.
JMJP 12/26/75; PR 19.1:7 (1/2/76); NCNA Peking 12/25/75;
SCMP 6009:171 (1/7/76).

75-136 12/25/75 — PEKING SAO TOME & PRINCIPE AGREEMENT
Economic and technical cooperation.
JMJP 12/26/75; PR 19.1:7 (1/2/76); NCNA Peking 12/25/75;
SCMP 6009:171 (1/7/76).

75-137 12/25/75 — KATMANDU NEPAL CERTIFICATE
Turning over of engineering circuits, power stations, repair
offices, and more than twenty other items of trolley bus built with
PRC aid, from Katmandu to Bhaktapur.
JMJP 1/2/76.

75-138 12/27/75 — PYONGYANG KOREA(N)
1976-77 plan for public health cooperation.
JMJP 12/30/75; NCNA Pyongyang 12/27/75; SCMP 6010:221
(1/8/76).

1976

76-1 1/3/76 — SOFIA BULGARIA AGREEMENT
Exchange of goods and payments for 1976.
JMJP 1/5/76; NCNA Sofia 1/3/76; SCMP 6015:175 (1/15/76).

76-2 1/14/76 — SHENYANG KOREA(N) AGREEMENT
Border railway transport.
Signed at fifteenth meeting of Sino-Korean Committee for Co-
operation in Border River Transport.
JMJP 1/15/76; NCNA Shenyang 1/14/76; SCMP 6022:47 (12/6/76).

76-3 1/18/76 — PEKING KOREA(N) AGREEMENT
Postal and telecommunications cooperation.
JMJP 1/19/76; NCNA Peking 1/18/76; SCMP 6026:287 (1/30/76).

76-4 1/19/76 — PEKING POLAND AGREEMENT
Exchange of goods and payments for 1976.
JMJP 1/20/76; NCNA Peking 1/18/76; SCMP 6026:291 (1/30/76).

76-5 1/26/76 — PEKING KOREA(N) RESOLUTION
Border river hydroelectric power corporation.
Signed at twenth-eighth session of Council of Sino-Korean Yalu
River Hydroelectric Power Corporation.
JMJP 1/27/76; NCNA Peking 1/25/76; SCMP 6029:121 (2/6/76).

76-6 1/29/76 — PEKING RUMANIA AGREEMENT
1976-80 long-term trade.
JMJP 1/30/76; PR 19. 6:3 (2/6/76); NCNA Peking 1/29/76;
SCMP 6031:93 (2/10/76).

76-7 1/29/76 — PEKING RUMANIA PROTOCOL
Exchange of goods and payments for 1976.
JMJP 1/30/76; PR 19. 6:3 (2/6/76); NCNA Peking 1/29/76;
SCMP 6031:93 (2/10/76).

76-8 2/5/76 — MANILA PHILIPPINES MEMORANDUM
Exhibition of PRC in Philippines.
JMJP 2/6/76; NCNA Manila 2/5/76; SCMP 6035:25 (2/17/76).

76-9 2/7/76 — TIRANA ALBANIA PROTOCOL
Exchange of goods and payments for 1976.
JMJP 2/9/76; NCNA Tirana 2/8/76; SCMP 6036:63 (2/18/76).

76-10 2/7/76 — TIRANA ALBANIA PROTOCOL
Albania's use of PRC loan for 1976.
JMJP 2/9/76; NCNA Tirana 2/8/76; SCMP 6036:63 (2/18/76).

76-11 2/9/76 — PYONGYANG KOREA(N) PROTOCOL
Mutual supply of goods for 1976.
JMJP 2/10/76; NCNA Pyongyang 2/9/76; SCMP 6037:109 (2/19/76).

76-12 2/20/76 — RABAT MOROCCO PROTOCOL
Construction of a sports complex in Morocco.
JMJP 2/22/76; NCNA Rabat 2/20/76; SCMP 6045:65 (3/2/76).

76-13 3/2/76 — ACCRA GHANA PROTOCOL
Trade for 1976.
JMJP 3/6/76; NCNA Accra 3/3/76; SCMP 6053:181 (3/12/76).

76-14 3/2/76 — ACCRA GHANA EXCHANGE OF NOTES
Extension to another year of Agreement of Sino-Ghana Long-Term
Trade and Payments [72-96].
JMJP 3/6/76; NCNA Accra 3/3/76; SCMP 6053:181 (3/12/76).

76-15 3/6/76 — PEKING HUNGARY AGREEMENT
Exchange of goods and payments for 1976.
JMJP 3/7/76; NCNA Peking 3/6/76; SCMP 6054:26 (3/15/76).

76-16 3/10/76 — PHNOMPENH CAMBODIA AGREEMENT
Economic cooperation.
JMJP 3/12/76; PR 19.12:5 (3/19/76); NCNA Peking 3/11/76;
SCMP 6058:181 (3/19/76).

76-17 3/12/76 — PEKING ALGERIA AGREEMENT
Maritime transport.
JMJP 3/13/76; NCNA Peking 3/12/76; SCMP 6058:179 (3/19/76).

76-18 3/18/76 — PEKING LAOS AGREEMENT
Economic and technical cooperation.
JMJP 3/19/76; NCNA Peking 3/18/76; SCMP 6062:203 (3/25/76).

76-19 3/20/76 — TANANARIVE MALAGASY MINUTES
Talks on PRC aid in construction of Moramanga-Andranonampang
highway in Malagasy.
JMJP 3/24/76; NCNA Tananarive 3/21/76; SCMP 6066:127 (3/31/76).

76-20 3/22/76 — PEKING ETHIOPIA AGREEMENT
Economic and technical cooperation.
JMJP 3/23/76; PR 19.13:5 (3/26/76); NCNA Peking 3/22/76;
SCMP 6066:119 (3/31/76).

76-21 3/27/76 — BELGRADE YUGOSLAVIA MINUTES
Trade.
Signed at first session of Sino-Yugoslav Trade Mixed Commission.
JMJP 3/28/76; NCNA Belgrade 3/27/76; SCMP 6069:37 (4/6/76).

76-22 3/31/76 — OUAGADOUGOU UPPER VOLTA PROTOCOL
Dispatch of medical teams to Upper Volta.
JMJP 4/4/76.

76-23 4/5/76 — MANILA PHILIPPINES EXCHANGE OF LETTERS
Development of trade.
JMJP 4/6/76; NCNA Manila 4/5/76; SCMP 6075:132 (4/14/76).

76-24 4/7/76 — KHARTOUM SUDAN PROTOCOL
Trade for 1976.
JMJP 4/9/76; NCNA Peking 4/7/76; SCMP 6077:245 (4/16/76).

76-25 4/8/76 — PEKING RUMANIA AGREEMENT
Marine transport.
JMJP 4/9/76; NCNA Peking 4/8/76; SCMP 6077:239 (4/16/76).

76-26 4/15/76 4/25/76 PEKING(?) CAPE VERDE JOINT COM-
MUNIQUÉ
Establishment of diplomatic relations.
JMJP 4/26/76(C); PR 19.18:5 (4/30/76)(E); NCNA Peking 4/25/76;
SCMP 6088:134 (5/5/76)(E).

76-27 4/16/76 — BUCHAREST RUMANIA PROTOCOL
Scientific and technical cooperation.
Signed at seventeenth session of Sino-Rumanian Joint Commission
on Scientific and Technical Cooperation.
JMJP 4/21/76; NCNA Bucharest 4/17/76; SCMP 6084:219 (4/29/76).

76-28 4/29/76 — TIRANA ALBANIA PROTOCOL
Shipping.
Signed at eleventh session of Board of Directors of Sino-Albanian
Joint Stock Shipping Company.
JMJP 5/6/76; NCNA Tirana 4/30/76; SCMP 6092:97 (5/11/76).

76-29 4/30/76 — KATMANDU NEPAL EXCHANGE OF LETTERS
Extension of validity of 1956 Agreement on Trade and Related

Questions between Tibet Autonomous Region of China and Nepal [56-104] for another ten years beginning from 5/2/76.
JMJP 5/5/76; NCNA Katmandu 4/30/76; SCMP 6092:106 (5/11/76).

76-30   5/1/76 — MALABO   EQUATORIAL GUINEA   MINUTES
Talks on PRC aid in building of a Bicomo hydroelectric power station.
JMJP 5/6/76; NCNA Peking 5/4/76; SCMP 6095:265 (5/14/76).

76-31   5/1/76 — MALABO   EQUATORIAL GUINEA   MINUTES
Talks on PRC aid in building a high tension power transformer and transmission line between Bicomo and Bata in Equatorial Guinea.
JMJP 5/6/76; NCNA Peking 5/4/76; SCMP 6095:265 (5/14/76).

76-32   5/1/76 — PEKING   NEW ZEALAND   EXCHANGE OF LET-TERS
Mutual granting of most-favored-nation treatment in shipping.
JMJP 5/2/76; PR 19.19:6 (5/7/76); NCNA Peking 5/1/76; SCMP 6093:158 (5/12/76).

76-33   5/11/76 — BISSAU   GUINEA-BISSAU   PROTOCOL
Dispatch of medical teams to Guinea-Bissau by PRC.
JMJP 5/13/76; NCNA Bissau 5/11/76; SCMP 6100:256 (5/21/76).

76-34   5/20/76 — FREETOWN   SIERRA LEONE   TRANSFER DOCUMENT
PRC aid in establishing Bo and Makeni aquatic rice stations and another vegetable station in Sierra Leone.
JMJP 5/24/76.

76-35   5/21/76 — PEKING   USSR   AGREEMENT
Exchange of goods and payments for 1976.
JMJP 5/22/76; NCNA Peking 5/21/76; SCMP 6106:40 (6/1/76).

76-36   5/28/76   5/28/76   NEW YORK   SURINAM   JOINT COM-MUNIQUÉ
Establishment of diplomatic relations.
JMJP 5/30/76(C); PR 19.23:5 (6/4/76)(E); NCNA Peking 5/30/76; SCMP 6111:181 (6/9/76)(E).

76-37   5/30/76 — PEKING   PAKISTAN   JOINT COMMUNIQUÉ
Talks during visit of Prime Minister Zulfikar Ali Bhutto: Indo-china, Arab, South Asian subcontinent, etc.
JMJP 5/31/76(C); PR 19.23:7 (6/4/76)(E); NCNA Peking 5/30/76; SCMP 6112:228 (6/10/76)(E).

76-38 5/30/76 — PEKING PAKISTAN AGREEMENT
Scientific and technical cooperation.
JMJP 5/31/76; PR 19. 23:3 (6/4/76); NCNA Peking 5/30/76;
SCMP 6112:227 (6/10/76).

76-39 5/30/76 — PEKING PAKISTAN PROTOCOL
Economic and technical cooperation.
JMJP 5/31/76; PR 19. 23:3 (6/4/76); NCNA Peking 5/30/76;
SCMP 6112:227 (6/10/76).

76-40 6/3/76 — PEKING VIETNAM(N)
1975-77 executive plan for scientific cooperation between PRC
Academy of Sciences and Vietnamese State Commission of Sciences and Technology and Academy of Social Science.
JMJP 6/4/76; NCNA Peking 6/3/76; SCMP 6115:124 (6/15/76).

76-41 6/5/76 — PEKING AFGHANISTAN PROTOCOL
Exchange of goods for 1976.
JMJP 6/6/76; NCNA Peking 6/5/76; SCMP 6116:157 (6/16/76).

76-42 6/6/76 — CAIRO EGYPT PROTOCOL
Trade for 1976.
JMJP 6/8/76; NCNA Cairo 6/6/76; SCMP 6117:218 (6/17/76).

76-43 6/10/76 — PEKING COMOROS AGREEMENT
Economic and technical cooperation.
JMJP 6/11/76; NCNA Peking 6/10/76; SCMP 6119:38 (6/21/76).

76-44 6/10/76 — HAVANA CUBA AGREEMENT
Trade.
JMJP 6/13/76; NCNA Havana 6/10/76; SCMP 6120:85 (6/22/76).

76-45 6/10/76 — HAVANA CUBA AGREEMENT
Payments.
JMJP 6/13/76; NCNA Havana 6/10/76; SCMP 6120:85 (6/22/76).

76-46 6/10/76 — HAVANA CUBA PROTOCOL
Trade for 1976.
JMJP 6/13/76; NCNA Havana 6/10/76; SCMP 6120:85 (6/22/76).

76-47 6/10/76 — PEKING PHILIPPINES AGREEMENT
Questions concerning exhibition in Philippines.
JMJP 6/12/76; NCNA Peking 6/10/76; SCMP 6119:43 (6/21/76).

76-48   6/13/76 — GILGIT   PAKISTAN   EXCHANGE OF NOTES
Border trade for 1976.
JMJP 6/14/76; NCNA Rawalpindi 6/13/76; SCMP 6121:158 (6/23/76).

76-49   6/13/76 — KUNMING   VIETNAM   PROTOCOL
Joint railway transport for 1976.
Signed at eighteenth session of Joint Sino-Vietnamese Boundary
Railway Commission.
JMJP 6/15/76; NCNA Kunming 6/14/76; SCMP 6122:210 (6/24/76).

76-50   6/18/76 — PEKING   IRAN   MEMORANDUM
1976 trade arrangements.
JMJP 6/19/76; NCNA Peking 6/18/76; SCMP 6125:81 (6/29/76).

76-51   6/19/76 — ADEN   YEMEN (PDRY)   CERTIFICATE
Turning over of PRC aid in expansion construction of Aden salt
works to Yemen.
JMJP 6/21/76.

76-52   6/19/76 — ADEN   YEMEN (PDRY)   EXCHANGE OF NOTES
Technical cooperation.
JMJP 6/21/76.

76-53   6/23/76 — PEKING   AUSTRALIA   AGREEMENT
PRC's unearthed relics exhibition in Australia.
JMJP 6/24/76; NCNA Peking 6/23/76; SCMP 6128:223 (7/2/76).

76-54   6/23/76   6/23/76   PEKING   AUSTRALIA   ARRANGEMENT
Exhibition of unearthed relics of PRC in Australia.
Signed by representatives of PRC State Administrative Bureau of
Museums and Archaeological Data and Australian Ambassador to
PRC.
JMJP 6/24/76; NCNA Peking 6/23/76; SCMP 6128:223 (7/2/76);
Aust. T. S. , 1976, No. 13(E).

76-55   6/26/76 — PEKING   LAOS   CONTRACT
Goods supply in accordance with 1976 Agreement of Economic
and Technical Cooperation [76-18].
JMJP 6/23/76; NCNA Peking 6/26/76; SCMP 6130:86 (7/7/76).

76-56   6/30/76 — PEKING   ETHIOPIA   AGREEMENT
Trade.
JMJP 7/1/76; NCNA Peking 6/30/76; SCMP 6133:43 (7/12/76).

76-57 6/30/76 — PEKING ETHIOPIA PROTOCOL
Trade for 1976-77.
JMJP 7/1/76; NCNA Peking 6/30/76; SCMP 6133:43 (7/12/76).

76-58 6/30/76 6/30/76 VICTORIA SEYCHELLES JOINT COM-
MUNIQUÉ
Establishment of diplomatic relations.
JMJP 7/13/76(C); PR 19. 30:5 (7/23/76)(E); NCNA Peking 7/12/76;
SCMP 6142:308 (7/23/76)(E).

76-59 7/4/76 — PEKING JAPAN PROTOCOL
"Exhibition of PRC on Lu Hsun" in Japan.
Signed by representatives of Japan-China Culture Exchange Asso-
ciation and "Nippon Keizai Shimbun" and PRC departments con-
cerned.
NCNA Peking 7/5/76; SCMP 6136:217 (7/15/76).

76-60 7/8/76 — KATMANDU NEPAL AGREEMENT
Construction of Pokhara water conservation and irrigation project.
JMJP 7/10/76; NCNA Katmandu 7/9/76; SCMP 6139:112 (7/20/76).

76-61 7/8/76 — MAGADISHU SOMALIA PROTOCOL
Dispatch of medical teams to Somalia by PRC.
JMJP 7/10/76; NCNA Mogadishu 7/8/76; SCMP 6139:115 (7/20/76).

76-62 7/8/76 — LUSAKA TANZANIA & ZAMBIA PROTOCOL
Railway technical cooperation.
Three other protocols were also signed.
JMJP 7/15/76; NCNA Lusaka 7/13/76; SCMP 6143:68 (7/26/76).

76-63 7/8/76 — LUSAKA TANZANIA & ZAMBIA MINUTES
Talks on eighth round of Tanzania-Zambia railway.
JMJP 7/15/76; NCNA Lusaka 7/13/76; SCMP 6143:68 (7/26/76).

76-64 7/12/76 — ADEN YEMEN (PDRY) MINUTES
Talks on building Aden friendship hospital in Yemen.
A gift to Yemen by PRC under notes exchanged in 1974 during
Chairman Salem Robaya Ali's visit.
JMJP 7/14/76; NCNA Aden 7/12/76; SCMP 6142:318 (7/23/76).

76-65 7/14/76 — NEW KAPIRI MPOSHI TANZANIA & ZAMBIA
CERTIFICATE
Handing over of Tanzania-Zambia railway to Tanzania and Zambia.
JMJP 7/16/76; NCNA Lusaka 7/14/76; SCMP 6144:134 (7/27/76).

76-66   7/20/76 — PEKING   BENIN   AGREEMENT
Economic and technical cooperation.
JMJP 7/21/76; PR 19. 30:5 (7/23/76); NCNA Peking 7/20/76;
SCMP 6174:287 (7/30/76).

76-67   7/20/76 — PEKING   BENIN   PROTOCOL
Supplement to 1976 Agreement of Economic and Technical Co-
operation [76-66].
JMJP 7/21/76; PR 19. 30:5 (7/23/76); NCNA Peking 7/20/76;
SCMP 6147:287 (7/30/76).

76-68   7/23/76 — CHINGCHI   KOREA(N)   PROTOCOL
Sino-Korean border railway meeting.
JMJP 8/3/76.

76-69   8/8/76 — PEKING   BOTSWANA   AGREEMENT
Economic and technical cooperation.
JMJP 8/9/76; PR 19. 32:3 (8/8/76); NCNA Peking 8/8/76;
SCMP 6159:94 (8/17/76).

76-70   8/10/76 — BANJUL   GAMBIA   PROTOCOL
Dispatch of medical team to Gambia by PRC.
JMJP 8/12/76; NCNA Peking 8/11/76; SCMP 6162:213 (8/20/76).

76-71   8/20/76   8/20/76   BANGUI   CENTRAL AFRICA   JOINT
COMMITTEE
Establishment of diplomatic relations.
JMJP 8/21/76(C); PR 19. 35:3 (8/27/76)(E); NCNA Peking
8/20/76; SCMP 6167:218 (8/27/76)(E).

76-72   8/25/76 — TOKYO   JAPAN   AGREEMENT
Reference to establishing reciprocal civil maritime liaison office.
Yearbook on Chinese Communism 8-46 (1977).

76-73   8/26/76 — PHNOMPENH   CAMBODIA   PROTOCOL
Implementation of 1976 Agreement of Economic Cooperation [76-16].
JMJP 8/29/76; NCNA Peking 8/28/76; SCMP 6174:74 (9/8/76).

76-74   8/28/76 — YAOUNDE   CAMEROON & CHAD   PROTOCOL
Construction of a highway bridge over the Chari River linking
Ndjamena of Chad and Kousseri in Cameroon.
JMJP 8/31/76; NCNA Yaounde 8/29/76; SCMP 6175:110 (9/9/76).

76-75   9/8/76 — PEKING   WESTERN SAMOA   AGREEMENT
Economic and technical cooperation.
JMJP 9/9/76; NCNA Peking 9/8/76; SCMP 6180:223 (9/16/76).

76-76 9/26/76 — PEKING JAMAICA AGREEMENT
Trade.
JMJP 9/27/76; PR 19.40:4 (9/30/76); NCNA Peking 9/26/76;
SCMP 6195:247 (10/7/76).

76-77 9/26/76 — PEKING JAMAICA PROTOCOL
Economic cooperation.
JMJP 9/26/76; PR 19.40:4 (9/30/76); NCNA Peking 9/26/76;
SCMP 6195:247 (10/7/76).

76-78 10/8/76 — PEKING AUSTRALIA EXCHANGE OF NOTES
An understanding on matters related to travel of PRC citizens to
Australia.
JMJP 10/9/76; NCNA Peking 10/8/76; SCMP 6203:150 (10/20/76).

76-79 10/12/76 10/12/76 PEKING PAPUA, NEW GUINEA
JOINT COMMUNIQUÉ
Establishment of diplomatic relations.
JMJP 10/13/76(C); PR 19.42:5 (10/15/76)(E); NCNA Peking
10/12/76; SCMP 6205:278 (10/22/76)(E).

76-80 10/19/76 — KINSHASA ZAIRE MINUTES
PRC aid in construction of sports stadium in Kinshasa.
JMJP 10/22/76.

76-81 10/23/76 — PEKING HUNGARY PROTOCOL
Scientific and technical cooperation.
Signed at fifteenth session of Sino-Hungarian Committee for Sci-
entific and Technical Cooperation.
JMJP 10/24/76; NCNA Peking 10/23/76; SCMP 6212:177 (11/4/76).

76-82 10/25/76 — MUONG SAI LAOS EXCHANGE OF NOTES
Turning over of PRC aid radio station to Laos.
JMJP 11/5/78; Yearbook on Chinese Communism: 8-43 (1977).

76-83 11/11/76 — PEKING MONGOLIA PROTOCOL
Mutual supply of goods for 1976.
JMJP 11/12/76; NCNA Peking 11/11/76; SCMP 6224:42 (11/22/76).

76-84 11/15/76 — MOGADISHU SOMALIA CERTIFICATE
Handing over of highway section between Belet Uen and Galcaio
to Somalia.
JMJP 11/18/76; NCNA Mogadishu 11/15/76; SCMP 6227:253
(11/26/76).

76-85 11/16/76 — PEKING CENTRAL AFRICA AGREEMENT
Trade.
JMJP 11/17/76; PR 19. 47:5 (11/19/76); NCNA Peking 11/16/76;
SCMP 6227:223 (11/26/76).

76-86 11/16/76 — PEKING CENTRAL AFRICA AGREEMENT
Economic and technical cooperation.
JMJP 11/17/76; PR 19/47:5 (11/19/76); NCNA Peking 11/16/76;
SCMP 6227:223 (11/26/76).

76-87 11/20/76 — PEKING BULGARIA PROTOCOL
Scientific and technical cooperation.
Signed at fourteenth session of Sino-Bulgarian Commission for
Scientific and Technical Cooperation.
JMJP 11/21/76; NCNA Peking 11/20/76; SCMP 6229:86 (11/30/76).

76-88 11/22/76 — PEKING CENTRAL AFRICAN REPUBLIC
PRESS COMMUNIQUÉ
Talks during visit of President Salah Addin Ahmed Bokassa: anti-
imperialism, colonialism, Angola, Namibia, Zimbabwe, Middle
East, etc.
JMJP 11/25/76; PR 19. 49:14 (12/3/76)(E); NCNA Peking 11/24/76;
SCMP 6232:240 (12/3/76)(E).

76-89 11/25/76 — PRAGUE CZECHOSLOVAKIA PROTOCOL
Scientific and technical cooperation.
Signed at eighteenth session of Sino-Czechoslovak Joint Commis-
sion for Scientific and Technical Cooperation.
JMJP 11/28/76; NCNA Prague 11/25/76; SCMP 6234:88 (12/7/76).

76-90 11/25/76 — MEXICO CITY MEXICO PROTOCOL
Scientific and technical cooperation.
Signed at second session of Sino-Mexican Committee for Scientific
and Technical Cooperation.
JMJP 12/6/76; NCNA Mexico City 12/4/76; SCMP 6239:82 (12/14/76).

76-91 11/25/76 — WARSAW POLAND PROTOCOL
The assessment of work of Sino-Polish shipping joint stock.
Signed at thirteenth session of shareholders' meeting of Sino-
Polish Shipping Joint Stock Company.
JMJP 11/28/76; NCNA Warsaw 11/26/76; SCMP 6234:90 (12/7/76).

76-92 12/13/76 — PEKING KOREA(N) PROTOCOL
Demarcation and maintenance of Yalu River border railway bridge.
JMJP 12/18/76; NCNA Peking 12/14/76; SCMP 6245:137 (12/22/76).

76-93 12/16/76 — GEORGETOWN GUYANA CERTIFICATE
Handing over of Bel–lu claybrick factory to Guyana.
NCNA Georgetown 12/16/76; SCMP 6247:36 (12/28/76).

76-94 12/16/76 — KIGALI RWANDA CERTIFICATE
Handing over of PRC–aid expansion project of Rwandan sugar
refinery to Rwanda.
NCNA Peking 12/18/76; SCMP 6248:90 (12/29/76).

76-95 12/19/76 — PEKING KOREA(N)
1977-78 plan for scientific cooperation between Academies of
Sciences.
JMJP 12/20/76; NCNA Peking 12/19/76; SCMP 6249:132 (12/30/76).

76-96 12/21/76 — HELSINKI FINLAND AGREEMENT
Trade for 1977.
JMJP 12/29/76; NCNA Helsinki 12/21/76; SCMP 6251:95 (1/4/77).

76-97 12/22/76 — PEKING ALGERIA MINUTES
Talks on enlarged draft of surgical instruments factory of Medea.
JMJP 12/27/76; NCNA Peking 12/23/76; SCMP 6252:170 (1/5/77).

76-98 12/23/76 — PEKING YEMEN(YAR) AGREEMENT
Economic and technical cooperation.
JMJP 12/24/76; NCNA Peking 12/23/76; SCMP 6251:114 (1/4/77).

76-99 12/25/76 — PHNOMPENH KAMPUCHEA (CAMBODIA)
AGREEMENT
Cooperation in science and technology.
JMJP 12/27/76; PR 20. 3:5 (1/14/77); NCNA Peking 12/28/76;
SCMP 6254:314 (1/7/77).

76-100 12/25/76 — PHNOMPENH KAMPUCHEA (CAMBODIA)
PROTOCOL
Supply of complete sets of equipment by PRC to Cambodia.
JMJP 12/27/76; PR 20. 3:25 (1/14/77); NCNA Peking 12/28/76;
SCMP 6254:314 (1/7/77).

76-101 12/27/76 — KATMANDU NEPAL AGREEMENT
PRC aid in construction of highway in Nepal.
Yearbook on Chinese Communism 8-44 (1977).

1977

77-1   1/4/77 — PEKING   BANGLADESH   AGREEMENT
Economic and technical cooperation.
JMJP 1/5/57; PR 20. 2:4 (1/7/77); NCNA Peking 1/4/77; SCMP
6259:279 (1/14/77).

77-2   1/4/77 — PEKING   BANGLADESH   AGREEMENT
Trade and payments.
JMJP 1/5/77; PR 20. 2:4 (1/7/77); NCNA Peking 1/4/77; SCMP
6259:279 (1/14/77).

77-3   1/6/77 — PEKING   BANGLADESH   PRESS COMMUNIQUÉ
Talks during visit of General Ziaur Rahman: self-determination,
Taiwan, etc.
JMJP 1/7/77(C); PR 20. 3:26 (1/14/77)(E); NCNA Peking 1/6/77;
SCMP 6260:44 (1/17/77)(E).

77-4   1/18/77 — PEKING   THAILAND   EXCHANGE OF NOTES
Agreement on Reciprocal Registration of Trademark.
JMJP 1/19/77; NCNA Peking 1/18/77; SCMP 6268:167 (1/27/77).

77-5   1/21/77 — PYONGYANG   KOREA(N)   AGREEMENT
Border river navigation cooperation.
Signed at sixteenth meeting of Sino-Korean Border River Naviga-
tion Cooperation Committee.
JMJP 1/23/77; NCNA Pyongyang 1/22/77; SCMP 6271:76 (2/1/77).

77-6   1/24/77 — BUCHAREST   RUMANIA   PROTOCOL
Exchange of goods and payments for 1977.
JMJP 1/26/77; NCNA Bucharest 1/25/77; SCMP 6273:154 (2/3/77).

77-7   1/27/77 — HELSINKI   FINLAND   AGREEMENT
Maritime transport.
JMJP 1/31/77; NCNA Helsinki 1/28/77; SCMP 6275:34 (2/7/77).

77-8   1/29/77 — ISLAMABAD   PAKISTAN   PROTOCOL
Program of scientific and technical cooperation for 1977.
JMJP 1/31/77; NCNA Rawalpindi 1/29/77; SCMP 6276:68 (2/8/77).

77-9   1/29/77 — LAMBYAMA STATION   SIERRA LEONE (EAST-
ERN PROVINCE)   CERTIFICATE
Handing over of PRC aid Lambyama, Kabala, and Newton agro-
technical stations to Sierra Leone.
JMJP 2/1/77; NCNA Freetown 1/30/77; SCMP 6277:111 (2/9/77).

77-10 2/1/77 — PEKING ALBANIA PROTOCOL
Exchange of goods and payments for 1977.
JMJP 2/2/77; NCNA Peking 2/1/77; SCMP 6277:101 (2/9/77).

77-11 2/1/77 — PEKING ALBANIA PROTOCOL
Albania's use of PRC loan in 1977.
JMJP 2/2/77; NCNA Peking 2/1/77; SCMP 6277:101 (2/9/77).

77-12 2/2/77 5/30/78 — BUENOS AIRES ARGENTINA AGREE-
MENT
Trade.
JMJP 2/6/77; NCNA Peking 2/3/77; SCMP 6279:182 (2/11/77).
Exchange of notes on ratification, Buenos Aires.
JMJP 5/31/77; NCNA Peking 5/30/78; FBIS (1) 106:A28 (6/1/78).

77-13 2/4/77 — BAMAKO MALI MINUTES
PRC aid in building four water conservation projects of a state
farm "Office of Niger."
JMJP 2/9/77; NCNA Bamako 2/6/77; SCMP 6282:105 (2/16/77).

77-14 2/5/77 — PEKING KOREA(N) PROTOCOL
Scientific and technical cooperation.
Signed at seventeenth meeting of Sino-Korean Scientific and
Technical Cooperation Committee.
JMJP 2/6/77; NCNA Peking 2/5/77; SCMP 6280:39 (2/14/77).

77-15 2/8/77 — PYONGYANG KOREA(N) PROTOCOL
Signed at twenty-ninth meeting of Board of Directors of Sino-
Korean Yalu River Hydroelectric Power Company.
JMJP 2/9/77; NCNA Pyongyang 2/8/77; SCMP 6282:112 (2/16/77).

77-16 2/17/77 2/17/77 MONROVIA LIBERIA JOINT COMMUNI-
QUÉ
Establishment of diplomatic relations.
JMJP 2/23/77(C); PR 20. 9:4 (2/25/77)(E); NCNA Peking 2/22/77;
SCMP 6290:138 (3/2/77)(E).

77-17 2/17/77 — MONROVIA LIBERIA AGREEMENT
Economic cooperation.
JMJP 2/23/77; NCNA Monrovia 2/21/77; SCMP 6290:138 (3/2/77).

77-18 2/17/77 — MONROVIA LIBERIA EXCHANGE OF NOTES
Economic and technical cooperation.
JMJP 2/23/77; NCNA Monrovia 2/21/77; SCMP 6290:138 (3/2/77).

77-19 2/24/77 — NIAMEY NIGER CERTIFICATE
Handing over of PRC-aid Saga Reclamation Area to Niger.
Built under 1975 Protocol of Agricultural Cooperation [75-80].
JMJP 3/9/77; NCNA Peking 2/26/77; SCMP 6293:28 (3/7/77).

77-20 2/25/77 — TUNIS TUNISIA EXCHANGE OF NOTES
PRC accord additional credit to Tunisia for Maedjerdah–Cape
Bon canal project.
JMJP 2/27/77; NCNA Tunis 2/25/77; SCMP 6293:36 (3/7/77).

77-21 3/1/77 — KHARTOUM SUDAN PROTOCOL
Trade for 1977.
JMJP 3/7/77; NCNA Khartoum 3/1/77; SCMP 6296:164 (3/10/77).

77-22 3/8/77 — MOGADISHU SOMALIA CERTIFICATE
Handing over of PRC-aid Benadir Gynecology, Obstetrics, and
Pediatrics Hospital to Somalia.
JMJP 3/12/77; NCNA Mogadishu 3/8/77; SCMP 6300:118 (3/16/77).

77-23 3/10/77 — PEKING VIETNAM
Annual executive plan for cooperation in public health work.
JMJP 3/11/77; NCNA Peking 3/10/77; SCMP 6301:151 (3/17/77).

77-24 3/12/77 — PEKING KOREA(N) AGREEMENT
Long-term trade.
JMJP 3/13/77; PR 20.12:3 (3/18/77); NCNA Peking 3/12/77;
SCMP 6302:190 (3/18/77).

77-25 3/12/77 — PEKING KOREA(N) PROTOCOL
1977 trade.
JMJP 3/13/77; PR 20.12:3 (3/18/77); NCNA Peking 3/12/77;
SCMP 6302:190 (3/18/77).

77-26 3/15/77 — PEKING BULGARIA AGREEMENT
Exchange of goods and payments for 1977.
JMJP 3/16/77; NCNA Peking 3/15/77; SCMP 6304:69 (3/22/77).

77-27 3/17/77 — CONAKRY GUINEA CERTIFICATE
Handing over of repaired hydroagricultural project with PRC
assistance on Guinean Island of Kaback to Guinea.
JMJP 3/20/77; NCNA Conakry 3/18/77; SCMP 6307:181 (3/25/77).

77-28 3/19/77 — PEKING VIETNAM(N) AGREEMENT
Exchange of goods and payments for 1977.
NCNA Peking 3/19/77; SCMP 6307:188 (3/25/77).

77-29 3/21/77 — PEKING EGYPT AGREEMENT
Long-term trade.
JMJP 3/22/77; NCNA Peking 3/21/77; SCMP 6308:30 (3/28/77).

77-30 3/21/77 — PEKING EGYPT AGREEMENT
Long-term payment from 1/1/77 to 12/31/80.
JMJP 3/22/77; NCNA Peking 3/21/77; SCMP 6308:30 (3/28/77).

77-31 3/21/77 — PEKING EGYPT PROTOCOL
1977 Trade.
JMJP 3/22/77; NCNA Peking 3/21/77; SCMP 6308:30 (3/28/77).

77-32 3/24/77 — PEKING NORWAY AGREEMENT
Cooperation in ship inspection.
JMJP 3/26/77; NCNA Peking 3/25/77; SCMP 6312:187 (4/1/77).

77-33 3/28/77 — NDJAMENA CHAD AGREEMENT
PRC aid in building of a stadium in Ndjamena.
JMJP 4/4/77; NCNA Peking 3/31/77; SCMP 6316:131 (4/8/77).

77-34 3/30/77 — JAPAN PROTOCOL
Agency on air cargo transport.
Yearbook on Chinese Communism 8-46 (1977).

77-35 4/3/77 — PEKING POLAND PROTOCOL
Signed at twenty-seventh session of Joint Standing Commission
of Sino-Polish Shipping Joint Stock Company.
JMJP 4/9/77; NCNA Peking 4/8/77; SCMP 6323:131 (4/20/77).

77-36 4/4/77 — PEKING AUSTRIA EXCHANGE OF NOTES
Affirming a recently concluded reciprocal agreement for trade-
mark registration.
JMJP 4/5/77; NCNA Peking 4/4/77; SCMP 6319:99 (4/14/77).

77-37 4/4/77 — NOUAKCHOTT MAURITANIA PROTOCOL
Dispatch of medical teams to Mauritania by PRC.
JMJP 4/9/77; NCNA Nouakchott 4/4/77; SCMP 6319:106 (4/14/77).

77-38 4/7/77 — WASHINGTON JORDAN JOINT COMMUNIQUÉ
Establishment of diplomatic relations.
JMJP 4/16/77(C); PR 20. 17:10 (4/22/77)(E); NCNA Peking
4/14/77; SCMP 6327:154 (4/27/77)(E).

77-39 4/13/77 — KABUL AFGHANISTAN PROTOCOL
Exchange of goods for 1977.
JMJP 4/16/77; NCNA Kabul 4/14/77; SCMP 6328:200 (4/28/77).

77-40 4/13/77 — KABUL AFGHANISTAN AGREEMENT
Trade and payments for 1977.
JMJP 4/16/77; NCNA Kabul 4/14/77; SCMP 6328:200 (4/28/77).

77-41 4/13/77 — PYONGYANG KOREA(N) PROTOCOL (RENEWED)
Renewal of 1956 Protocol of timber transportation on Yalu and
Tumen Rivers [56-10].
JMJP 4/14/77; NCNA Pyongyang 4/13/77; SCMP 6326:104 (4/26/77).

77-42 4/15/77 — PEKING CUBA PROTOCOL
1977 trade.
JMJP 4/19/77; NCNA Peking 4/18/77; SCMP 6330:28 (5/2/77).

77-43 4/15/77 — CONAKRY GUINEA CERTIFICATE
Handing over of PRC-aid fishing projects to Guinea.
JMJP 4/18/77; NCNA Conakry 4/16/77; SCMP 6329:247 (4/29/77).

77-44 4/20/77 — HAMBURG GERMANY(W) AGREEMENT
Cooperation in ship inspection.
JMJP 5/1/77; NCNA Peking 4/30/77; SCMP 6338:245 (5/12/77).

77-45 4/20/77 — BUDAPEST HUNGARY AGREEMENT
Exchange of goods and payments for 1977.
JMJP 4/22/77; NCNA Budapest 4/21/77; SCMP 6332:157 (5/4/77).

77-46 4/25/77 — CONAKRY GUINEA PROTOCOL
1977 trade.
JMJP 5/4/77; NCNA Conakry 4/26/77; SCMP 6335:37 (5/9/77).

77-47 4/26/77 — PEKING RUMANIA
1977-80 executive plan on health cooperation.
JMJP 4/27/77; NCNA Peking 4/26/77; SCMP 6335:48 (5/9/77).

77-48 4/28/77 4/28/77 PEKING AUSTRALIA EXCHANGE OF
NOTES
Amending Agreement on Exhibition of Archaeological Finds of
PRC [76-53].
Aust. T. S. 1977:1.

77-49 5/2/77 — PEKING INTERNATIONAL TELECOMMUNICA-
TIONS SATELLITE ORGANIZATION MINUTES
Talks on PRC joining International Telecommunications Satellite
Organization.
JMJP 5/3/77; NCNA Peking 5/2/77; SCMP 6340:59 (5/16/77).

77-50 5/3/77 — PEKING GERMANY(E) AGREEMENT
Exchange of goods and payments for 1977.
JMJP 5/6/77; NCNA Peking 5/3/77; SCMP 6340:40 (5/16/77).

77-51 5/6/77 — BRAZZAVILLE CONGO MINUTES
Talks on construction of a "People Palace" in Brazzaville.
JMJP 5/10/77; NCNA Brazzaville 5/6/77; SCMP 6343:249 (5/19/77).

77-52 5/10/77 — BAMAKO MALI PROTOCOL
Dispatch of PRC medical team to Mali.
JMJP 5/16/77; NCNA Bamako 5/11/77; SCMP 6345:41 (5/23/77).

77-53 5/13/77 — LOME TOGO CERTIFICATE
Handing over of a rice plantation center to Togo.
JMJP 5/16/77; NCNA Lome 5/13/77; SCMP 6348:234 (5/26/77).

77-54 5/18/77 — BAGHDAD IRAQ EXCHANGE OF LETTERS
Trade for 1977-81.
JMJP 5/25/77; NCNA Baghdad 5/19/77; SCMP 6351:78 (6/1/77).

77-55 5/19/77 — PRAGUE CZECHOSLOVAKIA AGREEMENT
Goods exchange and payments for 1977.
JMJP 5/24/77; NCNA Prague 5/19/77; SCMP 6351:75 (6/1/77).

77-56 5/23/77 — WARSAW POLAND AGREEMENT
Exchange of goods and payments for 1977.
JMJP 5/28/77; NCNA Warsaw 5/26/77; SCMP 6356:136 (6/8/77).

77-57 5/25/77 — BANJUL GAMBIA MINUTES
Talks on PRC aid in construction of a stadium and an athletic
center in Banjul.
JMJP 5/29/77; NCNA Peking 5/27/77; SCMP 6356:127 (6/8/77).

77-58 5/30/77 — NEW YORK BARBADOS JOINT COMMUNIQUÉ
Establishment of diplomatic relations.
JMJP 6/1/77(C); PR 20. 24:10 (6/10/77)(E); NCNA Peking 6/1/77;
SCMP 6358:236 (6/10/77)(E).

77-59 5/31/77 — MALABO EQUATORIAL GUINEA PROTOCOL
Dispatch of a new medical team to Equatorial Guinea by PRC.
NCNA Peking 6/3/77; SCMP 6360:78 (6/14/77).

77-60 6/1/77 — KINSHASA ZAIRE MINUTES
Talks on joint construction of a station for popularizing rice-
growing technique in Zaire.
JMJP 6/11/77; NCNA Kinshasa 6/2/77; SCMP 6360:95 (6/14/77).

77-61 6/4/77 — PEKING YUGOSLAVIA AGREEMENT
1977-78 scientific and technical cooperation.
JMJP 6/5/77; NCNA Peking 6/4/77; SCMP 6360:95 (6/14/77).

77-62 6/4/77 — OUAGADOUGOU UPPER VOLTA MINUTES
PRC and Upper Volta joint construction of a stadium in Ouagadougou.
JMJP 6/11/77; NCNA Peking 6/7/77; SCMP 6363:252 (6/17/77).

77-63 6/7/77 — SANAA YEMEN (YAR) PROTOCOL
Dispatch of another medical team to Yemen by PRC.
JMJP 6/13/77; NCNA Sanaa 6/7/77; SCMP 6364:60 (6/20/77).

77-64 6/9/77 — PEKING SUDAN AGREEMENT
Economic and technical cooperation.
JMJP 6/10/77; PR 20. 26:7 (6/24/77); NCNA Peking 6/9/77;
SCMP 6364:48 (6/20/77).

77-65 6/?/77 — PEKING FRANCE DRAFT
Reciprocal exemption of duties and taxes for aviation enterprises.
JMJP 6/9/77; NCNA Peking 6/8/77; SCMP 6363:232 (6/17/77).

77-66 6/10/77 — BISSAU GUINEA-BISSAU MINUTES
Talks on PRC aid in construction of a water conservation project
on Udunduma River.
JMJP 6/16/77; NCNA Bissau 6/14/77; SCMP 6368:38 (6/27/77).

77-67 6/10/77 — PEKING SPAIN EXCHANGE OF INSTRUMENTS
Agreement of Trademark, Registration, and Protection.
JMJP 6/11/77; NCNA Peking 6/10/77; SCMP 6365:107 (6/22/77).

77-68 6/11/77(?) — KIGALI RWANDA MINUTES
Talks on cooperation in developing a rice cultivation project in
Rubindi of Rwanda.
JMJP 6/13/77; NCNA Peking 6/11/77; SCMP 6366:150 (6/23/77).

77-69 6/11/77 — HANOI VIETNAM PROTOCOL
Railway transportation for 1977.
Signed at nineteenth railway conference between PRC and Vietnam.
JMJP 6/13/77; NCNA Hanoi 6/11/77; SCMP 6366:162 (6/23/77).

77-70 6/17/77 — ULAN BATOR MONGOLIA PROTOCOL
Supply of goods for 1977.
JMJP 6/20/77; NCNA Ulan Bator 6/18/77; SCMP 6370:148 (6/29/77).

77-71 6/18/77 — PEKING CONGO AGREEMENT
Economic and technical cooperation.
JMJP 6/19/77; PR 20. 26:4 (6/24/77); NCNA Peking 6/18/77;
SCMP 6370:137 (6/29/77).

77-72 6/18/77 — ADDIS ABABA ETHIOPIA MINUTES
Talks on opening air service between Peking and African countries
via Addis Ababa.
JMJP 6/23/77; NCNA Addis Ababa 6/20/77; SCMP 6372:239 (7/1/77).

77-73 6/23/77 — PEKING SOMALIA PROTOCOL
Economic and technical cooperation.
JMJP 6/24/77; NCNA Peking 6/23/77; SCMP 6373:43 (7/5/77).

77-74 6/24/77 — RABAT MOROCCO MINUTES
Trade.
Signed at a meeting of Sino-Morocco Joint Trade Committee.
JMJP 7/5/77; NCNA Rabat 6/27/77; SCMP 6376:177 (7/8/77).

77-75 6/28/77 — NOUAKCHOTT MAURITANIA MINUTES
Talks on construction of a port in Nouakchott.
JMJP 6/30/77; NCNA Nouakchott 6/29/77; SCMP 6378:74 (7/12/77).

77-76 6/29/77 — KARACHI PAKISTAN MEMORANDUM
Opening up of an air route to Africa via Karachi.
JMJP 7/1/77; NCNA Karachi 6/30/77; SCMP 6378:75 (7/12/77).

77-77 6/30/77 — ADDIS ABABA ETHIOPIA PROTOCOL
1977-78 trade.
JMJP 7/4/77; NCNA Addis Ababa 6/30/77; SCMP 6378:69 (7/12/77).

77-78 7/21/77 — MOSCOW U. S. S. R. AGREEMENT
Exchange of goods and payments for 1977.
JMJP 7/22/77; NCNA Moscow 7/21/77; SCMP 6392:40 (8/1/77).

77-79 8/2/77 — URUMCHI PAKISTAN EXCHANGE OF LETTERS
Border trade.
JMJP 8/6/77; NCNA Peking 8/5/77; SCMP 6402:33 (8/15/77).

77-80 8/12/77 — PRAIA CAPE VERDE AGREEMENT
Economic and technical cooperation.
JMJP 8/14/77; NCNA Praia 8/13/77; SCMP 6408:66 (8/23/77).

77-81 8/25/77(?) — KIRIN KOREA(N) PROTOCOL
Border railway transport.

Signed at regular meeting on Sino-Korean Railway Transport for 1977.
JMJP 9/7/77; NCNA Peking 9/5/77; SCMP 6424:225 (9/16/77).

77-82 8/30/77(?) — HUHEHOT MONGOLIA PROTOCOL
Border railway.
Signed at regular meeting of Sino-Mongolian Border Railway Joint Commission.
JMJP 9/1/77; NCNA Huhehot 8/30/77; SCMP 6420:29 (9/12/77).

77-83 9/10/77 — TUNIS TUNISIA CONTRACT
Building Medjerda-Cape Bon Canal for Tunisia.
Signed under 1974 Exchange of Notes [74-96] on implementing 1972 Agreement on Economic and Technical Cooperation [72-92].
JMJP 9/18/77; NCNA Tunis 9/12/77; SCMP 6429:377 (9/23/77).

77-84 9/21/77 — PEKING NIGER PROTOCOL
Economic and technical cooperation.
JMJP 9/22/77; NCNA Peking 9/21/77; SCMP 6434:386 (9/30/77).

77-85 9/23/77 — PEKING EQUATORIAL GUINEA AGREEMENT
Economic and technical cooperation.
JMJP 9/24/77; NCNA Peking 9/23/77; FBIS (1). 186:A15 (9/26/77).

77-86 9/23/77 — PEKING MOZAMBIQUE PROTOCOL
Economic and technical cooperation.
JMJP 9/24/77; NCNA Peking 9/23/77; FBIS (1). 186:A24 (9/26/77).

77-87 9/24/77 — PEKING RUMANIA PROTOCOL
Handing over a new building for Rumanian Embassy.
JMJP 9/25/77; NCNA Peking 9/24/77; FBIS (1). 186:A13 (9/26/77).

77-88 9/25/77 — PEKING JAPAN AGREEMENT
Metrological circuit between PRC and Japan.
JMJP 9/26/77; NCNA Peking 9/25/77; FBIS (1). 188:A4 (9/28/77).

77-89 9/29/77 1/31/78 — PEKING JAPAN AGREEMENT
Trademark protection.
JMJP 10/2/77; NCNA Peking 9/29/77; FBIS (1). 193:A10 (10/5/77).
Exchange of notes on entering into force.
JMJP 2/1/78; NCNA Peking 1/31/78; FBIS (1). 23:A4 (2/2/78).

77-90 10/6/77(?) — HEIHO U.S.S.R. MINUTES
Border river navigation.
Signed at twentieth regular session of Sino-Soviet Joint Commis-

sion for Navigation on Boundary waters.
JMJP 10/7/77; NCNA Peking 10/6/66; FBIS (1). 195:A6 (10/7/77).

77-91 10/7/77 — PEKING CAMEROON AGREEMENT
Economic and technical cooperation.
JMJP 10/8/77; PR 20. 42:4 (10/14/77); NCNA Peking 10/7/77;
FBIS (1)196:A13 (10/11/77).

77-92 10/20/77 — MOGADISHU SOMALIA CERTIFICATE
Handing over a highway between Galcaio and Garowe built with
PRC aid to Somalia.
JMJP 10/23/77; NCNA Peking 10/21/77; FBIS (1). 204:A17
(10/21/77).

77-93 10/27/77 — PEKING SRI LANKA AGREEMENT
Trade and payments.
JMJP 10/28/77; NCNA Peking 10/27/77; FBIS (1). 207:A15
(10/27/77).

77-94 10/27/77 — PEKING SRI LANKA PROTOCOL
Exchange of goods for 1978.
JMJP 10/28/77; NCNA Peking 10/27/77; FBIS (1). 207:A15
(10/27/77).

77-95 10/29/77 — VIENTIANE LAOS AGREEMENT
PRC providing free interest loan to Laos.
JMJP 10/31/77.

77-96 11/1/77 — TEHRAN IRAN MEMORANDUM
Trade.
JMJP 11/3/77; NCNA Peking 11/2/77; FBIS (1). 211:A27 (11/2/77).

77-97 11/3/77 — TIRANA ALBANIA PROTOCOL
Scientific and technical cooperation.
Signed at seventeenth session of Sino-Albanian Joint Committee
for Scientific and Technical Cooperation.
JMJP 11/6/77; NCNA Peking 11/4/77; FBIS (1). 214:A22 (11/7/77).

77-98 11/6/77 — PEKING MALTA PROTOCOL
Economic and technical cooperation.
JMJP 11/7/77; PR 20. 46:4 (11/11/77); NCNA Peking 11/6/77;
FBIS (1). 214:A18 (11/7/77).

77-99 11/15/77 — MOGADISHU SOMALIA CERTIFICATE
Turnover of Mogadishu stadium to Somalia, built with PRC aid.
JMJP 11/16/77.

77-100 11/18/77 — PEKING   FINLAND   AGREEMENT
  1978 trade.
  JMJP 11/20/77; NCNA Peking 11/18/77; FBIS (1)224:A20 (11/21/77).

77-101 11/24/77 — FREETOWN   SIERRA LEONE   CERTIFICATE
  Turnover of six rice agriculture technical expansion stations to
  Sierra Leone.
  JMJP 12/11/77.

77-102 11/25/77 — SOFIA   BULGARIA   PROTOCOL
  Scientific and technical cooperation.
  Signed at fifteenth session of Sino-Bulgarian Joint Committee for
  Scientific and Technical Cooperation.
  JMJP 11/29/77; NCNA Peking 11/26/77; FBIS (1) . 229:A12
  (11/29/77).

77-103 11/25/77 — BUDAPEST   HUNGARY   PROTOCOL
  Scientific and technical cooperation.
  Signed at sixteenth session of Sino-Hungarian Committee for Sci-
  entific and Technical Cooperation.
  JMJP 12/2/77; NCNA Peking 11/27/77; FBIS (1) . 229:A12 (11/29/77).

77-104 12/?/77 — LONDON   UK   AGREEMENT
  Technical cooperation in ship inspection.
  JMJP 12/15/77; NCNA Peking 12/14/77; FBIS (1) . 240:A9 (12/14/77).

77-105 12/10/77 — ULAN BATOR   MONGOLIA   PROTOCOL
  Talks between two groups of specialists in meteorological com-
  munications.
  JMJP 12/16/77; NCNA Peking 12/11/77; FBIS (1) . 239:A4 (12/13/77).

77-106 12/14/77 — BUCHAREST   RUMANIA
  Scientific cooperation plan for 1977-79.
  JMJP 12/17/77; NCNA Peking 12/16/77; FBIS (1) . 242:A13
  (12/16/77).

77-107 12/16/77 — PEKING   MEXICO   PROTOCOL
  Scientific and technical cooperation.
  Signed at third session of Sino-Mexican Scientific and Technical
  Cooperation.
  JMJP 12/17/77; NCNA Peking 12/16/77; FBIS (1) . 243:A24
  (12/19/77).

77-108 12/17/77 — PEKING   CZECHOSLOVAKIA   AGREEMENT
  Goods exchange and payments for 1978.
  JMJP 12/19/77; NCNA Peking 12/17/77; FBIS (1) . 244:A15 (12/20/77).

77-109 12/18/77 — PEKING CZECHOSLOVAKIA PROTOCOL
Scientific and technical cooperation.
Signed at nineteenth session of Sino-Czechoslovak Joint Commission for Scientific and Technical Cooperation.
JMJP 12/19/77; NCNA Peking 12/18/77; FBIS (1).244:A16 (12/20/77).

77-110 12/19/77 — PEKING GHANA AGREEMENT
Long-term trade and payments.
JMJP 12/20/77; NCNA Peking 12/19/77; FBIS (1).244:A22 (12/20/77).

77-111 12/19/77 — PEKING GHANA PROTOCOL
1978 trade.
JMJP 12/20/77; NCNA Peking 12/19/77; FBIS (1).244:A22 (12/20/77).

77-112 12/19/77 — ADDIS ABABA ETHIOPIA MINUTES
PRC and Ethiopia will jointly build Awassa cotton mill.
JMJP 12/21/77; NCNA Peking 12/20/77; FBIS (1).244:A22 (12/20/77).

77-113 12/21/77 — PEKING RUMANIA PROTOCOL
Exchange of goods and payments in 1978.
JMJP 12/22/77; PR 20.52:5 (12/26/77); NCNA Peking 12/21/77; FBIS (1).245:A11 (12/21/77).

77-114 12/26/77 — KUWAIT KUWAIT AGREEMENT
Economic and technical cooperation.
JMJP 12/27/77; NCNA Peking 12/26/77; FBIS (1).248:A13 (12/27/77).

77-115 12/ /77 — COLOMBO SRI LANKA MINUTES
Shipping.
Talks on fifth regular session of Sino-Sri Lanka Joint Commission for Joint Shipping Services.
JMJP 12/27/77.

77-116 12/28/77 — PEKING PAKISTAN PROTOCOL
Trade.
JMJP 12/29/77; NCNA Peking 12/28/77; FBIS (1).250:A9 (12/29/77).

<u>1978</u>

78-1   1/6/78 — — UPPER VOLTA   CERTIFICATE
Handing over of a Banfora rice plantation developed cooperatively
by PRC and Upper Volta.
JMJP 1/14/78.

78-2   1/7/78 — PEKING   BRAZIL   AGREEMENT
Trade.
JMJP 1/9/78; NCNA Peking 1/7/78; FBIS (1).6:A12 (1/10/78)

78-3   1/10/78 — PEKING   VIETNAM   AGREEMENT
Mutual supply of goods and payments in 1978.
JMJP 1/12/78; NCNA Peking 1/10/78; FBIS (1).7:A4 (1/11/78).

78-4   1/14/78 — SOFIA   BULGARIA   AGREEMENT
Exchange of goods and payments in 1978.
JMJP 1/17/78; NCNA Peking 1/15/78; FBIS (1).10:A6 (1/16/78).

78-5   1/15/78 — KARACHI   PAKISTAN   EXCHANGE OF NOTES
Handing over of the 13,500 ton cargo ship <u>Ho Tien</u> built by Karachi
shipyard.
JMJP 1/18/78.

78-6   1/19/78 — BERLIN   GERMANY(E)   AGREEMENT
Exchange of goods and payments.
JMJP 1/21/78; NCNA Peking 1/20/78; FBIS (1).14:A19 (1/20/78).

78-7   1/20/78 — VIENTIANE   LAOS   PROTOCOL
PRC aid to Laos in the form of complete projects.
JMJP 1/24/78; NCNA Peking 1/21/78; FBIS (1).15:A6 (1/23/78).

78-8   1/20/78 — VIENTIANE   LAOS   PROTOCOL
Treatment and work conditions of PRC engineering and technical
personnel in Laos.
JMJP 1/24/78.

78-9   1/21/78 — PEKING   FRANCE   AGREEMENT
Scientific and technical cooperation.
JMJP 1/22/78; PR 21.4:3 (1/27/78); NCNA Peking 1/21/78;
FBIS (1).15:A9 (1/23/78).

78-10   1/22/78 — — U.S.A.   ACCORD
Trade payments between China Bank and First National Bank of
Chicago, U.S.A.
Wen-hui Pao 1/29/78.

78-11 1/24/78 — DACCA BANGLADESH PROTOCOL
Trade.
JMJP 1/26/78; NCNA Peking 1/25/78; FBIS (1).18:A10 (1/26/78).

78-12 1/24/78 — PEKING KOREA(N) RESOLUTION
Signed at thirtieth session of Board of Directors of Sino-Korean
Yalu River Hydroelectric Power Co.
JMJP 1/25/78; NCNA Peking 1/24/78; FBIS (1).17:A4 (1/25/78).

78-13 1/26/78 — SHENYANG KOREA(N) ARRANGEMENT
Border river navigation.
Signed at seventeenth session of Sino-Korean Border River
Navigation Cooperation Committee.
JMJP 1/28/78; NCNA Peking 1/27/78; FBIS (1).20:A3 (1/30/78).

78-14 1/29/78 — MANILA PHILIPPINES AGREEMENT
Continuing supply of crude oil by PRC.
NCNA Peking 1/31/78; FBIS (1).22:A6 (2/1/78).

78-15 1/30/78 — PEKING POLAND AGREEMENT
Exchange of goods and payments in 1978.
JMJP 2/3/78; NCNA Peking 2/2/78; FBIS (1).24:A7 (2/3/78).

78-16 2/3/78 — BELGRADE YUGOSLAVIA PROTOCOL
Opening direct flight route between China and Yugoslavia.
JMJP 2/4/78; NCNA Peking 2/3/78; FBIS (1).26:A11 (2/7/78).

78-17 2/3/78 — BRUSSELS EUROPEAN COMMON MARKET
DRAFT TRADE AGREEMENT
JMJP 2/6/78; Kyodo Tokyo 2/4/78; FBIS (1).25:A16 (2/6/78).

78-18 2/15/78 — FREETOWN SIERRA LEONE CERTIFICATE
Handing over of Kambia highway bridge built with PRC aid.
JMJP 2/22/78; NCNA Peking 2/19/78; FBIS (1).36:A17 (2/22/78).

78-19 2/15/78 — BONGO ETHIOPIA CERTIFICATE
Handing over of Bongo diesel power station built by PRC.
JMJP 2/19/78; NCNA Peking 2/18/78; FBIS (1).35:A15 (2/21/78).

78-20 2/16/78 — PEKING JAPAN ACCORD
Long-term trade (1978-85).
JMJP 2/17/78; PR 21.8:4 (2/24/78); NCNA Peking 2/16/78;
FBIS (1).33:A5 (2/16/78).

78-21 2/20/78 — ADDIS ABABA ETHIOPIA MINUTES
Talks on constructing Addis Ababa Gymansium.
JMJP 2/22/78; NCNA Peking 2/21/78; FBIS (1). 36:A17 (2/22/78).

78-22 2/24/78 — MANILA PHILIPPINES EXCHANGE OF NOTES
Trade for 1978.
JMJP 3/2/78; NCNA Peking 2/25/78; FBIS (1). 39:A11 (2/27/78).

78-23 2/27/78 — PEKING HUNGARY AGREEMENT
Exchange of goods and payments in 1978.
JMJP 2/28/78; NCNA Peking 2/27/78; FBIS (1). 40:A10 (2/28/78).

78-24 2/28/78 — KHARTOUM SUDAN CERTIFICATE
Handing over of the Hassaheisa Friendship Textile Mill in
Gezira Province built with PRC aid to Sudan.
JMJP 3/3/78; PR 21. 21:27 (5/26/78); NCNA Peking 3/1/78;
FBIS (1). 43:A10 (3/3/78).

78-25 3/1/78 — PEKING MONGOLIA PROTOCOL
Mutual supply of goods in 1978.
JMJP 3/3/78; NCNA Peking 3/1/78; FBIS (1). 42:A6 (3/2/78).

78-26 3/5/78 — PEKING YUGOSLAVIA MINUTES
Talks on friendship sports cooperation.
JMJP 3/6/78; NCNA Peking 3/5/78; FBIS (1). 44:A10 (3/6/78).

78-27 3/8/78 — RANGOON BURMA DOCUMENT
Completion of the second stage of expansion project of Meiktila
People's Textile Mill.
NCNA Peking 3/10/78; FBIS (1). 53:A10 (3/17/78).

78-28 3/9/78 — MONROVIA LIBERIA PROTOCOL
Expansion project of Barreke Sugar Refinery.
JMJP 3/17/78; PR 21. 21:27 (5/26/78).

78-29 3/10/78 — PEKING SOMALIA AGREEMENT
Radio and television cooperation between PRC Broadcasting
Bureau and Somalia News Agency.
JMJP 3/11/78; NCNA Peking 3/10/78; FBIS (1). 49:A19 (3/13/78).

78-30 3/10/78 — PEKING SOMALIA AGREEMENT
News cooperation between New China News Agency and Somalian
News Agency.
JMJP 3/11/78; NCNA Peking 3/10/78; FBIS (1). 49:A19 (3/13/78).

78-31   3/13/78 — LOME   TOGO   CERTIFICATE
Handing over of two rice plantation centers built by PRC for Togo.
JMJP 3/20/78; PR 21. 21:27 (5/26/78).

78-32   3/13/78 — LOME   TOGO   PROTOCOL
PRC aid in building agro-technique popularization center for Togo.
JMJP 3/20/78; PR 21. 21:27 (5/26/78).

78-33   3/14/78 — MANILA   PHILIPPINES   AGREEMENT
Scientific and technical cooperation.
JMJP 3/16/78; PR 21. 12:4 (3/24/78); NCNA Peking (3/14/78);
FBIS (1). 51:A16 (3/15/78).

78-34   3/17/78 — PEKING   GUINEA   PROTOCOL
Trade in 1978.
JMJP 3/18/78; NCNA Peking 3/17/78; FBIS (1). 56:A20 (3/22/78).

78-35   3/18/78 — HAVANA   CUBA   PROTOCOL
1978 Trade.
NCNA Peking 3/21/78; FBIS (1). 57:A29 (3/23/78).

78-36   3/21/78 — DACCA   BANGLADESH   AGREEMENT
Economic and technical cooperation.
JMJP 3/22/78; PR 21. 13:3 (3/31/78); NCNA Peking 3/21/78;
FBIS (1). 56:A11 (3/22/78).

78-37   3/21/78 — DACCA   BANGLADESH   AGREEMENT
Scientific and technical cooperation.
JMJP 3/22/78; PR 21. 13:3 (3/31/78); NCNA Peking 3/21/78;
FBIS (1). 56:A11 (3/22/78).

78-38   3/21/78 — PEKING   AFGHANISTAN   PROTOCOL
Exchange of goods in 1978.
JMJP 3/22/78; NCNA Peking 3/21/78; FBIS (1). 57:A19 (3/23/78).

78-39   3/25/78 — BANJUL   GAMBIA   MINUTES
Talks on construction of four health centers in Gambia.
NCNA Peking 3/26/78; FBIS (1). 60:A18 (3/28/78).

78-40   3/25/78 — CAIRO   EGYPT   AGREEMENT
Trade in 1978.
JMJP 3/28/78; NCNA Peking 3/28/78; FBIS (1). 61:A12 (3/29/78).

78-41   3/31/78 — PEKING   THAILAND   AGREEMENT
Trade.

JMJP 4/1/68; PR 21.14:4 (4/7/78); NCNA Peking 3/31/78; FBIS (1).64:A7 (4/3/78).

78-42 3/31/78 8/18/78* — PEKING THAILAND AGREEMENT
Scientific and technical cooperation.
JMJP 4/1/78; PR 21.14:4 (4/7/78); NCNA Peking 3/31/78; FBIS (1).64:A7 (4/3/78).
*Exchange of instrument on ratification.
JMJP 9/12/78; NCNA Peking 8/18/78; FBIS (1).164:A11 (8/23/78).

78-43 3/31/78 — LOME TOGO PROTOCOL
Dispatch of PRC medical team to Togo.
JMJP 4/2/78; Domestic Service in Mandarin Peking 4/2/78; FBIS (1).68:A8 (4/7/78).

78-44 3/31/78 — KUALA LUMPUR MALAYSIA CONTRACT
Purchase of PRC rice by Malaysia.
JMJP 4/4/78; NCNA Peking 4/2/78; FBIS (1).65:A8 (4/4/78).

78-45 4/1/78 — NDJAMENA CHAD & CAMEROON MINUTES
Handing over of Chari River highway bridge.
JMJP 4/4/78.

78-46 4/3/78 — BRUSSELS EUROPEAN COMMON MARKET
AGREEMENT
Trade.
JMJP 4/5/78; PR 21.15:5 (4/14/78); NCNA Peking 4/4/78; FBIS (1).65:A9 (4/4/78).

78-47 4/7/78 — DAKAR SENEGAL MINUTES (SUPPLEMENTARY)
Talks on drilling wells with PRC assistance.
JMJP 4/10/78; NCNA Peking 4/9/78; FBIS (1).70:A17 (4/11/78).

78-48 4/8/78 — MUONG LAO CERTIFICATE
Handing over of the Na Sang-Boun Hai Highway built with PRC aid.
JMJP 4/11/78; NCNA Peking 4/10/78; FBIS (1).70:A3 (4/11/78).

78-49 4/10/78 — MONROVIA LIBERIA PROTOCOL
Cooperation in building agricultural technology.
JMJP 4/12/78; NCNA Peking 4/11/78; FBIS (1).71:A10 (4/12/78).

78-50 4/12/78 — PEKING GERMANY(W) & FRANCE EXCHANGE
OF INSTRUMENTS
Agreement on Utilization of Symphonic System for Communication
Transmission Experiments.
JMJP 4/15/78; NCNA Peking 4/12/78; FBIS (1).72:A8 (4/13/78).

78-51 4/12/78 — NANNING VIETNAM PROTOCOL
Border railway — Signed at twentieth session of Sino-Vietnamese
Boundary Railway Commission.
JMJP 4/22/78; NCNA Peking 4/13/78; FBIS (1). 73:A7 (4/14/78).

78-52 4/12/78 — WARSAW POLAND PROTOCOL
Signed at twenty-eighth session of Joint Standing Commission of
Sino-Polish Shipbroker's Company.
JMJP 4/18/78; NCNA Peking 4/13/78; FBIS (1). 73:A10 (4/14/78).

78-53 4/14/78 — GABERONES BOTSWANA EXCHANGE OF
NOTES
Providing PRC technical aid in building experimental state farm.
JMJP 4/19/78.

78-54 4/15/78 — ADEN YEMEN(S) PROTOCOL
Continuing dispatch of PRC medical team to Southern Yemen.
JMJP 4/19/78; NCNA Peking 4/16/78; FBIS (1). 76:A23 (4/19/78).

78-55 4/17/78 — PEKING U. S. S. R. AGREEMENT
Exchange of goods and payments in 1978.
JMJP 4/19/78; NCNA Peking 4/17/78; FBIS (1). 75:A5 (4/18/78).

78-56 4/18/78 — PEKING SOMALIA AGREEMENT
Economic and technical cooperation.
JMJP 4/20/78; NCNA Peking 4/18/78; FBIS (1). 75:A21 (4/18/78).

78-57 4/19/78 — PEKING ETHIOPIA MINUTES
Talks on sports exchange and cooperation.
JMJP 4/22/78; NCNA Peking 4/19/78; FBIS (1). 78:A18 (4/21/78).

78-58 4/24/78 — PEKING SPAIN AGREEMENT
Trade.
Madrid Domestic Service in Spanish 4/24/78; FBIS (1). 81:A16
(4/26/78).

78-59 4/25/78 — NDJAMENA CHAD PROTOCOL
Dispatch of PRC medical team to Chad.
JMJP 4/29/78; NCNA Peking 4/26/78; FBIS (1). 86:A24 (5/3/78).

78-60 4/26/78 — PEKING YEMEN(S) AGREEMENT
Economic and technical cooperation.
JMJP 4/27/78; PR 21. 18:4 (5/5/78); NCNA Peking 4/26/78;
FBIS (1). 82:A15 (4/27/78).

78-61 4/28/78 — PEKING BANGLADESH AGREEMENT
News exchange cooperation between New China News Agency and Bangladesh Sangbad Sangstha.
JMJP 4/30/78; NCNA Peking 4/28/78; FBIS (1). 86:A10 (5/3/78).

78-62 5/2/78 — PYONGYANG KOREA(N) PROTOCOL
Exchange of goods in 1978.
JMJP 5/6/78; PR 21. 19:4 (5/12/78); NCNA Peking 5/2/78; FBIS (1). 86:A5 (5/3/78).

78-63 5/2/78 — PEKING SEYCHELLES AGREEMENT
Economic and technical cooperation.
JMJP 5/3/78; PR 21. 19:4 (5/12/78); NCNA Peking 5/2/78; FBIS (1). 85:A19 (5/2/78).

78-64 5/2/78 — RANGOON BURMA CERTIFICATE
Gift of two motor driven "Eastwind II" planting machines.
JMJP 5/12/78.

78-65 5/4/78 — BELGRADE YUGOSLAVIA MINUTES
Talks on third meeting of Sino-Yugoslav Trade Joint Committee.
NCNA Peking 5/5/78; FBIS (1). 90:A16 (5/9/78).

78-66 5/ /78 — PEKING BULGARIA EXCHANGE OF NOTE
Extension of Scientific and Technical Cooperation Agreement signed on 3/22/55 [55-18].
JMJP 5/13/78; NCNA Peking 5/12/78; FBIS (1). 95:A23 (5/16/78).

78-67 5/19/78 — PEKING RUMANIA DOCUMENT
Consular and cultural cooperation.
JMJP 5/20/78; PR 21. 21:4 (5/26/78); NCNA Peking 5/19/78; FBIS (1). 99:A11 (5/22/78).
Exchange of instrument on ratification.
JMJP 8/22/78; NCNA Peking 8/21/78; FBIS (1). 162:A19 (8/21/78).

78-68 5/19/78 — PEKING RUMANIA AGREEMENT
Long-term economic and technical cooperation.
JMJP 5/20/78; PR 21. 21:4 (5/26/78); NCNA Peking 5/19/78; FBIS (1). 99:A11 (5/22/78).
Exchange of instrument on ratification.
JMJP 8/22/78; NCNA Peking 8/21/78; FBIS (1). 162LA19 (8/21/78).

78-69 5/19/78 — PEKING RUMANIA PROTOCOL
Long-term Agreement on Economic and Technical Cooperation.
JMJP 5/20/78; PR 21. 21:4 (5/26/78); NCNA Peking 5/19/78; FBIS (1). 99:A11 (5/22/78).

78-70 5/23/78 — NAIROBI KENYA AGREEMENT
Trade.
JMJP 5/26/78; NCNA Peking 5/24/78; FBIS (1). 101:A18 (5/24/78).

78-71 5/23/78 — PEKING JAPAN PROTOCOL
Building the Paoshan General Iron and Steel Plant in Shanghai.
JMJP 5/24/78; PR 21. 22:4 (6/2/78); NCNA Peking 5/23/78;
FBIS (1). 101:A5 (5/24/78).

78-72 5/23/78 — PEKING JAPAN CONTRACT
Technical cooperation.
JMJP 5/24/78; PR 21. 22:4 (6/2/78); NCNA Peking 5/23/78;
FBIS (1). 101:A5 (5/24/78).

78-73 5/25/78 5/25/78 LONDON OMAN JOINT COMMUNIQUÉ
Establishment of diplomatic relation.
JMJP 5/27/78; PR 21. 22:3 (6/2/78); NCNA Peking 5/26/78;
FBIS (1). 103:A37 (5/26/78).

78-74 5/25/78 6/1/78 — BRUSSELS EEC EXCHANGE OF IN-
STRUMENTS
Notification of accomplishment of internal procedure necessary
for implementation of trade agreement [78-46].
JMJP 5/30/78; NCNA Peking 5/26/78; FBIS (1). 103:A20 (5/26/78).

78-75 5/27/78(?) — VALLETTA(?) MALTA AGREEMENT
Joint shipping arrangements.
NCNA Peking 5/27/78; FBIS (1). 105:A19 (5/31/78).

78-76 5/28/78 — PEKING MOZAMBIQUE PROTOCOL
Agreement on Economic and Technical Cooperation [75-47].
JMJP 5/29/78; PR 21. 22:3 (6/2/78); NCNA Peking 5/28/78;
FBIS (1). 105:A22 (5/31/78).

78-77 5/28/78 — KATMANDU NEPAL AGREEMENT
Border inspection.
Signed at first session of China-Nepal Boundary Joint Inspection
Committee.
JMJP 5/31/78; NCNA Peking 5/30/78; FBIS (1). 106:A15 (6/1/78).

78-78 5/30/78 — PEKING ARGENTINA MINUTES
Exchange of documents on the entry into force of Trade Agree-
ment [77-12].
JMJP 5/31/78; NCNA Peking 5/30/78; FBIS (1). 106:A28 (6/1/78).

78-79 5/30/78 — PEKING   ARGENTINA   DOCUMENT
Registration of trademark.
JMJP 5/31/78; NCNA Peking 5/30/78; FBIS (1). 106:A29 (6/1/78).

78-80 5/30/78 — PEKING   ARGENTINA   DOCUMENT
Reciprocal exemption of maritime enterprise tax.
JMJP 5/31/78; NCNA Peking 5/30/78; FBIS (1). 106:A29 (6/1/78).

78-81 5/30/78 — PEKING   ARGENTINA   AGREEMENT
Maritime transport.
JMJP 5/31/78; PR 21. 23:4 (6/9/78); NCNA Peking 5/30/78;
FBIS (1). 106:A29 (6/1/78).

78-82 5/30/78 — PEKING   ARGENTINA   EXCHANGE OF NOTES
Establishing tax advantages to facilitate and enlarge maritime
transportation.
Buenos Aires TELAM in Spanish 5/30/78; FBIS (1). 106:A29
(6/1/78).

78-83 5/30/78 — PEKING   ARGENTINA   EXCHANGE OF NOTES
Reciprocal registry of wheat, corn, and cotton.
Buenos Aires TELAM in Spanish 5/30/78; FBIS (1). 106:A29
(6/1/78).

78-84 5/30/78 — PEKING   ARGENTINA   AGREEMENT
Establishment of long-term purchase from Argentina of 25,000
tons of cotton fiber per year between 1979 and 1980.
Buenos Aires TELAM in Spanish 5/30/78; FBIS (1). 106:A29
(6/1/78).

78-85 6/6/78 — PYONGYANG   KOREAN(N)   PROTOCOL
Scientific and technical cooperation.
Signed at eighteenth meeting of Sino-Korean Scientific and Tech-
nical Cooperation Committee.
JMJP 6/9/78; NCNA Peking 6/6/78; FBIS (1). 110:A6 (6/7/78).

78-86 6/7/78 — SANTIAGO   CHILE   AGREEMENT
Sports exchange and cooperation.
JMJP 6/12/78; NCNA Peking 6/11/78; FBIS (1). 115:A27 (6/14/78).

78-87 6/8/78 — PEKING   SPAIN   DRAFT
Civil Air Transport Agreement.
JMJP 6/10/78; NCNA Peking 6/8/78; FBIS (1). 112:A19 (6/9/78).

78-88 6/10/78 — GILGIT   PAKISTAN   AGREEMENT
Border trade.
JMJP 6/12/78; NCNA Peking 6/11/78; FBIS (1). 114:A11 (6/13/78).

78-89 6/10/78 — PEKING   RWANDA   AGREEMENT
Economic and technical cooperation.
JMJP 6/11/78; PR 21. 24:4 (6/16/78); NCNA Peking 6/10/78;
FBIS (1). 113:A29 (6/12/78).

78-90 6/13/78 — PEKING   IRAN   AGREEMENT
News cooperation between New China News Agency and Bars
News Agency (Iran).
JMJP 6/18/78; NCNA Peking 6/14/78; FBIS (1). 117:A25 (6/16/78).

78-91 6/14/78 — PEKING   FRANCE   AGREEMENT
Scientific and technical cooperation in petroleum.
AFP Paris 6/15/78; FBIS (1). 117:A21 (6/16/78).

78-92 6/18/78 — THAKOT   PAKISTAN   PROTOCOL
Handing over of the Karakoram Highway built by PRC for Pakistan.
PR 21. 27:4 (7/7/78); NCNA Peking 6/18/78; FBIS (1). 118:A16
(6/19/78).

78-93 6/19/78 — PEKING   SPAIN   AGREEMENT
Trade.
JMJP 6/20/78; PR 21. 26:3 (6/30/78); NCNA Peking 6/19/78;
FBIS (1). 118:A30 (6/19/78).

78-94 6/19/78 — PEKING   SPAIN   AGREEMENT
Civil air transport.
JMJP 6/20/78; PR 21. 26:3 (6/30/78); NCNA Peking 6/19/78;
FBIS (1). 118:A30 (6/19/78).

78-95 6/21/78 — YAOUNDE   CAMEROON   MINUTES
Talks on building a hydroelectric power station and high voltage
transmission line in Lagdo.
JMJP 6/23/78.

78-96 6/ /78 — PEKING   U. S. A.   CONTRACT
PRC accept on a regular basis, starting from January 1, 1979,
one hundred American tourists a week.
Signed between Pan American Airways and China Travel Service.
AFP Hong Kong 6/22/78; FBIS (1). 122:A9 (6/23/78).

78-97 6/28/78 — PEKING LIBERIA AGREEMENT
Economic and technical cooperation.
JMJP 6/29/78; NCNA Peking 6/28/78; FBIS (1).126:A16 (6/29/78).

78-98 6/28/78 — VIENTIANE LAOS AGREEMENT
Civil air transport.
JMJP 6/30/78; NCNA Peking 6/29/78; FBIS (1).127:A9 (6/30/78).

78-99 6/30/78 — PEKING KOREA(N) AGREEMENT
Cooperation in hydrological projects along Yalu and Tumen River.
JMJP 7/1/78; NCNA Peking 7/3/78; FBIS (1).131:A4 (7/7/78).

78-100 7/24/78 — GEORGETOWN GUYANA JOINT PRESS COM-
MUNIQUÉ
Talks during visit of Vice Premier Keng Piao: strengthening eco-
nomic, technical, and cultural cooperation.
JMJP 7/26/78; NCNA Peking 7/24/78; FBIS (1).143:A18 (7/25/78).

78-101 7/24/78 — KANGGYE CITY KOREA(N) PROTOCOL
Border railway transport.
Signed at regular meeting on Sino-Korean Border Railway Trans-
port for 1978.
JMJP 8/5/78; NCNA Peking 8/2/78; FBIS (1).150:A4 (8/3/78).

78-102 7/28/78 — PEKING JAPAN PROTOCOL
Cooperation in production of color picture tube and integrated
circuit.
JMJP 8/1/78.

78-103 7/28/78 — PEKING JAPAN CONTRACT
Cooperation in production of color picture tube and integrated
circuit.
JMJP 8/1/78.

78-104 7/31/78 — DAR ES SALAAM TANZANIA & ZAMBIA
PROTOCOL
Technical cooperation in the second phase of building Tanzania-
Zambia railway.
JMJP 8/7/78; NCNA Peking 8/1/79; FBIS (1).150:A22 (8/3/78).

78-105 7/31/78 — DAR ES SALAAM TANZANIA & ZAMBIA
PROTOCOL
Technical cooperation in building Tanzania-Zambia railway train-
ing school.
JMJP 8/7/78; NCNA Peking 8/1/78; FBIS (1).150:A22 (8/3/78).

78-106 7/31/78 — DAR ES SALAAM   TANZANIA & ZAMBIA
MINUTES
Talks on technical cooperation in building Tanzania-Zambia railway.
JMJP 8/7/78; NCNA Peking 8/1/78; FBIS (1). 150:A22 (8/3/78).

78-107 8/1/78 — BURAO   SOMALIA   PROTOCOL
Handing over of the Belet Uin-Burao highway built with PRC aid.
JMJP 8/3/78; NCNA Peking 8/1/78; FBIS (1). 150:A19 (8/3/78).

78-108 8/9/78 — PEKING   LIBYA   JOINT COMMUNIQUÉ
Establishment of diplomatic relations.
JMJP 8/10/78(C); PR 21. 33:3 (8/18/78)(E); NCNA Peking 8/9/78;
FBIS (1). 154:A18 (8/9/78)(E).

78-109 8/9/78 — PEKING   LIBYA   AGREEMENT
Economic and technical cooperation.
JMJP 8/10/78; PR 21. 33:3 (8/18/78); NCNA Peking 8/9/78;
FBIS (1). 154:A18 (8/9/78).

78-110 8/9/78 — PEKING   LIBYA   AGREEMENT
Scientific and technical cooperation.
JMJP 8/10/78; PR 21. 33:3 (8/18/78); NCNA Peking 8/9/78;
FBIS (1). 154:A18 (8/9/78).

78-111 8/9/78 — PEKING   LIBYA   AGREEMENT
Trade.
JMJP 8/10/78; PR 21. 33:3 (8/18/78); NCNA Peking 8/9/78;
FBIS (1). 154:A18 (8/9/78).

78-112 8/12/78   10/23/78*   PEKING   JAPAN   TREATY
PRC-Japan Peace and Friendship Treaty.
JMJP 8/13/78(C); PR 21. 33:6 (8/18/78)(C); NCNA Peking 8/12/78;
FBIS (1). 157:A4 (8/14/78).
*Exchange of instruments on ratification.
JMJP 10/24/78; PR 21. 43:3 (10/27/78); NCNA Peking 10/23/78;
FBIS (1). 205:A13 (10/23/78).

78-113 8/14/78 — PEKING   JAPAN   CONTRACT
Coking Coal (Contract concluded under PRC-Japan long-term
Trade Agreement (78-20).
JMJP 8/15/78; NCNA Peking 8/14/78; FBIS (1). 160:A7 (8/17/78).

78-114 8/21/78 — BUCHAREST   RUMANIA   AGREEMENT
Establishment of a committee on economic and technical cooperation.

JMJP 8/22/78; PR 21. 34:7 (8/25/78); NCNA Peking 8/21/78;
FBIS (1). 162:A19 (8/21/78).

78-115 8/21/78 — BUCHAREST RUMANIA PROTOCOL
Cooperation in production and technology.
JMJP 8/22/78; PR 21. 34:7 (8/25/78); NCNA Peking 8/21/78;
FBIS (1). 162:A19 (8/21/78).

78-116 8/21/78 — BUCHAREST RUMANIA AGREEMENT
Scientific and technical cooperation.
JMJP 8/22/78; PR 21. 34:7 (8/25/78); NCNA Peking 8/21/78;
FBIS (1). 162:A19 (8/21/78).

78-117 8/21/78 — BUCHAREST RUMANIA PROTOCOL
Exchange of engineering technicians and students.
JMJP 8/22/78; PR 21. 34:7 (8/25/78); NCNA Peking 8/21/78;
FBIS (1). 162:A19 (8/21/78).

78-118 8/21/78 — BUCHAREST RUMANIA PROTOCOL
Trade in 1979.
JMJP 8/22/78; PR 21. 34:7 (8/25/78); NCNA Peking 8/21/78;
FBIS (1). 162:A19 (8/21/78).

78-119 8/21/78 — BUCHAREST RUMANIA AGREEMENT
Cooperation in tourism.
JMJP 8/22/78; PR 21. 34:7 (8/25/78); NCNA Peking 8/21/78;
FBIS (1). 162:A19 (8/21/78).

78-120 8/21/78 — BUCHAREST RUMANIA PROTOCOL
Cooperation in animal quarantine.
JMJP 8/22/78; PR 21. 34:7 (8/25/78); NCNA Peking 8/21/78;
FBIS (1). 162:A19 (8/21/78).

78-121 8/21/78 — BUCHAREST RUMANIA PROTOCOL
Cooperation in plant quarantine.
JMJP 8/22/78; PR 21. 34:7 (8/25/78); NCNA Peking 8/21/78;
FBIS (1). 162:A19 (8/21/78).

78-122 8/21/78 — BUCHAREST RUMANIA AGREEMENT
Opening shipping routes.
JMJP 8/22/78; PR 21. 34:7 (8/25/78); NCNA Peking 8/21/78;
FBIS (1). 162:A19 (8/21/78).

78-123 8/26/78 — BELGRADE YUGOSLAVIA AGREEMENT
Establishment of a PRC-Yugoslav Committee on Economic, Sci-

entific, and Technical Cooperation.
JMJP 8/27/78; PR 21.35:4 (9/1/78); NCNA Peking 8/26/78;
FBIS (1).167:A21 (8/28/78).

78-124 8/26/78 — BELGRADE YUGOSLAVIA AGREEMENT
Long-term economic, scientific, and technical cooperation.
JMJP 8/27/78; PR 21.35:5 (9/1/78); NCNA Peking 8/26/78;
FBIS (1).167:A21 (8/28/78).

78-125 8/ /78 — PEKING JAPAN AGREEMENT
Silk trade for 1978.
NCNA Peking 8/26/78; FBIS (1).169:A4 (8/30/78).

78-126 8/31/78 — TEHRAN IRAN AGREEMENT
Cultural cooperation.
JMJP 9/1/78; PR 21.3:5 (9/8/78); NCNA Peking 8/31/78; FBIS
(1).171:A23 (9/1/78).

78-127 8/31/78 — PEKING NEPAL AGREEMENT
Civil air transport.
JMJP 9/1/78; PR 21.36:4 (9/8/78); NCNA Peking 8/31/78; FBIS
(1).170:A13 (8/31/78).

78-128 9/ /78 — PEKING U.S.A. AGREEMENT
Development of undersea oil resources.
KYODO Tokyo 9/6/78; FBIS (1).174:A2 (9/7/78).

78-129 9/12/78 — PARIS FRANCE AGREEMENT
Exchange of TV programs and further development of professional
cooperation.
JMJP 9/21/78; NCNA Peking 9/13/78; FBIS (1).181:A22 (9/18/78).

78-130 9/14/78 — PEKING TANZANIA PROTOCOL
Further development of economic and technical cooperation.
JMJP 9/15/78; PR 21.38:4 (9/22/78); NCNA Peking 9/14/78;
FBIS (1).180:A15 (9/15/78).

78-131 9/15/78 — PEKING GERMANY(W) ACCORD
Scientific cooperation between PRC Academy of Sciences and
Max Planck Institute.
JMJP 9/16/78; NCNA Peking 9/15/78; FBIS (1).181:A20 (9/18/78).

78-132 9/17/78 — PEKING NEPAL MINUTES
Border inspection.
Talks at second session of China-Nepal Border Inspection Joint

Committee.
JMJP 9/19/78; NCNA Peking 9/18/78; FBIS (1). 183:A13 (9/20/78).

78-133 9/18/78 — PEKING AUSTRALIA EXCHANGE OF NOTES
Mutual agreement on establishing consulate-general.
JMJP 9/19/78; NCNA Peking 9/18/78; FBIS (1). 183:A12 (9/20/78).

78-134 9/18/78 — PEKING YGUOSLAVIA ACCORD
Scientific cooperation between PRC Academy of Science and
Academy of Social Science and Commission of Academies of
Sciences and Arts of Yugoslavia.
JMJP 9/19/78; NCNA Peking 9/18/78; FBIS (1). 182:A19 (9/19/78).

78-135 9/20/78 — PEKING SUDAN PROTOCOL
1978-79 trade.
JMJP 9/21/78; NCNA Peking 9/20/78; FBIS (1). 184:A22 (9/21/78).

78-136 9/21/78 — KINGSTON JAMAICA CONTRACT
Supply of equipment and materials for Jamaican Cotton Polyester
Textile Company Limited to be built with PRC aid.
JMJP 10/4/78; NCNA Peking 9/22/78; FBIS (1). 187:A25 (9/26/78).

78-137 9/22/78 — ATHENS GREECE AGREEMENT
Cultural cooperation.
JMJP 9/24/78; NCNA Peking 9/23/78; FBIS (1). 186:A16 (9/25/78).

78-138 9/22/78 — PEKING GERMANY(W) PROTOCOL
PRC will conclude long-term credit transactions with firms in
FRG amounting to over DM 8 billion.
DPA in German Hamburg 9/22/78; FBIS (1). 186:A17 (9/25/78).

78-139 9/23/78 — PEKING CHAD PROTOCOL
Economic and technical cooperation.
JMJP 9/24/78; PR 21. 39:4 (9/29/78); NCNA Peking 9/23/78;
FBIS (1). 186:A24 (9/25/78).

78-140 9/23/78 — PEKING MALAYSIA COMMUNIQUÉ
Talks during visit of Foreign Minister Tengku Ahmad Rithauddeen:
ASEAN, zone of peace, freedom and neutrality in Southeast Asia,
etc.
AFP Hong Kong 9/23/78; FBIS (1). 186:A9 (9/25/78).

78-141 9/23/78 — ISLAMABAD PAKISTAN AGREEMENT
Purchase and sale of ships.
JMJP 9/26/78; NCNA Peking 9/23/78; FBIS (1). 187:A14 (9/26/78).

78-142 9/26/78 — PEKING POLAND PROTOCOL
Shipping cooperation.
Signed at fourteenth session of shareholders' meeting of Chinese-Polish Joint-Stock Shipping Company.
JMJP 9/28/78; NCNA Peking 9/27/78; FBIS (1).189:A22 (9/28/78).

78-143 9/28/78 — BRAZZAVILLE CONGO AGREEMENT
Trade.
JMJP 10/5/78; NCNA Peking 9/29/78; FBIS (1).192:A22 (10/3/78).

78-144 9/30/78 — PEKING BULGARIA PROTOCOL
Scientific and technical cooperation.
Signed at sixteenth session of Sino-Bulgaria Committee on Scientific and Technical Cooperation.
JMJP 10/2/78; NCNA Peking 9/30/78; FBIS (1).192:A19 (10/3/78).

78-145 10/1/78 — PEKING NEPAL AGREEMENT
Establishment of complete projects.
JMJP 10/2/78; PR 21.40:4 (10/6/78); NCNA Peking 10/1/78;
FBIS (1).191:A24 (10/2/78).

78-146 10/4/78 — HELSINKI FINLAND AGREEMENT
Trade in 1979.
JMJP 10/6/78; NCNA Peking 10/5/78; FBIS (1).195:A14 (10/6/78).

78-147 10/4/78 — ROME ITALY ACCORD
Cooperation in ship inspection.
JMJP 10/7/78; NCNA Peking 10/5/78; FBIS (1).195:A13 (10/6/78).

78-148 10/5/78 — PEKING WORLD HEALTH ORGANIZATION
MEMORANDUM
Cooperation in public health.
JMJP 10/7/78; NCNA Peking 10/5/78; FBIS (1).195:A2 (10/6/78).

78-149 10/5/78 — SANTIAGO CHILE ACCORD
Three-year sale of copper to PRC.
JMJP 10/7/78; NCNA Peking 10/6/78; FBIS (1).201:A25 (10/17/78).

78-150 10/5/78 — HONG KONG HONG KONG ACCORD
Charter flight between Canton and Hong Kong effective in mid-October.
JMJP 10/8/78.

78-151 10/6/78 — PEKING GERMANY(W) AGREEMENT
Television cooperation between Central Television Station of PRC

and Z. D. F. of West Germany.
PR 21.45:25 (11/10/78); DPA in German Hamburg 10/6/78;
FBIS (1).195:A11 (10/6/78).

78-152 10/6/78 — ROME ITALY AGREEMENT
Cultural cooperation.
JMJP 10/8/78; NCNA Peking 10/7/78; FBIS (1).197:A17 (10/11/78).

78-153 10/6/78 — ROME ITALY AGREEMENT
Scientific and technical cooperation.
JMJP 10/8/78; NCNA Peking 10/7/78; FBIS (1).197:A17 (10/11/78).

78-154 10/7/78 — BAMAKO MALI AGREEMENT
Trade.
JMJP 10/10/78; NCNA Peking 10/8/78; FBIS (1).197:A26 (10/11/78).

78-155 10/9/78 — PEKING ITALY AGREEMENT
News cooperation between New China News Agency and Agenzia
Nazionale Stampa Asociata of Italy.
JMJP 10/10/78; NCNA Peking 10/9/78; FBIS (1).197:A17 (10/11/78).

78-156 10/9/78 — BONN GERMANY(W) AGREEMENT
Scientific and technical cooperation.
JMJP 10/11/78; NCNA Peking 10/9/78; FBIS (1).198:A10 (10/12/78).

78-157 10/9/78 — BONN GERMANY(W) MINUTES
Talks on executing Scientific and Technical Cooperation Agreement
[78-156].
JMJP 10/11/78; NCNA Peking 10/9/78; FBIS (1).198:A11 (10/12/78).

78-158 10/19/78 — STOCKHOLM SWEDEN AGREEMENT
Cooperation in science and technology between Chinese Academy
of Sciences and Royal Swedish Academy of Engineering Sciences.
NCNA Peking 10/21/78; FBIS (1).206:A19 (10/24/78).

78-159 10/20/78 — PARIS FRANCE PROTOCOL (SUPPLE-
MENTARY)
Scientific and technical exchange.
JMJP 10/22/78; NCNA Peking 10/20/78; FBIS (1).205:A23 (10/23
(10/23/78).

78-160 10/20/78 — PARIS FRANCE ACCORD
Scientific cooperation between PRC Academy of Sciences and
French State Center of Science and Research.
JMJP 10/22/78; NCNA Peking 10/20/78; FBIS (1).205:A23
(10/23/78).

78-161 10/20/78 — RANGOON BURMA MINUTES
Talks on building state stadium in Burma.
JMJP 10/23/78; NCNA Peking 10/20/78; FBIS (1).209:A17
(10/27/78).

78-162 10/23/78 — LISBON PORTUGAL AGREEMENT
News cooperation between Hsinhua News Agency and Portuguese
News Agency (ANOP).
NCNA Peking 10/24/78; FBIS (1).208:A23 (10/26/78).

78-163 10/24/78(?) — PYONGYANG KOREA(N)
1979-80 plan for scientific cooperation between academies of
sciences.
JMJP 11/3/78; NCNA domestic service in Chinese 10/25/78;
FBIS (1).208:A16 (10/26/78).

78-164 10/27/78 — PEKING MEXICO AGREEMENT
Cultural cooperation.
JMJP 10/28/78; PR 21.44:3 (11/3/78); NCNA Peking 10/27/78;
FBIS (1).210:A22 (10/30/78).

78-165 10/27/78 — PEKING MEXICO AGREEMENT
Cooperation in tourism.
JMJP 10/28/78; PR 21.44:3 (11/3/78); NCNA Peking 10/27/78;
FBIS (1).210:A22 (10/30/78).

78-166 11/1/78 — PEKING KOREA(N) AGREEMENT
Plant quarantine and insect pest control.
JMJP 11/3/78; NCNA Peking 11/2/78; FBIS (1).214:A7 (11/3/78).

78-167 11/9/78 — BANGKOK THAILAND MINUTES
Talks on first session of Sino-Thai Joint Committee on Scientific
and Technical Cooperation.
JMJP 11/10/78; PR 21.46:4 (11/17/78); NCNA Peking 11/9/78;
FBIS (1).218:A16 (11/9/78).

78-168 11/9/78 — BANGKOK THAILAND PROTOCOL
Import and export of commodities for 1979.
JMJP 11/10/78; PR 21.46:4 (11/17/78); NCNA Peking 11/9/78;
FBIS (1).218:A16 (11/9/78).

78-169 11/9/78 — BANGKOK THAILAND PROTOCOL
Establishment of a joint trade committee.
JMJP 11/10/78; PR 21.46:4 (11/17/78); NCNA Peking 11/9/78;
FBIS (1).218:A16 (11/9/78).

78-170 11/9/78 — HONG KONG   U. S. A.   AGREEMENT
Building a chain of hotels in Peking, Shanghai, Canton, and
several other Chinese cities with around 500 million U. S. dollars.
AFP Hong Kong 11/9/78; FBIS (1). 219:A3 (11/13/78).

78-171 11/10/78 — LONDON   UNITED KINGDOM   AGREEMENT
Scientific cooperation between Chinese Academy of Sciences and
Royal Society of Britain.
NCNA Peking 11/11/78; FBIS (1). 221:A17.

78-172 11/12/78 — PEKING   HUNGARY   PROTOCOL
Scientific and technical cooperation.
Signed at seventeenth session of Sino-Hungary Committee on
Scientific and Technical Cooperation.
JMJP 11/13/78; NCNA Peking 11/12/78; FBIS (1). 220:A27
(11/14/78).

78-173 11/15/78   11/15/78   LONDON   UNITED KINGDOM   AGREE-
MENT
Scientific and technical cooperation.
JMJP 11/17/78; PR 21. 48:4 (12/1/78); British T. S. , 1979, No. 8(E);
NCNA Peking 11/15/78; FBIS (1). 222:A9 (11/16/78).

78-174 11/15/78   11/15/78   LONDON   UNITED KINGDOM   PRO-
TOCOL
Scientific and technical cooperation.
JMJP 11/17/78; British T. S. 1979, No. 9(E); NCNA Peking
11/15/78; FBIS (1). 222:A9 (11/16/78).

78-175 11/16/78 — BUCHAREST   RUMANIA   PROTOCOL
Scientific and technical cooperation.
Signed at the nineteenth session of PRC-Rumania Scientific and
Technical Cooperation Committee.
JMJP 11/25/78; NCNA Peking 11/17/78; FBIS (1). 223:A14
(11/17/78).

78-176 11/18/78 — PEKING   PHILIPPINES   AGREEMENT
Postal and parcel services.
JMJP 11/19/78.

78-177 11/18/78 — ULAN BATOR   MONGOLIA   PROTOCOL
Border railway.
Signed at 1978 annual meeting of Sino-Mongolian Border Railway
Joint Commission.
NCNA Peking 11/18/78; FBIS (1). 224:A7 (11/20/78).

78-178 11/25/78 — ULAN BATOR MONGOLIA MINUTES
Talks on changes in measures concerning nontrade payments.
JMJP 11/27/78; NCNA Peking 11/26/78; FBIS (1).228:A13
(11/27/78).

78-179 11/27/78 — THE HAGUE NETHERLANDS DRAFT
Civil Air Transport Agreement.
JMJP 11/29/78; NCNA Peking 11/27/78; FBIS (1).231:A14
(11/30/78).

78-180 11/29/78 — PEKING BANGLADESH AGREEMENT
Maritime transport.
JMJP 11/30/78; NCNA Peking 11/29/78; FBIS (1).231:A10
(11/30/78).

78-181 12/4/78 — PEKING FRANCE AGREEMENT
Seven-year cooperation on developing economic relations and
cooperation.
JMJP 12/5/78; PR 21.50:6 (12/15/78); NCNA Peking 12/4/78;
FBIS (1).233:A14 (12/4/78).

78-182 12/5/78 — PEKING SWEDEN AGREEMENT
Ten-year cooperation in industry, science, and technology.
JMJP 12/6/78; PR 21.50:6 (12/15/78); NCNA Peking 12/5/78;
FBIS (1).235:A15 (12/6/78).

78-183 12/5/78(?) — PEKING AUSTRALIA MINUTES
Exchange of data on ionosphere.
JMJP 12/6/78; NCNA Peking 12/5/78; FBIS (1).235:A13 (12/6/78).

78-184 12/6/78 — LONDON UNITED KINGDOM AGREEMENT
Seven separate "deposit facilities" between the Bank of China and
banks of the United Kingdom.
PR 21.50:6 (12/15/78); NCNA Peking 12/7/78; FBIS (1).236:A16
(12/7/78).

78-185 12/9/78 — PEKING JAPAN PROTOCOL
Arbitrating the disputes of maritime transportation between PRC
and Japan.
JMJP 12/13/78; NCNA Peking 12/9/78; FBIS (1).239:A9 (12/12/78).

78-186 12/10/78 — PEKING BANGLADESH PROTOCOL
1979 trade.
JMJP 12/11/78; NCNA Peking 12/10/78; FBIS (1).239:A13
(12/12/78).

78-187 12/15/78 — PRAGUE CZECHOSLOVAKIA PROTOCOL
Scientific and technical cooperation.
Signed at twentieth session of Sino–Czechoslovak Joint Committee
for Scientific and Technical Cooperation.
NCNA Peking 12/15/78; FBIS (1). 243:A31 (12/18/78).

78-188 12/16/78 1/1/79 PEKING U. S. A. JOINT COMMUNIQUÉ
Establishment of diplomatic relations effective 1/1/79.
JMJP 12/17/78(C); PR 21. 51:8 (12/22/78)(E); NCNA Peking
12/16/78; FBIS (1). 243:A1 (12/18/78)(E).

78-189 12/19/78 — SANAA YEMEN(N) PROTOCOL
PRC aid in building international conference hall.
JMJP 12/28/78; NCNA Peking 12/20/78; FBIS (1). 245:A31 (12/20/78).

78-190 12/20/78 — BELGRADE YUGOSLAVIA
Plan for 1979 and 1980 education and cultural cooperation.
JMJP 12/26/78; NCNA Peking 12/21/78; FBIS (1). 246:A23 (12/21/78).

78-191 12/20/78 — COLOMBO SRI LANKA PROTOCOL
Exchange of goods in 1979.
JMJP 12/26/78; NCNA Peking 12/21/78; FBIS (1). 247:A11 (12/22/78).

78-192 12/22/78 — SHANGHAI JAPAN PROTOCOL
Purchase of complete facilities for Paoshan Steel Plant in Shanghai.
JMJP 12/23/78; NCNA Peking 12/22/78; FBIS (1). 248:A9 (12/26/78).

78-193 12/23/78 — PEKING KOREA(N) PROTOCOL
Mutual supply of goods in 1979.
JMJP 12/24/78; NCNA Peking 12/23/78; FBIS (1). 249:A7 (12/27/78).

78-194 12/30/78 — KATMANDU NEPAL DOCUMENT
Handing over Hetauda cotton textiles printing and dyeing mill built
with PRC aid.
NCNA Peking 12/30/78; FBIS (1). 4:A18 (1/5/79).

1979

79-1 1/5/79 1/8/79 PARIS DJIBOUTI JOINT COMMUNIQUÉ
Establishment of diplomatic relations.

Note for 1979 and 1980 listings: Since January 1, 1979, the PRC
has used the Pinyin transcription system to romanize Chinese names,

JMJP 1/10/79; PR 22. 3:5 (1/19/79); NCNA Peking 1/9/79; FBIS (1). 6:A27 (1/9/79).

79-2　1/8/79 — PEKING　BULGARIA　AGREEMENT
1979 goods exchange and payments.
JMJP 1/10/79; NCNA Peking 1/8/79; FBIS (1). 6:A23 (1/9/79).

79-3　1/11/79 — PRAGUE　CZECHOSLOVAKIA　AGREEMENT
Goods exchange and payments in 1979.
JMJP 1/18/79; NCNA Peking 1/12/79; FBIS (1). 9:A13 (1/12/79).

79-4　1/14/79 — PEKING　THAILAND　PROTOCOL
Long-term crude oil trade.
JMJP 1/15/79; NCNA Peking 1/14/79; FBIS (1). 10:A30 (1/15/79).

79-5　1/15/79 — LUSAKA　ZAMBIA　AGREEMENT
Scientific and technical cooperation.
JMJP 1/17/79; NCNA Peking 1/16/79; FBIS (1). 11:A33 (1/16/79).

79-6　1/15/79 — CONAKRY　GUINEA　PROTOCOL
1979 trade.
NCNA Peking 1/16/79; FBIS (1). 12:A28 (1/17/79).

79-7　1/16/79 — BUDAPEST　HUNGARY　AGREEMENT
Goods exchange and payments in 1979.
JMJP 1/18/79; NCNA Peking 1/16/79; FBIS (1). 12:A22 (1/17/79).

79-8　1/16/79 — PEKING　JAPAN　EXCHANGE OF INSTRUMENTS
Amendments to China-Japan Fishery Agreement.
JMJP 11/17/79; Peking 1/16/79; FBIS (1). 12:A12 (1/17/79).

79-9　1/17/79 — PEKING　CUBA　PROTOCOL
1979 trade.
JMJP 1/19/79; NCNA Peking 1/18/79; FBIS (1). 14:A25 (1/19/79).

places, and publications. For consistent listing, however, I have continued to use the Wade-Giles system. The following is a list of the important terms in both the Wade-Giles and Pinyin system:

Conventional or Wade-Giles	Pinyin
NCNA or Hsinhua News Agency	Xinhua
Peking Review (PR)	Beijing Review (BR)
Jen-min jih-pao	Rinmin ribao
Peking	Beijing

79-10 1/19/79 — GEORGETOWN GUYANA AGREEMENT
PRC providing with interest-free commodity loan of two million
renminbi.
NCNA Peking 1/20/79; FBIS (1). 33:A19 (2/15/79).

79-11 1/20/79 — PEKING NETHERLANDS AGREEMENT
Civil air transport.
JMJP 11/21/79; NCNA Peking 1/20/79; FBIS (1). 15:A30 (1/22/79).

79-12 1/20/79 — PEKING GERMANY(E) AGREEMENT
Goods exchange and payments in 1979.
JMJP 11/21/79; NCNA Peking 1/20/79; FBIS (1). 15:A33 (1/22/79).

79-13 1/20/79 — KINSHASA ZAIRE PROTOCOL
Concerning PRC's supply of diversified commodities to Zaire.
NCNA Peking 1/20/79; FBIS (1). 15:A36 (1/22/79).

79-14 1/22/79 — WARSAW POLAND AGREEMENT
Goods exchange and payments in 1979.
JMJP 1/24/79; NCNA Peking 1/22/79; FBIS (1). 16:A22 (1/23/79).

79-15 1/29/79 — PEKING LUXEMBOURG PRESS COMMUNIQUÉ
Talks during visit of Prime Minister Gaston Thorn strengthening
economic, commercial, cultural, and personal exchange, cooperation in iron and steel industry, establishment of an Office of Diplomatic Representative in Peking, etc.
JMJP 1/30/79; PR 22. 5:6 (2/2/79); NCNA Peking 1/29/79(Chinese);
FBIS (1). 22:A25 (1/31/79).

79-16 1/31/79 1/31/79 WASHINGTON, D.C. U.S.A. AGREEMENT
Cultural cooperation.
JMJP 2/2/79; PR 22. 6:12 (2/9/79); NCNA Peking 2/1/79(Chinese);
FBIS (1). 23:A5 (2/1/79); TIAS 9178(E)(C).

79-17 1/31/79 1/31/79 WASHINGTON, D.C. U.S.A. AGREEMENT
Scientific and technological cooperation.
JMJP 2/2/79; PR 22. 6:12 (2/9/79); NCNA Peking 2/1/79; FBIS
(1). 23:A5 (2/1/79); TIAS 9179(E)(C).

79-18 2/1/79 — WASHINGTON, D.C. U.S.A. JOINT PRESS COM-
MUNIQUÉ
Talks during visit of Vice-Premier Deng Xiaoping (Teng Hsiao-
ping): hegemony, agreements on cooperation in science and technology, cultural, high energy physics, agriculture, space, etc.
JMJP 2/2/79; PR 22. 6:3 (2/9/79); NCNA Peking 2/1/79; FBIS
(1). 24:A3 (2/2/79).

79-19 2/1/79 — WASHINGTON, D.C. U.S.A. LETTERS OF
UNDERSTANDING
Cooperation in education, agriculture, and space.
JMJP 2/2/79; NCNA Peking 2/1/79; FBIS (1).24:A4 (2/2/79).

79-20 2/1/79* 2/1/79* WASHINGTON, D.C. U.S.A. ACCORD
Cooperation in high energy physics.
JMJP 2/2/79; NCNA Peking 2/1/79; FBIS (1).24:A4 (2/2/79).
*DSB 79.2024:68 (March 1979) reported the date as 1/31/79.

79-21 2/1/79 — WASHINGTON, D.C. U.S.A. AGREEMENT
Mutual establishment of consular relations and opening of con-
sulates general.
JMJP 2/2/79; NCNA Peking 2/1/79; FBIS (1).24:A4 (2/2/79).

79-22 2/6/79 — PEKING JAPAN EXCHANGE OF NOTES
Agreement providing for Japanese technical cooperation in modern-
izing PRC's railway system.
KYODO Tokyo 2/6/79; FBIS (1).27:A10 (2/7/79).

79-23 2/6/79 — SINUIJU KOREA(N) AGREEMENT
Border river transport.
Signed at eighteenth meeting of PRC-Korea Committee for Co-
operation in Border River Transport.
JMJP 2/9/79; NCNA Peking 2/7/79; FBIS (1).27:A11 (2/7/79).

79-24 2/8/79 2/8/79 PARIS PORTUGAL JOINT COMMUNIQUÉ
Establishment of diplomatic relations.
JMJP 2/9/79; PR 22.7:3 (2/16/79); NCNA Peking 2/8/79; FBIS
(1).28:A12 (2/8/79).

79-25 2/24/79 — PEKING YUGOSLAVIA PROTOCOL
Scientific and technical cooperation in 1979.
JMJP 2/25/79; NCNA Peking 2/24/79; FBIS (1).40:A24 (2/27/79).

79-26 2/27/79 — KATMANDU NEPAL NOTES
Boundary inspection.
Signed at third session of Nepal-China Boundary Joint Inspection
Committee.
JMJP 3/1/79; NCNA Peking 2/27/79; FBIS (1).42:A14 (3/1/79).

79-27 3/2/79 — PEKING YUGOSLAVIA AGREEMENT
Scientific and technological cooperation.
JMJP 3/3/79; NCNA Peking 3/2/79; FBIS (1).44:A27 (3/5/79).

79-28 3/2/79 — PEKING   YUGOSLAVIA   AGREEMENT
Cooperation in veterinary science.
JMJP 3/3/79; NCNA Peking 3/2/79; FBIS (1). 44:A27 (3/5/79).

79-29 3/2/79 — PEKING   YUGOSLAVIA   PROTOCOL
Economic, scientific, and technological cooperation.
Signed at first meeting of Sino-Yugoslavian Joint Committee for
Economical, Scientific, and Technological Cooperation.
JMJP 3/3/79; NCNA Peking 3/2/79; FBIS (1). 44:A27 (3/5/79).

79-30 3/4/79 3/4/79 PEKING U.K.   AGREEMENT
Economic cooperation.
JMJP 3/5/79; NCNA Peking 3/4/79; FBIS (1). 44:A25 (3/5/79);
British Treaty Series, 1979, no. 61(E).

79-31 3/9/79 — NIAMEY   NIGER   DOCUMENT
Handing over of Niger Kolo Agricultural Project built with PRC
aid.
NCNA Peking 3/10/79; FBIS (1). 58:I7 (3/23/79).

79-32 3/14/79 — PEKING   JAPAN   AGREEMENT
Friendship between cities of Peking and Tokyo.
NCNA Peking 3/14/79; FBIS (1). 52:A4 (3/15/79).

79-33 3/19/79 — PEKING   BURUNDI   AGREEMENT
Economic and technical cooperation.
NCNA Peking 3/19/79; FBIS (1). 55:I8 (3/20/79).

79-34 3/27/79(?) — BLAGOVESHCHENSK U.S.S.R.   MINUTES
Talks on twenty-first regular meeting of Sino-Soviet Joint Com-
mission for Boundary River Navigation.
JMJP 3/27/79; NCNA Peking 3/27/79; FBIS (1). 62:C1 (3/29/79).

79-35 3/29/79 — DACCA   BANGLADESH   PROTOCOL
Scientific and technical cooperation.
JMJP 3/31/79; NCNA Peking 3/29/79; FBIS (1). 63:F1 (3/30/79).

79-36 3/29/79 — TOKYO   JAPAN   MINUTES
Talks on long-term Trade Agreement [78-20].
JMJP 3/30/79; PR 22. 14:2 (4/6/79); Peking 3/29/79; FBIS
(1). 63:D1 (3/30/79).

79-37 4/14/79 — PEKING   CHILE   AGREEMENT (VERBAL)
Cooperation in exploration of subsoil of Antarctic and possible
exploitation of minerals and other resources discovered.
AFP Paris 4/14/79; FBIS (1). 75:J1 (4/17/79).

79-38 4/19/79 — PEKING EGYPT PROTOCOL
1979 trade.
JMJP 4/20/79; NCNA Peking 4/19/79; FBIS (1). 80:I1 (4/24/79).

79-39 4/23/79 — ROME ITALY AGREEMENT
Economic cooperation.
JMJP 4/24/79; NCNA Peking 4/23/79; FBIS (1). 80:G2 (4/24/79).

79-40 5/1/79 — PEKING EGYPT PROGRAM
An executive program of cultural cooperation for 1979-81.
JMJP 5/2/79; NCNA Peking 5/1/79; FBIS (1). 86:I1 (5/2/79).

79-41 5/2/79 — PEKING FRANCE MINUTES
Talks on scientific and technical cooperation and exchange in
metrology.
JMJP 5/8/79; NCNA Peking 5/2/79; FBIS (1). 87:G1 (5/3/79).

79-42 5/2/79 — DAKA SENEGAL DOCUMENT
Handing over of agricultural projects to Senegal built with PRC
aid.
NCNA Peking 5/3/79; FBIS (1). 97:I4 (5/17/79).

79-43 5/8/79 — PEKING U.S.A. PROTOCOL
Cooperation in fields of management in science and technology
and scientific and technical information.
JMJP 5/9/79; PR 22. 20:2 (5/18/79); NCNA Peking 5/8/79;
FBIS (1). 91:B1 (5/9/79).

79-44 5/8/79 — MANILA PHILIPPINES AGREEMENT (DRAFT)
Civil air transport.
JMJP 5/9/79; NCNA Peking 5/8/79; FBIS (1). 92:E6 (5/10/79).

79-45 5/8/79 — PEKING U.S.A. PROTOCOL
Cooperation in field of atmospheric science and technology.
JMJP 5/9/79; PR 22. 20:2 (5/18/79); NCNA Peking 5/8/79;
FBIS (1). 91:B1 (5/9/79).

79-46 5/8/79 — PEKING U.S.A. PROTOCOL
Cooperation in field of metrology and standards.
JMJP 5/9/79; PR 22. 20:2 (5/18/79); NCNA Peking 5/8/79;
FBIS (1). 91:B1 (5/9/79).

79-47 5/8/79 — PEKING U.S.A. PROTOCOL
Cooperation in fishery and marine science and technology.
JMJP 5/9/79; PR 22. 20:2 (5/18/79); NCNA Peking 5/8/79;
FBIS (1). 91:B1 (5/9/79).

79-48 5/10/79 — PEKING   U. S. A.   AGREEMENT
Trade exhibition in 1980.
JMJP 5/11/79; PR 22. 20:2 (5/18/79); NCNA Peking 5/10/79;
FBIS (1). 93:B1 (5/11/79); TIAS 9470(E)(C).

79-49 5/11/79 — MISSION TOVE(?)   TOGO   DOCUMENT
Handing over of agrotechnical cooperation projects built with PRC
aid.
JMJP 5/13/79; NCNA Peking 5/12/79; FBIS (1). 95:I3 (5/15/79).

79-50 5/11/79 5/1/79 PEKING   U. S. A.   AGREEMENT
Settlement of claims on assets.
JMJP 5/12/79; PR 22. 20:2 (5/18/79); NCNA Peking 5/10/79.

79-51 5/12/79 — PEKING   JORDAN   AGREEMENT
Trade.
JMJP 5/14/79; NCNA Peking 5/12/79; FBIS (1). 95:I1 (5/15/79);
FBIS (1). 93:B2 (5/11/79); TIAS 9306(E)(C).

79-52 5/14/79 — PEKING   U. S. A.   DRAFT
Agreement on Trade Relations.
JMJP 5/15/79; PR 22. 20:2 (5/18/79); NCNA Peking 5/14/79;
FBIS (1). 95:B1 (5/15/79) [See also 79-77].

79-53 5/14/79 — PEKING   ITALY   AGREEMENT
Scientific cooperation between Chinese Academy of Sciences and
Italian National Research Committee.
JMJP 5/15/79; NCNA Peking 5/14/79; FBIS (1). 96:G4 (5/16/79).

79-54 5/15/79 — TOKYO   JAPAN   AGREEMENT
Credit to PRC for development of oil and coal resources and
export to Japan by Export-Import Bank of Japan.
JMJP 5/16/79; NCNA Peking 5/15/79; FBIS (1). 96:D7 (5/16/79).

79-55 5/16/79 — MONROVIA   LIBERIA   AGREEMENT
Trade.
JMJP 5/18/79; NCNA Peking 5/17/79; FBIS (1). 97:I3 (5/17/79).

79-56 5/17/79 — PEKING   TUNISIA   AGREEMENT
Trade.
JMJP 5/18/79; NCNA Peking 5/17/79; FBIS (1). 98:I2 (5/18/79).

79-57 5/19/79 — PEKING   CANADA   AGREEMENT (IN PRINCIPLE)
Extend credit of 200 million Canadian dollars (230 million U. S.
dollars) to PRC to cover purchases of Canadian goods and services.
AFP Paris 5/19/79; FBIS (1). 99:J1 (5/21/79).

79-58 5/19/79 — PEKING ALGERIA AGREEMENT
Long-term trade.
JMJP 5/20/79; NCNA Peking 5/19/79; FBIS (1).100:I2 (5/22/79).

79-59 5/22/79 — PEKING RUMANIA PROTOCOL
Economic and technical cooperation.
Signed at first meeting of Economic and Technical Cooperation
Committee between PRC and Rumania.
JMJP 5/23/79; NCNA Peking 5/22/79; FBIS (1).101:H2 (5/23/79).

79-60 5/22/79 — BRASILIA BRAZIL AGREEMENT
Maritime transport.
JMJP 5/24/79; NCNA Peking 5/23/79; FBIS (1).101:J2 (5/23/79).

79-61 5/24/79 — PEKING MALI PROTOCOL
Economic and technical cooperation.
JMJP 5/25/79; NCNA Peking 5/24/79; FBIS (1).103:I2 (5/25/79).

79-62 5/26/79 — PEKING JAPAN PROTOCOL
Increasing weekly flights and expanding civil air routes to Hangzhou
and Nagasaki.
KYODO Tokyo 5/26/79; FBIS (1).108:D2 (6/4/79).

79-63 5/29/79 — HELSINKI FINLAND AGREEMENT
Economic, industrial, scientific, and technical cooperation.
JMJP 5/31/79; NCNA Peking 5/29/79; FBIS (1).105:G1 (5/30/79).

79-64 6/6/79 — PEKING AUSTRALIA DRAFT
Scientific and technical cooperation.
JMJP 6/7/79; NCNA Peking 6/6/79; FBIS (1).111:E5 (6/7/79).

79-65 6/11/79 — PEKING GERMANY(W) PROTOCOL
Scientific and technical cooperation between Chinese Academy of
Sciences and Foaunhofer Society for Advancement of Research in
Applied Sciences of FRG.
JMJP 6/12/79; NCNA Peking 4/11/79; FBIS (1).115:G1 (6/13/79).

79-66 6/19/79 — PEKING GERMANY(W) AGREEMENT
Cooperation in field of geological science and technology between
Chinese State Geological Bureau and Federal Ministry of Eco-
nomics of FRG.
JMJP 6/20/79; NCNA Peking 6/19/79; FBIS (1).121:G2 (6/21/79).

79-67 6/19/79 — SKOPLJE CITY YUGOSLAVIA PLAN
1979-80 radio and TV implementation plan.
JMJP 6/22/79; NCNA Peking 6/21/79; FBIS (1).122:H1 (6/22/79).

79-68   6/19/79 — SKOPLJE CITY   YUGOSLAVIA   AGREEMENT
Radio and TV cooperation.
JMJP 6/22/79; NCNA Peking 6/21/79; FBIS (1). 122:H1 (6/22/79).

79-69   6/22/79 — PEKING   U. S. A.   PROTOCOL
Scientific and technical cooperation in medical and public health.
JMJP 6/23/79; NCNA Peking 6/22/79; FBIS (1). 123:B1 (6/25/79).

79-70   6/22/79 — NEW YORK   IRELAND   JOINT COMMUNIQUÉ
Establishment of diplomatic relations.
JMJP 6/24/79; PR 22. 26:7 (6/29/79); NCNA Peking 6/23/79;
FBIS (1). 124:G1 (6/26/79)(E).

79-71   6/27/79 — PEKING   BELGIUM-LUXEMBOURG ECONOMIC
UNION   DRAFT
Agreement on Development of Economic, Industrial, and Scientific
and Technical Cooperation.
JMJP 7/5/79; NCNA Peking 6/28/79; FBIS (1). 134:G1 (7/11/79).

79-72   6/27/79 — PEKING   BELGIUM-LUXEMBOURG ECONOMIC
UNION   PROTOCOL (DRAFT)
Cooperation in economy, industry, and technology.
JMJP 7/5/79; NCNA Peking 6/28/79; FBIS (1). 134:G1 (7/11/79).

79-73   6/27/79 — PEKING   BELGIUM-LUXEMBOURG ECONOMIC
UNION   PROTOCOL (DRAFT)
Cooperation in science and technology.
JMJP 7/5/79; NCNA Peking 6/28/79; FBIS (1). 134:G1 (7/11/79).

79-74   7/6/79 — PARIS   FRANCE   PROTOCOL
Establishment of a joint working committee and on sports exchange.
NCNA Peking 7/8/79; FBIS (1). 132:G1 (7/9/79).

79-75   7/7/79   2/1/80*   PEKING   U. S. A.   AGREEMENT
Trade relations.
JMJP 7/8/79; GRGGG 1980. 1:13 (3/8/80)(C); PR 22. 28:2 (7/13/79);
NCNA Peking 7/7/79; FBIS (1). 132:B1 (7/9/79); TIAS 9630;
*GRGGG 1980. 1:18(C); JMJP 2/2/80.

79-76   7/8/79 — PEKING   PHILIPPINES   AGREEMENT
Long-term trade.
JMJP 7/9/79; PR 22. 28:2 (7/13/79); NCNA Peking 7/8/79; FBIS
(1). 132:E10 (7/9/79).

79-77 7/8/79 — PEKING PHILIPPINES AGREEMENT
Cultural cooperation.
JMJP 7/9/79; PR 22.28:2 (7/13/79); NCNA Peking 7/8/79;
FBIS (1).132:E10 (7/9/79).

79-78 7/8/79 — PEKING PHILIPPINES AGREEMENT
Civil air transport.
JMJP 7/9/79; PR 22.28:2 (7/13/79); NCNA Peking 7/8/79;
FBIS (1).132:E10 (7/9/79).

79-79 7/8/79 — PEKING PHILIPPINES MEMORANDUM
Understanding on cooperative construction of tourist hotels.
JMJP 7/9/79; PR 22.28:2 (7/13/79); NCNA Peking 7/8/79;
FBIS (1).132:E10 (7/9/79).

79-80 7/8/79 — HANGCHOW (HANGZHOU IN PINYIN) FRANCE
AGREEMENT
Standardization cooperation between Bureau of Standards of China
and Commission of Standardization of France.
JMJP 7/16/79; NCNA Peking 7/8/79; FBIS (1).132:G1 (7/9/79).

79-81 7/8/79 — HANCHOW FRANCE PROTOCOL
1979-80 standardization cooperation.
NCNA Peking 7/8/79; FBIS (1).132:G1 (7/9/79).

79-82 7/12/79 — PEKING BURMA AGREEMENT
Economic and technical cooperation.
JMJP 7/13/79; PR 22.29:4 (7/20/79); NCNA Peking 7/12/79;
FBIS (1).136:E8 (7/13/79).

79-83 7/18/79 — PEKING EUROPEAN ECONOMIC COMMUNITY
DRAFT
Shipment of Chinese textiles to EEC.
AFP Hong Kong 7/18/79; FBIS (1).140:G1 (7/19/79).

79-84 7/22/79 — PEKING FRANCE MEMORANDUM
Listing thirteen projects being negotiated with PRC.
AFP Paris 7/22/79; FBIS (1).142:G1 (7/23/79).

79-85 7/25/79 — PEKING PAKISTAN EXCHANGE OF LETTERS
Agreement on Reciprocal Registration of Trademark.
JMJP 7/27/79; NCNA Peking 7/26/79; FBIS (1).146:F2 (7/27/79).

79-86 8/6/79 — MOSCOW U.S.S.R. AGREEMENT
Goods exchange and payment for 1979.
JMJP 8/8/79; NCNA Peking 8/6/79; FBIS (1).153:C1 (8/7/79).

79-87 8/6/79 — PEKING ITALY AGREEMENT
Chinese manpower will be made available for civil engineering
projects abroad.
AFP Hong Kong 8/6/79; FBIS (1).153:G1 (8/7/79).

79-88 8/6/79 — KHARTOUM SUDAN PROTOCOL
1979-80 trade.
NCNA Peking 8/6/79; FBIS (1).155:I3 (8/9/79).

79-89 8/10/79 — UBN KAATAR MONGOLIA PROTOCOL
Mutual supply of goods for 1979.
JMJP 8/13/79; NCNA Peking 8/11/79; FBIS (1).157:D4 (8/13/79).

79-90 8/15/79 — BELGRADE YUGOSLAVIA AGREEMENT
Exchange of news items and cooperation between Hsinhua.
[Xinhua in Pinyin] News Agency and Yugoslav Telegraph Agency.
JMJP 8/17/79; NCNA Peking 8/16/79; FBIS (1).161:H2 (8/17/79).

79-91 8/16/79 — DAR ES SALAAM TANZANIA PROTOCOL
Signed at thirteenth meeting of board of Directors of Chinese-
Tanzanian Joint Shipping Company.
JMJP 8/23/79; NCNA Peking 8/17/79; FBIS (1).163:I1 (8/21/79).

79-92 8/17/79 — PEKING FRANCE AGREEMENT (PRELIMINARY)
Exchange of information and opening way to negotiations on mutual
copyright recognition.
AFP Paris 8/18/79; FBIS (1).169:G2 (8/29/79).

79-93 8/18/79 — BUCHAREST ROMANIA AGREEMENT
Cooperation between Hsinhua [Xinhua in Pinyin] News Agency and
Romanian news agency (AGERPRES).
JMJP 8/19/79; NCNA Peking 8/18/79; FBIS (1).162:H1 (8/20/79).

79-94 8/18/79 — SANA YEMEN (YAR) CONTRACT
Designing road construction in urban areas of Sana.
JMJP 8/23/79; NCNA Peking 8/19/79; FBIS (1).163:I2 (8/21/79).

79-95 8/28/79 — PEKING U.S.A. PROTOCOL
Cooperation in hydroelectric power and related water resource
management.
JMJP 8/29/79; NCNA Peking 8/28/79; FBIS (1).168:B8 (8/28/79).

79-96 8/28/79 — PEKING U.S.A. ACCORD (IMPLEMENTATION)
Cultural exchange in 1980 and 1981.
JMJP 8/29/79; NCNA Peking 8/28/79; FBIS (1).168:B8 (8/28/79).

79-97 8/28/79 — SHENYANG KOREA(N) PROTOCOL
Border railway transport for 1979.
Signed at regular meeting of Sino-Korean Border Railway Transport.
JMJP 8/29/79; NCNA Peking 8/28/79; FBIS (1).169:D1 (8/29/79).

79-98 9/3/79 — PEKING NEPAL NOTES
Boundary inspection.
Signed at fourth session of China-Nepal Joint Boundary Inspection
Committee.
JMJP 9/6/79; NCNA Peking 9/5/79; FBIS (1).176:F1 (9/10/79).

79-99 9/5/79 — BUCHAREST RUMANIA AGREEMENT
Cooperation in building a coking plant in Huo County, China's
Shanxi Province.
JMJP 9/7/79; NCNA Peking 9/6/79; FBIS (1).175:H1 (9/7/79).

79-100 9/14/79 — PEKING DENMARK AGREEMENT
Economic and technical cooperation.
JMJP 9/15/79; NCNA Peking 9/14/79; FBIS (1).181:G1 (9/17/79).

79-101 9/17/79 — TOKYO JAPAN MEMORANDUM
Science exchange between Academy of Sciences of PRC and
Japanese Society for Promotion of Science.
JMJP 9/17/79; NCNA Peking 9/17/79; FBIS (1).182:D1 (9/18/79).

79-102 9/25/79 — RABAT MOROCCO PROTOCOL
Sending of medical team by PRC to Morocco.
JMJP 9/27/79; NCNA Peking 9/26/79; FBIS (1).190:I1 (9/28/79).

79-103 9/28/79 — HOHHOT MONGOLIA PROTOCOL
Border railway.
Signed at 1979 annual meeting of Sino-Mongolian Border Railway
Joint Commission.
JMJP 10/2/79; NCNA Peking 9/29/79; FBIS (1).194:D5 (10/4/79).

79-104 10/8/79 — THE HAGUE NETHERLANDS DECLARATION
OF INTENT
Development of agricultural cooperation.
JMJP 10/10/79; NCNA Peking 10/8/79; FBIS (1).197:G7 (10/10/79).

79-105 10/9/79 — PEKING FRANCE CONTRACT
Turbo generators for new 600-megawatt thermal electrical plant
in Yuan Broshan with French aid.
AFP Paris 10/9/79; FBIS (1).202:G9 (10/17/79).

79-106 10/10/79 — BAGHDAD IRAQ AGREEMENT
Information cooperation between New China News Agency and
Iraqi News Agency.
JMJP 10/11/79; NCNA Peking 10/10/79; FBIS (1). 199:I2 (10/12/79).

79-107 10/15/79 — — HONG KONG AGREEMENT
Joint venture construction project in Guangzhou by Chrysobesyl.
River Development Ltd. , Hong Kong and Guangzhou authorities.
NCNA Peking 11/21/79; FBIS (1). 232:E5 (11/30/79).

79-108 10/19/79 — ROME ITALY
1980-81 program of cultural, scientific, and technical cooperation.
JMJP 10/23/79; PR 22:45:13; NCNA Peking 10/20/79; FBIS
(1). 210:G9 (10/29/79).

79-109 10/19/79 — BANGKOK THAILAND PROTOCOL
Importation and exportation of commodities in 1980.
JMJP 10/23/79; NCNA Peking 10/19/79; FBIS (1). 205:E11
(10/22/79).

79-110 10/20/79 — PEKING PHILIPPINES PROTOCOL
Scientific and technical cooperation.
Signed at second meeting on scientific and technical cooperation.
JMJP 10/21/79; NCNA Peking 10/20/79; FBIS (1). 209:E5 (10/26/79).

79-111 10/24/79 — BONN GERMANY(W) AGREEMENT
Economic cooperation.
JMJP 10/26/79; PR 22. 44:9 (11/2/79); NCNA Peking (10/25/79);
FBIS (1). 208:G1 (10/25/79).

79-112 10/24/79 — BONN GERMANY(W) AGREEMENT
Cultural cooperation.
JMJP 10/26/79; PR 22. 44:9 (11/2/79); NCNA Peking 10/25/79;
FBIS (1). 208:G1 (10/25/79).

79-113 10/24/79 — BONN GERMANY(W) AGREEMENT
Mutual establishment of a consulate-general in Hamburg and
Shanghai.
JMJP 10/26/79; PR 22. 44:9 (11/2/79); NCNA Peking 10/25/79;
FBIS (1). 208:G1 (10/25/79).

79-114 10/26/79 — PEKING FINLAND AGREEMENT
1980 trade.
JMJP 10/29/79; NCNA Peking 10/27/79; FBIS (1). 211:G4
(10/30/79).

79-115 10/29/79 — BANJUL GAMBIA PROTOCOL
Dispatch of a Chinese medical team to Gambia.
JMJP 11/5/79; NCNA Peking 10/30/79; FBIS (1). 212:I2 (10/31/79).

79-116 10/29/79 — BRANNSCHWEIG GERMANY(W) AGREEMENT
Technical cooperation in weights and measures.
JMJP 11/5/79; NCNA Peking 10/29/79; FBIS (1). 211:G4 (10/30/79).

79-117 10/31/79 — WUHAN U. S. A. PROTOCOL
Establishing friendly relations between Hupeh [Hubei in Pinyin]
Province and Ohio State.
JMJP 11/3/79; NCNA Peking 10/3/79; 11/2/79; FBIS (1). 213:B1
(11/9/79); FBIS (1). 216:B1 (11/6/79)(E).

79-118 11/11/79(?) — PEKING(?) U. N. HIGH COMMISSION FOR
REFUGEES AGREEMENT
18 million aid program for integration into southern China of
more than 250,000 refugees from Vietnam.
AFP Hong Kong 11/11/79; FBIS (1). 221:A3 (11/14/79).

79-119 11/12/79 — SOFIA BULGARIA PROTOCOL
Scientific and technical cooperation.
Signed at seventeenth meeting of Commission for Scientific and
Technical Cooperation.
JMJP 11/15/79; NCNA Peking 11/12/79; FBIS (1). 222:H1 (11/15/79).

79-120 11/15/79 — PEKING GREECE AGREEMENT
Scientific and technological cooperation.
JMJP 11/16/79; NCNA Peking 11/15/79; FBIS (1). 223:G3 (11/16/79).

79-121 11/17/79 — PEKING BANGLADESH AGREEMENT
Cultural cooperation.
JMJP 11/18/79; NCNA Peking 11/17/79; FBIS (1). 224:F1 (11/19/79).

79-122 11/20/79 — KATMANDU NEPAL PROTOCOL
Joint border inspection.
JMJP 11/21/79; PR 22. 48:2 (11/30/79); NCNA Peking 11/20/79;
FBIS (1). 226:F1 (11/21/79).

79-123 11/24/79 — PEKING GERMANY(W) AGREEMENT
Cooperation in broadcasting and television between Central Broadcasting Administration of PRC and the Broadcasting Association
of FRG.
NCNA Peking 11/9/79; FBIS (1). 232:G3 (11/30/79).

79-124 11/26/79 — DAMASCUS SYRIA AGREEMENT
Sports cooperation.
JMJP 12/3/79; NCNA Peking 11/29/79; FBIS (1). 236:I7 (12/6/79).

79-125 11/28/79 — MELBOURNE AUSTRALIA EXCHANGE OF
LETTERS
Establishment of official links of friendship between Kiangsu
[Jiangsu in Pinyin] Province of PRC and Victorian State of the
Commonwealth of Australia.
JMJP 11/29/79; NCNA Peking 11/28/79; FBIS (1). 232:E5 (11/30/79).

79-126 12/5/79 — SYDNEY AUSTRALIA JOINT STATEMENT
Friendly cooperation between Kwangtung [Guangdong in Pinyin]
Province of PRC and New South Wales State of Australia.
JMJP 12/7/79; NCNA Peking 12/5/79; FBIS (1). 241:E7 (12/13/79).

79-127 12/11/79 — PEKING DJIBOUTI AGREEMENT
Economic and technical cooperation.
JMJP 12/12/79; NCNA Peking 12/11/79; FBIS (1). 241:I5 (12/13/79).

79-128 12/13/79 — PEKING CZECHOSLOVAKIA PROTOCOL
Scientific and technical cooperation.
Signed at twenty-first session of Sino-Czechoslovak Joint Commis-
sion for Scientific and Technical Cooperation.
NCNA Peking 12/13/79; FBIS (1). 242:H1 (12/14/79).

79-129 12/15/79 — PEKING FRANCE PROTOCOL (MINUTES?)
Affirmed achievements so far in scientific and technical coopera-
tion and reviewed prospects for development of such cooperation.
JMJP 12/16/79; NCNA Peking 12/15/79; FBIS (1). 243:G1 (12/17/79).

79-130 12/15/79 — PEKING FRANCE AGREEMENT
Scientific and technical cooperation in geological sphere.
JMJP 12/16/79; NCNA Peking 12/15/79; FBIS (1). 243:G1 (12/17/79).

79-131 12/19/79 — CAIRO EGYPT AGREEMENT
Scientific cooperation.
JMJP 12/21/79; NCNA Peking 12/20/79; FBIS (1). 247:I1 (12/21/79).

79-132 12/21/79 — BUDAPEST HUNGARY PROTOCOL
Scientific and technical cooperation.
Signed at eighteenth meeting of Sino-Hungarian Committee for
Scientific and Technical Cooperation.
JMJP 12/25/79; NCNA Peking 12/21/79; FBIS (1). 01:H3 (1/2/80).

79-133 12/21/79(?) — PEKING GERMANY(W) AGREEMENT
Providing a complete set of agricultural machinery for a modern
farm in Ningxia Hui Autonomous Region by Germany.
NCNA Peking 12/21/79; FBIS (1). 006:G1 (1/9/80).

79-134 12/22/79 — PEKING FRANCE ACCORD
Promotion of joint ventures.
NCNA Peking 12/22/79; FBIS (1). 06:G1 (1/9/80)(E. Sum).

79-135 12/24/79 1/2/80 NEW YORK ECUADOR JOINT COM-
MUNIQUÉ
Establishment of diplomatic relations.
PR 23. 1:4 (1/7/80); NCNA Peking 12/26/70; FBIS (1). 250:J1
(12/27/79).

79-136 12/26/79 12/9/79 PEKING YEMEN ACCORD
Transformation and expansion of the San'a' textile factory.
NCNA Peking 12/26/79; FBIS (1). 01:I3 (1/2/80).

79-137 12/27/79 — PEKING GERMANY(W) AGREEMENT
Compensation trade agreement.
NCNA Peking 12/27/79; FBIS (1). 08:G1 (1/11/80).

79-138 12/29/79 — PEKING SINGAPORE AGREEMENT
Trade Agreement—reciprocal most-favored-nation status.
NCNA Peking 12/29/79; FBIS . 08:E4 (1/11/80).

<u>1980</u>

80-1 1/2/80 — BRAZZAVILLE CONGO AGREEMENT
Technical cooperation on boat-building in Congo.
NCNA Peking 1/2/80; FBIS (1). 23:I4 (2/1/80).

80-2 1/3/80 — BANGKOK THAILAND AGREEMENT
Oil supply contract.
NCNA Peking 1/3/80; FBIS (1). 03:E3 (1/4/80).

80-3 1/5/80 (December?) — PEKING U. S. S. R. CONTRACT(?)
Purchase of Soviet transport planes, helicopters.
AFP: Hong Kong (1/6/80); FBIS (1). 04:C8 (1/7/80).

80-4 1/18/80 — PEKING JAPAN AGREEMENT
Establishment of joint economic council.
Tokyo: Kyodo 1/18/80; FBIS (1). 14:D3 (1/21/80).

80-5   1/18/80 — COLOMBO   SRI LANKA   AGREEMENT
Economic and technical cooperation.
NCNA Peking 1/18/80; FBIS (1). 18:F5 (1/25/80)(E. Sum).

80-6   1/19/80 — PEKING   JAPAN   AGREEMENT
Soybean trade.
NCNA Peking 1/19/80; FBIS (1). 16:D6 (1/23/80)(E. Sum).

80-7   1/19/80 — PEKING   JAPAN   PROTOCOL
Purchasing machinery.
JMJP 1/21/80; NCNA Peking 1/19/80; FBIS (1). 16:D6 (1/23/80).
(E. Sum).

80-8   1/19/80 — PEKING   JAPAN   ACCORD
Cooperation in land reclamation.
JMJP 1/21/80; NCNA Peking 1/19/80; FBIS (1). 16:D6 (1/23/80)
(E. Sum).

80-9   1/19/80 — PEKING   JAPAN   ACCORD
Loan.
JMJP 1/21/80; NCNA Peking 1/19/80; FBIS (1). 16:D6 (1/23/80)
(E. Sum).

80-10   1/22/80 — PEKING   JAPAN   AGREEMENT
Trade and economic cooperation.
NCNA Peking 1/22/80; FBIS (1). 16:D3 (1/23/80).

80-11   1/24/80 — PEKING   U.S.A.   PROTOCOL
Scientific and technological cooperation in earth sciences.
JMJP 1/25/80; NCNA Peking 1/24/80; FBIS (1). 17:B1 (1/24/80).

80-12   1/24/80 — PEKING   U.S.A.   PROTOCOL
Scientific and technological cooperation in earthquake studies.
JMJP 1/25/80; NCNA Peking 1/24/80; FBIS (1). 17:B1 (1/24/80).

80-13   1/24/80 — PEKING   U.S.A.   ACCORD
Conference report on First Meeting of the Joint Committee on
Sino-American Scientific & Technological Cooperation.
JMJP 1/25/80; NCNA Peking 1/24/80; FBIS (1). 17:B1 (1/24/80).

80-14   1/24/80 — PEKING   U.S.A.   DOCUMENT
Cooperation in agriculture.
JMJP 1/25/80; NCNA Peking 1/24/80; FBIS (1). 17:B1
(1/24/80).

80-15   1/24/80 — PEKING   U. S. A.   MEMORANDUM
Understanding between Chinese and American academies of
sciences.
JMJP 1/25/80; NCNA Peking 1/24/80; FBIS (1). 17:B1 (1/24/80).

80-16   1/24/80 — PEKING   U. S. A.   MEMORANDUM
Understanding on establishing land resource satellite ground
station in China.
JMJP 1/25/80; NCNA Peking 1/24/80; FBIS (1).17:B1 (1/24/80).

80-17   1/28/80 — SHENYANG   KOREA(N)   ACCORD
Nineteenth Meeting of Committee on Cooperation in Border River
Transport.
JMJP 1/30/80; NCNA Peking 1/28/80; FBIS (1). 20:D1 (1/29/80).

80-18   1/29/80 — SHANGHAI   U. S. A.   AGREEMENT
Freight service.
NCNA Peking 1/29/80; FBIS (1). 28:B1 (2/8/80).

80-19   1/30/80 — PEKING   NORWAY   AGREEMENT
Export credit.
NCNA Peking 1/30/80; FBIS (1). 25:G1 (2/5/80).

80-20   1/31/80 — SAN FRANCISCO   U. S. A.   AGREEMENT
Sister-city relations between Shanghai and San Francisco.
Shanghai City Service 1/31/80; FBIS (1). 40:B4 (2/27/80).

80-21   2/1/80 — VALLETTA   MALTA   AGREEMENT
Exchange of information and material on the development of
tourism.
NCNA Peking 2/1/80; FBIS (1). 24:G1 (2/4/80).

80-22   2/1/80 — PEKING   JAPAN   AGREEMENT
Exchange of consuls-general.
NCNA Peking 2/1/80; FBIS (1). 23:D2 (2/1/80).

80-23   2/1/80 — PEKING   U. S. A.   AGREEMENT
Trade Agreement (including the granting of most-favored-nation
status).
NCNA Peking 2/1/80; FBIS (1). 23:B1 (2/1/80)(E. Sum).

80-24   2/5/80 — PEKING   U. S. A.   PROTOCOL
Scientific and technical cooperation between Chinese State Council
and U. S. Environmental Protection Agency concerning environmental protection.

JMJP 2/6/80; NCNA Peking 2/5/80; FBIS (1).27:B8 (2/7/80)
(E. Sum).

80-25   2/7/80 — SAN'A   YAR   PROTOCOL
Trade in 1980-84.
JMJP 2/13/80; NCNA Peking 2/7/80; FBIS (1).28:I1 (2/8/80).

80-26   2/8/80   2/7/80   BEIJING   COLOMBIA   COMMUNIQUÉ
Establishment of diplomatic relations.
JMJP 2/9/80(C); ZAGGG 1980. 2:51 (4/16/80)(C); PR 23.7:8
(2/18/80)(E. Sum); NCNA Peking 2/8/80; FBIS (1).29:J1 (2/11/80)
(E).

80-27   2/9/80 — MUSCAT   OMAN   AGREEMENT
Trade relations.
NCNA Peking 2/10/80; FBIS (1).30:I2 (2/12/80).

80-28   2/12/80 — PEKING   U.S.A.   AGREEMENT
Minting and marketing of Olympic coins.
NCNA Peking 2/12/80; FBIS (1).32:A3 (2/14/80).

80-29   2/13/80 — PARIS   FRANCE   PLAN
Establishment of French-Chinese cultural organizations to
increase cultural exchanges.
NCNA Peking 2/14/80; FBIS (1).33:G1 (2/15/80).

80-30   2/22/80 — NANKING   ITALY   ACCORD
Sister-city relations between Nanking (Nanjing in Pinyin) and
Florence.
JMJP 2/23/80.

80-31   2/25/80 — PEKING   U.S.A.   AGREEMENT
Sister-city relations between Peking (Beijing in Pinyin) and New
York.
JMJP 2/26/80; PR 23.10:6 (3/10/80)(E. Sum); NCNA Peking
2/25/80; FBIS (1).40:B4 (2/27/80).

80-32   2/29/80 — BEIJING   RUMANIA   PROTOCOL
Exchange of goods and methods of payments in 1980.
JMJP 3/1/80; NCNA Peking 2/29/80; FBIS (1).44:H1 (3/4/80).

80-33   3/1/80 — DACCA   BANGLADESH   AGREEMENT
Five-year long-term trade.
JMJP 3/4/80; NCNA Peking 3/1/80; FBIS (1).44:F3 (3/4/80).

80-34 3/1/80 — DACCA BANGLADESH PROTOCOL
Five-year long-term trade.
JMJP 3/4/80; NCNA Peking 3/1/80; FBIS (1) . 44:F3 (3/4/80).

80-35 3/2/80 — OTTAWA CANADA AGREEMENT
Formation of friendship association.
NCNA Peking 3/2/80; FBIS (1). 47:J1 (3/7/80).

80-36 3/3/80 — HAVANA CUBA PROTOCOL
Trade.
NCNA Peking 3/4/80; FBIS (1) . 44:J1 (3/4/80).

80-37 3/5/80 — DAR ES SALAAM TANZANIA PROTOCOL
China's planning, designing, and construction of the headquarters
of the Revolutionary Party of Tanzania.
JMJP 3/19/80; NCNA Peking 3/6/80; FBIS (1) . 47:I4 (3/7/80).

80-38 3/6/80 — TOKYO(?) FRANCE AGREEMENT
Exploration for oil in Tsing Hai Province (Qinghai in Pinyin).
Tokyo: Kyodo 3/6/80; FBIS (1) . 49:G1 (3/11/80).

80-39 3/13/80 — PEKING UNITED KINGDOM MEMORANDUM
Understanding in health cooperation.
NCNA Peking 3/13/80; FBIS (1) . 54:G1 (3/18/80).

80-40 3/14/80 — PYONGYANG KOREA(N) PROTOCOL
Protocol on goods exchange for 1980.
JMJP 3/15/80; NCNA Peking 3/14/80; FBIS (1) . 53:D2 (3/17/80).

80-41 3/15/80 — PEKING U.S.A. PROTOCOL
Annex to U.S.-Sino Hydroelectric Protocol (See 79-97).
JMJP 3/16/80; NCNA Peking 3/15/80; FBIS (1). 53:B1 (3/17/80)
(E. Sum).

80-42 3/19/80 — PEKING SWITZERLAND HONG KONG
AGREEMENT
Joint venture elevator company.
JMJP 3/29/80; NCNA Peking 3/26/80; FBIS (1). 61:A1 (3/27/80)
(E. Sum).

80-43 3/21/80 — PEKING HONG KONG AGREEMENT
New joint shipping company.
NCNA Peking 3/21/80; FBIS (1). 66:E3 (4/3/80).

80-44 3/22/80 — PEKING CZECHOSLOVAKIA AGREEMENT
Goods exchange and payments for 1980.
NCNA Peking 3/22/80; FBIS (1). 60:H1 (3/26/80).

80-45 3/24/80 — VENICE ITALY AGREEMENT
Sister-city relations between Venice and Soochow (Suzhou in Pinyin).
JMJP 3/26/80; NCNA Peking 3/25/80; FBIS (1). 66:G3 (4/3/80).

80-46 3/25/80 — PEKING POLAND AGREEMENT
Exchange of goods and schedule for payments in 1980.
JMJP 3/26/80; NCNA Peking 3/25/80; FBIS (1). 60:H1 (3/26/80).

80-47 3/26/80 — PEKING ZAIRE AGREEMENT
Cultural exchanges and cooperation.
JMJP 3/27/80; NCNA Peking 3/26/80; FBIS (1). 61:I2 (3/27/80)
(E. Sum).

80-48 3/28/80 — SOFIA BULGARIA AGREEMENT
Goods exchange and payments agreement for 1980.
JMJP 3/30/80; NCNA Peking 3/29/80; FBIS (1). 63:H1 (3/31/80).

80-49 4/2/80 — BERLIN GERMANY(E) AGREEMENT
Goods exchange and payments for 1980.
NCNA Peking 4/3/80; FBIS (1). 66:H1 (4/3/80).

80-50 4/11/80 — CANTON(GUANGZHOU IN PINYIN) AUSTRALIA
AGREEMENTS
Technical and economic cooperation between New South Wales
and Kuangtung (Guandong in Pinyin) Province.
Canton-Kuangtung Provincial Service 4/11/80; FBIS (1). 76:E4
(4/17/80).

80-51 4/11/80 — PEKING ZAMBIA PROTOCOL
Economic and technical cooperation.
NCNA Peking 4/11/80; FBIS (1). 73:I1 (4/14/80)(E. Sum).

80-52 4/14/80 — TOKYO JAPAN AGREEMENT
Cooperation in news service.
JMJP 4/17/80; NCNA Peking 4/14/80; FBIS (1). 76:D2 (4/17/80).

80-53 4/15/80 — PEKING HUNGARY AGREEMENT
Exchange of goods and arrangements for payments in 1980.
JMJP 4/17/80; NCNA Peking 4/16/80; FBIS (1). 76:H1 (4/17/80).

80-54 4/17/80 — PEKING MONGOLIA PROTOCOL
Supply of goods for 1980.
JMJP 4/21/80; NCNA Peking 4/17/80; FBIS (1). 81:D1 (4/24/80).

80-55 4/18/80 4/18/80 SALISBURY ZIMBABWE AGREEMENT
Establishment of diplomatic relations.
JMJP 4/18/80; NCNA Peking 4/17/80; FBIS (1). 77:I1 (4/18/80).

80-56 4/21/80 — BELGRADE YUGOSLAVIA PROTOCOL
Scientific and technical cooperation in 1980.
JMJP 4/23/80; NCNA Peking 4/22/80; FBIS (1). 79:H1 (4/22/80).

80-57 4/21/80 — MANILA PHILIPPINES PROTOCOL
Trade for 1980.
JMJP 4/23/80; NCNA Peking 4/21/80; FBIS (1). 80:E5 (4/23/80)
(E. Sum).

80-58 4/23/80 — PEKING YAR AGREEMENT
Cultural exchanges and cooperation.
JMJP 4/26/80; NCNA Peking 4/23/80; FBIS (1). 81:I2 (4/24/80).

80-59 4/23/80 — PEKING SOMALIA AGREEMENT
Trade.
JMJP 4/24/80; NCNA Peking 4/23/80; FBIS (1). 81:I4 (4/24/80).

80-60 4/25/80 — PEKING JAPAN EXCHANGE OF NOTES
Extension of credit by Japan to China.
Kyodo Tokyo 4/25/80; FBIS (1). 82:D3 (4/25/80).

80-61 4/30/80 — PEKING BELGIUM AGREEMENT
Provision for interest-free government loans of 300 million
Belgian Fr. from Belgium to China.
JMJP 5/1/80; NCNA Peking 4/30/80; FBIS (1). 86:G1 (5/1/80).

80-62 4/30/80 — PEKING JAPAN AGREEMENT
Fifty billion Yen Loan to China for fiscal 1979 year.
JMJP 5/1/80; NCNA Peking 4/30/80; FBIS (1). 87:D4 (5/2/80)
(E. Sum).

80-63 4/30/80 — PEKING YUGOSLAVIA AGREEMENT
Cooperation for peaceful use of atomic energy.
JMJP 5/1/80; NCNA Peking 4/30/80; FBIS (1). 185:H1 (4/30/80).

80-64 5/2/80 — SHANGHAI YUGOSLAVIA AGREEMENT
Cooperation in compiling photo album on PRC.
NCNA Peking 5/2/80; FBIS (1). 100:A5 (5/21/80).

80-65 5/3/80 — PEKING FINLAND AGREEMENT
Cultural cooperation for 1980-81.
NCNA Peking 5/3/80; FBIS (1). 89:G1 (5/6/80).

80-66   5/9/80   6/27/80*   BANGKOK   THAILAND   AGREEMENT
(INITIAL)
Civil air transport.
JMJP 5/10/80; *JMJP 6/27/80.

80-67   5/9/80 — BANGKOK   THAILAND   MEMORANDUM
Understanding on civil air transport.
JMJP 5/10/80.

80-68   5/10/80 — PEKING   OMAN   AGREEMENT (PRELIMINARY)
Possibility of cooperation in electrical engineering work.
JMJP 5/12/80.

80-69   5/10/80 — SIDNEY   AUSTRALIA   AGREEMENT
Holding Canton Trade Fair at Sidney.
JMJP 5/12/80.

80-70   5/11/80 — ISLAMABAD   PAKISTAN   PROTOCOL
Scientific and technical cooperation.
NCNA Peking 5/11/80; FBIS (1). 93:F1 (5/12/80).

80-71   5/14/80 — PEKING   MAURITANIA   AGREEMENT
Economic and technical cooperation.
JMJP 5/15/80.

80-72   5/15/80 — CANTON (GUANGZHOU IN PINYIN)   HONG KONG
PROTOCOL
Supplement to agreement Kuangtung (Guangdong in Pinyin)
Province on water supply from Tung-chiang (Dongjiang in Pinyin)
River to Hong Kong and Kowloon.
NCNA Peking 5/15/80; FBIS (1). 96:E4 (5/15/80)(E. Sum).

80-73   5/16/80 — PEKING   GERMANY(E)   AGREEMENT
Health cooperation.
JMJP 5/17/80; NCNA Peking 5/16/80; FBIS (1). 99:61 (5/20/80).

80-74   5/19/80 — ROME   ITALY   PROTOCOL
Scientific and technical cooperation for peaceful uses of nuclear
energy.
JMJP 5/21/80; NCNA Peking 5/20/80; FBIS (1). 99:61 (5/20/80)
(E. Sum).

80-75   5/19/80 — ROME   ITALY   PROGRAM
Cooperation for peaceful use of nuclear energy.
JMJP 5/21/80; NCNA Peking 5/20/80; FBIS (1). 99:61 (5/27/80)
(E. Sum).

80-76 5/27/80 — OSLO NORWAY AGREEMENT
Widening of bilateral economic, industrial, and technical co-
operation.
NCNA Peking 5/31/80; FBIS (1). 107:62 (6/2/80).

80-77 5/28/80 — TOKYO JAPAN AGREEMENT
Scientific and technical cooperation.
JMJP 5/29/80 and 6/4/80; NCNA Peking 5/28/80; FBIS
(1). 104:D4 (5/28/80)(E. Sum).

80-78 5/29/80 — BUCHAREST RUMANIA PROTOCOL
Second meeting of conference on bilateral, economic, and tech-
nical cooperation.
JMJP 5/31/80; NCNA Peking 5/29/80; FBIS (1). 106:H2 (5/30/80).

80-79 5/29/80 — PEKING IRAQ PLAN
Cultural cooperation from 1980-81.
JMJP 5/30/80; NCNA Peking 5/29/80; FBIS (1). 106:I1 (5/30/80).

80-80 6/6/80 — PEKING ARGENTINA AGREEMENT
Granting of $300 million of financial credit to PRC.
Telam Buenos Aries 6/7/80; FBIS (1). 113:J5 (6/10/80)(E. Sum).

80-81 6/6/80 — BUCHAREST RUMANIA AGREEMENT
Cooperation and coordination in the exchange of goods, experience,
specialists, and information.
NCNA Peking 6/6/80; FBIS (1). 114:H1 (6/11/80).

80-82 6/6/80 — PEKING U. S. S. R. AGREEMENT
Trade and payments agreement for 1980.
JMJP 6/11/80; Kyodo: Tokyo 6/6/80; FBIS (1). 111:C1 (6/6/80);
NCNA Peking 6/6/80; FBIS (1). 112:C1 (6/9/80).

80-83 6/6/80 — LAGOS NIGERIA PROTOCOL
Extension of service of Chinese technical team in Nigeria and
"certificate of job completion. "
NCNA Peking 6/6/80; FBIS (1). 112:I3 (6/9/80).

80-84 6/6/80 — BELGRADE YUGOSLAVIA ACCORD
Plant protection and quarantine.
NCNA Peking 6/7/80; FBIS (1). 113:H1 (6/10/80).

80-85 6/6/80 — BELGRADE YUGOSLAVIA ACCORD
Economic cooperation.
JMJP 6/8/80; NCNA Peking 6/7/80; FBIS (1). 113:H1 (6/10/80).

80-86 6/7/80 — PEKING ARGENTINA AGREEMENT
Economic cooperation.
JMJP 6/8/80; NCNA Peking 6/7/80; FBIS (1).112:J8 (6/9/80).

80-87 6/7/80 — PEKING ARGENTINA AGREEMENT
Scientific and technical cooperation.
JMJP 6/8/80; NCNA Peking 6/7/80; FBIS (1).112:J8 (6/9/80).

80-88 6/7/80 — PEKING ARGENTINA EXCHANGE OF NOTES
Cultural exchange.
JMJP 6/8/80.

80-89 6/7/80 — PEKING GERMANY(W) PROTOCOL
Cooperation in electronics research and production.
JMJP 6/8/80; NCNA Peking 6/7/80; FBIS (1).113:G5 (6/10/80).

80-90 6/9/80 — RABAT MOROCCO ACCORD
Public health and medical service.
NCNA Peking 6/9/80; FBIS (1).114:I3 (6/11/80)(E. Sum).

80-91 6/10/80 — HO-FEI(HEFEI IN PINYIN) U.S.A. ACCORD
Friendship between Anhui Province and the State of Maryland.
JMJP 6/11/80.

80-92 6/13/80 — PEKING BARBADOS AGREEMENT
Cultural cooperation.
JMJP 6/14/80; NCNA Peking 6/13/80; FBIS (1).117:J1 (6/16/80).

80-93 6/14/80 — PEKING SINGAPORE AGREEMENT
Establishing trade mission.
JMJP 6/15/80.

80-94 6/18/80 — PEKING YUGOSLAVIA AGREEMENT
Establishing friendship city relations between Shanghai and Zagreb.
JMJP 6/22/80.

80-95 6/19/80 — PEKING WESTERN SAMOA PROTOCOL
Economic and technical cooperation.
JMJP 6/20/80; NCNA Peking 6/19/80; FBIS (1).121:E4 (6/20/80).

80-96 6/21/80 — TIENTSIN(TIANJIN IN PINYIN) AUSTRALIA
AGREEMENT (?)
Establishing friendship city relations between Tientsin (Tianjin
in Pinyin) and Melbourne.
JMJP 6/24/80.

80-97 6/22/80 — PEKING YAR ACCORD
Repayment by Yemen on Chinese loans.
NCNA Peking 6/22/80; FBIS (1).125:I3 (6/26/80).

80-98 6/25/80 6/25/80 TARAWA KIRIBATI EXCHANGE OF
NOTES
Establishing diplomatic relations.
JMJP 6/29/80; ZRGGG 1980. 8:232 (8/14/80)(C); PR 23. 27:8
(7/7/80).

80-99 7/1/80 — PEKING GERMANY(W) PROTOCOL
Set up jointly financed China Jewelry Co. , Ltd. , in Bremen,
West Germany.
NCNA Peking 7/1/80; FBIS (1).129:G1 (7/2/80)(E. Sum).

80-100 7/2/80 — PEKING FRANCE AGREEMENT
Industrial cooperation for the construction of helicopters.
AFP: Hong Kong 7/2/80; FBIS (1).130:61 (7/3/80).

80-101 7/2/80 — MEXICO CITY MEXICO PROTOCOL
Cultural exchanges and cooperation.
NCNA Peking 7/3/80; FBIS (1).140:J2 (7/18/80)(E. Sum).

80-102 7/3/80 — RANGOON BURMA PROTOCOL
Economic and technical cooperation.
NCNA Peking 7/4/80; FBIS (1).132:E6 (7/8/80).

80-103 7/4/80 — PEKING PORTUGAL AGREEMENT
Trade and reciprocal most-favored-nation trade status.
JMJP 7/5/80; NCNA Peking 7/4/80; FBIS (1).131:G1 (7/7/80).
(E. Sum).

80-104 7/8/80 — PEKING CONGO AGREEMENT
Cultural cooperation.
JMJP 7/9/80; NCNA Peking 7/8/80; FBIS (1).133:I1 (7/9/80)
(E. Sum).

80-105 7/8/80 — PEKING CONGO AGREEMENT
Technical and economic cooperation.
JMJP 7/9/80; NCNA Peking 7/8/80; FBIS (1).133:I1 (7/9/80)
(E. Sum).

80-106 7/8/80 — PEKING CONGO SUMMARY
Talks on arrangement for technical cooperation.
JMJP 7/9/80; NCNA Peking 7/8/80; FBIS (1).133:I1 (7/9/80)
(E. Sum).

80-107 7/10/80 — PEKING GERMANY(W) AGREEMENT
Mutual provision of navigational, communications, meterological, and other technical services.
NCNA Peking 7/10/80; FBIS (1). 135:G1 (7/11/80).

80-108 7/10/80 — WASHINGTON, D. C. U. S. A. PROGRAM
High Energy Physics Collaboration (See also 79-20).
NCNA Peking 7/11/80; FBIS (1). 135:B1 (7/11/80).

80-109 7/10/80 — NIAMEY NIGER PROTOCOL
Sending another Chinese medical team to Niger.
NCNA Peking 7/12/80; FBIS (1). 145:I3 (7/25/80).

80-110 7/10/80 — KHARTOUM SUDAN PROTOCOL
Dispatch of PRC medical team to Sudan.
NCNA Peking 7/10/80; FBIS (1). 145:I3 (7/25/80).

80-111 7/10/80 — WASHINGTON, D. C. U. S. A. PLAN
Cooperation in high energy physics.
JMJP 7/12/80(C).

80-112 7/24/80 — PEKING BANGLADESH AGREEMENT
Extension of PRC loans to Bangladesh.
JMJP 7/25/80; NCNA Peking 7/24/80; FBIS (1). 144:F2 (7/24/80).

80-113 7/24/80 — PEKING BANGLADESH AGREEMENT
Civil air transport.
JMJP 7/25/80; NCNA Peking 7/24/80; FBIS (1). 144:F2 (7/24/80).

80-114 7/25/80 7/25/80 PEKING U. S. A. AGREEMENT
Annual quotas and control measures on exports of six categories of Chinese textile products to the U. S.
NCNA Peking 7/25/80; FBIS (1). 146:B5 (7/28/80).

80-115 7/25/80 — PEKING CAPE VERDE PROTOCOL
Economic and technical cooperation.
JMJP 7/26/80.

80-116 7/28/80 — DJIBOUTI DJIBOUTI AGREEMENT
Rules on accounts between national banks.
JMJP 7/31/80.

80-117 7/28/80 — DJIBOUTI DJIBOUTI PROTOCOL
Economic and technical cooperation.
JMJP 7/31/80.

80-118 8/6/80 — BERNE SWITZERLAND PROTOCOL
Radio and TV operation.
JMJP 8/7/80; NCNA Peking 8/6/80; FBIS (1). 155:61 (8/8/80)
(E. Sum).

80-119 8/14/80 — PYONGYANG KOREA(N) AGREEMENT
Cultural exchange for 1980.
NCNA Peking 8/14/80; FBIS (1). 160:D1 (8/15/80).

80-120 8/18/80 — ISLAMABAD PAKISTAN AGREEMENT
Implementation program of cultural exchange for 1980-81.
NCNA Peking 8/18/80; FBIS (1). 162:F3 (8/19/80).

80-121 8/19/80 — PEKING NICARAGUA AGREEMENT
Sale of 10,000 tons of cotton to China in 1981.
JMJP 8/20/80.

80-122 8/20/80 — CONAKRY GUINEA AGREEMENT
Technical cooperation.
NCNA Peking 8/21/80; FBIS (1). 172:I1 (9/3/80).

80-123 8/22/80 — TOKYO JAPAN AGREEMENT
Cooperation in technical survey of ships.
JMJP 9/9/80; NCNA Peking 9/6/80; FBIS (1). 176:D1 (9/9/80).

80-124 8/25/80 — OTTAWA CANADA NOTE OF UNDERSTANDING
Establishment of consulate-general in Toronto.
JMJP 8/27/80; NCNA Peking 8/26/80; FBIS (1). 168:J1 (8/27/80).

80-125 8/26/80 — SAN MARINO SAN MARINO AGREEMENT
Cultural and educational cooperation.
JMJP 8/28/80; NCNA Peking 8/26/80; FBIS (1). 183:G5 (9/18/80).
(E. Sum).

80-126 8/26/80 — MANILA PHILIPPINES PROGRAM
Executive program of the cultural agreement for 1980-81.
JMJP 8/27/80; NCNA Peking 8/26/80; FBIS (1). 169:E4 (8/28/80).

80-127 8/29/80 — LUSAKA TANZANIA ZAMBIA PROTOCOL
Third term of technical cooperation on Tazara Railway.
NCNA Peking 8/30/80; FBIS (1). 174:I2 (9/5/80).

80-128 8/30/80 — PYONGYANG KOREA(N) PROTOCOL
Twentieth meeting of Conference on scientific and technical co-
operation.
JMJP 8/31/80; NCNA Peking 8/30/80; FBIS (1). 173:D7 (9/4/80).

80-129 9/8/80 — PEKING CANADA MEMORANDUM
Understanding between agricultural ministers.
JMJP 9/9/80.

80-130 9/8/80 — PEKING U. S. A. AGREEMENT (INITIAL)
Civil air transport.
JMJP 9/8/80; NCNA Peking 9/8/80; FBIS (1). 177:B1 (9/10/80).

80-131 9/9/80 9/9/80 PEKING UN FUND FOR POPULATION
ACTIVITIES AGREEMENT
Program agreement for technical assistance to China.
NCNA Peking 9/9/80; FBIS (1). 177:A3 (9/10/80).

80-132 9/14/80 — BRUSSELS BELGIUM AGREEMENT
Establishment of joint venture for sale of Chinese coal to Belgium.
NCNA Peking 9/15/80; FBIS (1). 183:G5 (9/18/80).

80-133 9/16/80 — PEKING KENYA AGREEMENT
Economic and technical cooperation.
JMJP 9/17/80; NCNA Peking 9/16/80; FBIS (1). 182:I2 (9/17/80).

80-134 9/16/80 — PEKING CANADA MEMORANDUM
Scientific and technical cooperation.
JMJP 9/17/80.

80-135 9/16/80 — PEKING GERMANY(W) PROTOCOL
Statement of intent for cultural cooperation.
NCNA Peking 9/16/80; FBIS (1). 182:63 (9/17/80)(E. Sum).

80-136 9/16/80 — PRAGUE CZECHOSLOVAKIA PROTOCOL
Scientific and technical cooperation.
NCNA Peking 9/16/80; FBIS (1). 182:H1 (9/17/80).

80-137 9/16/80 — PEKING KENYA AGREEMENT
Cultural cooperation.
NCNA Peking 9/16/80; FBIS (1). 182:I2 (9/17/80).

80-138 9/17/80 9/17/80 WASHINGTON, D. C. , U. S. A. AGREE-
MENT
Civil aviation.
JMJP 9/19/80; PR 23. 39:4 (9/29/80); NCNA Peking 9/17/80;
FBIS (1). 183:B1 (9/18/80)(E. Sum); ILM 19:1106 (1980)(E).

80-139 9/17/80 — WASHINGTON, D. C. , U. S. A. AGREEMENT
Establishing consulates.

JMJP 9/19/80; PR 23.39:4 (9/29/80); NCNA Peking 9/17/80; FBIS (1).183:B1 (9/18/80)(E. Sum); ILM 19:1114 (1980)(E).

80-140 9/17/80 1/1/80 WASHINGTON, D.C. , U.S.A. AGREE-
MENT
Textiles.
JMJP 9/19/80; PR 23.39:4 (9/29/80); NCNA Peking 9/17/80; FBIS (1).183:B1 (9/18/80)(E. Sum); ILM 19:1119 (1980)(E).

80-141 9/17/80 9/17/80 WASHINGTON, D.C. , U.S.A. AGREE-
MENT
Maritime trade.
JMJP 9/19/80; PR 23.39:4 (9/29/80); NCNA Peking 9/17/80; FBIS (1).183:B1 (9/18/80)(E. Sum); ILM 19:1117 (1980)(E).

80-142 9/17/80 — PEKING ALGERIA AGREEMENT
Strengthening friendly relations and promoting cultural exchanges.
NCNA Peking 9/17/80; FBIS (1).183:I1 (9/18/80)(E. Sum).

80-143 9/23/80 — PEKING NETHERLANDS MEMORANDUM
Understanding on agricultural matters.
JMJP 9/24/80.

80-144 9/25/80 — PEKING KOREA(N) AGREEMENT
Cooperation in broadcasting and television between the Central Broadcasting Administration of the PRC and the Central Broad-casting Committee of the Democratic People's Republic of Korea.
JMJP 9/26/80; NCNA Peking 9/25/80; FBIS (1).189:D4 (9/26/80).

80-145 9/25/80 — PEKING NORWAY AGREEMENT
Economic, industrial, and technical cooperation.
JMJP 9/26/80; NCNA Peking 9/25/80; FBIS (1).189:G3 (9/26/80).

80-146 9/26/80 — HELSINKI FINLAND AGREEMENT
Trade agreement for 1981.
JMJP 9/30/80; NCNA Peking 9/27/80; FBIS (1).191:G2 (9/30/80).

80-147 9/30/80 — PEKING SRI LANKA MINUTES
Eighth joint committee meeting of Sino-Sri Lanka joint shipping service.
NCNA Peking 9/30/80; FBIS (1).193:F1 (10/2/80); Also reported in FBIS (1).197:F1 (10/8/80).

80-148 10/3/80 — PARIS FRANCE AGREEMENT
Exchanging recording materials on news items, cultural life and

music, organizing special programs and exchanging reporting groups between the Central People's Broadcasting Station of China and the National Society of Radio Broadcasting of France.
JMJP 10/6/80; NCNA Peking 10/4/80; FBIS (1). 195:G3 (10/6/80).

80-149 10/4/80 — PEKING WORLD FOOD PROGRAM AGREEMENT
Providing food assistance in support of China's economic and social development projects or to meet emergency food needs arising from natural disasters or as the result of other emergencies.
JMJP 10/5/80; NCNA Peking 10/4/80; FBIS (1). 195:A2 (10/6/80).

80-150 10/6/80 — KUWAIT KUWAIT AGREEMENT
Trade agreement to expand trade and to provide for each other necessary convenience for importing commodities and labor power.
JMJP 10/9/80; NCNA Peking 10/6/80; FBIS . 197:I1 (10/8/80).

80-151 10/9/80 — WASHINGTON, D. C. , U. S. A. AGREEMENT
International express mail.
JMJP 10/11/80; NCNA Peking 10/10/80; FBIS (1). 199:B1 (10/10/80).

80-152 10/9/80 11/10/80* WASHINGTON, D. C. , U. S. A. AGREE-MENT
Parcel post.
JMJP 10/11/80; NCNA Peking 10/10/80; FBIS (1). 199:B1 (10/10/80); *NCNA Peking 11/10/80; FBIS (1). 220:B4 (11/12/80).

80-153 10/13/80 — TOKYO JAPAN MEMORANDUM
Promoting scientific and technological exchange between the Scientific and Technical Association of China and the Japan Techno-Economics Society.
NCNA Peking 10/13/80; FBIS (1). 201:D5 (10/15/80).

80-154 10/13/80 — MANILA PHILIPPINES AGREEMENT
Supplying hydroelectric equipment between the China National Machinery and Equipment Import and Export Corporation and the National Electrification Administration of the Philippines.
NCNA Peking 10/13/80; FBIS (1). 201:E5 (10/15/80); (E. Sum. in FBIS (1). 221:E4 (11/13/80).

80-155 10/14/80 — PEKING OMAN AGREEMENT
Trade.
JMJP 10/15/80; NCNA Peking 10/14/80; FBIS (1). 201:I1 (10/15/80).

80-156 10/14/80 — BELGRADE YUGOSLAVIA AGREEMENT
Establishing friendly city-to-city relations between Peking and

Belgrade.
NCNA Peking 10/15/80; FBIS . 201:H1 (E. Sum) (10/15/80).

80-157 10/17/80 — — FRANCE AGREEMENT
Principle for the construction of two nuclear power stations.
Paris Domestic Service in French, 10/17/80; FBIS (1). 204:G1
(10/20/80).

80-158 10/17/80 — PEKING FRANCE AGREEMENT
Establishing consulates in Shanghai and Marseilles.
JMJP 10/18/80; NCNA Peking 10/17/80; FBIS (1). 204:G1 (10/20/80).

80-159 10/22/80 — PEKING U. S. A. AGREEMENT
Grain trade.
JMJP 10/23/80; NCNA Peking 10/22/80; FBIS (1). 206:B1 (10/22/80).

80-160 10/24/80 — PEKING JAPAN JOINT DECLARATION
Further development of Tokyo-Peking sister-city relations
established in March 1979.
Kyodo: Tokyo 10/24/80; FBIS (1). 208:D4 (10/24/80).

80-161 10/30/81 — PEKING NETHERLANDS AGREEMENT
Cultural cooperation.
JMJP 10/31/80; NCNA Peking 10/30/80; FBIS (1). 213:G1 (10/31/80).

80-162 10/30/81 — PEKING NETHERLANDS AGREEMENT
Economic and technological cooperation.
JMJP 10/31/80; NCNA Peking 10/30/80; FBIS (1). 213:G1 (10/31/80).

80-163 10/30/80* — PEKING U. S. A. EXCHANGE OF NOTES
Investment insurance and guarantees by U. S. Overseas Private
Insurance Corporation (OPIC).
JMJP 10/31/80; NCNA Peking 10/30/80; FBIS (1). 212:B3
(10/30/80*); ILM 19:1482 (1980)(E); (Initiated 10/7/80; JMJP
10/11/80).

80-164 11/5/80 — VIENNA AUSTRIA AGREEMENT
Economic, industrial, and technological cooperation for 10-year
period.
JMJP 11/7/80; NCNA Peking 11/6/80; FBIS (1). 217:G1 (11/6/80).

80-165 11/7/80 — COLOMBO SRI LANKA EXECUTIVE PROGRAM
Implementing cultural agreement for 1981.
JMJP 11/9/80; NCNA Peking 11/7/80; FBIS (1). 221:F1 (11/13/80).

80-166 11/7/80 — PYONGYANG KOREA(N) EXECUTIVE PROGRAM
Implementing health cooperation program for 1981.
JMJP 11/9/80.

80-167 11/8/80 — PEKING YUGOSLAVIA AGREEMENT
Cooperation in marine shipping.
NCNA Peking 11/8/80; FBIS (1). 219:H3 (11/10/80).

80-168 11/11/80 — MANILA PHILIPPINES ARRANGEMENT
Mutual deposit facility.
JMJP 11/13/80; NCNA Peking 11/11/80; FBIS (1). 221:E3
(11/13/80)(E. Sum).

80-169 11/11/80 — PEKING UNITED KINGDOM MEMORANDUM
OF UNDERSTANDING
Cooperation in agricultural science and technology between
Chinese Ministry of Agriculture and the British Ministry of
Agriculture.
JMJP 11/12/80; NCNA Peking 11/11/80; FBIS (1). 220:G6 (11/12/80).

80-170 11/18/80 — ANKARA TURKEY (PROGRAM) AGREEMENT
Program of cultural exchange for 1981 and 1982.
JMJP 11/21/80; NCNA Peking 11/18/80; FBIS (1). 226:G1 (11/20/80).

80-171 11/20/80 — PEKING RUMANIA PROTOCOL
Broadcasting and television cooperation for 1981-82.
JMJP 11/21/80.

80-172 11/24/80 — PEKING SWEDEN AGREEMENT
Academic cooperation between Chinese Academy of Social Sciences
and Stockholm University of Sweden.
JMJP 11/26/80.

80-173 11/29/80 — CONTONOU BENIN DOCUMENT
Handing over a Chinese-aid project at Malanville paddy area to
Benin Government.
NCNA Peking 11/30/80; FBIS (1). 223:I1 (12/2/80).

80-174 12/1/80 — PEKING KOREA(N) PLAN
1981-82 scientific cooperation between the Academy of Sciences
of China and the Academy of Sciences of the Democratic People's
Republic of Korea.
JMJP 12/2/80; NCNA 12/1/80; FBIS (1). 233:D2 (12/2/80).

80-175 12/1/80 — MANILA PHILIPPINES PROTOCOL
Third session in implementing 1978 agreement on scientific and
technical cooperation.
JMJP 12/2/80; NCNA Peking 12/3/80; FBIS (1). 234:E2 (12/3/80).

80-176 12/3/80 — PEKING BELGIUM MINUTES
Talks between Chinese Minister Fang Yi, in charge of the State
Scientific and Technological Commission, and Raymond Scheyven,
Belgian Minister of State (implementing 1979 protocol on scientific
and technical cooperation; see 79-75.)
NCNA Peking 12/3/80; FBIS (1). 235:G2 (12/4/80).

80-177 12/5/80 — PEKING JAPAN EXCHANGE OF NOTES
Japanese loan of fifty-six billion Japanese Yen to China for 1980.
JMJP 12/6/80.

80-178 12/5/80 — PEKING JAPAN PRESS COMMUNIQUÉ
First meeting of the Sino-Japanese Government Officials Confer-
ence.
JMJP 12/6/80; PR 23. 50:7-8 (12/15/80); NCNA Peking 12/5/80;
FBIS (1). 236:D2-D4 (12/5/80)(E).

80-179 12/5/80 — PEKING POLAND PROTOCOL
Scientific and technical cooperation for 1981.
PAP, Warsaw, 12/5/80; FBIS (1). 238:H3 (12/9/80).

80-180 12/7/80 — PEKING BULGARIA PROTOCOL
Eighteenth session of Sino-Bulgarian Commission for Scientific
and Technical Cooperation.
NCNA Peking 12/7/80; FBIS (1). 238:H3 (12/9/80).

80-181 12/9/80* — BRUSSELS BELGIUM AGREEMENT
Cultural cooperation.
JMJP 12/12/80; NCNA Peking 12/10/80; FBIS (1). 241:G7 (12/12/80).
*NCNA's date is 12/10/80.

80-182 12/11/80(?) — BANGKOK THAILAND PROTOCOL
Trade.
Voice of Free Asia, Bangkok, FBIS (1). 249:E4 (12/24/80).

80-183 12/11/80 — WASHINGTON, D.C., U.S.A. AGREEMENT
Scientific cooperation (exchange and personnel information) be-
tween the Chinese Academy of Sciences and the Smithsonian
Institution in Washington, D. C.
JMJP 12/17/80; NCNA Peking 12/12/80; FBIS (1). 241:B2 (12/12/80).

80-184 12/19/80 — COLOMBO SRI LANKA PROTOCOL
Trade for 1981.
JMJP 12/21/80; NCNA Peking 12/19/80; FBIS (1). 249:F1 (12/24/80).

80-185 12/20/80 — PEKING CUBA AGREEMENT
Trade for 1981-85.
JMJP 12/21/80.

80-186 12/20/80 — PEKING CUBA PROTOCOL
Trade for 1981.
JMJP 12/21/80.

80-187 12/20/80 PEKING CUBA AGREEMENT
Payment.
JMJP 12/21/80.

80-188 12/22/80 — BANGKOK THAILAND MINUTES
Third Session of Sino-Thai Scientific and Technical Cooperation
Committee.
JMJP 12/24/80.

80-189 12/30/80 — PYONGYANG KOREA(N) AGREEMENT
Border television frequencies.
JMJP 1/1/81.

CALENDAR OF MULTILATERAL TREATIES

PRC'S ACCESSION/ RATIFICATION	TITLE OF MULTILATERAL TREATIES
M-1 10/25/71	Charter of United Nations with Statute of International Court of Justice.
	6/26/45 10/24/45
UNYB 25:126 (1971).	STAT 59:1031; TS 993; BEVANS 3:1153; KCTYC (1945-47):35(C).
M-2 10/29/71	Constitution of United Nations Educational, Scientific, and Cultural Organization.
	11/16/45 11/4/46
UNYB 25:701 (1971).	STAT 6:2495; TIAS 1580; BEVANS 3:1311; UNTS 4:275.
M-3 2/24/72	Convention of World Meteorological Organization.
	10/11/47 3/23/56
UNYB 26:807 (1972).	UST 1:281; TIAS 2052; UNTS 77:143.
M-4 5/10/72	Constitution of World Health Organization.
	7/22/46 4/7/48
UNYB 26:765 (1972).	STAT 62:2679; TIAS 1808; BEVANS 4:119; UNTS 14:185.
M-5 11/16/72 (accession deposited with reservation).	1965 International Telecommunication Convention.
	11/12/65 1/1/67
DSB 68:1752:100 (1/22/75).	UST 18:575; TIAS 6257.
M-6 2/7/73 (acceptance deposited).	1969 additional protocol to Constitution of Universal Postal Union with final protocol, general regulations with final protocol and annex, and Universal Postal Convention with final protocol and detailed regulations.
	1/14/69 7/1/71
DSB 68.1763:440 (4/9/73).	UST 22:1056; TIAS 7150; UNTS 810:7.

M-7   3/1/73 (acceptance deposited).

DSB 68. 1762:410 (4/2/73); ILM 12. 2:468 (March, 1973).

Convention of Intergovernmental Maritime Consultative Organization. 3/6/48   3/17/58 UST 9:621; TIAS 4044; UNTS 289:48; KCTYC (1958-59):732(C).

M-8   3/2/73   3/2/73 Signed by twelve nations: U. S. , France, Indonesia, Hungary, Poland, Vietnam(N), U. K. , Vietnam(S), U. S. S. R. , Canada, China, Vietnam (R. S. V. N.) at Paris. JMJP 3/3/73(C); PR 16. 10:6 (3/9/73)(E); NCNA Paris 3/2/73; SCMP 5333:110 (3/14/73)(E).

Act of International Conference on Vietnam.

M-9   4/1/73 (resumption of membership).

DSB 69. 1800:775 (12/24/73).

Constitution of Food and Agriculture Organization. 10/16/45   10/16/45 UST 12:980; TIAS 4803.

M-10   8/21/73 (signature).

DSB 69. 1785:359 (9/10/73).

Additional Protocol II to the Treaty of February 14, 1967 for the Prohibition of Nuclear Weapons. 2/14/67   — UST 22:754; TIAS 7137; UNTS 634:364.

M-11   10/5/73 (acceptance deposited with a declaration).

DSB 69. 1800:776 (12/24/73).

1960 International Convention for Safety of Life at Sea. 6/17/60   5/26/65 UST 16:185; TIAS y80; UNTS 536:27.

M-12   10/5/73 (ratification deposited with following reservation: PRC withdrew from 1930 International Convention on Load Lines and with respect to delimitation of coastal territory, PRC did not consider itself bound by provisions

1966 International Convention on Load Lines. 4/5/66   7/21/68 UST 18:1857; TIAS 633; UNTS 640:133.

of Articles 49 and 50 of the
second additional protocol of
the convention). Bureau of
Ship Inspection of PRC, trans.
I-chiu-liu-lin-nien-kuo-chi-
ch'uan-opo-tsai-chung-hsien-
kung-yueh (1966 International
Convention on Load Lines)
1974(C).

M-13   1/14/74 (acceptance
deposited).

MTSGPDF 1977:243.

1967 Amendments to Articles 24
and 25 of the Constitution of the
World Health Organization.
5/23/67   5/21/75
UST 26:990; TIAS 8086.

M-14   2/28/74 (ratification
deposited).

DSB 71.1834:304 (8/19/74).

Protocol relating to Amendment
of Article 56 to the Convention
on International Civil Aviation to
enlarge membership of the Air
Navigation Commission.
7/7/71   12/19/74
UST 26:1061; TIAS 8092.

M-15   2/28/74 (ratification
deposited).

DSB 71.1843:304 (8/19/74).

Protocol relating to Amendment
of Article 50(a) of the Convention
on International Civil Aviation to
increase membership of the International Civil Aviation Organization (ICAO) council from twenty-
seven to thirty.
3/12/71   1/16/73
UST 24:1019; TIAS 7616.

M-16   2/28/74 (ratification
deposited).

ICAOCAR 1974:89.

Protocol relating to Amendments
of Articles 48(a), 49(e), and 61
of the Convention on International
Civil Aviation.
6/14/54   12/12/56
UST 8:179; TIAS 3756;
UNTS 320:217.

M-17   2/28/74 (acceptance
deposited).

Protocol on Authentic Trilingual
Text of the Convention on International Civil Aviation.

ICAOCAR 1974:89

9/24/68 10/24/68
UST 19:7693; TIAS 6605;
UNTS 740:21.

M-18 2/28/74 (ratification
deposited).

Protocol relating to an Amendment of Article 48(a) of the Convention on International Civil
Aviation.
9/15/62 9/11/75

ICAOCAR 1974:89.

UST 26:2374; TIAS 8162.

M-19 2/28/74 (ratification
deposited).

Protocol relating to an Amendment of Article 50(a) of the Convention on International Civil
Aviation.
6/21/61 7/17/62

ICAOCAR 1974:89.

UST 13:2105; TIAS 5170.

M-20 2/28/74 (ratification
deposited).

Protocol relating to an Amendment of Article 45 of the Convention on International Civil
Aviation.
6/14/54 5/16/58

ICAOCAR 1974:89.

UNTS 320:210.

M-21 2/28/74 (ratification
deposited).

Protocol relating to an Amendment of Article 56 of the Convention on International Civil
Aviation.
7/7/71 12/19/74

ICAOCAR 1974:89.

UST 26:1061; TIAS 8092.

M-22 6/12/74 (ratification
deposited).

Additional Protocol II to Treaty
for Prohibition of Nuclear
Weapons in Latin America
2/4/67
UST 22:754; TIAS 7137;
UNTS 634:364.

DSB 71.1832:255 (8/5/74).
Signed on 8/21/73. JMJP
8/23/73(C); NCNA Mexico
City 8/21/73; SCMP 5447:161
(8/21/73); DSB 69.1785:359
(9/10/73).

M-23 4/28/75 (ratification
deposited).

Amendments to Articles 10, 16,
17, 18, 20, 28, 31, and 32 of the

Convention on Intergovernmental
Maritime Consultative Organization.
10/17/74 —
TIAS 8606.

MTSGPDF 1977:405; DSB
DSB 73.1884:195 (8/4/75).

M-24 6/20/75 (signature).

1974 International Convention for
Safety of Life at Sea.
11/1/74 —
ILM 14.4:963 (July, 1975).

DSB 73.1885:231 (8/11/75);
ILM 14.4:959 (July, 1975).

M-25 8/20/75 (adherence
deposited with declaration).
Entry in force: 11/18/75;
International Conference on
Air Law, Vol: 1, p. 7
(Montreal September, 1975).

The Hague Protocol to amend
Warsaw Convention.
9/28/55 8/1/63
UNTS 478:373.

M-26 11/26/75 (accession
deposited with a declaration).

Vienna Convention on Diplomatic
Relations.
4/18/61 4/24/64
UST 23:3227; TIAS 7502;
UNTS 500:95.

MTSGPDF 1977:51;
DSB 1905:947 (12/29/75).

M-27 3/5/76 (acceptance
deposited).

Amendments to Articles 34 and
55 of the Constitution of World
Health Organization.
5/22/73 —
TIAS 8534;

MTSGPDF 1977:245;
DSB 74.1919:456 (4/5/76).

M-28 12/29/76 (ratification
deposited).

1973 International Telecommunication Convention.
10/25/73 1/1/75
TIAS 8575.

TYC 20:138(C);
DSB 76.1970:304 (3/8/77).

M-29 5/20/77 (adherence
deposited).

Convention concerning creation
of an International Office of
Weights and Measures.
5/29/1875 1/1/1876
STAT 20:709; TS 378;
BEVANS 1:39.

DSB 77.1994:363 (9/12/77).

M-30   5/29/77 (adherence deposited).

DSB 77. 1994:363 (9/12/77).

Convention amending Convention relating to Weights and Measures
10/6/21   6/23/22
STAT 43:1686; TS 673;
BEVANS 2:323; LNTS 17:45.

M-31   6/2/77 (acceptance deposited).

MTSGPDF 1977:562.
Signed on 10/25/76.

Constitution of Asia-Pacific Telecommunity.
3/27/76   —

M-32   8/16/77 (accession deposited).

DSB 77. 1993:327 (9/5/77).
Minutes of talks on the PRC joining the International Tele-communication Satellite Orga-nization were held at Peking on 5/2/77. JMJP 5/3/77; NCNA Peking 5/2/77; SCMP 6340:59 (5/16/77).

Agreement relating to the Inter-national Telecommunications Satellite Organization.
8/20/71   2/12/73
UST 23:3813; TIAS 7532

M-33   8/16/77 (signature).

DSB 77. 1993:327 (9/5/77).
Signed with Peking Adminis-tration of Long-Distance Telecommunications for PRC.

Operating agreement relating to the International Telecommunica-tions Satellite Organization.
8/20/71   2/12/73
UST 23:4091; TIAS 7532.

M-34   11/14/78 (accession deposited with reservation).

DSB 79. 2025:67 (April 1979);
JMJP 12/14/78; FBIS
(1). 241:A2 (12/14/78).

Convention on Offenses & Certain Other Acts Committed on Board Aircraft.
9/14/63   12/4/69
UST 20:2941; TIAS 6768;
UNTS 704:219.

M-35   7/2/79 (accession deposited).
DSB 79. 2029:66 (Aug. 1979).

Convention on Consular Relations.
4/24/63   3/19/67
UST 21:77; TIAS 6820; UNTS 596:261.

M-36 7/13/79 (signature).

DSB 80. 2035:75 (Feb. 1980).

Convention on the International
Maritime Satellite Organization
(INMARSAT).
9/3/76
TIAS 9605.

M-37 9/11/79 (accession
deposited).

DSB 79. 2032:60 (Nov. 1979);
U. N. Chronicle 16. 6:71
(July-Oct. 1979).

Convention on the Privilege and
Immunities of the Specialized
Agencies.
2/13/46 (For China) 9/11/79
UST 21:1418; TIAS 6900;
UNTS 1:15.

M-38 10/30/79 (acceptance
deposited).

DSB 79. 2033:67 (Dec. 1979).

Amendments to the Convention on
the Intergovernmental Maritime
Consultative Organization (IMCO).
11/17/77 —

M-39 1/15/80 (accession
deposited).

DSB 80. 2036:70 (Mar. 1980).
U. N. Chronicle 17. 2: (Mar.
1980).

Agreement Establishing the International Fund for Agricultural
Development.
6/18/76 —
TIAS 8765.

M-40 1/30/80 (accession
deposited).

DSB 80. 2038:68 (May 1980).

International Convention on Civil
Liability for Oil Pollution Damage.
11/29/69 6/19/75
Text published by IMCO, Sales
No. 77. 16. E.

M-41 3/3/80 (accession
deposited, entered into force
6/3/80). (Date of Approval by
the PRC: 2/14/80);
JMJP 7/12/80: U.N. Chronicle
17. 4:59 (May 1980).

Convention Establishing the World
Intellectual Property Organization.
7/14/67 4/26/70

UST 21:1749; TIAS 6932.

M-42 4/17/80 (Resolution of
IMF to transfer China's seat
to PRC).
JMJP 4/20/80.

Articles of Agreement of the
International Monetary Fund.
12/27/45 12/27/45
STAT 60:1401; TIAS 1501;
BEVANS 3:1531; UNTS 2:39.

M-43 5/15/80 (Resolution of
World Bank Executive Council
to transfer China's Seat to
PRC).

JMJP 5/17/80.

Articles of Agreement of the
International Bank for Reconstruc-
tion and Development (World
Bank). [1]
12/24/45   12/27/45
STAT 60:1440; TIAS 1502;
BEVANS 3:1390; UNTS 2:134.

M-44 5/15/80 (Resolution of
World Bank Executive Council
to transfer China's seat to
PRC).
JMJP 5/17/80.

Articles of Agreement of International Development Association. [2]
1/26/60   9/?/60

UST 11:2284; TIAS 4607;
UNTS 439:249.

M-45 5/15/80 (Resolution of
World Bank Executive Council
to transfer China's seat to
PRC).
JMJP 5/17/80.

Articles of Agreement of the
International Finance Corporation. [3]
5/25/55   ?/?/56

UST: 2197; TIAS 3620;
UNTS 264:117.

M-46 9/15/80 (Ratification)
UN Chronicle 17. 9:89 (Nov.
1980).

International Rubber Agreement
1/79 Not yet in force; Convention
on the Elimination of all Forms
of Discrimination against Women.

M-47 9/29/80 (Ratification by
standing committee of the
National People's Congress,
with reservation to Article 29,
paragraph 1).
JMJP 9/30/80; ZRGGG 1980.
15:454 (12/20/80)(C).

1/79 Not yet in force.

M-48 10/10/80 (accession
deposited).

Convention for the Suppression of
Unlawful Acts against the Safety
of Civil Aviation.
9/23/71   1/26/73
UST 24:564; TIAS 7570.

JMJP 10/15/80; NCNA Peking
10/14/80; FBIS (1). 201:A2
(10/14/80).

M-49   10/10/80 (accession
    deposited).

JMJP 10/15/80; NCNA Peking
10/14/80; FBIS (1) . 201:A2
(10/14/80).

Convention for the Suppression of
Unlawful Seizure of Aircraft.
12/16/70   10/14/71
UST 22:1641; TIAS 7192.

NOTES

1. The World Bank is a group of three institutions—the International Bank for Reconstruction and Development (IBRD), the International Development Association (IDA), and the International Finance Corporation (IFC). IBRD and IDA have the same officers, directors, and staff. The IFC, while closely associated with IBRD, is a separate legal entity, and its staff and funds are distinct from those of the bank.

    2. See note 1.

    3. See note 1.

TABLE 1

Topical Distribution of PRC Agreements: 1966-78

	1966	1967	1968	1969	1970	1971	1972	1973	1974	1975	1976	1977	1978	Total
Trade	M 43	M 28	M 37	30	M 32	M 52	M 46	36	M 35	35	M 28	35	45	482
Cultural	M 28	5	M 6	—	—	1	M 5	5	5	M 1	5	M 1	M 15	77
Science & Technology	18	8	1	—	M 6	5	8	M 14	10	M 14	9	M 11	M 39	143
Economic & Technical Aid	M 15	M 10	M 13	M 14	M 32	M 29	35	M 31	20	21	28	34	38	320
Friendship & Foreign Policy Alignment	8	5	5	3	9	19	13	14	9	9	2	1	1	97
Finance	4	2	4	1	7	5	9	2	2	3	1	2	—	42
Postal Services & Telecommunications	—	—	—	—	—	3	—	—	1	1	1	1	1	8
Railway & Highway	2	2	M 5	M 3	M 4	M 3	M 2	M 4	M 3	M 8	M 9	M 3	M 10	M 58
Boundary	—	1	—	1	—	M 2	2	1	3	—	2	—	5	18
Aviation	M 6	—	—	—	—	1	M 9	1	3	M 5	2	M 4	7	50
Navigation	1	—	—	M 1	M 4	—	1	M 5	6	M 6	M 3	M 3	7	35
Fishery	—	—	—	—	1	1	1	1	6	2	3	3	5	6
Military	—	—	—	—	M 3	M 5	M 6	M 3	—	—	—	—	—	20
Shipping & Joint Stock Companies	3	1	1	1	1	—	4	1	1	2	3	6	5	29
Diplomatic & Consular	—	—	1	—	5	17	20	2	8	10	5	2	6	76
Medical aid	—	3	1	1	4	—	3	5	3	3	4	6	4	37
Trademark	—	1	—	—	—	—	—	2	2	8	—	4	1	18
Sports	—	—	—	—	—	—	—	3	—	—	—	—	3	6
Miscellaneous	—	2	—	1	2	5	1	6	—	1	1	4	12	35
Total	128	68	74	57	110	148	165	145	117	129	101	117	197	1556

Note: M Category also represented in one or more agreements listed in miscellaneous column.

TABLE 2

National Treaty Contacts with PRC: 1966–78
(This table includes both single contacts, in bilateral agreements, and plural contacts, in trilateral and other multilateral agreements.)

Partner (in order of total volume)	1966	1967	1968	1969	1970	1971	1972	1973	1974	1975	1976	1977	1978	Total
Vietnam (N)	13	7	5	5	9	13	10	9	8	5	2	3	2	91
Korea (N)	7	3	1	1	9	12	13	8	7	4	7	7	9	88
Japan	5	1	7	7	10	8	6	5	5	4	2	3	10	73
Rumania	2	5	—	2	5	10	5	7	4	4	4	5	13	66
Albania	8	5	8	—	11	3	7	3	3	6	3	3	—	60
Pakistan	6	3	3	—	6	4	4	—	2	2	4	4	4	42
Nepal	5	4	7	—	1	4	3	4	1	3	3	—	5	40
Sri Lanka	2	2	2	2	3	7	11	1	1	5	—	3	1	40
Tanzania	5	1	6	5	6	1	—	1	1	5	3	—	4	38
Guinea	8	1	4	3	3	2	5	1	3	3	—	3	1	37
Zambia	2	4	5	5	7	1	—	1	1	5	3	—	3	37
Poland	4	3	2	2	3	3	4	2	2	1	2	2	3	33
Hungary	4	2	2	2	2	2	3	2	2	2	2	2	2	29
Mongolia	4	1	1	1	1	2	4	3	2	2	1	3	3	28
Yemen (S)	—	—	4	2	4	5	3	2	2	1	3	—	2	28
Afghanistan	4	1	1	3	4	—	3	3	3	1	1	2	1	27
Czechoslovakia	3	1	2	1	2	2	1	4	2	2	1	3	1	25
Bulgaria	2	2	1	1	1	2	1	3	3	2	2	2	3	24
U.S.S.R.	5	1	—	2	4	1	1	3	2	1	1	2	1	24
Egypt	2	1	4	1	1	4	1	1	1	2	1	3	1	22
Cuba	3	1	2	1	1	3	2	1	1	1	3	1	1	21
Finland	—	3	2	1	1	2	—	1	3	3	1	2	1	20
Yugoslavia	1	1	1	1	1	2	1	1	1	2	1	1	7	20
Kampuchea	2	—	2	2	—	—	1	2	2	2	4	—	—	19
Somalia	2	2	—	1	2	1	1	—	—	1	2	4	4	19
Germany (E)	6	1	1	1	1	1	1	1	1	2	—	1	1	18
Sudan	2	—	1	1	4	2	1	2	—	—	1	2	2	18
Laos	—	—	—	—	—	—	—	—	3	6	3	1	4	17
Algeria	1	—	—	—	1	4	3	1	3	1	2	—	—	16

(continued)

Table 2, continued

Partner (in order of total volume)	1966	1967	1968	1969	1970	1971	1972	1973	1974	1975	1976	1977	1978	Total
France	2	—	—	2	—	1	—	2	—	2	—	1	6	16
Congo	1	1	2	2	1	1	1	2	—	1	—	2	1	15
Ethiopia	—	—	—	—	1	2	1	2	—	—	3	3	3	15
Mauritania	—	7	—	1	1	1	2	—	1	1	—	2	—	15
Burma	6	—	—	—	—	3	1	1	—	1	—	1	3	14
Germany (W)	—	—	—	—	—	—	1	—	—	5	—	1	6	14
Mali	2	3	3	—	1	—	1	2	—	—	—	2	1	14
Cameroon	—	—	—	—	—	—	2	2	—	4	1	1	2	13
Guyana	—	—	—	—	—	3	4	1	—	3	1	—	1	13
Sierra Leone	—	—	—	—	—	4	2	3	—	—	1	2	1	13
Iraq	2	—	—	1	—	1	1	1	1	4	—	1	—	12
Mexico	—	—	—	—	—	—	2	3	—	3	1	1	2	12
Australia	—	—	—	—	1	—	1	3	1	—	3	—	2	11
Italy	—	—	—	—	—	2	1	2	—	1	—	1	4	11
Philippines	—	—	—	—	—	—	—	—	1	3	3	3	4	11
Bangladesh	—	—	—	—	—	—	—	—	—	1	—	—	6	10
Canada	—	—	—	—	1	1	2	5	1	—	—	—	—	10
Chile	—	—	—	—	1	2	4	1	—	—	—	—	2	10
Ghana	—	—	—	—	—	—	4	—	1	1	2	2	—	10
Yemen (N)	2	—	1	—	—	—	3	—	—	1	1	1	1	10
Argentina	—	—	—	—	—	—	1	—	—	—	—	1	7	9
Equatorial Guinea	—	—	—	—	1	2	1	1	—	—	2	2	—	9
Iran	—	—	—	—	—	1	1	2	—	1	1	1	2	9
U.S.A.	—	—	—	—	—	—	1	2	1	—	—	—	5	9
Zaire	—	—	—	—	—	—	1	3	3	—	1	1	—	9
Benin	—	—	—	—	—	—	3	—	2	1	2	—	—	8
Chad	—	—	—	—	—	—	1	2	—	—	1	1	3	8
Greece	—	—	—	—	—	—	—	5	—	1	—	—	1	8
Morocco	2	—	—	—	—	1	—	—	—	3	1	1	—	8
Rwanda	—	—	—	—	—	1	3	1	—	—	1	1	1	8
Tunisia	—	—	—	—	—	—	2	1	3	—	1	2	—	8
Madagascar	1	—	1	—	—	1	1	—	3	1	1	—	—	7
Syria	1	1	1	—	—	1	1	—	—	2	—	—	—	7
Thailand	—	—	—	—	—	—	1	—	—	1	—	1	5	7

224

Country	1	2	3	4	5	6	7	8	9	10	11	12	Total
Togo	3	1	—	—	1	—	2	—	—	—	—	—	7
United Kingdom	4	1	—	—	1	1	—	—	—	—	—	—	7
Upper Volta	1	1	1	—	1	3	—	—	—	1	—	—	7
Vietnam (S)	—	—	—	2	1	5	—	—	1	—	—	—	7
Gambia	1	1	1	—	1	—	—	—	—	—	—	—	6
Liberia	3	3	—	—	—	1	3	—	—	—	—	—	6
Malta	1	1	—	2	—	—	—	—	1	—	—	—	6
Niger	—	2	—	—	3	1	1	—	—	—	—	—	6
Norway	—	1	—	—	—	—	—	—	—	—	—	1	6
Peru	1	—	—	—	2	2	—	—	—	—	—	—	6
Senegal	—	—	—	3	—	1	5	—	—	—	—	—	6
Spain	4	1	2	1	1	2	1	—	—	—	—	—	5
Austria	—	1	1	1	—	1	1	—	—	—	—	—	5
Belgium	1	—	1	—	2	—	—	—	—	—	—	—	5
Jamaica	—	—	—	1	—	2	1	—	—	—	—	—	5
New Zealand	1	—	4	—	1	2	—	—	—	—	—	—	5
Sweden	—	1	1	2	—	—	2	—	—	—	—	—	4
Turkey	2	—	—	2	2	—	—	—	—	—	—	—	4
Central African Republic	—	1	—	—	—	—	—	—	—	—	—	—	4
Gabon	1	—	—	2	4	3	—	—	—	—	—	—	4
Guinea-Bissau	—	—	—	1	1	—	—	—	—	—	—	—	4
Libya	4	—	—	1	—	—	—	—	—	—	—	—	4
Malaysia	2	—	—	—	—	—	—	—	—	—	—	—	4
Mozambique	1	—	—	1	—	—	—	—	—	—	—	—	4
Netherlands	—	—	—	—	2	—	—	—	—	—	—	—	4
Nigeria	1	—	—	1	2	1	1	—	—	—	—	—	4
Switzerland	—	1	1	—	—	—	—	—	—	—	—	—	4
Trinidad & Tobago	—	—	—	1	—	—	1	—	—	—	—	—	4
Botswana	1	—	—	—	—	—	—	—	—	—	—	—	4
Brazil	—	—	1	—	—	3	—	—	—	—	—	—	3
Burundi	—	—	—	1	—	—	—	—	—	—	—	—	3
Denmark	—	—	—	—	1	—	—	—	—	—	—	—	3
Lebanon	1	—	1	2	2	1	—	—	—	—	—	—	3
Mauritius	—	1	—	1	—	—	—	—	—	—	—	—	3
Papua New Guinea	—	—	—	—	—	—	—	—	—	—	—	—	3
Sao Tome & Principe	—	—	1	2	—	—	—	—	—	—	—	—	3
Cape Verde	—	—	1	3	—	—	—	—	—	—	—	—	3
Comoros	—	—	—	1	—	—	—	—	—	—	—	—	2

(continued)

225

Table 2, continued

Partner (in order of total volume)	1966	1967	1968	1969	1970	1971	1972	1973	1974	1975	1976	1977	1978	Total
Cyprus	—	—	—	—	—	1	—	1	—	—	—	—	—	2
Ecuador	—	—	—	—	—	—	—	—	—	2	—	—	—	2
Hong Kong	—	1	—	—	—	1	—	—	—	—	—	1	—	2
Kuwait	—	—	—	—	—	1	1	—	—	1	—	1	—	2
Luxemburg	—	—	—	—	1	—	—	1	—	—	1	—	1	2
Seychelles	—	—	—	—	—	—	—	—	—	—	1	—	—	2
Uganda	—	—	—	—	—	—	1	—	1	1	1	1	—	2
Venezuela	—	—	—	—	—	—	—	—	—	—	—	—	—	2
West Samoa	—	—	—	—	—	1	—	—	—	1	—	1	1	1
Barbados	—	—	—	—	—	—	—	—	—	—	—	—	—	1
Fiji	—	—	—	—	—	—	—	—	—	—	—	—	—	1
Iceland	—	—	—	—	—	—	—	—	—	—	—	1	1	1
Jordan	—	—	—	—	—	—	1	—	—	—	—	—	—	1
Kenya	—	—	—	—	—	—	1	—	—	—	—	—	1	1
Maldives	—	—	—	—	—	—	—	—	—	—	—	—	1	1
Oman Sudan	—	—	—	—	—	1	—	—	—	—	—	—	—	1
Portugal	—	—	—	—	—	—	—	—	—	—	1	—	—	1
San Marino	—	—	—	—	—	—	—	—	—	—	1	—	—	1
Surinam	—	—	—	—	—	—	—	—	—	—	—	—	—	1
Total	128	69	81	60	113	146	166	146	114	148	105	115	194	1585

TABLE 3

Topical Distribution of Agreements Listed in PRC's Official Treaty Series (TYC), 1966–73
(The classification is the same as the classification used in the TYC.)

	1966	1967	1968	1969	1970	1971	1972	1973	Total
Political									
Joint Communiqué	1				5**	4;13**	5;21**	7;2**	60
Others	2	2							7
Boundary Problems						1***; 3*	1††		2
Economic									
Commerce & Navigation					1		1		2
Economic Aid, Loan, and Technical Cooperation						1		1	2
Trade and Payment		1	2	1	2	1	7	7	21
General Conditions for Delivery of Goods	33	21	27	19	19	39	33	29	220
Registration of Trademark	4	4	3	3	4	3	4	3	28
Others	1†††		1*	1*	1*			2	28
Culture									
Cultural Cooperation		1	1						4
Broadcasting and Television Cooperation		1					1	5	8
Others	2		1*		1	1			5

(continued)

Table 3, continued

	1966	1967	1968	1969	1970	1971	1972	1973	Total
Science and Technology	1	1						2	4
Agriculture and Forest	1						1		2
Fishery					3				3
Health and Sanitation		3	1	1	2		3	5	15
Postal and Telecommunication						2		1	3
Communication and Transportation									
Air Transportation	6						6	6	18
Water Transportation	1					2	1	1	5
Ship Inspection								2	2
Multilateral		1						2	3
Total	52	34	37	25	37	70	85	75	415

*Indicates semiofficial agreements.

†Protocol establishing consular relations between the PRC and San Marino, May 5, 1971.

††Extension of Economic and Cultural Cooperation Agreement between the PRC and Mongolia (52-54).

**Indicates communiqué establishing, normalizing, elevating diplomatic relations.

†††Economic and Cultural Cooperation Agreement between the PRC and Cambodia, April 29, 1966.

228

TABLE 4

National Distribution of Agreements Listed in PRC Official Treaty Series (TYC), 1966–73

Country	1966	1967	1968	1969	1970	1971	1972	1973	Total
Afghanistan	1			1				1	6
Albania	2	1					2	1	9
Algeria			1		1		3		7
Argentina					3	3	1		1
Austria						1**	1**		3
Australia						1**	1	1	3
Belgium							1**	2	1
Benin (Dahomey)						1**	1**		2
Bulgaria	1		1	1	1	1	1;1**		8
Burma	5	1		1		1	1	2	7
Burundi						1			2
Cambodia	1						2		1
Cameroun									4
Canada					1**	1**	2	1	5
Chad								4	3
Chile					1**		1**	2	4
Congo (B)		1				1	2		3
Cuba	2	1	2			2	2	1	11
Cyprus				1		1**		1	2

(continued)

Table 4, continued

Country	1966	1967	1968	1969	1970	1971	1972	1973	Total
Czechoslovakia	1	1	1	1	2	2	1	2	11
Egypt	1	1	4	1		4	1		12
Equatorial Guinea					1**	1		1	3
Ethiopia				1	1**			1	3
Finland		1	2		1	2		2	8
France	1						1	1	3
Germany (E)	4	1	1	1	2	1	1**	1	12
Germany (W)							2;1**		2
Ghana							1**	3	3
Greece	3	1	2	2		2	3	1	4
Guinea	2	2			2	2	1;1**		14
Guyana			2	2	2		2	2	2
Hungary						1**			16
Iceland						1**	1	1	1
Iran	1								3
Iraq					1**	1	1	2	1
Italy							1**		5
Jamaica			2*	1*	4*	3*	1**	1	1
Japan	4	1	1	1	4	6	2		12
Korea (N)						1**			19
Kuwait						1**	2		1
Lebanon							2		3
Luxembourg							1**		1

(continued)

Country	1	2	3	4	5	6	7	8	Total
Madagascar							1**		1
Maldive							1**		1
Mali		2	1					2	5
Malta							1**		1
Mauritania		4					2		6
Mauritius							1**		1
Mexico		1			1		1**		3
Mongolia	2	1				1	3	1	11
Morocco	2					1		1	4
Nepal	2		3					1	6
Netherlands							1**		1
New Zealand							1**	1	2
Nigeria						1**	1		2
Pakistan	2		1				2		5
Peru						3;1*			4
Poland	2	2	2	2	3	3	2	2	18
Romania		4		2	3	4	4	4	21
Rwanda						1**	1		2
San Marino						1***			1
Sierra Leone						2;1**	1		4
Senegal						1**		1	2
Soviet Union	4	1			2	1	1	2	11
Spain	1							1**	1
Sri Lanka (Ceylon)		2	2	2	1	3	5	1	17
Sudan	2		1	1	1	1	1	1	8

Table 4, continued

Country	1966	1967	1968	1969	1970	1971	1972	1973	Total
Sweden								1	1
Switzerland								2	2
Tanzania			1						1
Togo							1**		1
Tunisia								1	1
Turkey						1**			2
United Kingdom							1**	1	2
United Nations								1	1
United States							1	2	3
Upper Volta								1;1**	2
Vietnam	5	4	3	2	1	3	1	2	21
Yemen (ARY)							1	1	2
Yemen (PDY)			1	1			1	1	4
Yugoslavia	1	1	1	1			1	1	6
Zaire							1**	2	3
Total	52	33	37	25	37	70	85	73	412

*Indicates semiofficial agreements.
†Protocol establishing consular relations between the PRC and San Marino, May 5, 1971.
**Indicates communiqués establishing, normalizing, elevating diplomatic relations.

APPENDIX:
QUESTIONABLE AGREEMENTS

The following agreements were listed in Wolfgan Bartke, The Agreements of the PR China (Hamburg: Des Instituts fur Asienkunde Hamburg, 1976). Since the compiler is unable to locate the reported agreements in the People's Daily, Peking Review, and Survey of China Mainland Press, they are not included in the Calendar.

Sources (with abbreviations) as appearing in Bartke's Agreements of the PR China 1949-75

NNA   Not listed in Bartke's
BBC   British Broadcasting Co.
CBC   Canadian Broadcasting Co.
DPA   Deutsche - Presse - Agentur
EPAKL   Entwicklungspolitische Aktivitaten der Kommunistischen Lander, a monthly review of Forschungsinstitut der Friedrich Ebert-stiftung, Bonn
FAZ   Not listed in Bartke's
KYODO   News Agency, Tokyo
NCNA   New China News Agency, Peking
NZZ   Neue Zurcher Zeitung, Zurich, Switzerland
SWB   Summary of World Broadcasts, as edited by The Monitoring Service of the British Broadcasting Co. , Caversham Park, Reading, Berks.
TANYNG   News Agency of Yugoslavia
TASS   Soviet Russian News Agency
UPI   United Press International, USA

1. 1/17/66 — — CONGO   PROTOCOL
Construction of a broadcasting station with PRC aid.
Peking Radio 1/20/66.

2. 9/25/66 — — AFGHANISTAN   PROTOCOL
Economic and technical cooperation relating to Chinese aid on construction of a silkworm station.
NCNA 9/8/66.

3. 9/26/66 — — ALGERIA   PROTOCOL
Economic and technical cooperation relating to construction of a ceramics factory.
NCNA 9/26/66.

4. 1/24/67 — — CONGO   PROTOCOL
Medical aid.
NCNA 1/25/67.

5. 4/1/67 — — AFGHANISTAN   PROTOCOL
Economic and technical cooperation relating to a fishbreed
experimental station.
NCNA 4/2/67.

6. 4/28/67 — — AFGHANISTAN   PROTOCOL
Economic and technical cooperation relating to a poultry farm.
NCNA 4/28/67.

7. 5/26/67 — — ZAMBIA   AGREEMENT
Loan.
EPAKL 2/69, at 68.

8. 12/23/67 — — PAKISTAN   AGREEMENT
PRC providing a loan of US $40 million.
Karachi Radio 12/28/67.

9. 9/24/68 — — YEMEN(S)
PRC grants a loan of US $9.6 million.
Aden Radio 9/29/68.

10. 12/26/68 — — PAKISTAN
PRC granting an interest-free loan of US $42 million.
Karachi Radio 12/26/68.

11. 7/14/69 — — YEMEN(N)   PROTOCOL
Construction of a secondary school with PRC aid.
NCNA 7/14/69.

12. 12/17/69 — — U.S.S.R.   PROTOCOL
Establishing 1970-71 timetables for running of passenger trains
and through coaches on Moscow-Zabaykalsk-Peking, Moscow-
Ulan Bator-Peking, and other international trains.
TASS 12/18/69.

13. 4/12/70 — — VIETNAM(N)   PROTOCOL
Border railway.
Signed at twelfth Sino-Vietnamese Railway Conference.
Nanning Radio 4/13/70.

14. 11/17/70 — — AFGHANISTAN   EXCHANGE OF LETTERS
Supply of commodities by PRC under Loan Agreement (70-95).
NCNA 11/17/70.

15. 1/22/71 — — KOREA(N) AGREEMENT
Border river transport.
NCNA 1/23/71.

16. 3/7/71 — — NEPAL PROTOCOL
Relating to Agreement on Economic and Technical Cooperation.
NCNA 3/7/71.

17. 4/12/71 — — VIETNAM(N) AGREEMENT
Boundary railway.
NCNA 4/14/71.

18. 5/5/71 — — PAKISTAN
PRC providing a new loan of U. S. $300 million.
NZZ 5/18/71.

19. 6/ /71 — — SUDAN PROTOCOL
Construction of Medani-Gederef road project with PRC aid.
Omdurman Radio 6/10/71.

20. 7/11/71 — — PAKISTAN AGREEMENT
Transactions of goods between Gilgit Agency and Sinkiang via
ancient silk road.
Pakistan Radio 7/13/71.

21. 7/14/71 — — YEMEN(S) PROTOCOL
Trade.
ANA 7/14/71.

22. 8/24/71 — — SUDAN AGREEMENT
PRC providing a loan of U. S. $35 million.
UPI 8/24/71.

23. 9/14/71 — — CONGO AGREEMENT
PRC military aid.
Brazzaville Radio 9/14/71.

24. 12/23/71 — — YUGOSLAVIA AGREEMENT
Convertibility of "manipulative credits" between Bank of China
and bank representatives from Yugoslavia.
TANYUG 12/25/71.

25. 1/29/72 — — CHILE
PRC granting a loan of U. S. $70 million.
UPI 1/29/72.

26. 3/20/72 — — VIETNAM(N) PROTOCOL
Railway.
Signed at fourteenth Sino-Vietnamese Railway Conference.
Kumning Radio 3/22/72.

27. 3/29/72 — — PAKISTAN AGREEMENT
Promotion of mutual cooperation in civil aviation.
Karachi Radio 3/20/72.

28. 4/13/72 — — GUYANA
PRC granting a loan of US $52 million.
Japan Times 6/30/72.

29. 4/27/72 — — IRAN AGREEMENT
Establishment of an air link.
NCNA 4/27/72.

30. 8/1/72 — — MAURITIUS
PRC granting a loan of US $33 million.
NZZ 1/6/73.

31. 8/20/72 — — MAURITANIA PROTOCOL
Cultural cooperation.
NCNA 8/21/72.

32. 8/21/72 — — PAKISTAN AGREEMENT
Cooperation in re-insurance.
Karachi Radio 8/22/72.

33. 10/23/72 — — SRI LANKA AGREEMENT
Rubber - rice.
Colombo Radio 10/23/72.

34. 11/18/72 — — JAPAN AGREEMENT
News exchange between New China News Agency and Kyoto News
Agency.
KYODO 11/18/72.

35. 12/13/72 — — CONGO PROTOCOL
Building of Bouenza dam with Chinese aid.
Brazzaville Radio 12/13/72.

36. 1/ /73 — — AFGHANISTAN
$44 million loan to Afghanistan.
NZZ (?) 1/7/73.

37. 1/14/73 — — ZAIRE
PRC granting Zaire a loan of U. S. $115 million.
NZZ 2/1/73.

38. 2/ /73 — — CHILE
PRC granting a loan of U. S. $52 million.
FAZ 2/12/73.

39. 4/ /73 — — GHANA PROTOCOL
1973 Trade.
Ghana News Agency 5/16/73.

40. 5/22/73 — — PAKISTAN PROTOCOL
Construction of Tarbela-Wah transmission line.
Karachi Radio 5/22/73.

41. 5/ /73 — — CHAD
PRC offering a loan of U. S. $10 million to Chad.
NZZ 5/23/73.

42. 5/ /73(?) — — ZAMBIA
PRC donates US $10 million to Zambia for overcoming transport
problems in connection with closure of frontiers between Zambia
and Rhodesia.
NZZ 5/30/73.

43. 6/17/73(?) — — UNITED KINGDOM AGREEMENT
Civil air transport.
NZZ 6/20/73.

44. 7/15/73 — — U. S. S. R. PROTOCOL
Simultaneous regular direct flights on Moscow-Peking route.
TASS 7/16/73.

45. 7/16/73 — — VENEZUELA AGREEMENT
Trade.
Prensa Latina, Havana 7/17/73.

46. 8/10/73(?) — — PAKISTAN PROTOCOL
Extension of validity of trade agreement.
Karachi Radio 8/10/73.

8/16/73 — — TANZANIA PROTOCOL
Agreement of joint shipping company.
NCNA 8/18/73.

9/15/73(?) — — UGANDA   CONTRACT
Goods exchange.
NCNA 9/16/73.

47. 9/20/73 — — PAKISTAN   PROTOCOL
Construction of Tarbela cotton spinning mill.
Karachi Radio 9/20/73.

48. 10/15/73 — — CANADA   AGREEMENT
Civil aviation.
CBC Montreal 10/15/73.

49. 10/24/73(?) — — GUYANA   AGREEMENT
1973 trade.
NCNA 10/25/73.

50. 11/ /73 1/21/74 — ARGENTINA
Program for medical cooperation.
NZZ 11/15/73. The ratification was reported in NCNA 1/22/74.

51. 11/26/73 — — YEMEN(S)   AGREEMENT
Trade.
SWB/ME/W 753.

52. 1/18/74 — — MADAGASCAR   AGREEMENT
Trade.
NCNA 1/18/74.

53. 1/18/74 — — MADAGASCAR   AGREEMENT
Economic and technical cooperation.
NCNA 1/18/74.

54. 2/9/74 — — SUDAN   PROTOCOL
1974 trade.
SWB/ME/W 763.

55. 3/ /74 — — CANADA   AGREEMENT
Emigration to Canada of Chinese inhabitants of PRC to their
relatives.
BBC 3/25/74.

56. 4/13/74 — — CONGO   PROTOCOL
Medical team sent by PRC.
Peking Radio 4/17/74.

57. 4/19/74 — — PAKISTAN   PROTOCOL
Sharing of servicing facilities throughout world.
Karachi Radio 4/19/74.

58. 4/26/74 — — GERMANY(W)   CONTRACT
Exchange of service between Deutsche-Presse-Agentur and New
China News Agency.
DPA 4/20/74.

59. 4/30/74 — — GHANA   PROTOCOL
1974 trade.
NCNA 4/30/74.

60. 5/24/74 — — PAKISTAN   AGREEMENT
Border trade.
Karachi Radio 5/25/74.

61. 5/26/74 — PEKING   CAMBODIA   AGREEMENT
PRC's gratis provision of military equipment and supplies to
Cambodia in 1974.
NCNA 5/26/74.

62. 7/10/74 — — SIERRA LEONE   PROTOCOL
Construction of agrotechnical stations.
NCNA 11/7/74.

63. 7/24/74 — — SUDAN   PROTOCOL
Expanding rice cultivation in Sudan.
SWB/ME/W 786.

64. 8/10/74 — — PAKISTAN   PROTOCOL
Setting up of fertilizer works in Northwest Frontier Province
and a sports complex in Islamabad.
SWB 789, cit. Karachi Radio 8/10/74.

65. 9/7/74 — — KOREA(N)   AGREEMENT
Method of operation of joint international passenger traffic and
through service (among PRC, Korean(N), Vietnam(N), Mongolia,
and U. S. S. R.).
NCNA 9/7/74.

66. 9/7/74 — — MONGOLIA   AGREEMENT
Method of operation of joint international passenger traffic and
through passenger service for 1975-77.
NCNA 9/7/74.

67. 9/29/74 — — IRAN PROTOCOL
Trade.
Teheran Radio, cit. BBC ME/W 796.

68. 11/7/74 — — AUSTRALIA AGREEMENT
Cultural exchange program.
Melbourne Radio 11/7/74, cit. SWB.

69. 11/12/74 — — BRAZIL AGREEMENT
Mutual supply of commodities.
NCNA 11/12/74.

70. 11/14/74 — — JAPAN TREATY
Consular relations.
KYODO 11/14/74.

71. 12/8/74 — — ZAIRE COMMUNIQUÉ
News exchange.
NCNA 12/9/74.

72. 1/22/75 — — SRI LANKA PROTOCOL
Setting up a freshwater fish-breeding research center.
SWB/W 812, cit. Colombo Radio 1/23/75.

73. 2/5/75(?) — — PAKISTAN PROTOCOL
Extension of 1968 loan of U. S. $42 million to 11/30/75.
SWB/W 814, cit. Karachi Radio 2/5/75.

74. 2/5/75 — — LAOS AGREEMENT
Trade.
Vientiane Radio, cit. SWB 4831 2/15/75.

75. 4/4/75 — — TUNISIA PROTOCOL
Construction of a canal linking Siti Salem dam to Cap-Bon;
delivery of 1,000 railway vans by PRC for transport of phosphates.
SWB 4875.

76. 4/5/75 — — SUDAN PROTOCOL
1975 trade.
SWB/ME/W 822.

77. 4/16/75 — — PAKISTAN AGREEMENT
Supply of forty-one diesel generating sets by PRC.
SWB/W 823, cit. Karachi Radio 4/17/75.

78. 4/16/75 — — JAPAN AGREEMENT
Reciprocal yen-yuan toward transactions between Bank of China
and Bank of Tokyo.
KYODO 4/17/75.

4/18/75 — — SRI LANKA EXCHANGE OF LETTERS
Mutual exemption from income and other taxes on freight
earnings by vessels.
NCNA 4/18/75.

79. 4/25/75 — — PAKISTAN PROTOCOL
Establishment of a textile mill in Punjab.
SWB/W 824, cit. Karachi Radio 9/25/75.

80. 4/30/75 — — CONGO AGREEMENT
Supply of military equipment by PRC and assistance in training
of cadres.
NZZ 5/3/75.

81. 5/31/75 — — VIETNAM(N) PROTOCOL
PRC's nonrefundable emergency aid.
SWB/FE/4927 6/12/75.

82. 6/25/75 — — MOZAMBIQUE JOINT COMMUNIQUÉ
Establishment of diplomatic relations.
NCNA 7/2/75.

83. 7/23/75 — — TUNISIA AGREEMENT
News exchange.
NCNA 7/23/75.

9/3/75(?) — — PAPUA NEW GUINEA AGREEMENT
Trade.
NCNA 9/4/75.

9/25/75 — — SYRIA AGREEMENT
Broadcasting and television cooperation.
NCNA 9/22/75.

84. 10/11/75(?) — — SUDAN PROTOCOL
Exploiting fishery resources in Nuba Lake with PRC aid.
SWB/ME/W 849, cit. Omdurman Radio 10/11/75.

85. 11/26/75 — — YEMEN(S) EXCHANGE OF NOTES
Construction of a mill with an annual production of sixty tons of yarn.
SWB/ME/W 856.

The following agreement was reported in Dieter Heinzig, "PRC-Soviet Relations After Mao," in Jurgen Domes, ed. , Chinese Politics After Mao, Great Britain: University College Cardiff Press, in association with Christopher Davies, Ltd. , 52 Mansel St. , Swansea, Wales, 1979, pp. 277 and 283. (Excerpts).

SECRET TREATY ON THE CONFLUENCE OF THE AMUR AND THE USSURI

In June or July, 1977, a Sino-Soviet treaty on navigation along the main confluence of the Amur and the Ussuri rivers was concluded, with the Chinese side initiating the negotiations.[1] It is assumed that the Chinese were led to take this step by, above all, their need to transport more coal on the rivers.

The treaty is said to include the following points:

(1) China is to give notice of its intention to dispatch ships along the main junctions; the Soviet Union agrees to permit the ships to pass.
(2) This notice is to be given to the joint Sino-Soviet Border Navigation Commission.
(3) The passage of Chinese ships is to take place during daylight.
(4) During passage internal Soviet law is applicable.
(5) The treaty does not affect the standpoints of the two parties on the border question.

The treaty is not to be confused with agreements reached at the twentieth session of the Border Navigation Commission (27 July to 6 October 1977).[2] These agreements (effective 6 October 1977) deal with technical matters such as placement of buoys, the dredging of silted sections of the river bed, as well as the regulation of navigation (apart from that of the main junction) on the Kazakevich tributary.[3]

The treaty of June or July is an attempt at reaching a modus vivendi on a question under dispute for several years.

NOTES (renumbered)

1. Information from diplomatic sources in Peking. — The conclusion of a treaty about the passage of Chinese ships along the main confluence of the Amur and the Ussuri rivers was confirmed in December, 1977, in Harbin in a statement made by a deputy chairman of the Department of Foreign Affairs of the Revolutionary Committee of Heilungkiang Province to foreign correspondents (see South China Morning Post, Hong Kong, 14 December 1977). According to this statement, the treaty was concluded between the foreign ministries

of the two countries and does not affect the border navigation agreement of 6 October 1977, which regulates 'technical details. ' As regards the contents of the treaty about passage along the main junction, the functionary merely said that the treaty has made it possible for Chinese ships to use the main junction once again, if the Kazakevich (Fu-yuan) should become too shallow. The passage of Chinese ships up to 500 tons began in September, 1977. This date confirms the information that the treaty on the passage of Chinese ships along the main confluence was concluded <u>before</u> the border navigation agreement of 6 October 1977.

    2. <u>TASS</u>, 7 October 1977, <u>Summary of World Broadcasts</u> SU/5636/A3/1; <u>Hsinhua</u>, 6 October 1977, <u>News from Hsinhua News Agency</u>, 7 October 1978, p. 20. The <u>TASS</u> and <u>Hsinhua</u> reports are not identical. The <u>TASS</u> announcement was broadcast by Radio Moscow in its English-language service and in its Russian service aimed at listeners abroad, but not in its domestic service; neither was it published in <u>Pravda</u> or <u>Izvestiya</u>. The <u>Hsinhua</u> announcement was made public both in the English-language foreign broadcast service and in <u>Jen-min jih-pao</u> of 7 October 1977, p. 4.

    3. Information from diplomatic sources in Peking.

INDEX:
BILATERAL AND TRILATERAL AGREEMENTS BY PARTNERS

Partners

Afghanistan
Albania
Algeria
Argentina
Australia
Austria
Bangladesh
Barbados
Belgium
Benin
Botswana
Brazil
Bulgaria
Burma
Burundi
Cameroon
Canada
Cape Verde
Central African
  Republic
Chad
Chile
Colombia
Comoros
Congo
Cuba
Cyprus
Czechoslovakia
Denmark
Djibouti
Ecuador
Egypt
Equatorial Guinea
Ethiopia
Fiji
Finland
France
Gabon
Gambia
Germany (E)
Germany (W)
Ghana
Greece

Guinea
Guinea-Bissau
Guyana
Hong Kong
Hungary
Iceland
Iran
Iraq
Ireland
Italy
Jamaica
Japan
Jordan
Kampuchea
Kenya
Kiribati
Korea (N)
Kuwait
Laos
Lebanon
Liberia
Libya
Luxembourg
Madagascar
Malaysia
Maldives
Mali
Malta
Mauritania
Mauritius
Mexico
Mongolia
Morocco
Mozambique
Nepal
Netherlands
New Zealand
Nicaragua
Niger
Nigeria
Norway
Oman
Pakistan

Papua New Guinea
Peru
Philippines
Poland
Portugal
Rumania
Rwanda
Samoa (W)
San Marino
Sao Tome and Principe
Senegal
Seychelles
Sierra Leone
Singapore
Somalia
Spain
Sri Lanka
Sudan
Surinam
Sweden
Switzerland
Syria
Tanzania
Thailand
Togo
Trinidad and Tobago
Tunisia
Turkey
Uganda
United Kingdom
U.S.A.
U.S.S.R.
Upper Volta
Venezuela
Vietnam (N)
Vietnam (S-National
  Liberation Front)
Yemen (N) (YAR)
Yemen (S)
Yugoslavia
Zaire
Zambia
Zimbabwe

Afghanistan

(66-25)	4/8/66	Joint Communiqué: Visit of Chairman Liu Shao-ch'i
(66-48)	5/24/66	Plan for cultural cooperation
(66-87)	7/29/66	Protocol: Economic and technical cooperation
(66-126)	12/28/66	Protocol: Exchange of goods
(67-60)	12/6/67	Exchange of Letters: Technical cooperation in tea planting
(68-1)	1/11/68	Protocol: Exchange of goods
(69-4)	1/26/69	Protocol: Exchange of goods
(69-10)	3/8/69	Notes: Aquaculture
(69-56)	12/20/69	Minutes: Tea planting
(70-17)	3/23/70	Certificate: Soil construction, etc.
(70-95)	11/14/70	Exchange of Letters: Loan
(70-107)	12/26/70	Agreement: Trade and payments
(70-108)	12/26/70	Protocol: Exchange of goods
(72-34)	4/4/72	Protocol: Exchange of goods
(72-81)	7/25/72	Exchange of Instruments: Construction of a hospital
(72-82)	7/26/72	Agreement: Air transportation
(73-13)	1/25/73	Protocol: Exchange of goods
(73-23)	2/ /73	Notes: Expansion of Bagrami textile mill
(73-129)	11/21/73	Notes: Constructing a hospital
(74-30)	4/21/74	Protocol: Exchange of goods
(74-31)	4/21/74	Agreement: Trade and payments
(74-101)	12/8/74	Agreement: Economic and technical cooperation
(75-42)	5/11/75	Protocol: Exchange of goods
(76-41)	6/5/76	Protocol: Exchange of goods
(77-39)	4/13/77	Protocol: Exchange of goods
(77-40)	4/13/77	Agreement: Trade and payments
(78-38)	3/21/78	Protocol: Exchange of goods

Albania

(66-38)	5/4/66	Protocol: Shipping
(66-42)	5/11/66	Joint Statement: Visit of Premier Shehu
(66-49)	5/24/66	Plan for cooperation between academies of sciences
(66-71)	6/28/66	Communiqué: Visit of Chinese Communist Party
(66-103)	10/20/66	Agreement: Loan for the petroleum industry
(66-114)	11/21/66	Protocol: Exchange of goods and payments
(66-115)	11/21/66	Protocol: Loans

(66–122)	11/30/66	Protocol: Scientific and technical cooperation
(67–15)	4/24/67	Plan for cultural cooperation
(67–22)	5/28/67	Protocol: Shipping
(67–48)	10/14/67	Press Communiqué: Visit of Chairman Shehu
(67–61)	12/9/67	Protocol: Exchange of goods and payments
(67–62)	12/9/67	Protocol: Credit
(68–5)	2/26/68	Protocol: Scientific and technical cooperation
(68–43)	6/11/68	Protocol: Sino-Albanian Shipping Joint Stock Company
(68–68)	11/20/68	Agreement: Loan
(68–69)	11/20/68	Press Communiqué: Trade talks
(68–70)	11/20/68	Protocol: Technical aid and equipment
(68–71)	11/20/68	Protocol: Providing machines and ships, etc.
(68–72)	11/20/68	Protocol: Exchange of goods and payments
(68–73)	11/29/68	Protocol: Loan
(70–1)	1/30/70	Protocol: Scientific and technical cooperation
(70–2)	1/19/70	Protocol: Barter and payments
(70–3)	1/19/70	Protocol: Credits
(70–22)	4/9/70	Protocol: Sino-Albanian Shipping Joint Stock Company
(70–73)	10/16/70	Agreement: Loan
(70–74)	10/16/70	Agreement: Exchange of goods and payments
(70–75)	10/16/70	Protocol: Providing equipment for projects
(70–76)	10/16/70	Protocol: Supply of general materials
(70–77)	10/16/70	Protocol: Loan
(70–78)	10/16/70	Protocol: Delivery of goods and payments
(70–79)	10/17/70	Plan for scientific cooperation
(71–106)	10/19/71	Protocol: Scientific and technical cooperation
(71–132)	12/5/71	Protocol: Loan
(71–133)	12/5/71	Protocol: Exchange of goods and payments
(72–33)	3/28/72	Agreement: Air transport
(72–37)	4/8/72	Protocol: Sino-Albanian Shipping Joint Stock Company
(72–40)	4/11/72	Agreement: Loan for the farm machinery
(72–107)	10/5/72	Plan for scientific cooperation
(72–114)	10/12/72	Protocol: Aviation
(72–131)	11/9/72	Protocol: Exchange of goods and payments
(72–132)	11/9/72	Protocol: Delivery of goods
(73–131)	11/21/73	Agreement: Scientific cooperation
(73–132)	11/21/73	Executive plan of scientific cooperation
(73–142)	12/11/73	Protocol: Scientific and technical cooperation
(74–4)	1/15/74	Protocol: Loan
(74–5)	1/15/74	Protocol: Exchange of goods and payments
(74–66)	9/30/74	Protocol: Exchange of goods and payments
(75–23)	3/28/75	Plan for scientific cooperation

(75-55)	7/3/75	Agreement: Loan
(75-56)	7/3/75	Agreement: Exchange of goods and payments
(75-57)	7/3/75	Protocol: Providing equipment for projects
(75-58)	7/3/75	Protocol: Providing general materials
(75-95)	10/16/75	Protocol: Technical science cooperation
(76-9)	2/7/76	Protocol: Exchange of goods and payments
(76-10)	2/7/76	Protocol: Loan
(76-28)	4/29/76	Protocol: Shipping
(77-10)	2/1/77	Protocol: Exchange of goods and payments
(77-11)	2/1/77	Protocol: Loan
(77-97)	11/3/77	Protocol: Scientific and technical cooperation

Algeria

(66-66)	6/20/66	Memorandum: Construction of exhibition hall
(70-13)	3/17/70	Protocol: Medical cooperation
(71-70)	7/27/71	Agreement: Economic and technical cooperation
(71-77)	8/1/71	Joint Communiqué: Visit of government delegation of Algeria
(71-107)	10/27/71	Agreement: Trade
(71-109)	10/28/71	Joint Press Communiqué: Visit of PRC government trade delegation
(72-125)	11/6/72	Press Communiqué: Trade talks
(72-126)	11/6/72	Protocol: Trade
(72-127)	11/6/72	Documents: Economic and technical cooperation
(73-54)	5/4/73	Agreement: Insurance
(74-17)	2/23/74	Protocol: Trade
(74-19)	3/2/74	Joint Communiqué: Visit of President Boumediene
(74-97)	11/29/74	Protocol: Trade
(75-98)	10/20/75	Draft: Shipping
(76-17)	3/12/76	Agreement: Maritime transport
(76-97)	12/22/76	Minutes: Surgical instrument factory
(79-58)	5/19/79	Agreement: Long-term trade
(80-142)	9/17/80	Agreement: Strengthen friendly relations and promote cultural exchanges

Argentina

(72-12)	2/16/72	Joint Communiqué: Establishment of diplomatic relations
(77-12)	2/2/77	Agreement: Trade
(78-78)	5/30/78	Minutes: Trade Agreement

(78-79)	5/30/78	Document: Trademark registration
(78-80)	5/30/78	Document: Exemption of maritime tax
(78-81)	5/30/78	Agreement: Maritime transport
(78-82)	5/30/78	Exchange of Notes: Tax Advantages for maritime transportation
(78-83)	5/30/78	Exchange of Notes: Reciprocal registry of wheat, corn, and cotton
(78-84)	5/30/78	Exchange of Notes: Long-term purchase of cotton
(80-80)	6/6/80	Agreement: Granting of $300 million of financial credit to PRC
(80-86)	6/7/80	Agreement: Economic cooperation
(80-87)	6/7/80	Agreement: Scientific and technical cooperation
(80-88)	6/7/80	Exchange of Notes: Cultural exchange

Australia

(72-157)	12/21/72	Joint Communiqué: Establishment of diplomatic relations
(73-58)	5/19/73	Press Communiqué: Trade talks
(73-89)	7/24/73	Agreement: Trade
(73-118)	11/4/73	Joint Press Communiqué: Visit of Prime Minister Whitlam
(74-72)	10/12/74	Exchange of Notes: Registration of trade marks
(76-53)	6/23/76	Agreement: Relics exhibition
(76-54)	6/23/76	Arrangement: Relics exhibition
(76-78)	10/8/76	Exchange of Notes: Travel
(77-48)	4/28/77	Exchange of Notes: Relics Exhibition
(78-133)	9/18/78	Exchange of Notes: Establishing general consulate
(78-183)	12/5/78	Minutes: Exchange of data on ionosphere
(79-64)	6/6/79	Draft: Scientific and technical cooperation
(79-125)	11/28/79	Exchange of Letters: Establishment of official links of friendship between Kiangsu Province and Victorian State
(79-126)	12/5/79	Joint Statement: Friendly cooperation between Kwangtung Province and New South Wales State
(80-50)	4/11/80	Agreement: Technical and economic cooperation between Kwangtung Province and New South Wales
(80-69)	5/10/80	Agreement: Holding Canton Trade Fair at Sidney
(80-96)	6/21/80	Agreement(?): Establishing friendship city relations between Tientsin and Melbourne

Austria

(71-47)	5/26/71	Joint Communiqué: Establishment of diplomatic relations
(72-122)	11/2/72	Agreement: Trade and payments
(73-41)	4/2/73	Exchange of Notes: Trade and payment
(73-117)	10/30/73	Agreement: Exhibition of PRC archaelogical finds
(77-36)	4/4/77	Exchange of Notes: Trademark registration
(80-164)	11/5/80	Agreement: Economic, industrial, and technological cooperation for ten-year period

Bangladesh

(75-84)	10/4/75	Joint Communiqué: Establishment of diplomatic relations
(77-1)	1/4/77	Agreement: Economic and technical cooperation
(77-2)	1/4/77	Agreement: Trade and payments
(77-3)	1/ 6/77	Press Communiqué: Visit of General Rahman
(78-11)	1/24/78	Protocol: Trade
(78-36)	3/21/78	Agreement: Economic and technical cooperation
(78-37)	3/21/78	Agreement: Scientific and technical cooperation
(78-61)	4/28/78	Agreement: News exchange
(78-180)	11/29/78	Agreement: Maritime transport
(78-186)	12/10/78	Protocol: Trade
(79-35)	3/29/79	Protocol: Scientific and technical cooperation
(79-121)	11/17/79	Agreement: Cultural cooperation
(80-33)	3/1/80	Agreement: Five-year long term trade
(80-34)	3/1/80	Protocol: Five-year long term trade
(80-112)	7/24/80	Agreement: Extension of PRC loans to Bangladesh
(80-113)	7/24/80	Agreement: Civil air transport

Barbados

(77-58)	5/30/77	Joint Communiqué: Establishment of diplomatic relations
(80-92)	6/13/80	Agreement: Cultural cooperation

Belgium

(71-106)	10/25/71	Joint Communiqué: Establishment of diplomatic relations

(73–50)	4/22/73	Press Communiqué: Establishment of Sino-Belgium Trade Joint Committee
(75–29)	4/10/75	Exchange of Notes: Trademark registration
(75–36)	4/20/75	Agreement: Maritime transport
(75–37)	4/20/75	Agreement: Civil air transport
(80–61)	4/30/80	Agreement: Interest-free government loans
(80–132)	9/14/80	Agreement: Joint venture for sale of coal
(80–176)	12/3/80	Minutes: Talks between ministers in charge of the State Scientific and Technological Commission
(80–181)	12/9/80	Agreement: Cultural cooperation

Benin

(72–166)	12/29/72	Joint Communiqué: Resumption of diplomatic relations
(72–167)	12/29/72	Agreement: Economic and technical cooperation
(72–168)	12/29/72	Agreement: Trade and payments
(74–116)	12/30/74	Protocol: Agricultural project
(74–117)	12/30/74	Exchange of Letters: Local expenses
(75–76)	8/28/75	Minutes: Construction of a tobacco factory
(76–66)	7/20/76	Agreement: Economic and technical cooperation
(76–67)	7/20/76	Protocol: Economic and technical cooperation
(80–173)	11/29/80	Document: Chinese-aid project at Malanville paddy area

Botswana

(75–1)	1/6/75	Joint Communiqué: Establishment of diplomatic relations
(76–69)	8/8/76	Agreement: Economic and technical cooperation
(78–53)	4/14/78	Exchange of Notes: Building an experimental state farm

Brazil

(74–56)	8/15/74	Joint Communiqué: Establishment of diplomatic relations
(75–52)	6/23/75	Agreement: Representation of pharmaceuticals
(78–2)	1/7/78	Agreement: Trade
(79–62)	5/22/79	Agreement: Maritime transport

Bulgaria

(66-13)	3/16/66	Agreement: Exchange of goods and payments
(66-73)	7/1/66	Plan for cultural cooperation
(67-3)	1/31/67	Agreement: Exchange of goods and payments
(67-10)	2/25/67	Protocol: Scientific and technical cooperation
(68-20)	4/2/68	Agreement: Exchange of goods and payments
(69-27)	7/4/69	Agreement: Trade
(70-65)	8/31/70	Agreement: Exchange of goods and payments
(71-28)	4/9/71	Agreement: Exchange of goods and payments
(72-44)	4/18/72	Agreement: Exchange of goods and payments
(73-19)	2/19/73	Agreement: Trade
(73-48)	4/20/73	Exchange of Notes: Scientific and technical cooperation
(73-106)	9/22/73	Protocol: Scientific and technical cooperation
(74-11)	2/15/74	Agreement: Exchange of goods and payments
(74-42)	6/4/74	Agreement: Maritime transport
(74-63)	9/21/74	Protocol: Scientific and technical cooperation
(75-19)	3/11/75	Agreement: Exchange of goods and payments
(75-109)	11/4/75	Protocol: Scientific and technical cooperation
(76-1)	1/3/76	Agreement: Exchange of goods and payments
(76-87)	11/20/76	Protocol: Scientific and technical cooperation
(77-26)	3/15/77	Agreement: Exchange of goods and payments
(77-102)	11/25/77	Protocol: Scientific and technical cooperation
(78-4)	1/14/78	Agreement: Exchange of goods and payments
(78-66)	5/ /78	Note: Extension of Scientific and technical cooperation agreement
(78-144)	9/30/78	Protocol: Sino-Bulgarian Joint Committee for Scientific and Technical Cooperation
(79-2)	1/8/79	Agreement: 1979 goods exchange and payments
(79-119)	11/12/79	Protocol: Scientific and technical cooperation
(80-48)	3/28/80	Agreement: Goods exchange and payments for 1980
(80-180)	12/7/80	Protocol: Eighteenth Session of Sino-Bulgaria Commission for Scientific and Technical Cooperation

Burma

(66-12)	3/12/66	Exchange of Notes: Trade and payments
(66-26)	4/8/66	Protocol: Purchase of rice
(66-28)	4/19/66	Joint Communiqué: Visit of Chairman Liu Shao-ch'i and Vice Premier Ch'en Yi
(66-54)	6/1/66	Exchange of Notes: Air transport

(66–74)	7/2/66	Exchange of Notes: Payments
(66–128)	12/31/66	Protocol: Purchase of rice
(71–97)	10/7/71	Exchange of Letters: Economic and technical cooperation
(71–124)	11/19/71	Agreement: Trade
(71–125)	11/19/71	Agreement: Loan
(72–56)	5/19/72	Agreement: News agencies
(75–120)	11/15/75	Joint Communiqué: Visit of President Win
(78–27)	3/8/78	Document: Meiktila People's Textile Mill
(78–64)	5/2/78	Certificate: Motor-driven planting machines
(78–161)	10/20/78	Minutes: Building a national stadium in Burma
(79–82)	7/12/79	Agreement: Economic and technical cooperation
(80–102)	7/3/80	Protocol: Economic and technical cooperation

Burundi

(71–101)	10/13/71	Joint Communiqué: Diplomatic relations
(72–1)	1/6/72	Agreement: Economic and technical cooperation
(72–2)	1/6/72	Agreement: Trade
(79–33)	3/19/79	Agreement: Economic and technical cooperation

Cambodia

(See Kampuchea)

Cameroon

(71–26)	3/26/71	Joint Communiqué: Establishment of diplomatic relations
(72–89)	8/17/72	Agreement: Economic and technical cooperation
(72–90)	8/17/72	Agreement: Trade
(73–39)	3/28/73	Agreement: Economic and technical cooperation
(73–42)	4/2/73	Press Communiqué: Visit of President Ahidjo
(75–39)	5/7/75	Protocol: Dispatch of medical teams
(75–100)	10/21/75	Agreement: News exchange
(75–131)	12/19/75	Document: Construction of cultural palace
(75–132)	12/19/75	Documents: Construction of a power station
(76–74)	8/28/76	Protocol (with Chad): Bridge construction
(77–91)	10/7/77	Agreement: Economic and technical cooperation
(78–45)	4/1/78	Minutes (with Chad): Hand-over of Chari highway bridge
(78–95)	6/21/78	Minutes: Talks on building a hydroelectric power station

Canada

(70-70)	10/30/70	Joint Communiqué: Establishment of diplomatic relations
(71-62)	7/2/71	Press Communiqué: Trade talks
(72-60)	5/20/72(?)	Agreement (initial): Air traffic
(72-113)	10/13/72	Agreement: Air transport
(73-71)	6/4/73	Agreement: Settling Canadian Bank loan
(73-76)	6/11/73	Agreement: Air transport
(73-77)	6/11/73	Protocol: Air transport
(73-87)	7/16/73	Exchange of Notes: Trademark registration
(73-110)	10/13/73	Agreement: Trade
(74-22)	3/15/74	Agreement: Exhibition of archaeological finds
(79-57)	5/19/79	Agreement (in principle): Extend credit of 2,000 million Canadian dollars to PRC to cover purchases of Canadian goods and services
(80-35)	3/2/80	Agreement: Formation of friendship association
(80-124)	8/25/80	Note of Understanding: Establishment of consulate-general in Toronto
(80-129)	9/8/80	Memorandum: Understanding between agricultural ministers
(80-134)	9/16/80	Memorandum: Scientific and technical cooperation

Cape Verde

(76-26)	4/15/76	Joint Communiqué: Establishment of diplomatic relations
(77-80)	8/12/77	Agreement: Economic and technical cooperation
(80-115)	7/25/80	Protocol: Economic and technical cooperation

Central African Republic

(76-71)	8/20/76	Joint Communiqué: Establishment of diplomatic relations
(76-85)	11/16/76	Agreement: Trade
(76-86)	11/16/76	Agreement: Economic and technical cooperation
(76-88)	11/22/76	Press Communiqué: Visit of President Bokassa

Ceylon

(See Sri Lanka)

Chad

(72–146)	11/28/72	Joint Communiqué: Establishment of diplomatic relations
(73–104)	9/20/73	Agreement: Trade
(73–105)	9/20/73	Agreement: Economic and technical cooperation
(76–74)	8/28/76	Protocol (with Cameroon): Bridge construction
(77–33)	3/28/77	Agreement: Building a stadium
(78–45)	4/1/78	Minutes (with Cameroon): Handing over of Chari highway bridge
(78–59)	4/25/78	Protocol: Dispatch of a medical team
(78–139)	9/23/78	Protocol: Economic and technical cooperation

Chile

(70–103)	12/15/70	Joint Communiqué: Establishment of diplomatic relations
(71–29)	4/20/71	Agreement: Trade
(71–90)	8/19/71	Agreement: Telecommunication
(72–64)	6/8/72	Agreement: Economic and technical cooperation
(72–65)	6/8/72	Agreement: Exchange of commodities
(72–66)	6/8/72	Agreement: Trade and payments
(72–67)	6/8/72	Agreement: Long-term trade
(73–15)	1/26/73	Agreement: Maritime transport
(78–86)	6/7/78	Agreement: Sports exchange
(78–149)	10/5/78	Accord: Sale of copper to PRC
(79–37)	4/14/79	Agreement (Verbal): Cooperation in exploration of subsoil and exploitation of minerals and other resources discovered

Colombia

(80–26)	2/8/80	Communiqué: Establishment of diplomatic relations

Comoros

(75–118)	11/13/75	Joint Communiqué: Establishment of diplomatic relations
(76–43)	6/10/76	Agreement: Economic and technical cooperation

Congo

(66-27)	4/14/66	Plan for cultural cooperation
(67-47)	10/10/67	Joint Press Communiqué: Visit of Prime Minister Noumazalay
(68-5)	2/7/68	Minutes (Summary): Constructing a shipyard
(68-55)	8/12/68	Summary: Building a state farm
(69-37)	9/6/69	Agreement: Construction of a boat building yard
(69-41)	10/10/69	Agreement: Economic and technical cooperation
(70-47)	7/9/70	Protocol: Dispatch of medical teams
(71-6)	1/27/71	Minutes: Hospital construction
(72-118)	10/19/72	Agreement: Economic and technical cooperation
(73-64)	5/24/73	Protocol: Economic and technical cooperation
(73-90)	7/30/73	Agreement: Loan
(75-16)	3/2/75	Exchange of Letters: Economic and technical cooperation
(77-51)	5/6/77	Minutes: Construction of "People Palace"
(77-71)	6/18/77	Agreement: Economic and technical cooperation
(78-143)	9/28/78	Agreement: Trade
(80-1)	1/2/80	Agreement: Technical cooperation on boat-building
(80-104)	7/8/80	Agreement: Cultural cooperation
(80-105)	7/8/80	Agreement: Technical and economic cooperation
(80-106)	7/8/80	Summary: Arrangement for technical cooperation

Cuba

(66-50)	5/26/66	Protocol: Trade
(66-51)	5/27/66	Plan for cooperation between academies of sciences
(66-81)	7/6/66	Agreement: Scientific and technical cooperation
(67-12)	3/21/67	Protocol: Trade
(68-52)	7/19/68	Protocol: Trade
(68-53)	7/19/68	Exchange of Letters: Delivery of goods
(69-5)	2/14/69	Protocol: Trade
(70-41)	6/29/70	Protocol: Trade
(71-39)	5/11/71	Agreement: Trade
(71-40)	5/11/71	Agreement: Payments
(71-41)	5/11/71	Protocol: Trade
(72-18)	3/4/72	Agreement: Loan
(72-19)	3/4/72	Protocol: Trade
(73-32)	3/23/73	Protocol: Trade
(74-48)	7/10/74	Protocol: Trade

(75–40)	5/8/75	Protocol: Trade
(76–44)	6/10/76	Agreement: Trade
(76–45)	6/10/76	Agreement: Payments
(76–46)	6/10/73	Protocol: Trade
(77–42)	4/15/77	Protocol: Trade
(78–35)	3/18/78	Protocol: Trade
(79–9)	1/17/79	Protocol: 1979 Trade
(80–36)	3/3/80	Protocol: Trade
(80–185)	12/20/80	Agreement: Trade for 1981-85
(80–186)	12/20/80	Protocol: Trade for 1981
(80–187)	12/20/80	Agreement: Payment

Cyprus

(71–141)	12/14/71	Communiqué: Establishment of diplomatic relations
(73–102)	9/19/73	Agreement: Trade and payments

Czechoslovakia

(66–6)	2/4/66	Agreement: Exchange of goods and payments
(66–43)	5/11/66	Plan for cultural cooperation
(66–107)	10/28/66	Protocol: Scientific and technical cooperation
(67–31)	7/5/67	Agreement: Exchange of goods and payments
(68–18)	3/26/68	Agreement: Exchange of goods and payments
(68–45)	6/16/68	Agreement: Exchange of goods and payments
(69–24)	6/6/69	Agreement: Trade
(70–36)	6/16/70	Agreement: Exchange of goods and payments
(70–37)	6/16/70	Exchange of Notes: Changing ruble account into Swiss franc account
(71–43)	5/18/71	Agreement: Exchange of goods and payments
(71–44)	5/18/71	Exchange of Notes: Change of Swiss franc
(72–10)	2/10/72	Agreement: Exchange of goods and payments
(73–16)	2/2/73	Protocol: Banking formalities for settling accounts of goods exchange and payments
(73–30)	3/20/73	Agreement: Exchange of goods and payments
(73–49)	4/20/73	Protocol: Scientific and technical cooperation
(73–144)	12/17/73	Agreement: Exchange of goods and payments
(74–65)	9/24/74	Protocol: Scientific and technical cooperation
(74–107)	12/20/74	Agreement: Exchange of goods and payments
(75–96)	10/18/75	Protocol: Scientific and technical cooperation
(75–126)	12/9/75	Agreement: Exchange of goods and payments
(76–89)	11/25/76	Protocol: Scientific and technical cooperation

(77-55)	5/19/77	Agreement: Exchange of goods and payments
(77-108)	12/17/77	Agreement: Exchange of goods and payments
(77-109)	12/18/77	Protocol: Scientific and technical cooperation
(78-187)	12/15/78	Protocol: Scientific and technical cooperation
(79-3)	1/11/79	Agreement: Goods exchange and payments in 1979
(79-128)	12/13/79	Protocol: Scientific and technical cooperation
(80-44)	3/22/80	Agreement: Goods exchange and payments for 1980
(80-136)	9/16/80	Protocol: Scientific and technical cooperation

Dahomey

(See Benin)

Denmark

(73-57)	5/18/73	Agreement: Air transport
(74-75)	10/21/74	Agreement: Maritime transport
(74-76)	10/21/74	Exchange of Letters: Trade promotion
(79-100)	9/14/79	Agreement: Economic and technical cooperation

Djibouti

(79-1)	1/5/79	Joint Communiqué: Establishment of diplomatic relations
(79-127)	12/11/79	Agreement: Economic and technical cooperation
(80-114)	7/28/80	Agreement: Rules on accounts between national banks
(80-117)	7/28/80	Protocol: Economic and technical cooperation

Ecuador

(75-64)	7/10/75	Agreement: Trade
(75-65)	7/10/75	Agreement: Establishment of commercial offices
(79-135)	12/24/79	Joint Communiqué: Establishment of diplomatic relations

Egypt

(66-39)	5/4/66	Protocol: Trade
(66-41)	5/7/66	Plan for cultural cooperation
(67-20)	5/25/67	Protocol: Trade
(68-47)	7/4/68	Protocol: Trade
(68-48)	7/4/68	Exchange of Letters: Trade and payments
(68-49)	7/4/68	Exchange of Letters: Payments
(68-50)	7/4/68	Exchange of Letters: Payments
(69-9)	3/5/69	Protocol: Trade
(70-14)	3/19/70	Protocol: Trade
(71-78)	8/2/71	Protocol: Trade
(71-79)	8/2/71	Exchange of Notes: Payments
(71-80)	8/2/71	Exchange of Notes: Payments
(71-81)	8/2/71	Exchange of Notes: Trade and payments
(72-30)	1/1/72	Protocol: Trade
(73-83)	6/26/73	Minutes: Building a claybrick factory
(75-45)	5/31/75	Protocol: Trade
(75-46)	5/31/75	Exchange of Letters: Trade and payments
(76-42)	6/6/76	Protocol: Trade
(77-29)	3/21/77	Agreement: Trade
(77-30)	3/21/77	Agreement: Payment
(77-31)	3/21/77	Protocol: Trade
(78-40)	3/25/78	Agreement: Trade
(79-38)	4/19/79	Protocol: 1979 Trade
(79-40)	5/1/79	Program: Cultural cooperation for 1979-81
(79-131)	12/19/79	Agreement: Scientific cooperation

Equatorial Guinea

(70-71)	10/15/70	Joint Communiqué: Establishment of diplomatic relations
(71-4)	1/22/71	Agreement: Economic and technical cooperation
(71-5)	1/22/71	Agreement: Trade
(72-119)	10/24/72	Protocol (supplementary): Economic and technical cooperation
(73-67)	5/29/73	Protocol: Dispatch of medical teams
(76-30)	5/1/76	Minutes: Building a power station
(76-31)	5/1/76	Minutes: Building transmission line
(77-59)	5/31/77	Protocol: Dispatch of medical teams
(77-85)	9/23/77	Agreement: Economic and technical cooperation

Ethiopia

(70-98)	11/24/70	Joint Communiqué: Establishment of diplomatic relations
(71-98)	10/9/71	Agreement: Trade
(71-99)	10/9/71	Agreement: Economic and technical cooperation
(72-85)	7/30/72	Agreement: Air transport
(73-20)	2/20/73	Protocol: Economic and technical cooperation
(73-134)	11/22/73	Exchange of Notes: Dispatch of medical team
(76-20)	3/22/76	Agreement: Economic and technical cooperation
(76-56)	6/30/76	Agreement: Trade
(76-57)	6/30/76	Protocol: Trade
(77-72)	6/18/77	Minutes: Air service
(77-77)	6/30/77	Protocol: Trade
(77-112)	12/19/77	Minutes: Jointly build cotton mill
(78-19)	2/15/78	Certificate: Handing over of Bako thermal power station
(78-21)	2/20/78	Minutes: Constructing a stadium
(78-57)	4/19/78	Minutes: Sports exchange

Fiji

(75-110)	11/5/75	Joint Communiqué: Establishment of diplomatic relations

Finland

(67-2)	1/26/67	Exchange of Notes: Trademark registration
(67-16)	4/25/67	Agreement: Trade
(67-18)	4/25/67	Exchange of Letters: Converting ruble to Finnish mark
(68-2)	1/20/68	Agreement: Trade
(68-3)	1/20/68	Exchange of Letters: Payments
(69-18)	4/22/69	Agreement: Trade
(70-8)	1/31/70	Agreement: Trade
(71-8)	2/8/71	Agreement: Trade
(71-122)	11/18/71	Agreement: Trade
(73-25)	3/3/73	Agreement: Trade
(74-10)	2/12/74	Agreement: Trade
(74-105)	12/17/74	Draft: Air service
(74-108)	12/20/74	Agreement: Trade
(75-91)	10/2/75	Agreement: Air transport
(75-114)	11/8/75	Draft: Maritime transport

(75-125)	12/5/75	Agreement: Trade
(76-96)	12/21/76	Agreement: Trade
(77- 7)	1/27/77	Agreement: Maritime transport
(77-100)	11/18/77	Agreement: Trade
(78-146)	10/4/78	Agreement: Trade
(79-64)	5/29/79	Agreement: Economic, industrial, scientific, and technical cooperation
(79-114)	10/26/79	Agreement: 1980 Trade
(80-65)	5/3/80	Agreement: Cultural cooperation for 1980-81
(80-146)	9/26/80	Agreement: 1981 Trade

France

(66-55)	6/1/66	Agreement: Air communications
(66-85)	7/25/66	Protocol: Aviation
(69-13)	3/26/69	Agreement: Trade
(69-14)	3/26/69	Agreement: Technical problems concerning frozen meat
(71-61)	6/23/71	Contract: Locomotives
(73-36)	3/23/73	Agreement: Exhibition of PRC archaeological finds
(73-98)	9/14/73	Communiqué: Visit of President Pompidou
(75-66)	7/15/75	Exchange of Notes: Trademark registration
(75-90)	9/28/75	Agreement: Maritime transport
(77-65)	6/ /77	Draft: Aviation enterprises
(78-9)	1/21/78	Agreement: Scientific and technical cooperation
(78-50)	4/12/78	Accord (with W. Germany): "Symphony" satellite communications
(78-91)	6/14/78	Agreement: Scientific and technical cooperation
(78-159)	10/20/78	Protocol (supplementary): Scientific and technical exchange
(78-160)	10/20/78	Accord: Scientific cooperation between Academies of Sciences
(78-181)	12/4/78	Agreement: Economic cooperation
(79-41)	5/2/79	Minutes: Scientific and technical cooperation and exchange in metrology
(79-74)	7/6/79	Protocol: Joint working committee and sports exchange
(79-80)	7/8/79	Agreement: Standardization cooperation
(79-81)	7/8/79	Protocol: 1979-80 Standardization cooperation
(79-84)	7/22/79	Memorandum: Thirteen projects being negotiated with PRC
(79-92)	8/17/79	Agreement (preliminary): Exchange of information and opening way to negotiations on mutual copyright recognition

(79-105)	10/9/79	Contract: Turbo generators with French aid
(79-129)	12/15/79	Protocol (minutes?): Scientific and technical cooperation
(79-130)	12/15/79	Agreement: Scientific and technical cooperation in geological sphere
(79-134)	12/22/79	Accord: Promotion of joint ventures
(80-29)	2/13/80	Plan: Establishment of cultural organization
(80-38)	3/6/80	Agreement: Exploration for oil in Tsing Hai
(80-100)	7/2/80	Agreement: Industrial cooperation for construction of helicopters
(80-148)	10/3/80	Agreement: Radio broadcasting exchange
(80-157)	10/17/80	Agreement: Construction of nuclear power stations
(80-158)	10/17/80	Agreement: Establishing consulates

Gabon

(74-28)	4/20/74	Joint Communiqué: Establishment of diplomatic relations
(74-69)	10/6/74	Agreement: Trade
(74-70)	10/6/74	Agreement: Economic and technical cooperation
(74-71)	10/9/74	Press Communiqué: Visit of President Bongo

Gambia

(74-106)	12/17/74	Joint Communiqué: Establishment of diplomatic relations
(75-10)	2/2/75	Agreement: Economic and technical cooperation
(75-111)	11/5/75	Agreement: Trade
(76-70)	8/10/76	Protocol: Dispatch of medical teams
(77-57)	5/25/77	Minutes: Reconstruction of a stadium
(78-39)	3/25/78	Minutes: Construction of health centers
(79-115)	10/29/79	Protocol: Chinese medical team to Gambia

Germany (E)

(66-17)	3/25/66	Agreement: Exchange of goods and payments
(66-18)	3/25/66	Protocol: Delivery of goods
(66-76)	7/4/66	Protocol: Scientific and technical cooperation
(66-84)	7/22/66	Plan for cultural cooperation
(66-96)	8/23/66	Exchange of Notes: Exchange of goods and payments

(66-124)	12/20/66	Exchange of Notes: Noncommercial payments
(67-14)	4/14/67	Agreement: Exchange of goods and payments
(68-31)	5/3/68	Agreement: Exchange of goods and payments
(69-28)	7/7/69	Agreement: Exchange of goods and payments
(70-42)	6/30/70	Agreement: Exchange of goods and payments
(71-44)	5/18/71	Agreement: Exchange of goods and payments
(72-47)	4/24/72	Agreement: Exchange of goods and payments
(73-26)	3/5/73	Agreement: Exchange of goods and payments
(74-16)	2/21/74	Agreement: Exchange of goods and payments
(75-8)	1/25/75	Agreement: Exchange of goods and payments
(75-133)	12/20/75	Agreement: Exchange of goods and payments
(77-52)	5/3/77	Agreement: Exchange of goods and payments
(78-6)	1/19/78	Agreement: Exchange of goods and payments
(79-11)	1/20/79	Agreement: Goods exchange and payments in 1979
(80-49)	4/2/80	Goods exchange and payments for 1980
(80-73)	5/16/80	Agreement: Health cooperation

Germany (W)

(72-112)	10/11/72	Joint Communiqué: Establishment of diplomatic relations
(73-86)	7/5/73	Agreement: Trade and payments
(75-70)	8/8/75	Exchange of Letters: Trademark registration
(75-77)	8/30/75	Draft: Maritime transport
(75-95)	10/31/75	Exchange of Notes: Establishment of a committee for the promotion of trade
(75-105)	10/31/75	Agreement: Maritime transport
(75-106)	10/31/75	Agreement: Civil air transport
(77-44)	4/20/77	Agreement: Ship inspection
(78-50)	4/12/78	Accord (with France): "Symphony" satellite communications
(78-131)	9/15/78	Accord: Scientific cooperation
(78-138)	9/22/78	Protocol: Long-term credit transactions
(78-151)	10/6/78	Agreement: Television cooperation
(78-156)	10/9/78	Agreement: Scientific and technical cooperation
(78-157)	10/9/78	Minutes: Executing Scientific and Technical Cooperation Agreement
(79-65)	6/11/79	Protocol: Scientific and technical cooperation
(79-66)	6/19/79	Agreement: Scientific and technological cooperation
(79-111)	10/24/79	Agreement: Economic cooperation
(79-112)	10/24/79	Agreement: Cultural cooperation
(79-113)	10/24/79	Agreement: Establishment of consulate-general

(79-116)   10/29/79   Agreement: Technical cooperation
(79-123)   11/24/79   Agreement: Cooperation in broadcasting and
                         TV
(79-133)   12/21/79(?)   Agreement: Agricultural machinery to PRC
(79-137)   12/27/79   Agreement: Trade
(80-89)   6/7/80   Protocol: Cooperation in electronics and
                         production
(80-99)   7/1/80   Protocol: Set up joint-financed jewelery co. ltd.
(80-107)   7/10/80   Agreement: Mutual provision of navigational,
                         communications, meteorological, and other
                         technical services
(80-135)   9/16/80   Protocol: Statement of intent for cultural co-
                         operation

Ghana

(72-16)   2/29/72   Press Communiqué: Diplomatic relations
(72-96)   1/14/72   Agreement: Trade and payments
(72-97)   9/14/72   Protocol: Trade
(72-98)   9/14/72   Exchange of Letters: Economic and technical
                         cooperation
(74-34)   4/30/74   Protocol: Trade
(75-44)   5/20/76   Protocol: Trade
(76-13)   3/2/76   Protocol: Trade
(76-14)   3/2/76   Exchange of Notes: Trade and payments
(77-110)   12/19/77   Agreement: Long-term trade and payments
(77-111)   12/19/77   Protocol: Trade

Greece

(72-63)   6/5/72   Joint Communiqué: Establishment of diplo-
                         matic relations
(73-61)   5/23/73   Agreement: Trade and payments
(73-62)   5/23/73   Agreement: Maritime transport
(73-63)   5/23/73   Agreement: Air transport
(73-65)   5/27/73   Communiqué: Visit of Deputy Prime Minister
                         Macarezos
(73-95)   8/12/73   Minutes: Establishing satellite communications
                         service
(75-33)   4/19/75   Exchange of Notes
(78-137)   9/22/78   Agreement: Cultural cooperation
(79-121)   11/15/79   Agreement: Scientific and technological co-
                         operation

Guinea

(66-5)	2/1/66	Protocol: Trade
(66-34)	4/30/66	Plan for cultural cooperation
(66-58)	6/2/66	Agreement: News agencies
(66-59)	6/2/66	Memorandum: Construction of a cinema
(66-110)	11/16/66	Agreement: Economic and technical cooperation
(66-111)	11/16/66	Protocol: Economic and technical cooperation
(66-112)	11/16/66	Protocol: Trade
(66-113)	11/16/66	Agreement: Loan
(67-66)	12/30/67	Protocol: Dispatch of medical teams
(68-37)	5/14/68	Protocol: Trade
(68-38)	5/24/68	Agreement (with Mali): Railway construction
(68-39)	5/25/68	Joint Communiqué (with Mali): Visit of Foreign Ministers Ousman Ba and Lansana Beavogui
(68-56)	8/26/68	Agreement: Cultural construction
(69-7)	2/28/69	Agreement: Loan
(69-8)	2/28/69	Protocol: Trade
(69-40)	10/9/69	Agreement: Economic and technical cooperation
(70-7)	1/30/70	Protocol: Trade
(70-11)	3/10/70	Protocol: Medical cooperation
(70-91)	11/2/70	Protocol: Economic and technical cooperation agreement
(71-9)	2/8/71	Protocol: Trade
(71-95)	9/29/71	Exchange of Notes: Trade and payments
(72-8)	2/5/72	Agreement: Loan
(72-9)	2/5/72	Protocol: Trade
(72-101)	9/18/72	Protocol: Dispatch of medical teams
(72-151)	12/13/72	Agreement: Credit
(72-152)	12/13/72	Agreement: Credit
(73-18)	2/16/73	Agreement: Trade
(74-13)	2/15/74	Agreement: Loan
(74-14)	2/15/74	Protocol: Trade
(74-103)	12/11/74	Protocol: Dispatch of medical teams
(75-20)	3/11/75	Agreement: Loan
(75-21)	3/11/75	Protocol: Trade
(75-97)	10/18/75	Protocol: Trade
(77-27)	3/17/77	Certificate: Handing over the hydroagricultural project
(77-43)	4/15/77	Certificate: Handing over fishing projects
(77-46)	4/25/77	Protocol: Trade
(78-34)	3/17/78	Protocol: Trade
(79-6)	1/15/79	Protocol: 1979 Trade
(80-122)	8/20/80	Technical cooperation

Guinea-Bissau

(74-21)	3/15/74	Joint Communiqué: Establishment of diplomatic relations
(75-62)	7/9/75	Agreement: Economic and technical cooperation
(76-33)	5/11/76	Protocol: Dispatch of medical teams
(77-66)	6/10/77	Minutes: Construction of water conservancy project

Guyana

(71-118)	11/14/71	Agreement: Import and export
(71-119)	11/14/71	Agreement: Developing trade, etc.
(71-120)	11/16/71	Press Communiqué: Trade talks
(73-39)	4/9/72	Agreement: Economic and technical cooperation
(72-71)	6/27/72	Joint Communiqué: Establishment of diplomatic relations
(72-129)	11/8/72	Agreement: Import and export
(72-130)	11/8/72	Protocol: Economic and technical cooperation
(73-116)	10/25/73	Agreement: Import and export
(75-23)	3/14/75	Agreement: Economic and technical cooperation
(75-24)	3/17/75	Press Communiqué: Visit of Prime Minister Burnham
(75-92)	10/23/75	Agreement: Imports and exports
(76-93)	12/16/76	Certificate: Handing over a claybrick factory
(78-100)	7/24/78	Joint Communiqué: Visit of Vice Premier Keng Piao
(79-10)	1/19/79	Agreement: Interest-free commodity loan by PRC

Hong Kong

(67-59)	11/25/67	Agreement: Border
(78-150)	10/5/78	Accord: Charter flight between Canton and Hong Kong
(79-107)	10/15/79	Agreement: Joint venture construction project
(80-42)	3/19/80	Agreement: Joint venture elevator company
(80-44)	3/21/80	Agreement: New joint shipping company
(80-72)	5/15/80	Protocol: Supplement to agreement on water supply

Hungary

(66-8)	2/20/66	Agreement: Exchange of goods and payments
(66-9)	2/20/66	Protocol: Delivery of goods
(66-83)	7/20/66	Plan for cultural cooperation
(66-90)	8/9/66(?)	Protocol: Scientific and technical cooperation
(67-25)	6/21/67	Protocol: Delivery of goods
(67-26)	6/22/67	Agreement: Exchange of goods and payments
(68-32)	5/3/68	Protocol: Delivery of goods
(68-33)	5/4/68	Agreement: Exchange of goods and payments
(69-32)	8/2/69	Protocol: Delivery of goods
(69-33)	8/5/69	Agreement: Exchange of goods and payments
(70-53)	7/24/70	Agreement: Exchange of goods and payments
(70-54)	7/24/70	Protocol: Delivery of goods
(71-33)	4/28/71	Agreement: Exchange of goods and payments
(71-34)	4/28/71	Protocol: Delivery of goods
(72-21)	3/14/72	Agreement: Exchange of goods and payments
(72-22)	3/14/72	Protocol: Delivery of goods
(72-53)	5/16/72	Protocol: Scientific and technical cooperation
(73-28)	3/7/73	Agreement: Exchange of goods and payments
(73-70)	6/2/73	Protocol: Scientific and technical cooperation
(74-25)	3/25/74	Agreement: Exchange of goods and payments
(74-83)	10/26/74	Protocol: Scientific and technical cooperation
(75-18)	3/3/75	Agreement: Exchange of goods and payments
(75-112)	11/5/75	Protocol: Scientific and technical cooperation
(76-15)	3/6/76	Agreement: Exchange of goods and payments
(76-81)	10/23/76	Protocol: Scientific and technical cooperation
(77-45)	4/20/77	Agreement: Exchange of goods and payments
(77-103)	11/25/77	Protocol: Scientific and technical cooperation
(78-23)	2/27/78	Agreement: Exchange of goods and payments
(78-172)	11/12/78	Protocol: Sino-Hungarian Committee for Scientific and Technical Cooperation
(79-7)	1/16/79	Agreement: Goods exchange and payments in 1979
(79-132)	12/21/79	Protocol: Scientific and technical cooperation
(80-53)	4/15/80	Agreement: Exchange of goods and payments in 1980

Iceland

(71-139)	12/8/71	Joint Communiqué: Establishment of diplomatic relations

Iran

(71–89)	8/16/71	Joint Communiqué: Establishment of diplomatic relations
(72–137)	11/18/72	Agreement: Air transport
(73–46)	4/8/73	Agreement: Trade
(73–47)	4/8/73	Agreement: Payments
(75–127)	12/15/75	Exchange of Notes: Trademark registration
(76–50)	6/18/76	Memorandum: Trade
(77–96)	11/1/77	Memorandum: Trade
(78–90)	6/13/78	Agreement: News cooperation
(78–126)	8/31/78	Agreement: Cultural cooperation

Iraq

(66–60)	6/4/66	Plan for cultural cooperation
(66–61)	6/4/66	Protocol: Radio and television cooperation
(69–47)	11/7/69	Agreement: Air transport
(71–60)	6/21/71	Agreement: Economic and technical cooperation
(72–156)	12/20/72	Protocol: Economic and technical cooperation
(73–139)	11/25/73	Minutes: Building a bridge
(74–15)	2/16/74	Minutes: Trade talks
(75–59)	7/6/75	Document: Development of trade
(75–60)	7/6/75	Document: Economic and technical cooperation
(75–61)	7/7/75	Press Communiqué: Developing friendship
(75–113)	11/30/75	Protocol: Trade
(77–54)	5/18/77	Exchange of Letters: Trade
(79–106)	10/10/79	Agreement: Information cooperation
(80–79)	5/29/80	Plan: Cultural cooperation 1980–81

Ireland

(79–70)	6/22/79	Joint Communiqué: Establishment of diplomatic relations

Italy

(70–92)	11/6/70	Joint Communiqué: Establishment of diplomatic relations
(71–46)	5/25/71	Joint Press Communiqué: Trade talks
(71–112)	10/29/71	Agreement: Trade and payments
(72–109)	10/8/72	Agreement: Maritime transport

(73-2)	1/8/73	Agreement: Air transport
(73-3)	1/8/73	Exchange of Notes: Trademark registration
(75-9)	1/29/75	Exchange of Letters: Establishment of Sino-Italian Amalgamated Committee to promote trade
(78-147)	10/4/78	Accord: Ship inspection
(78-152)	10/6/78	Agreement: Cultural cooperation
(78-153)	10/6/78	Agreement: Scientific and technical cooperation
(78-155)	10/9/78	Agreement: News cooperation
(79-39)	4/23/79	Agreement: Economic cooperation
(79-53)	5/14/79	Agreement: Scientific cooperation
(79-87)	8/6/79	Agreement: Chinese manpower for civil engineering
(79-108)	10/19/79	Program: Cultural, scientific, and technical cooperation
(80-30)	2/22/80	Accord: Sister-city relations between Nanking and Florence
(80-45)	3/24/80	Agreement: Sister-cities relation between Venice and Soochow
(80-74)	5/19/80	Protocol: Scientific and technical cooperation
(80-75)	5/19/80	Program: Cooperation for peaceful use of nuclear energy

Jamaica

(72-141)	11/21/72	Joint Communiqué: Establishment of diplomatic relations
(74-11)	2/12/74	Agreement: Economic and technical cooperation
(76-76)	9/26/76	Agreement: Trade
(76-77)	9/26/76	Protocol: Economic cooperation

Japan

(66-4)	1/22/66	Joint Statement: Promotion of trade, maritime transport, etc.
(66-45)	5/19/66	Minutes: Trade talks
(66-80)	7/5/66	Joint Statement: Cultural exchange
(66-101)	10/12/66	Joint Statement: Cultural exchange
(66-116)	11/21/66	Trade
(67-57)	11/10/67	Joint Statement: Promotion of trade
(68-9)	3/6/68	Communiqué: Japan-PRC Memorandum Trade Office
(68-10)	3/6/68	Agreement: Trade

(68–11)	3/6/68	Accord: Exchange of correspondents
(68–14)	3/19/68	Protocol: Industrial exhibition
(68–15)	3/19/68	Minutes: Promotion of trade
(68–27)	4/10/68	Minutes: Japan–PRC Friendship Association
(68–67)	11/14/68	Agreement: Japan importing meat from PRC
(69–16)	4/4/69	Communiqué: Japan–PRC Memorandum Trade Office
(69–17)	4/4/69	Agreement: Trade
(69–19)	5/15/69	Minutes: Japan importing meat from PRC
(69–21)	5/28/69	Protocol: Steel project
(69–26)	6/25/69	Agreement: Purchase of fertilizer
(69–39)	9/28/69	Contract: Machines
(69–48)	11/13/69	Contract: Papers
(70–24)	4/14/70	Joint Statement: Promotion of trade
(70–25)	4/19/70	Communiqué: Japan–PRC Memorandum Trade Office
(70–26)	4/19/70	Agreement: Trade
(70–39)	6/20/70	Communiqué: Fishery Association
(70–46)	7/8/70	Contract: Soybeans
(70–62)	8/17/70	Agreement: Purchase of fertilizers
(70–64)	8/25/70	Contract: Urea
(70–90)	11/1/70	Joint Statement: Visit of Chairman of Central Executive Committee of Japanese Socialist Party
(70–109)	12/31/70	Communiqué: Japan–PRC Fishery Association
(70–110)	12/31/70	Regulation: Purse–Seining with lighting ships
(71–7)	2/1/71	Summary: Table Tennis Association
(71–16)	3/1/71	Communiqué: Japan–PRC Memorandum Trade offices
(71–17)	3/1/71	Agreement: 1971 Memorandum trade
(71–63)	7/2/71	Joint Statement: Delegation of Japanese Komei Party
(71–96)	10/2/71	Joint Statement: Visit of delegation of Japanese Dietmen's League
(71–103)	10/16/71	Joint Statement: Visit of Delegation of Japan–China Friendship Association
(71–126)	11/20/71	Joint Statement: Visit of Japanese delegation of National Council
(71–143)	12/21/71	Communiqué: Japan–PRC Memorandum Trade Office
(72–25)	3/15/72	Communiqué: Table Tennis Association
(72–26)	3/15/72	Communiqué: Table Tennis Association
(72–31)	3/24/72	Summary: Visit of Japanese Volleyball Association
(72–41)	4/13/72	Joint Statement: Visit of Chairman of Central

		Executive Committee of Japanese Democratic Socialist Party
(72-106)	9/29/72	Joint Statement: Establishment of diplomatic relations
(72-121)	10/29/72	Agreement: Trade
(73-6)	1/13/73	Minutes: Ice hockey exchange
(73-7)	1/13/73	Minutes: Energetic exchange (badminton)
(73-43)	4/3/73	Minutes: Talks between PRC and Japan football organizations
(73-55)	5/4/73	Agreement: Seabed cable
(73-81)	6/21/73	Exchange of Notes: Fishery
(74-1)	1/5/74	Agreement: Trade
(74-29)	4/20/74	Agreement: Air transport
(74-58)	8/27/74	Agreement: Aviation
(74-59)	8/27/74	Agreement: Technical problems of aviation
(74-93)	11/13/74	Agreement: Maritime transport
(75-43)	5/12/75	Joint Statement: Visit of Chairman of Central Executive Committee of Japanese Socialist Party
(75-72)	8/15/75	Agreement: Fishery
(75-73)	8/15/75	Exchange of Notes: Establishment of consulates-general
(75-85)	9/22/75	Protocol: Fishing
(76-59)	7/4/76	Protocol: Exhibition
(76-72)	8/25/76	Agreement: Maritime liaison office
(77-34)	3/30/77	Protocol: Air cargo agency
(77-88)	9/25/77	Agreement: Metrological circuit
(77-89)	9/29/77	Agreement: Trademark protection
(78-20)	2/16/78	Accord: Trade
(78-71)	5/23/78	Protocol: Building Paoshan Steel Plant
(78-72)	5/23/78	Contract: Technical cooperation
(78-102)	7/28/78	Protocol: Color picture tube and integrated circuit
(78-103)	7/28/78	Contract: Color picture tube and integrated circuit
(78-112)	8/12/78	Treaty: China-Japan Peace and Friendship Treaty
(78-113)	8/14/78	Contract: Coal
(78-125)	8/ /78	Agreement: Silk trade
(78-185)	12/9/78	Protocol: Arbitrating the disputes of maritime transportation
(78-192)	12/22/78	Protocol: Purchase of complete facilities for Paoshan Steel Plant
(79-8)	1/16/79	Exchange of Instruments: Amendments to China-Japan Fishery Agreement

(79-22)	2/6/79	Exchange of Notes: Technical cooperation in modernizing PRC's railway system
(79-32)	3/14/79	Agreement: Friendship between Peking and Tokyo
(79-36)	3/29/79	Minutes: Long-term trade agreement (78-20)
▷ (79-54)	5/15/79	Agreement: Development of oil and coal resources and export to Japan
(79-62)	5/26/79	Protocol: Civil air
(79-101)	9/17/79	Memorandum: Science exchange
(80-4)	1/18/80	Agreement: Establishment of joint economic council
(80-6)	1/19/80	Agreement: Soybean trade
(80-7)	1/19/80	Protocol: Purchasing machinery
(80-8)	1/19/80	Accord: Cooperation in land reclamation
(80-9)	1/19/80	Accord: Loan
(80-10)	1/22/80	Agreement: Trade and economic cooperation
(80-22)	2/1/80	Agreement: Exchange of consuls-general
(80-52)	4/14/80	Agreement: Cooperation in news service
(80-60)	4/25/80	Exchange of Notes: Extension of credit to China
(80-62)	4/30/80	Agreement: Fifty billion Yen loan to PRC for 1979
(80-77)	5/28/80	Agreement: Scientific and technical cooperation
(80-123)	8/22/80	Agreement: Cooperation in technical survey of ships
(80-153)	10/13/80	Memorandum: Promoting scientific and technical exchange
(80-160)	10/24/80	Joint Declaration: Further development of Tokyo-Peking sister-cities relation
(80-177)	12/5/80	Exchange of Notes: Fifty-six billion Yen to PRC for 1980
(80-178)	12/5/80	Press Communiqué: First meeting of government official conference

Jordan

| (77-38) | 4/7/77 | Joint Communiqué: Establishment of diplomatic relations |
| (79-51) | 5/12/79 | Agreement: Trade |

Kampuchea

| (66-21) | 3/31/66 | Plan for cultural and scientific cooperation |

(66–33)	4/29/66	Agreement: Economic and cultural cooperation
(68–19)	3/30/68	Document: Turnover of a textile factory
(68–65)	10/5/68	Document: Turnover of an airport
(69–2)	1/22/69	Document: Turnover of a glass factory
(69–20)	5/21/69	Document: Turnover of a paper mill
(70–33)	5/?/70	Agreement: Loan
(70–63)	8/17/70	Agreement: Military aid
(72–11)	2/11/72	Agreement: Economic and military aid
(73–4)	1/13/73	Agreements: Supply of military equipment
(73–5)	1/13/73	Agreement: Economic aid
(74–40)	5/26/75	Agreement: Granting military equipment
(74–41)	5/27/75	Joint Communiqué: Visit of Deputy Prime Minister Samphan
(75–74)	8/18/75	Joint Communiqué: Visit of Deputy Prime Minister Samphan
(75–75)	8/18/75	Agreement: Economic and technical cooperation
(76–16)	3/10/76	Agreement: Economic cooperation
(76–73)	8/26/76	Protocol: Economic cooperation
(76–99)	12/25/76	Agreement: Scientific and technical cooperation
(76–100)	12/25/76	Protocol: Supply of equipment

Kenya

(78–70)	5/23/78	Agreement: Trade
(80–133)	9/16/80	Agreement: Economic and technical cooperation
(80–137)	9/16/80	Agreement: Cultural cooperation

Kiribati

(80–98)	6/28/80	Exchange of Notes: Establishing diplomatic relations

Korea (N)

(66–10)	2/25/66	Plan for cultural cooperation
(66–56)	6/1/66	Agreement: Animal quarantine
(66–79)	7/5/66	Protocol: Scientific and technical cooperation
(66–88)	7/30/66	Plan for cooperation between Academies of Sciences
(66–108)	11/5/66	Protocol: Air transport
(66–123)	12/3/66	Protocol: Mutual supply of goods
(66–127)	12/30/66	Agreement: Radio and television cooperation

(67-43)	10/18/67	Exchange of Notes: Scientific and technical cooperation
(67-58)	11/23/67	Protocol: Scientific and technical cooperation
(67-67)	12/30/67	Plan for sanitary cooperation
(68-8)	3/5/68	Protocol: Exchange of goods
(69-3)	1/24/69	Protocol: Exchange of goods
(70-4)	1/29/70	Accord: Border river navigation
(70-10)	3/2/70	Protocol: Delivery of goods
(70-21)	4/7/70	Joint Communiqué: Visit of Premier Chou En-lai
(70-34)	6/3/70	Exchange of Notes: Transporting wood in Yalu and Tumen Rivers
(70-80)	10/17/70	Agreement: Economic and technical aid
(70-81)	10/17/70	Agreement: Mutual supply of goods
(70-82)	10/17/70	Protocol: Mutual supply of goods
(70-84)	10/31/70	Protocol: Border railway transport
(70-101)	12/9/70	Protocol: Scientific and technical cooperation
(71-21)	3/17/71	Decision: China-Korea Yalu River Power Co.
(71-30)	4/20/71	Exchange of Notes: Changing currency used in trade
(71-31)	4/22/71	Plan for scientific cooperation between academies of sciences
(71-64)	7/3/71	Agreement: Rescue at sea
(71-88)	8/15/71	Agreement: Economic cooperation
(71-91)	8/25/71	Protocol: Mutual supply of goods
(71-93)	9/6/71	Agreement: Military aid
(71-102)	10/15/71	Agreement: Broadcasting and television co-operation
(71-121)	11/17/71	Agreement: Ship overhaul
(71-123)	11/18/71	Protocol: Border river transport
(71-145)	12/27/71	Protocol: Scientific and technical cooperation
(71-148)	12/30/71	Protocol: Exchange of goods
(72-25)	3/15/72	Communiqué: Table Tennis Association
(72-35)	4/5/72	Agreement: Fisheries
(72-45)	4/19/72	Agreement: Newsreel materials
(72-83)	7/27/72	Resolution: Yalu River Power Co.
(72-105)	9/?/72	Protocol: Border railway
(72-110)	10/9/72	Agreement: Economic and technical cooperation in geology
(72-134)	11/14/72	Plan for scientific cooperation between academies of sciences
(72-149)	12/5/72	Agreement: Plant quarantine and insect pests
(72-150)	12/7/72	Plan for cooperation in public health
(72-153)	12/13/72	Protocol: Mutual supply of goods
(72-155)	12/19/72	Agreement: Fish resources management

(72-160)	12/23/72	Protocol: Scientific and technical cooperation
(72-162)	12/25/72	Press Communiqué: Visit of Foreign Minister Chi Peng-fei
(73-10)	1/19/73	Protocol: Border river transport
(73-17)	2/14/73	Press Communiqué: Visit of Foreign Minister Ho Dam
(73-79)	6/18/73	Agreement: Economic and technical cooperation
(73-80)	6/18/73	Protocol: Economic and technical cooperation
(73-91)	7/31/73	Resolution: Sino-Korean Yalu River Power Company
(73-97)	9/10/73	Protocol: Border railway
(73-120)	11/6/73	Protocol: Scientific and technical cooperation
(73-147)	12/31/73	Protocol: Border river transport
(74-3)	1/5/74	Protocol: Mutual supply of goods
(74-77)	10/22/74	Protocol: Border railway
(74-87)	11/4/74	Plan for scientific cooperation between academies of sciences
(74-89)	11/6/74	Protocol: Scientific and technical cooperation
(74-110)	12/21/74	Protocol: Mutual supply of goods
(74-113)	12/24/74	Agreement: Border river transport
(74-114)	12/26/74	Protocol: Yalu River power corporation
(75-38)	4/26/75	Joint Communiqué: Visit of President Sung
(75-108)	11/3/75	Protocol: Border railway
(75-124)	12/2/75	Protocol: Scientific and technical cooperation
(75-138)	12/27/75	Plan for public health cooperation
(76-2)	1/14/76	Agreement: Border railway
(76-3)	1/18/76	Agreement: Post and telecommunications
(76-5)	1/26/76	Resolution: Border river power corporation
(76-11)	2/9/76	Protocol: Mutual supply of goods
(76-68)	7/23/76	Protocol: Border railway
(76-92)	12/13/76	Protocol: Demarcation, etc.
(76-95)	12/19/76	Plan for scientific cooperation between academies of sciences
(77-5)	1/21/77	Agreement: Border river navigation
(77-14)	2/5/77	Protocol: Scientific and technical cooperation
(77-15)	2/8/77	Protocol: Sino-Korean Yalu River Power Company
(77-24)	3/12/77	Agreement: Trade
(77-25)	3/12/77	Protocol: Trade
(77-41)	4/13/77	Protocol (renewed): Timber transportation
(77-81)	8/25/77	Protocol: Border railway transport
(78-12)	1/24/78	Decision: Sino-Korean Yalu River Hydro-Electric Power Company
(78-13)	1/26/78	Arrangement: Sino-Korean Border River Navigation Cooperation Committee

(78-62)	5/2/78	Protocol: Exchange of goods
(78-85)	6/6/78	Protocol: Scientific and Technical Cooperation Committee
(78-99)	6/30/78	Agreement: Hydraulic projects
(78-101)	7/24/78	Protocol: Border railway transport
(78-163)	10/24/78	Plan for scientific cooperation
(78-166)	11/1/78	Agreement: Plant quarantine and insect pest control
(78-193)	12/23/78	Protocol: Mutual supply of goods
(79-23)	2/6/79	Agreement: Border river transport
(79-97)	8/28/79	Protocol: Border railway transport for 1979
(80-17)	1/28/80	Accord: Cooperation in border river transport
(80-40)	3/14/80	Protocol: Goods exchange for 1980
(80-119)	8/14/80	Agreement: Cultural exchange for 1980
(80-128)	8/30/80	Protocol: Scientific and technical cooperation
(80-144)	9/25/80	Agreement: Cooperation in broadcasting and TV
(80-166)	11/7/80	Executive Program: Health cooperation for 1981
(80-174)	12/1/80	Plan: 1981–82 scientific cooperation
(80-189)	12/30/80	Agreement: Border television frequencies

Kuwait

(71-21)	3/22/71	Joint Communiqué: Establishment of diplomatic relations
(77-114)	12/26/77	Agreement: Economic and technical cooperation
(80-150)	10/6/80	Agreement: Trade

Laos

(74-57)	8/27/74	Agreement: Air transport
(74-68)	10/3/74	Agreement: Economic and technical cooperation
(74-74)	10/20/74	Agreement: Post and telecommunications
(75-2)	1/10/75	Protocol: Technical service on aviation
(75-3)	1/10/75	Agreement(2): Civil air transport
(75-4)	1/17/75	Minutes: Building of dwellings
(75-5)	1/17/75	Minutes: Building a highway
(75-6)	1/17/75	Protocol: Working conditions and living standards of Chinese personnels
(76-18)	3/18/76	Agreement: Economic and technical cooperation
(76-55)	6/26/76	Contract: Goods supply
(76-82)	10/25/76	Exchange of Notes: Turning over a radio station

(77-95)	10/29/77	Agreement: Loan
(78-7)	1/20/78	Protocol: Aid
(78-8)	1/20/78	Protocol: Work conditions of PRC experts
(78-48)	4/8/78	Certificate: Handing over of highway
(78-98)	6/28/78	Agreement: Civil air transport

Lebanon

(71-115)	11/9/71	Joint Communiqué: Establishment of diplomatic relations
(72-147)	11/29/72	Agreement: Trade
(72-148)	11/29/72	Exchange of Notes: Purchase of commodities

Liberia

(77-16)	2/17/77	Joint Communiqué: Establishment of diplomatic relations
(77-17)	2/17/77	Agreement: Economic cooperation
(77-18)	2/17/77	Exchange of Notes: Economic and technical cooperation
(78-28)	3/9/78	Protocol: Expansion project of a sugar refinery
(78-49)	4/10/78	Protocol: Building agricultural technology
(78-97)	6/28/78	Agreement: Economic and technical cooperation
(79-55)	5/16/79	Agreement: Trade

Libya

(78-108)	8/9/78	Joint Communiqué: Establishment of diplomatic relations
(78-109)	8/9/78	Agreement: Economic and technical cooperation
(78-110)	8/9/78	Agreement: Scientific and technical cooperation
(78-111)	8/9/78	Agreement: Trade

Luxembourg

(72-133)	11/13/72	Joint Communiqué: Establishment of diplomatic relations
(75-30)	4/10/75	Exchange of Notes: Trademark registration
(79-14)	1/29/79	Press Communiqué: Talks during visit of Prime Minister Gaston Thorn

Madagascar

(66-91)	8/13/66(?)	Technical aid
(72-128)	11/16/72	Joint Communique: Establishment of diplomatic relations
(74-6)	1/18/74	Agreement: Economic and technical cooperation
(74-7)	1/18/74	Agreement: Trade
(74-102)	12/9/74	Protocol: Dispatch of medical teams
(75-68)	7/23/75	Agreement: Economic and technical cooperation
(76-19)	3/20/76	Minutes: Highway construction

Malagasy

(See Madagascar)

Malaysia

(71-92)	8/28/71	Joint Communiqué: Trade talks
(74-42)	5/31/74	Joint Communiqué: Establishment of diplomatic relations
(78-44)	3/31/78	Contract: Rice

Maldives

(72-116)	10/14/72	Joint Communiqué: Establishment of diplomatic relations

Mali

(66-44)	5/13/66	Plan for cultural cooperation
(66-63)	6/9/66	Agreement: Loans
(67-36)	8/14/67	Agreement(s): Economic aid
(67-37)	8/14/67	Agreement: Loan
(67-64)	12/14/67	Protocol: Dispatch of medical teams
(68-35)	5/13/68	Exchange of Notes: Radio cooperation
(68-38)	5/24/68	Agreement (with Guinea): Railway construction
(68-39)	5/25/68	Joint Communiqué (with Guinea): Visit of Foreign Ministers Ousman Ba and Lansana Beavogui
(70-105)	12/21/70	Agreement: Economic and technical cooperation
(73-44)	4/4/73	Protocol: Dispatch of medical teams

(73–82)	6/24/73	Agreement: Economic and technical cooperation
(77–13)	2/4/77	Minutes: Water conservancy
(77–52)	5/10/77	Protocol: Dispatch of medical teams
(78–154)	10/7/78	Agreement: Trade
(79–61)	5/24/79	Protocol: Economic and technical cooperation

Malta

(72–6)	1/31/72	Joint Communiqué: Establishment of diplomatic relations
(72–38)	4/8/72	Agreement: Loan
(72–135)	11/16/72	Protocol: Technical aid
(73–103)	9/19/73	Protocol: Technical aid
(77–98)	11/6/77	Protocol: Economic and technical cooperation
(78–75)	5/27/78	Agreement: Joint Shipping Arrangement
(80–21)	2/1/80	Agreement: Exchange of information and material on the development of tourism

Mauritania

(67–6)	2/16/67	Agreement: Trade
(67–7)	2/16/67	Agreement: Economic and technical cooperation
(67–8)	2/16/67	Agreement: Cultural cooperation
(67–9)	2/17/67	Joint Press Communiqué: Visit of Foreign Minister Wane
(67–49)	10/14/67	Protocol: Economic and technical cooperation
(67–53)	10/24/67	Joint Communiqué: Visit of President Daddah
(67–56)	11/8/67	Protocol: Dispatch of a medical team
(69–54)	11/27/69	Contract: Sinking wells
(70–100)	11/27/70	Certificate: Turnover of a "youth home"
(71–27)	4/1/71	Agreement: Economic and technical cooperation
(72–54)	5/16/72	Protocol (supplementary): Trade
(72–90)	8/17/72	Protocol: Dispatch of medical teams
(74–62)	9/19/74	Agreement: Economic and technical cooperation
(77–37)	4/4/77	Protocol: Dispatch of medical teams
(77–75)	6/28/77	Minutes: Port construction
(80–71)	5/14/80	Agreement: Economic and technical cooperation

Mauritius

(72–43)	4/15/72	Joint Communiqué: Establishment of diplomatic relations

(72-86)   8/9/72   Agreement: Economic and technical cooperation
(75-83)   9/10/75   Exchange of Letters: Agricultural cooperation

Mexico

(72-12)   2/14/72   Joint Communiqué: Establishment of diplo-
                       matic relations
(72-120)   10/27/72   Press Communiqué: Trade talks
(73-51)   4/22/73   Agreement: Trade
(73-52)   4/22/73   Exchange of Notes: Cultural, scientific, and
                       technical exchanges
(73-53)   4/24/73   Joint Communiqué: Visit of President
                       Echeverria
(75-81)   9/9/75   Agreement: Scientific and technical cooperation
(75-82)   9/9/75   Exchange of Notes: Cultural Exchange
(75-115)   11/8/75   Protocol: Scientific and technical cooperation
(76-90)   11/25/76   Protocol: Scientific and technical cooperation
(77-107)   12/16/77   Protocol: Scientific and technical cooperation
(78-164)   10/27/78   Agreement: Cultural cooperation
(78-165)   10/27/78   Agreement: Tourism cooperation
(80-101)   7/2/80   Protocol: Cultural exchanges and cooperation

Mongolia

(66-19)   3/28/66   Protocol: Mutual supply of goods
(66-20)   3/28/66   Protocol: Delivery of goods
(66-53)   5/30/66   Protocol: Scientific and technical cooperation
(66-97)   9/29/66   Plan for cultural cooperation
(67-32)   7/26/67   Protocol: Mutual supply of goods
(68-36)   5/13/68   Protocol: Mutual supply of goods
(69-31)   7/24/69   Protocol: Delivery of goods
(70-52)   7/14/70   Protocol: Mutual supply of goods
(71-54)   6/5/71   Protocol: Exchange of goods
(71-130)   11/30/71   Protocol: Border railway
(72-51)   5/12/72   Protocol: Mutual supply of goods
(72-88)   8/16/72   Exchange of Notes: Economic and cultural
                       cooperation
(72-93)   9/7/72   Protocol: Boundary landmark
(72-104)   9/23/72   Protocol: Border railway
(73-24)   3/1/73   Protocol: Exchange of goods
(73-33)   3/23/73   Minutes: Handing over projects
(73-119)   11/4/73   Protocol: Border railway
(74-33)   4/26/74   Protocol: Mutual supply of goods

(74–84)	10/26/74	Protocol: Border railway
(75–34)	4/19/75	Protocol: Mutual supply of goods
(75–94)	10/14/75	Protocol: Border railway
(76–83)	11/11/76	Protocol: Mutual supply of goods
(77–70)	6/17/77	Protocol: Supply of goods
(77–82)	8/30/77(?)	Protocol: Border railway
(77–105)	12/10/77	Protocol: Meteorological communications
(78–25)	3/1/78	Protocol: Mutual supply of goods
(78–174)	11/18/78	Protocol: Border railway
(78–178)	11/25/78	Minutes: Change in measures concerning nontrade payments
(79–89)	8/10/79	Protocol: Mutual supply of goods for 1979
(79–103)	9/28/79	Protocol: Border railway
(80–54)	4/17/80	Protocol: Supply of goods for 1980

Morocco

(66–46)	5/20/68	Protocol (supplementary): Trade
(66–98)	9/30/66	Exchange of Notes: Payments
(71–32)	4/26/71	Protocol: Trade
(75–25)	3/19/75	Agreement: Constructing a sports complex
(75–26)	3/19/75	Agreement: Trade
(75–27)	3/19/75	Protocol: Dispatch of medical teams
(76–12)	2/20/76	Protocol: Building a sports complex
(77–74)	6/24/77	Minutes: Trade
(79–102)	9/25/79	Protocol: Sending a medical team to Morocco
(80–90)	6/9/80	Accord: Public health and medical services

Mozambique

(75–17)	3/2/75	Press Communiqué: Visit of President Machel
(75–54)	7/2/75	Agreement: Economic and technical cooperation
(77–86)	9/23/77	Protocol: Economic and technical cooperation
(78–76)	5/28/78	Protocol: Economic and technical cooperation

Nepal

(66–3)	1/16/66	Exchange of Notes: Friendship, trade and communication between Tibet and Nepal
(66–37)	5/2/66	Agreement: Trade and communication between Tibet and Nepal
(66–73)	6/30/66	Agreement (supplementary): Highway maintenance

(66-102)	10/18/66	Exchange of Notes: Economic aid
(66-125)	12/21/66	Agreement: Economic and technical cooperation
(67-11)	3/14/67	Contract: Rice
(67-21)	5/25/67	Protocol: Construction of a power station
(67-23)	5/28/67	Agreement(?): Highway extension
(67-65)	12/?/67	Exchange of Notes: Highway maintenance
(68-16)	3/20/68	Exchange of Letters: Economic aid
(68-17)	3/24/68	Plan for cultural and scientific exchange
(68-40)	5/28/68	Agreement: Trade
(68-41)	5/28/68	Protocol: Trade
(68-42)	6/1/68	Joint Communiqué: Visit of Deputy Prime Minister Bista
(68-44)	6/13/68	Agreement: News agencies
(68-61)	9/27/68	Agreement: Highway construction
(70-106)	12/24/70	Letters of Exchange: Construction of a power transmission line
(71-18)	3/3/71	Exchange of Letters: Highway repair
(71-68)	7/16/71	Exchange of Notes: Cotton planting survey team
(71-69)	7/16/71	Exchange of Notes: Highway construction
(71-108)	10/27/71	Exchange of Letters: Mineral deposits surveys
(72-4)	1/14/72	Exchange of Letters: Building a sports stadium
(72-23)	3/14/72	Exchange of Notes: Economic cooperation
(72-138)	11/18/72	Agreement: Economic and technical cooperation
(73-22)	2/26/73	Exchange of Letters: Technical aid
(73-31)	3/20/73	Summary: Road construction
(73-38)	3/26/73	Minutes: Trolley bus service
(73-143)	12/14/73	Joint Communiqué: Visit of King Dev
(74-43)	5/31/74	Agreement: Trade and payments
(75-11)	2/2/75	Agreement: Highway construction
(75-15)	2/7/75	Joint Press Communiqué: Economic and technical cooperation
(75-137)	12/25/75	Certificate: Turning over engineering circuits, power stations, etc.
(76-29)	4/30/76	Exchange of Letters: Trade communication between Tibet and Nepal
(76-60)	7/8/76	Agreement: Water conservancy and irrigation
(76-101)	12/27/76	Agreement: Highway construction
(78-77)	5/28/78	Agreement: Border inspection
(78-127)	8/31/78	Agreement: Civil air transport
(78-132)	9/17/78	Minutes: China-Nepal Border Inspection Joint Committee
(78-145)	10/1/78	Agreement: Establishment of complete projects
(78-194)	12/30/78	Document: Handing over cotton textiles mill
(79-27)	2/27/79	Notes: Boundary inspection

(79-98)   9/3/79   Notes: Boundary inspection
(79-122) 11/20/79   Protocol: Joint border inspection

Netherlands

(72-55)   5/16/72   Joint Communiqué: Diplomatic relations
(75-31)   4/10/75   Exchange of Notes: Trademark registration
(75-71)   8/14/75   Agreement: Maritime transport
(78-179) 11/27/78   Draft: Civil air transport
(79-10)   1/20/79   Agreement: Civil air transport
(79-104) 10/8/79   Declaration of Intent: Agricultural cooperation
(80-143) 9/23/80   Memorandum: Understanding on agricultural
                      matters
(80-161) 10/30/80   Agreement: Cultural cooperation
(80-162) 10/30/80   Agreement: Economic and technological co-
                      operation

New Zealand

(72-158) 12/21/72   Joint Communiqué: Establishment of diplo-
                      matic relations
(73-44)   4/3/73   Press Communiqué: Visit of Associate
                      Minister of Foreign Affairs
(73-110) 10/9/73   Agreement: Trade
(75-51)   6/18/75   Exchange of Notes: Trademark registration
(76-32)   5/1/76   Exchange of Letters: Shipping

Nicaragua

(80-121) 8/19/80   Agreement: Sale of cotton to PRC in 1981

Niger

(74-52)   7/20/74   Joint Communiqué: Establishment of diplo-
                      matic relations
(74-53)   7/20/74   Agreement: Economic and technical cooperation
(75-79)   9/5/75   Protocol: Sending a medical team
(75-80)   9/5/75   Protocol: Agricultural cooperation
(77-19)   2/24/77   Document: Handing over reclamation area to
                      Niger

(79-31)   3/9/79   Document: Agricultural project built with PRC aid

(80-109) 7/10/80   Protocol: Sending Chinese medical team to Niger

Nigeria

(71-10)   2/10/71   Joint Communiqué: Establishment of diplomatic relations

(72-123) 11/3/72   Agreement: Economic and technical cooperation

(72-124) 11/3/72   Agreement: Trade

(74-61)   9/15/74   Press Communiqué: Visit of General Gowon

(80-83)   6/6/80   Protocol: Extension of Chinese technical services and certificate of job completion in Nigeria

Norway

(66-35)   4/30/66   Plan for cultural exchange

(73-56)   5/12/73   Agreement: Air transport

(74-55)   8/2/74   Agreement: Maritime transport

(74-73) 10/19/74   Agreement: Establishment of trade committee

(74-90) 11/8/74   Exchange of Letters: Trademark registration

(77-32)   3/24/77   Agreement: Ship inspection

(80-19)   1/30/80   Agreement: Export credit

(80-76)   5/27/80   Agreement: Widening of bilateral economic, industrial, and technical cooperation

(80-145) 9/25/80   Agreement: Economic, industrial, technical cooperation

Oman

(78-73)   5/25/78   Joint Communiqué: Establishment of diplomatic relations

(80-27)   2/9/80   Agreement: Trade relations

(80-68)   5/10/80   Agreement (preliminary): Cooperation in electrical engineering work

(80-155) 10/14/80   Agreement: Trade

Pakistan

(66-22)   3/31/66   Joint Communiqué: Visit of Chairman Liu Shao-ch'i

(66–57)	6/1/66	Plan for cultural cooperation
(66–68)	6/23/66	Protocol: Construction of a heavy machinery complex
(66–77)	7/4/66	Agreement: Barter
(66–78)	7/4/66	Protocol: Trade
(66–104)	10/21/66	Agreement: Maritime transport
(67–1)	1/17/67	Supply of grain
(67–42)	9/14/67	Plan for cultural cooperation
(67–51)	10/21/67	Letters of Agreement: Border trade
(68–28)	4/27/68	Protocol: Trade
(68–66)	11/7/68	Exchange of Letters: Border trade
(68–74)	12/26/68	Agreement: Economic and technical cooperation
(70–23)	4/9/70	Protocol: Economic and technical cooperation
(70–27)	5/5/70	Protocol: Trade
(70–29)	5/21/70	Letters: Border trade
(70–32)	5/? /70	Contract: Airplanes
(70–93)	11/14/70	Joint Communiqué: Visit of President Khan
(70–94)	11/14/70	Agreement: Economic and technical cooperation
(71–35)	4/28/71	Minutes: Sugar Hill construction
(71–49)	5/29/71	Exchange of Notes: Border trade
(71–83)	8/5/71	Exchange of Notes: Giving of Bank
(71–131)	12/2/71	Minutes: Factory construction
(72–7)	2/2/72	Joint Communiqué: Visit of President Bhutto
(72–32)	3/24/72	Exchange of Letters: Loan
(72–50)	5/7/72	Exchange of Letters: Border trade
(72–69)	6/23/72	Protocol: Trade
(74–37)	5/14/74	Joint Communiqué: Visit of Prime Minister Bhutto
(74–54)	7/27/74	Protocol: Trade
(75–50)	6/16/75	Exchange of Letters: Border trade
(75–102)	10/25/75	Protocol: Trade
(76–37)	5/30/76	Joint Communiqué: Visit of Prime Minister Bhutto
(76–38)	5/30/76	Agreement: Scientific and technical cooperation
(76–39)	5/30/76	Protocol: Economic and technical cooperation
(76–48)	6/13/76	Exchange of Notes: Border trade
(77–8)	1/29/77	Protocol: Scientific and technical cooperation
(77–76)	6/29/77	Memorandum: Air route
(77–79)	8/2/77	Exchange of Letters: Border trade
(77–116)	12/28/77	Protocol: Trade
(78–5)	1/15/78	Exchange of Notes: Handing over of a cargo ship
(77–88)	6/10/78	Agreement: Border trade
(78–92)	6/18/78	Protocol: Handing over of Karakoram Highway
(78–141)	9/23/78	Agreement: Purchase and sale of ships

(79-85)	7/25/79	Exchange of Letters: Reciprocal registration of trademark
(80-70)	5/11/80	Protocol: Scientific and technical cooperation
(80-120)	8/18/80	Agreement: Cultural exchange for 1980-81

Papua New Guinea

(75-78)	9/3/75	Contract: Cocoa, copper ores
(75-117)	11/12/75	Contract: Timber
(76-79)	10/12/76	Joint Communiqué: Establishment of diplomatic relations

Peru

(71-36)	4/28/71	Minutes: Talks between PRC vice-minister of Foreign Trade and Peruvian secretary-general of the Foreign Ministry
(71-57)	6/15/71	Minutes: Fishery talks
(71-59)	6/16/71	Minutes: Trade talks
(71-114)	11/2/71	Joint Communiqué: Establishment of diplomatic relations
(71-129)	11/28/71	Agreement: Economic and technical cooperation
(72-87)	8/9/72	Agreement: Trade

Philippines

(74-64)	9/23/74	Exchange of Letters: Development of trade
(75-48)	6/9/75	Joint Communiqué: Establishment of diplomatic relations
(75-49)	6/9/75	Agreement: Trade
(75-119)	11/14/75	Agreement: Petroleum trade
(76-8)	2/5/76	Memorandum: Exhibition of PRC
(76-23)	4/5/76	Exchange of Letters: Development of trade
(76-47)	6/10/76	Agreement: Exhibition
(78-14)	1/29/78	Agreement: Supply of crude oil
(78-22)	2/24/78	Exchange of Notes: Trade
(78-33)	3/14/78	Agreement: Scientific and technical cooperation
(78-176)	11/18/78	Agreement: Postal and parcel services
(79-44)	5/8/79	Agreement (Draft): Civil air transport
(79-76)	7/8/79	Agreement: Long-term trade
(79-77)	7/8/79	Agreement: Cultural cooperation
(79-78)	7/8/79	Agreement: Civil air transport

(79–79)	7/8/79	Memorandum: Cooperative construction of tourist hotels
(79–110)	10/20/79	Protocol: Scientific and technical cooperation
(80–57)	4/21/80	Protocol: Trade for 1980
(80–126)	8/26/80	Program: Cultural agreement for 1980–81
(80–154)	10/13/80	Agreement: Supplying hydroelectric equipment
(80–168)	11/11/80	Arrangement: Mutual deposit facility
(80–175)	12/1/80	Protocol: Scientific and technical cooperation

Poland

(66–15)	3/22/66	Agreement: Exchange of goods and payments
(66–16)	3/22/66	Protocol: Delivery of goods
(66–67)	6/20/66	Protocol: Scientific and technical cooperation
(66–69)	6/24/66	Plan for cultural cooperation
(67–29)	6/30/67	Agreement: Exchange of goods and payments
(67–30)	6/30/67	Protocol: Delivery of goods
(67–50)	10/17/67	Protocol: Scientific and technical cooperation
(68–25)	4/9/68	Agreement: Exchange of goods and payments
(68–26)	5/9/68	Protocol: Delivery of goods
(69–34)	8/7/69	Agreement: Delivery of goods
(69–35)	8/7/69	Protocol: Delivery of goods
(70–43)	7/2/70	Agreement: Exchange of goods and payments
(70–44)	7/2/70	Protocol: Delivery of goods
(70–45)	7/2/70	Exchange of Notes: Opening Swiss franc account
(71–51)	5/31/71	Agreement: Exchange of goods and payments
(71–52)	5/31/71	Protocol: Delivery of goods
(71–53)	5/31/71	Exchange of Notes: Change of Swiss franc
(72–27)	3/16/72	Agreement: Exchange of goods and payments
(72–28)	3/16/72	Protocol: Delivery of goods
(72–48)	5/5/72	Protocol: Shipping
(72–117)	10/16/72	Protocol: Sino-Polish Shipbrokers' Company
(73–34)	3/23/73	Agreement: Exchange of goods and payments
(73–35)	3/23/73	Protocol: Delivery of goods
(74–20)	3/11/74	Agreement: Exchange of goods and payments
(74–35)	5/4/74	Protocol: Sino-Polish Shipbrokers' Company
(75–22)	3/11/75	Agreement: Exchange of goods and payments
(76–4)	1/19/76	Agreement: Exchange of goods and payments
(76–91)	11/25/76	Protocol: Sino-Polish Shipbrokers' Company
(77–35)	4/3/77	Protocol: Sino-Polish Shipbrokers' Company
(77–56)	5/23/77	Agreement: Exchange of goods and payments
(78–15)	1/30/78	Agreement: Exchange of goods and payments
(78–52)	4/12/78	Protocol: Sino-Polish Shipbrokers' Company
(78–142)	9/26/78	Protocol: Shipping Cooperation

(79–13)	1/22/79	Agreement: Goods exchange and payments in 1979
(80–46)	3/25/80	Agreement: Goods exchange and payments for 1980
(80–80)	12/5/80	Protocol: Scientific and technical cooperation in 1981

Portugal

(71–24)	3/22/71	Protocol: Equipment delivery
(71–25)	3/22/71	Protocol: Work conditions for PRC experts
(71–56)	6/9/71	Joint Communiqué: Visit of President Ceausescu
(71–104)	10/16/71	Protocol: Technical aid
(71–110)	10/28/71	Agreement: Loan
(71–128)	11/26/71	Protocol: Exchange of goods and payments
(72–17)	3/2/72	Agreement: Radio and television cooperation
(72–24)	3/14/72	Protocol: Scientific and technical cooperation
(72–36)	4/6/72	Agreement: Air transport
(78–162)	10/23/78	Agreement: News Cooperation
(79–24)	2/8/79	Joint Communiqué: Establishment of diplomatic relations
(80–103)	7/4/80	Agreement: Reciprocal most-favored-nation trade status

Rumania

(66–7)	2/11/66	Plan for cultural cooperation
(66–89)	7/31/66	Protocol: Scientific and technical cooperation
(67–4)	2/14/67	Agreement: Exchange of goods and payments
(67–5)	2/14/67	Protocol: Delivery of goods
(67–52)	10/23/67	Protocol: Scientific and technical cooperation
(67–63)	12/13/67	Plan for scientific cooperation between Academies of Sciences
(67–68)	12/30/67	Agreement: Goods exchange and payments
(69–22)	6/3/69	Agreement: Trade
(69–23)	6/3/69	Protocol: Delivery of goods
(70–18)	3/28/70	Agreement: Trade and payments
(70–19)	3/28/70	Protocol: Delivery of goods
(70–40)	6/29/70	Protocol: Material aid
(70–83)	10/20/70	Protocol: Scientific and technical cooperation
(70–99)	11/25/70	Agreement: Loan
(71–12)	2/18/71	Agreement: Trade

(71-13)	2/18/71	Agreement: Trade and payments
(71-14)	2/18/71	Protocol: Delivery of goods
(71-23)	3/22/71	Protocol: Supply of plants and technical aid
(72-144)	11/27/72	Protocol: Exchange of goods and payments
(72-145)	11/27/72	Protocol: Delivery of goods
(73-11)	1/19/73	Protocol: Technical aid
(73-40)	3/31/73	Plan for scientific cooperation
(73-60)	5/22/73	Agreement: Technical survey cooperation
(73-68)	5/31/73	Protocol: Scientific and technical cooperation
(73-133)	11/22/73	Protocol: Delivery of goods
(73-135)	11/23/73	Protocol: Exchange of goods and payments
(73-138)	11/24/73	Agreement: Exhibition of PRC archaeological finds
(74-9)	2/8/74	Agreement: Health cooperation
(74-67)	9/30/74	Protocol: Technical aid
(74-104)	12/14/74	Protocol: Exchange of goods and payments
(74-111)	12/21/74	Protocol: Scientific and technical cooperation
(75-47)	5/31/75	Agreement: Post and telecommunications
(75-67)	7/18/75	Draft: Maritime transport
(75-129)	12/18/75	Agreement: Scientific and technical cooperation
(75-130)	12/18/75	Plan for scientific cooperation
(76-6)	1/29/76	Agreement: Trade
(76-7)	1/29/76	Protocol: Exchange of goods and payments
(76-25)	4/8/76	Agreement: Maritime transport
(76-27)	4/16/76	Protocol: Scientific and technical cooperation
(77-6)	1/24/77	Protocol: Exchange of goods and payments
(77-47)	4/26/77	Plan on health cooperation
(77-87)	9/24/77	Protocol: Embassy building
(77-106)	12/14/77	Plan on scientific cooperation
(77-112)	12/21/77	Protocol: Exchange of goods and payments
(78-67)	5/19/78	Document: Consular and cultural cooperation
(78-68)	5/19/78	Agreement: Economic and technical cooperation
(78-69)	5/19/78	Protocol: Economic and technical cooperation
(78-114)	8/21/78	Agreement: Establishment of committee on economic and technical cooperation
(78-115)	8/21/78	Protocol: Production and technology cooperation
(78-116)	8/21/78	Agreement: Scientific and technical cooperation
(78-117)	8/21/78	Protocol: Exchange of technicians and students
(78-118)	8/21/78	Protocol: Trade
(78-119)	8/21/78	Protocol: Tourism
(78-120)	8/21/78	Protocol: Animal quarantine
(78-121)	8/21/78	Protocol: Plant quarantine
(78-122)	8/21/78	Agreement: Opening shipping routes
(78-175)	11/16/78	Protocol: Sino-Rumanian Committee for Scientific and Technical Cooperation

(79-59)	5/22/79	Protocol: Economic and technical cooperation
(79-94)	8/18/79	Agreement: News cooperation
(79-99)	9/5/79	Agreement: Cooperation in building a coking plant
(80-32)	2/29/80	Protocol: Goods exchange and payments in 1980
(80-78)	5/29/80	Protocol: Economic and technical cooperation
(80-81)	6/6/80	Agreement: Exchange of goods, experience, specialists, and information
(80-171)	11/20/80	Protocol: Broadcasting and TV cooperation 1981-82

Rwanda

(71-116)	11/12/71	Joint Communiqué: Establishment of diplomatic relations
(72-52)	5/13/72	Agreement: Economic and technical cooperation
(72-70)	6/23/72	Protocol: Trade
(72-113)	10/11/72	Protocol: Economic and technical cooperation
(73-74)	6/6/73	Minutes: Road, sugar refinery, etc.
(76-94)	12/16/76	Certificate: Handing over a sugar refinery
(77-68)	6/11/77	Minutes: Rice plantation
(78-89)	6/10/78	Agreement: Economic and technical cooperation

Samoa (W)

(75-113)	11/6/75	Joint Communiqué: Establishment of diplomatic relations
(76-75)	9/8/76	Agreement: Economic and technical cooperation
(80-95)	6/19/80	Protocol: Economic and technical cooperation

San Marino

(71-37)	5/6/71	Protocol: Establishment of consulates
(80-125)	8/26/80	Agreement: Cultural and educational cooperation

Sao Tome and Principe

(75-65)	7/12/75	Joint Communiqué: Establishment of diplomatic relations
(75-135)	12/25/75	Agreement: Trade
(75-136)	12/25/75	Agreement: Economic and technical cooperation

Senegal

(71-138)	12/7/71	Joint Communiqué: Establishment of diplomatic relations
(73-136)	11/23/73	Agreement: Trade

(73–137)	11/23/73	Agreement: Economic and technical cooperation
(74–39)	5/18/74	Joint Communiqué: Visit of President Senghor
(74–112)	12/23/74	Protocol: Dispatch of medical teams
(78–47)	4/7/78	Minutes (supplementary): Drilling wells
(79–42)	5/2/79	Document: Agricultural projects with PRC aid

Seychelles

(76–58)	6/30/76	Joint Communiqué: Establishment of diplomatic relations
(78–63)	5/2/78	Agreement: Economic and technical cooperation

Sierra Leone

(71–71)	7/29/71	Communiqué: Establishment of diplomatic relations
(71–72)	7/29/71	Agreement: Economic and technical cooperation
(71–73)	7/29/71	Agreement: Trade and payments
(71–74)	7/30/71	Communiqué: Visit of government delegation of Sierra Leone
(72–108)	10/6/72	Protocol: Dispatch of medical teams
(72–111)	10/9/72	Protocol: Economic and technical cooperation
(73–94)	8/3/73	Minutes: Construction of a national stadium
(73–118)	11/10/73	Protocol: Economic and technical cooperation
(73–119)	11/10/73	Summary: Trade relations
(76–34)	5/20/76	Document: Transferring rice stations
(77–9)	1/29/77	Document: Handing over agricultural development stations
(77–101)	11/24/77	Certificate: Rice agriculture stations
(78–18)	2/15/78	Certificate: Handing over of a highway bridge

Singapore

(79–138)	12/29/79	Agreement: Reciprocal most-favored-nation trade status
(80–93)	6/14/80	Agreement: Establishing trade mission

Somalia

(66–65)	6/11/66	Plan for a cultural cooperation
(66–105)	10/23/66	Exchange of Letters: Working conditions for PRC experts

(67-38)	8/16/67	Minutes: Building a rice and tobacco experiment station
(67-39)	8/19/67	Plan for cultural cooperation
(69-12)	3/18/69	Minutes: Drilling of wells
(70-20)	4/5/70	Document: Transferring a rice and tobacco experimental station
(70-38)	6/19/70	Protocol: Economic and technical cooperation
(71-55)	6/7/71	Agreement: Economic and technical cooperation
(75-134)	12/21/75	Minutes: Drilling of wells and water supply works
(76-61)	7/8/76	Protocol: Dispatch of medical teams
(76-84)	11/15/76	Certificate: Handing over a highway
(77-22)	3/8/77	Certificate: Handing over a hospital
(77-73)	6/23/77	Protocol: Economic and technical cooperation
(77-92)	10/20/77	Certificate: Handing over a highway
(77-99)	11/15/77	Certificate: Turnover of a stadium
(78-29)	3/10/78	Agreement: Radio and television cooperation
(78-30)	3/10/78	Agreement: News cooperation
(78-56)	4/18/78	Agreement: Economic and technical cooperation
(78-107)	8/1/78	Protocol: Handing over of a highway
(80-59)	4/23/80	Agreement: Trade

Spain

(73-29)	3/9/73	Joint Communiqué: Establishment of diplomatic relations
(77-67)	6/10/77	Exchange of Instruments: Trademark registration and protection
(78-58)	4/24/78	Agreement: Trade
(78-87)	6/8/78	Draft: Civil Air Transport Agreement
(78-93)	6/19/78	Agreement: Trade
(78-94)	6/19/78	Agreement: Civil air transport

Sri Lanka

(66-120)	11/29/66	Protocol: Exchange of goods
(66-121)	11/29/66	Contracts(2): Rubber and rice
(67-54)	11/6/67	Agreement: Trade and payments
(67-55)	11/6/67	Protocol: Exchange of goods
(68-7)	3/3/68	Exchange of Letters: Economic and technical cooperation
(68-12)	3/11/68	Exchange of Letters: Trade and payments
(69-1)	1/7/69	Protocol: Exchange of goods

(69–44)	10/22/69	Protocol: Exchange of goods
(70–9)	2/8/70	Exchange of Letters: Building of a spinning and weaving mill
(70–67)	9/12/70	Agreement: Loan
(70–72)	10/15/70	Exchange of Notes: Economic aid
(71–1)	1/21/71	Protocol: Exchange of goods
(71–2)	1/21/71	Contract: Rubber
(71–3)	1/21/71	Contract: Rice
(71–48)	5/27/71	Agreement: Loan
(71–98)	10/8/71	Agreement: Loan of rice
(71–146)	12/28/71	Agreement: Parcel
(71–147)	12/28/71	Exchange of Notes: Parcel
(72–14)	2/18/72	Protocol: Trade (exchange of goods)
(72–46)	4/20/72	Agreement: Shipping
(72–57)	5/19/72	Exchange of Notes: Economic aid
(72–58)	5/19/72	Exchange of Notes: Sending teachers
(72–75)	6/29/72	Agreement: Economic and technical cooperation
(72–76)	6/29/72	Agreement: Construction of a printing and dyeing mill
(72–77)	7/5/72	Joint Communiqué: Visit of Prime Minister Mrs. Sirimavo
(72–100)	9/16/72	Agreement: Loan for a cargo ship
(72–140)	11/21/72	Agreement: Loan for a cargo ship
(72–154)	12/18/72	Agreement: Trade and payments (1973–74)
(72–159)	12/22/72	Protocol: Exchange of commodities
(73–145)	12/20/73	Protocol: Exchange of goods
(74–49)	7/12/74	Protocol: River controlling project
(75–13)	2/4/75	Protocol: Trade
(75–32)	4/18/75	Exchange of Letters: Mutual exemption from taxes on freight
(75–104)	10/27/75	Minutes: Shipping
(75–121)	11/30/75	Protocol: Exchange of goods
(77–93)	10/27/77	Agreement: Trade and payments
(77–94)	10/27/77	Protocol: Exchange of goods
(77–115)	12/? /77	Minutes: Shipping
(78–191)	12/20/78	Protocol: Exchange of goods
(80–5)	1/18/80	Agreement: Economic and technical cooperation
(80–147)	9/30/80	Minutes: Sino–Sri Lanka joint shipping service
(80–165)	11/7/80	Executive Program: Cultural agreement for 1981
(80–184)	12/19/80	Protocol: Trade 1981

Sudan

| (66–11) | 3/7/66 | Protocol: Trade |
| (66–86) | 7/27/66 | Protocol: Trade |

(68-46)	6/20/68	Protocol: Trade
(69-15)	4/1/69	Protocol: Trade
(70-30)	5/21/70	Protocol: Trade
(70-59)	8/12/70	Agreement: Economic and technical cooperation
(70-60)	8/12/70	Agreement: Cultural, scientific, and technical cooperation
(70-102)	12/14/70	Protocol: Dispatch of medical teams
(71-20)	3/9/71	Protocol: Trade
(71-142)	12/20/71	Agreement: Economic and technical cooperation
(72-62)	5/27/72	Protocol: Trade
(73-14)	1/25/73	Note: Construction of factories
(73-85)	7/4/73	Protocol: Trade
(76-24)	4/7/76	Protocol: Trade
(77-21)	3/1/77	Protocol: Trade
(77-64)	6/9/77	Agreement: Economic and technical cooperation
(78-24)	2/28/78	Certificate: Handing over of a textile mill
(78-135)	9/20/78	Protocol: Trade
(79-88)	8/6/79	Protocol: 1979-80 Trade
(80-110)	7/10/80	Protocol: Sending medical team to Sudan

Surinam

(76-36)	5/28/76	Joint Communiqué: Establishment of diplomatic relations

Sweden

(73-69)	6/1/73	Agreement: Air transport
(73-121)	11/9/73	Agreement: Exhibition of PRC archaeological finds
(75-7)	1/18/75	Agreement: Maritime transport
(78-158)	10/19/78	Agreement: Science and technology cooperation
(78-182)	12/5/78	Agreement: Cooperation in industry, science, and technology
(80-172)	11/24/80	Agreement: Academic cooperation in social sciences

Switzerland

(73-124)	11/12/73	Agreement: Air transport
(73-125)	11/12/73	Agreements(2): Concerning air transport
(73-126)	11/12/73	Minutes: Air transport

(74–109)   12/20/74   Agreement: Trade
(80–42)   3/19/80   Agreement: Joint venture elevator company
(80–118)   8/6/80   Protocol: Radio and TV cooperation

Syria

(66–30)   4/20/66   Plan for cultural cooperation
(67–13)   4/13/67   Exchange of Letters: Construction of a cotton
                      spinning mill
(68–21)   4/6/68   Agreement: News agencies
(71–140)   12/13/71   Agreement: Construction of a spinning mill
(72–61)   5/24/72   Agreement: Economic and technical cooperation
(75–86)   9/22/75   Agreement: Broadcasting and television co-
                      operation
(75–107)   11/10/75   Agreement: Air transport
(79–124)   11/26/79   Agreement: Sports cooperation

Tanzania

(66–31)   4/22/66   Memorandum: Maritime Transport Company
(66–40)   5/7/66   Plan for cultural cooperation
(66–62)   6/8/66   Agreement: Economic cooperation
(66–82)   7/7/66   Accord: Establishment of Sino-Tanzanian
                      Maritime Transport Company
(66–99)   10/10/66   Contracts (3): Construction of a textile mill
(67–41)   9/5/67   Agreement (with Zambia): Tanzania-Zambia
                      railway construction
(68–22)   4/8/68   Protocol (with Zambia): Railway survey and
                      design
(68–23)   4/8/68   Protocol (with Zambia): Working conditions
                      for PRC experts
(68–24)   4/8/68   Protocol (with Zambia): Loan
(68–29)   4/27/68   Agreement (with Zambia): Railway loans
(68–30)   4/27/68   Protocol (with Zambia): Railway construction
(68–34)   5/6/68   Protocol: Dispatch of medical teams
(69–25)   6/24/69   Minutes: National stadium
(69–29)   7/12/69   Protocol: PRC-Tanzania Joint Ocean Shipping
                      Company
(69–49)   11/14/69   Agreement (supplementary) (with Zambia):
                      Railway construction
(69–50)   11/14/69   Proposal (supplementary) (with Zambia): Rail-
                      way
(69–51)   11/14/69   Minutes (with Zambia): Railway

(70-28)	5/8/70	Minutes: Construction of a state farm
(70-35)	6/4/70	Document: Transferring an agricultural machinery factory
(70-49)	7/12/70	Protocol (with Zambia): Loan for the railway construction
(70-50)	7/12/70	Protocol (with Zambia): Railway
(70-51)	7/12/70	Minutes (with Zambia): Railway construction
(70-57)	7/31/70	Minutes: Constructing a mill factory
(71-144)	12/22/71	Summary (with Zambia): Talks on railway construction
(73-96)	8/16/73	Protocol: Shipping
(74-26)	3/29/74	Agreement: Economic and technical cooperation
(75-84)	9/18/75	Minutes (with Zambia): Tanzania-Zambia Railway
(75-128)	12/15/75	Certificates (with Zambia): Handing over a railway training school, etc.
(76-62)	7/8/76	Protocol (with Zambia): Railway
(76-63)	7/8/76	Minutes (with Zambia): Railway
(76-65)	7/14/76	Certificate (with Zambia): Handing over Tanzania-Zambia railway
(78-104)	7/31/78	Protocol (with Zambia): Tanzania-Zambia railway
(78-105)	7/31/78	Protocol (with Zambia): Building Tanzania-Zambia railway training school
(78-106)	7/31/78	Minutes (with Zambia): Technical cooperation in building Tanzania-Zambia railway
(78-130)	9/14/78	Protocol: Economic and technical cooperation
(79-91)	8/16/79	Protocol: Joint shipping
(80-37)	3/5/80	Protocol: China is planning, designing, and constructing a headquarters for the Revolutionary Party of Tanzania.
(80-127)	8/29/80	Protocol: Technical cooperation in Tazara railway

Thailand

(75-47)	7/1/75	Joint Communiqué: Establishment of diplomatic relations
(77-4)	1/8/77	Exchange of Notes: Trademark registration
(78-41)	3/31/78	Agreement: Trade
(78-42)	3/31/78	Agreement: Scientific and technical cooperation
(78-167)	11/9/78	Minutes: Sino-Thai Joint Committee on Scientific and Technical Cooperation
(78-168)	11/9/78	Protocol: Import and export

(78-169)	11/9/78	Protocol: Establishment of a joint trade committee
(79-4)	1/14/79	Protocol: Long-term crude oil trade
(79-109)	10/19/79	Protocol: Importation and exportation of commodities
(80-2)	1/3/80	Agreement: Oil supply contract
(80-66)	5/9/80	Agreement (initial): Civil air transport
(80-67)	5/9/80	Memorandum: Understanding of civil air transport
(80-182)	12/11/80(?)	Protocol: Trade
(80-188)	12/22/80	Minutes: Scientific and technical cooperation

Togo

(72-102)	9/19/72	Joint Communiqué: Establishment of diplomatic relations
(72-103)	9/19/72	Agreement: Economic and technical cooperation
(74-60)	9/5/74	Protocol: Economic and technical cooperation
(77-53)	5/13/77	Document: Rice plantation center
(78-31)	3/13/78	Certificate: Handing over of rice plantation centers
(78-32)	3/13/78	Protocol: Building an agricultural development center
(78-43)	3/31/78	Protocol: Dispatch of medical teams
(79-49)	5/11/79	Document: Agrotechnical cooperation project

Trinidad and Tobago

(74-46)	6/20/74	Joint Communiqué: Establishment of diplomatic relations
(74-91)	11/11/74	Press Communiqué: Visit of Prime Minister Dr. Williams
(75-12)	2/3/75	Agreement: Establishment of embassies
(75-14)	2/6/75	Press Communiqué: Visit of Prime Minister Dr. Williams

Tunisia

(72-59)	5/19/72	Protocol: Trade
(72-92)	8/27/72	Agreement: Economic and technical cooperation
(73-72)	6/5/73	Protocol: Dispatch of medical teams
(74-8)	2/7/74	Protocol: Trade

(74-50)	7/14/74	Accord: Economic and technical cooperation
(74-99)	12/7/74	Exchange of Notes: Local expenditure
(77-20)	2/25/77	Exchange of Notes: Credit for the canal project
(77-83)	9/10/77	Contract: Canal building
(79-56)	5/17/79	Agreement: Trade

Turkey

(71-38)	5/8/71	Press Communiqué: Diplomatic relations
(71-82)	8/4/71	Joint Communiqué: Establishment of diplomatic relations
(72-99)	9/15/72	Agreement: Air transportation
(74-51)	7/16/74	Agreement: Trade
(74-85)	10/27/74	Agreement: News exchange
(80-170)	11/18/80	Agreement: Cultural exchange for 1981-82

Uganda

| (70-66) | 9/5/70 | Protocol: Economic and technical cooperation |
| (73-101) | 9/15/73 | Contract: Trade |

United Kingdom

(72-20)	3/13/72	Joint Communiqué: Exchange of ambassadors
(73-84)	7/2/73	Agreement: Exhibition of PRC archaeological finds
(77-104)	12/?/77	Agreement: Ship inspection
(78-171)	11/10/78	Agreement: Scientific Cooperation
(78-173)	11/15/78	Agreement: Scientific and technical cooperation
(78-174)	11/15/78	Protocol: Scientific and technical cooperation
(78-184)	12/6/78	Agreement: Deposit facilities
(79-30)	3/4/79	Agreement: Economic cooperation
(80-39)	3/13/80	Memorandum: Understanding in health cooperation
(80-169)	11/11/80	Memorandum of Understanding: Cooperation in agricultural science and technology

U.S.A.

| (72-15) | 2/28/72 | Joint Communiqué: Visit of President Nixon |
| (73-21) | 2/22/73 | Communiqué: Visit of Dr. Kissinger |

(73-127)	11/14/73	Communiqué: Visit of Dr. Kissinger
(74-98)	11/29/74	Communiqué: Visit of Dr. Kissinger
(78-10)	1/22/78	Accord: Trade payments among banks
(78-96)	6/ /78	Contract: Accepting regular tourists
(78-128)	9/ /78	Agreement: Development of undersea oil resources
(78-170)	11/9/78	Agreement: Building hotels
(78-188)	12/16/78	Joint Communiqué: Establishment of diplomatic relations effective 1/1/79
(79-16)	1/31/79	Agreement: Cultural cooperation
(79-17)	1/31/79	Agreement: Scientific, technological cooperation
(79-18)	2/1/79	Joint Press Communiqué: Visit of Vice-Premier Deng
(79-19)	2/1/79	Letters of Understanding: Cooperation in education, agriculture, and space
(79-20)	2/1/79	Accord: Cooperation in high energy physics
(79-21)	2/1/79	Agreement: Mutual establishment of consular relations and opening of consulates
(79-43)	5/8/79	Protocol: Cooperation in science and technology
(79-45)	5/8/79	Protocol: Atmospheric science and technology
(79-46)	5/8/79	Protocol: Metrology and standards
(79-47)	5/8/79	Protocol: Fishery and marine science and technology
(79-48)	5/10/79	Agreement: Trade exhibition in 1980
(79-50)	5/11/79	Agreement: Settlement of claims on assets
(79-52)	5/14/79	Draft: Agreement on trade relations
(79-69)	6/22/79	Protocol: Medicine and public health
(79-75)	7/7/79	Agreement: Trade relations
(79-95)	8/28/79	Protocol: Hydroelectric power and water resources
(79-96)	8/28/79	Accord (implementation): Cultural exchange 1980, 1981
(79-117)	10/31/79	Protocol: Friendly relationship of Hupeh and Ohio
(80-11)	1/24/80	Protocol: Cooperation in earth sciences
(80-12)	1/24/80	Protocol: Cooperation in earthquake studies
(80-13)	1/24/80	Accord: Scientific and technical cooperation
(80-14)	1/24/80	Document: Cooperation in agriculture
(80-15)	1/24/80	Memorandum: Understanding between two academies
(80-18)	1/29/80	Agreement: Freight service
(80-20)	1/31/80	Agreement: Sister-city relationship
(80-23)	2/1/80	Agreement: Most-favored-nation trade status
(80-24)	2/5/80	Protocol: Environmental protection

(80–28)	2/12/80	Agreement: Olympic coins
(80–31)	2/25/80	Agreement: Sister-city relationship
(80–41)	3/15/80	Protocol: Annex to U. S. –Sino Hydroelectric Protocol
(80–91)	6/10/80	Accord: Friendship between Anhui and Maryland
(80–108)	7/10/80	Program: High energy physics collaboration
(80–111)	7/10/80	Plan: Cooperation in high energy physics
(80–114)	7/25/80	Agreement: Exports of Chinese textile products to U. S.
(80–130)	9/8/80	Agreement (initial): Civil air transport
(80–138)	9/17/80	Agreement: Civil aviation
(80–139)	9/17/80	Agreement: Establishing consulates
(80–140)	9/17/80	Agreement: Textiles
(80–141)	9/17/80	Agreement: Maritime trade
(80–151)	10/9/80	Agreement: International express mail
(80–152)	10/9/80	Agreement: Parcel post
(80–159)	10/22/80	Agreement: Grain trade
(80–163)	10/30/80	Exchange of Notes: Investment insurance
(80–183)	12/11/80	Agreement: Scientific cooperation

U. S. S. R.

(66–23)	4/4/66	Agreement: Air transport
(66–24)	4/4/66	Exchange of Notes: Air transport
(66–29)	4/19/66	Protocol: Exchange of goods
(66–70)	6/27/66	Plan for cultural cooperation
(66–109)	11/6/66	Protocol: Scientific and technical cooperation
(67–33)	7/27/67	Protocol: Exchange of goods
(69–36)	8/8/69	Minutes: Border river navigation
(69–43)	10/18/69	Communiqué: Border
(70–48)	7/10/70	Agreement: Border river navigation
(70–96)	11/22/70	Agreement: Exchange of goods and payments
(70–97)	11/23/70	Protocol: Delivery of goods
(70–104)	12/19/70	Summary: Border river navigation
(71–84)	8/5/71	Agreement: Exchange of goods and payments
(72–68)	6/13/72	Agreement: Exchange of goods and payments
(73–27)	3/5/73	Summary: Navigation
(73–92)	8/1/73	Agreement: Exchange of goods and payments
(73–93)	8/1/73	Exchange of Notes: Mutual supply of goods
(74–23)	3/21/74	Minutes: Border river transport
(74–38)	5/15/74	Agreement: Exchange of goods and payments
(75–69)	7/24/75	Agreement: Exchange of goods and payments
(76–35)	5/21/76	Agreement: Exchange of goods and payments

(77–78)	7/21/77	Agreement: Exchange of goods and payments
(77–90)	10/6/77	Minutes: Border river navigation
(78–55)	4/17/78	Agreement: Exchange of goods and payments
(79–34)	3/27/79	Minutes: Boundary River Navigation
(79–86)	8/6/79	Agreement: Goods exchange and payment for 1979
(80–3)	1/5/80	Contract (?): Purchase of Soviet helicopters and planes
(80–82)	6/6/80	Agreement: Trade and payment agreement for 1980

Upper Volta

(73–99)	9/15/73	Joint Communiqué: Establishment of diplomatic relations
(73–100)	9/15/73	Agreement: Economic and technical cooperation
(73–141)	12/3/73	Agreement: Economic and technical cooperation
(74–96)	11/22/74	Protocol: Agricultural cooperation
(76–22)	3/31/76	Protocol: Dispatch of medical teams
(77–62)	6/4/77	Minutes: Building a stadium
(78–1)	1/6/78	Certificate: Handing over of Banford rice plantation center

Venezuela

(72–136)	11/17/72	Minutes: Foreign trade talks
(74–47)	6/28/74	Joint Communiqué: Establishment of diplomatic relations

Vietnam (N)

(66–1)	1/6/66	Exchange of Notes: Exchange of goods in the border area
(66–2)	1/6/66	Exchange of Notes: Small scale trading in the border area
(66–14)	3/21/66	Protocol: Border railway
(66–32)	4/22/66	Protocol: Scientific and technical cooperation
(66–52)	5/28/66	Plan for cultural cooperation
(66–75)	7/2/66	Agreement: Agricultural aid
(66–92)	8/21/66	Plan for cooperation between academies of sciences
(66–95)	8/29/66	Agreement: Economic and technical aid

(66-100)	10/12/66	Plan for cooperation in public health work
(66-106)	10/23/66	Minutes: Talks on scientific and technical cooperation
(66-117)	11/23/66	Agreement: Mutual supply of goods and payments
(66-118)	11/23/66	Exchange of Notes: Exchange of goods in the border area
(66-119)	11/23/66	Exchange of Notes: Small-scale trading in the border area
(67-17)	4/25/67	Plan for cultural cooperation
(67-24)	5/31/67	Exchange of Notes: Changing ruble to people currency
(67-34)	8/3/67	Protocol: Scientific and technical cooperation
(67-35)	8/5/67	Agreement: Economic and technical aid
(67-44)	10/5/67	Agreement: Mutual commodity supply and payment
(67-45)	10/5/67	Exchange of Notes: Small scale trading in the border area
(67-46)	10/5/67	Exchange of Notes: Exchange of goods in the border area
(68-13)	3/18/68	Protocol: Border railway
(68-54)	7/23/68	Agreement: Economic and technical aid
(68-62)	9/30/68	Agreement: Mutual supply of goods and payments
(68-63)	9/30/68	Exchange of Letters: Exchange of goods in the border area
(68-64)	9/30/68	Exchange of Letters: Small-scale trading in the border area
(69-38)	9/26/69	Agreement: Economic aid
(69-45)	10/23/69	Agreement: Exchange of goods and payments
(69-46)	10/25/69	Communiqué: Visit of Premier Pham Van Dong
(69-52)	11/23/69	Agreement: Mutual goods supply and payments
(69-53)	11/26/69	Exchange of Letters: Small scale trading in border areas
(70-12)	3/14/70	Protocol: Scientific and technical cooperation
(70-31)	5/25/70	Protocol (supplementary): Economic and military aid
(70-68)	10/6/70	Agreement: Economic and technical aid
(70-69)	10/6/70	Protocol: Military aid
(70-85)	10/31/70	Agreement: Mutual supply of goods and payments
(70-86)	10/31/70	Protocol: Supply of material
(70-87)	10/31/70	Protocol: Aid
(70-88)	10/31/70	Protocol: Working conditions for PRC experts
(70-89)	10/31/70	Protocol: Delivery of equipment, etc.

(71-11)	2/15/71	Agreement: Economic and military aid
(71-15)	2/22/71	Protocol: Economic and military aid
(71-18)	3/8/71	Joint Communiqué: Visit of Premier Chou En-lai
(71-49)	5/30/71	Agreement: Air transport
(71-65)	7/4/71	Protocol: Supply of military equipment
(71-74)	7/31/71	Protocol: Scientific and technical cooperation
(71-75)	7/31/71	Plan for scientific cooperation
(71-93)	9/27/71	Agreement: Economic and military aid
(71-127)	11/25/71	Joint Communiqué: Visit of Premier Pham Van Dong
(71-134)	12/5/71	Agreement: Mutual supply of goods and payments
(71-135)	12/5/71	Protocol: Supply of general goods
(71-136)	12/5/71	Protocol: Supply with complete projects
(71-137)	12/5/71	Protocol: Providing relief material
(72-5)	1/22/72	Protocol: Supply of military equipment
(72-72)	6/28/72	Agreement: Economic and military aid
(72-73)	6/28/72	Protocol: Supply of general materials
(72-74)	6/28/72	Protocol: Supply of military equipment
(72-142)	11/26/72	Agreement: Economic and military aid
(72-143)	11/26/72	Protocol: Military equipment
(72-161)	12/23/72	Protocol: Scientific and technical cooperation
(72-163)	12/27/72	Protocol: Supply of projects
(72-164)	12/27/72	Protocol: Supply of general goods
(72-165)	12/27/72	Agreement: Supply of goods and payments
(73-73)	6/5/73	Plan of public health cooperation
(73-75)	6/8/73	Agreement: Economic and military aid
(73-78)	6/11/73	Joint Communiqué: Visit of Premier Pham Van Dong
(73-108)	10/5/73	Protocol: Supply of military equipment
(73-113)	10/19/73	Agreement: Mutual supply of goods and payments
(73-114)	10/19/73	Protocol: Aid
(73-115)	10/19/73	Protocol: Supply of general goods
(73-140)	11/30/73	Plan for scientific cooperation
(74-24)	3/23/74	Protocol: Scientific and technical cooperation
(74-32)	4/21/74	Protocol: Border railway transport
(74-78)	10/24/74	Plan for public health cooperation
(74-79)	10/26/74	Agreement: Mutual supply of goods and payments
(74-80)	10/26/74	Agreement: Economic and military aid
(74-81)	10/26/74	Protocol: Supply of general goods
(74-82)	10/26/74	Protocol: Supply of military equipment
(74-88)	11/5/74	Agreement: Broadcasting and television cooperation

(75-35)	4/19/75	Protocol: Border railway
(75-80)	9/25/75	Agreement: Loan
(75-89)	9/25/75	Protocol: Supply of general goods
(75-103)	10/25/75	Agreement: Mutual supply of goods and payment
(75-123)	12/1/75	Protocol: Scientific and technical cooperation
(76-40)	6/3/76	Plan for scientific cooperation
(76-49)	6/13/76	Protocol: Railway transport
(77-23)	3/10/77	Plan for cooperation in public health
(77-28)	3/19/77	Agreement: Mutual supply of goods and payments
(77-69)	6/11/77	Protocol: Railway
(78-3)	1/10/78	Agreement: Mutual supply of goods and payments
(78-51)	4/12/78	Protocol: Border railway

Vietnam (S)

(69-42)	10/15/69	Joint Communiqué: Visit of President Hguyen Huu Tho
(73-1)	1/1/73	Joint Communiqué: Visit of Foreign Affairs Minister
(73-88)	7/19/73	Agreement: Economic aid
(73-128)	11/20/73	Agreement: Economic aid
(73-130)	11/21/73	Joint Communiqué: Visit of President Tho
(73-146)	12/28/73	Agreement: Mutual exemption of visa
(74-115)	12/28/74	Agreement: Economic aid

Yemen (N)

(66-36)	5/ /66	Protocol: Economic and technical cooperation
(66-47)	5/23/66	Plan for cultural cooperation
(68-51)	7/9/68	Settlement (Final): Printing and dyeing mill
(72-29)	3/16/72	Minutes: Building a hospital
(72-80)	7/21/72	Agreement: Economic and technical cooperation
(72-84)	7/27/72	Communiqué: Visit of Prime Minister Aini
(75-87)	9/24/75	Credentials: Handing over Sanaa Industrial Technical School
(76-98)	12/23/76	Agreement: Economic and technical cooperation
(77-63)	6/7/77	Protocol: Dispatch of medical teams
(78-189)	12/19/78	Protocol: Building conference hall
(79-94)	8/18/79	Contract: Road construction
(79-136)	12/26/79	Accord: Transformation and expansion of the San'a textile factory

(80–25)	2/7/80	Protocol: Trade in 1980-84
(80–58)	4/23/80	Agreement: Cultural exchanges and cooperation
(80–97)	6/22/80	Accord: Repayment by Yemen on Chinese loans

Yemen (S)

(68–4)	1/31/68	Joint Communiqué: Establishment of diplomatic relations
(68–58)	9/24/68	Joint Press Communiqué: Visit of Foreign Minister Dhalai
(68–59)	9/24/68	Agreement: Economic and technical cooperation
(68–60)	9/24/68	Agreement: Trade
(69–30)	7/14/69	Minutes: Secondary technical school
(69–55)	12/4/69	Protocol: Dispatch of medical teams
(70–55)	7/30/70	Protocol: Economic and technical cooperation
(70–56)	7/30/70	Exchange of Letters: Dispatch of PRC experts
(70–58)	8/7/70	Agreement: Economic and technical cooperation
(70–61)	8/14/70	Joint Communiqué: Visit of Chairman of Presidential Council of Southern Yemen
(71–66)	7/6/71	Minutes: Salt plants
(71–67)	7/6/71	Minutes: Cotton textile printing–dyeing enterprise
(71–85)	8/14/71	Minutes: Road construction
(71–86)	8/14/71	Minutes: Bridge construction
(71–87)	8/14/71	Minutes: Drilling wells
(72–3)	1/13/72	Minutes: Building an agricultural machinery factory
(72–78)	7/12/72	Agreement: Economic and technical cooperation
(72–79)	7/17/72	Communiqué: Visit of President Ismail
(73–37)	3/24/73	Minutes: Road construction
(73–112)	10/16/73	Protocol: Dispatch of medical team
(74–94)	11/13/74	Agreement: Economic and technical cooperation
(74–95)	11/20/74	Press Communiqué: Visit of Chairman Ali
(74–41)	5/8/75	Exchange of Notes: Road construction
(76–51)	6/19/76	Certificate: Turning over salt plants
(76–52)	6/19/76	Exchange of Notes: Technical cooperation
(76–64)	7/12/76	Minutes: Building a hospital (gift)
(78–54)	4/15/78	Protocol: Dispatch of a medical team
(78–60)	4/26/78	Agreement: Economic and technical cooperation

Yugoslavia

(66–64)	6/10/66	Protocol: Exchange of goods
(67–40)	8/31/67	Protocol: Exchange of goods

(68-57)	9/13/68	Exchange of Letters: Exchange of goods
(69-11)	3/17/69	Agreement: Trade and payments
(71-42)	5/13/71	Contract: Freighters
(71-58)	6/15/71	Communiqué: Visit of Yugoslavian government delegation
(72-42)	4/14/72	Agreement: Air transport
(73-107)	9/27/73	Agreement: Shipping registration
(74-92)	11/12/74	Agreement: Scientific and technical cooperation
(75-93)	10/12/75	Press Communiqué: Visit of President Bijedic
(75-99)	10/20/75	Protocol: Scientific and technical cooperation
(76-21)	3/27/76	Minutes: Trade
(77-61)	6/4/77	Agreement: Scientific and technical cooperation
(78-16)	2/3/78	Protocol: Opening flight routes
(78-26)	3/5/78	Minutes: Talks on sports cooperation
(78-65)	5/4/78	Minutes: Sino-Yugoslavian Trade Joint Committee
(78-123)	8/26/78	Agreement: Establishment of economic, scientific, and technical cooperation committee
(78-124)	8/26/78	Agreement: Economic, scientific, and technical cooperation
(78-134)	9/18/78	Accord: Scientific cooperation
(78-190)	12/20/78	Plan for education and cultural cooperation
(79-25)	2/24/79	Protocol: Scientific and technical cooperation 1979
(79-27)	3/2/79	Agreement: Scientific and technological cooperation
(79-28)	3/2/79	Agreement: Cooperation in veterinary science
(79-29)	3/2/79	Protocol: Economic, scientific, and technological cooperation
(79-67)	6/19/79	Plan: 1979-80 radio and TV implementation plan
(79-68)	6/19/79	Agreement: Radio and TV cooperation
(79-90)	8/15/79	Agreement: News cooperation and exchange
(80-56)	4/21/80	Protocol: Scientific and technical cooperation 1980
(80-63)	4/30/80	Agreement: Peaceful use of atomic energy
(80-64)	5/2/80	Agreement: Cooperation in compiling photo album
(80-84)	6/6/80	Accord: Plant protection and quarantine
(80-85)	6/6/80	Accord: Economic cooperation
(80-94)	6/18/80	Agreement: Friendship city between Shanghai and Zagreb
(80-156)	10/14/80	Agreement: Friendship between Peking and Belgrade
(80-167)	11/8/80	Agreement: Cooperation in marine shipping

Zaire

(72-139)	11/19/72	Joint Communiqué: Normalization of relations
(73-8)	1/14/73	Agreement: Economic and technical cooperation
(73-9)	1/14/73	Agreement: Trade
(73-12)	1/20/73	Press Communiqué: Visit of President Banga
(74-27)	4/10/74	Agreement: Maritime transport
(74-44)	5/31/74	Agreement: Air transport
(74-100)	12/8/74	Joint Communiqué: News exchange
(76-80)	10/19/76	Minutes: Constructing a sports stadium
(77-60)	6/1/77	Minutes: Building a rice growing station
(79-13)	1/20/79	Protocol: Supply of diversified commodities to Zaire
(80-47)	3/26/80	Agreement: Cultural exchange and cooperation

Zambia

(66-93)	8/22/66	Joint Press Communiqué: Visit of Vice-President Kamanga
(66-94)	8/22/66	Agreement: Cultural cooperation
(67-19)	4/28/67	Agreement: Trade
(67-27)	6/23/67	Agreement: Economic and technical aid
(67-28)	6/26/67	Joint Communiqué: Visit of President Kaunda
(67-41)	9/5/67	Agreement (with Tanzania): Tanzania-Zambia railway construction
(68-22)	4/8/68	Protocol (with Tanzania): Railway survey and design
(68-23)	4/8/68	Protocol (with Tanzania): Working conditions for experts
(68-24)	4/8/68	Protocol (with Tanzania): Loan
(68-29)	4/27/68	Agreement (with Tanzania): Loans for railway construction
(68-30)	4/27/68	Protocol (with Tanzania): Railway construction
(69-6)	2/14/69	Exchange of Letters: Road construction
(69-49)	11/14/69	Agreement (supplementary) (with Tanzania): Railway construction
(69-50)	11/14/69	Proposal (supplementary) (with Tanzania): Railway
(69-51)	11/14/69	Minutes (with Tanzania): Railway
(69-57)	12/31/69	Exchange of Letters: Providing broadcasting equipment
(70-5)	1/30/70	Minutes: Highway construction
(70-6)	1/30/70	Exchange of Notes: Working conditions for experts

(70-15)	3/23/70	Minutes: Construction of a broadcasting station
(70-16)	3/23/70	Plan for construction of a broadcasting station
(70-49)	7/12/70	Protocol (with Tanzania): Loan for railway construction
(70-50)	7/12/70	Protocol (with Tanzania): Railway
(70-51)	7/12/70	Minutes (with Tanzania): Railway construction
(71-144)	12/22/71	Summary (with Tanzania): Talks on the railway construction
(73-66)	5/28/73	Certificate: Transferring a broadcasting station
(74-18)	2/24/74	Agreement: Economic and technical cooperation
(75-84)	9/18/75	Minutes (with Tanzania): Tanzania-Zambia Railway
(75-128)	12/15/75	Certificates (with Tanzania): Handing over the railway training school, etc.
(76-62)	7/8/76	Protocol (with Tanzania): Railway
(76-63)	7/8/76	Minutes (with Tanzania): Railway
(76-65)	7/14/76	Certificate (with Tanzania): Handing over Tanzania-Zambia railway
(78-104)	7/31/78	Protocol (with Tanzania): Tanzania-Zambia Railway
(78-105)	7/31/78	Protocol (with Tanzania): Building Tanzania-Zambia railway training school
(78-106)	7/31/78	Minutes (with Tanzania): Technical cooperation in building Tanzania-Zambia railway
(79-5)	1/15/79	Agreement: Scientific and technical cooperation
(80-51)	4/11/80	Protocol: Economic and technical cooperation
(80-127)	8/29/80	Protocol: Cooperation on Tazara railway

Zimbabwe

| (80-55) | 4/18/80 | Agreement: Establishment of diplomatic relations |

BILATERAL AGREEMENTS WITH INTERNATIONAL ORGANIZATIONS

Organizations

Afro-Asian Table Tennis
Asian Table Tennis Union
Belgium-Luxembourg Economic Union
European Economic Community
International Satellite-Communications Organization
UN Fund for Population Activities
UN High Commission for Refugees
World Health Organization
World Food Program

Afro-Asian Table Tennis

(71-111)	10/29/71	Press Communiqué: Afro-Asian Table Tennis Tournament
(71-113)	11/1/71	Press Communiqué: Table tennis delegations
(71-117)	11/13/71	Communiqué: Afro-Asian Table Tennis Tournament

Asian Table Tennis Union

(72-49)	5/7/72	Communiqué: ATTU Inauguration meeting
(72-94)	9/11/72	Communiqué: Table Tennis Tournament
(72-95)	9/13/72	Communiqué: Asian Table Tennis Union

Belgium-Luxembourg Economic Union

(79-71)	6/27/79	Draft: Economic, industrial, scientific, and technical cooperation
(79-72)	6/27/79	Protocol (Draft): Cooperation in economy, industry, and technology
(79-73)	6/27/79	Protocol (Draft): Cooperation in science and technology

European Economic Community

(78-17)	2/3/78	Draft: Trade Agreement
(78-46)	4/3/78	Agreement: Trade
(79-83)	7/18/79	Draft: Shipment of Chinese textiles to EEC

International Satellite-Communications Organization

(77-49)   5/2/77   Minutes: Talks on PRC joining International
                        Satellite-Communications Organization

World Health Organization

(78-148) 10/5/78   Memorandum: Public health cooperation

UN Fund for Population Activities

(80-131) 9/9/80   Agreement: Technical assistance to China

UN High Commission for Refugees

(79-118) 11/11/79(?) Agreement: Eighteen million aid program for
                        integration into southern China of more than
                        250,000 refugees

World Food Program

(80-149) 10/4/80   Agreement: Providing food assistance

AGREEMENTS BY
SUBJECT MATTER

This index is based on the general description of subject matter for the entries in the Calendar. Limited mostly to title categories, the headings and subheadings below do not constitute an exhaustive reference to the contents of the PRC agreements. This index should not, therefore, be used as a complete research tool, but only as a reference to the contents of the Calendar.

Reference here is to entry number only. Descriptive references are supplied in the two preceding indexes.

In most cases, in this index we have adhered to the official title of the agreement, but some minor modifications have been made to clarify the exact nature of the contents. General aid agreements, for example, are often described officially as cooperation agreements, in accordance with diplomatic euphemism. Where they are economic or technical in nature, the euphemism is discarded and they are indexed here as aid agreements. Agreements officially described as providing for cooperation in science and technology are indexed under scientific and technical cooperation.

Academies of Sciences, etc.
(see Scientific and technical cooperation)

Accords (see under subject matter and party)

Agreements (see under subject matter and party)

Agriculture (see Scientific and technical cooperation; Aid)

Aid, economic and technical/ general assistance (see headnote); economic, 66-62, 66-102, 67-36, 68-16, 69-38, 70-31, 70-72, 71-88, 72-23, 72-57, 73-5, 73-88, 73-128, 74-112, 76-16, 76-73, 76-77, 77-17; economic and cultural, 66-33, 68-56; economic and military, 71-11, 71-15, 71-94, 72-5, 72-11, 72-72, 72-142, 73-75, 74-80; economic and technical, 66-36, 66-87, 66-95, 66-110, 66-111, 66-125, 67-7, 67-28, 67-35, 67-49, 68-7, 68-54, 68-59, 68-74, 69-40, 69-41, 70-23, 70-38, 70-55, 70-58, 70-59, 70-66, 70-68, 70-80, 70-87, 70-91, 70-94, 70-105, 70-106, 71-4, 71-27, 71-55, 71-60, 71-70, 71-72, 71-97, 71-100, 71-129, 71-142, 72-1, 72-39, 72-52, 72-61, 72-64, 72-75, 72-78, 72-80, 72-86, 72-89, 72-92, 72-98, 72-103, 72-110, 72-111, 72-113, 72-118, 72-119, 72-123, 72-127, 72-130, 72-138, 72-156, 72-167, 73-8, 73-20, 73-39, 73-64, 73-79, 73-80, 73-82, 73-100, 73-105, 73-122, 73-137, 73-141, 74-6, 74-11, 74-18, 74-26, 74-50, 74-53, 74-60, 74-62, 74-68, 74-70, 74-94, 74-99, 74-101, 75-10, 75-15, 75-16, 75-23, 75-62, 75-68, 75-75, 76-18, 76-20, 76-39, 76-43, 76-55, 76-66, 76-67, 76-69, 76-75, 76-86, 76-98, 77-1, 77-18, 77-64, 77-71, 77-73, 77-80, 77-84, 77-91, 77-98, 77-114, 78-36, 78-55,

78-58, 78-62, 78-67, 78-68, 78-75, 78-87, 78-95, 78-105, 78-110, 78-126, 78-134; economic and trade, 76-74; material, 70-31, 70-40, 70-76, 70-86, 71-24, 71-94, 71-137, 72-71, 75-58; medical (see Medical aid); technical, 66-91, 68-70, 71-23, 71-104, 72-135, 73-11, 73-103, 74-67, 76-52, 78-71, 79-49, 80-83, 80-131; unspecified, 71-104, 71-136, 73-111

Aid, economic and technical/ specific forms and problems; agriculture, 66-75, 72-3, 74-116, 74-117, 78-48, 79-31, 79-42; certificate of job completion, 80-83; commodities, 79-13; credit, 67-62, 70-3, 72-151, 72-152, 79-54, 79-54, 79-57, 80-60, 80-80; experts and technical training, 66-105, 70-6, 70-56, 70-88, 71-25, 71-68, 78-8; food, 80-149; gift, 71-83, 78-63; goods, 71-135, 72-164, 73-107, 74-81, 75-89; handing over (turnover), 68-19, 68-65, 69-2, 69-20, 70-17, 70-35, 70-100, 73-33, 75-77, 75-116, 75-124, 76-63, 76-81, 76-91, 77-9, 77-19, 77-22, 77-27, 77-42, 77-52, 77-99, 77-101, 78-1, 78-5, 78-18, 78-19, 78-24, 78-30, 78-42, 78-45, 78-80, 78-93, 78-194, 79-31, 79-42, 79-49, 80-173; loan, 66-63, 66-102, 66-112, 66-114, 67-37, 68-23, 68-28, 68-65, 68-69, 69-7, 70-33, 70-67, 70-73, 70-77, 70-95, 70-99, 71-48, 71-110, 71-125, 71-132, 72-8, 72-18, 72-32, 72-38, 73-90, 74-4, 74-13, 75-

20, 75-55, 75-88, 76-10, 77-11, 77-95, 80-9, 80-61, 80-62, 80-97, 80-112, 80-177; loan (settlement), 73-71; loan (specific projects), 70-49, 72-40, 72-100, 72-140, 77-20, 79-10; military aid, 70-63, 70-69, 71-93, 74-37; military and material aid, 71-65, 72-74, 72-143, 73-4, 73-108, 74-82; miscellaneous, 73-74, 78-27, 78-112, 78-113, 78-191; specific aid projects, 66-59, 66-66, 66-68, 66-99, 67-13, 67-21, 67-23, 67-38, 67-41, 67-60, 67-65, 68-5, 68-51, 68-55, 68-61, 69-6, 69-10, 69-12, 69-25, 69-30, 69-37, 69-49, 69-54, 69-56, 70-5, 70-15, 70-16, 70-20, 70-28, 70-57, 71-6, 71-18, 71-35, 71-66, 71-67, 71-69, 71-85, 71-86, 71-87, 71-131, 71-140, 72-4, 72-29, 72-76, 72-81, 72-114, 73-14, 73-22, 73-23, 73-31, 73-37, 73-38, 73-66, 73-83, 73-94, 73-129, 73-139, 74-49, 75-4, 75-5, 75-11, 75-25, 75-41, 75-76, 75-131, 75-132, 75-134, 76-12, 76-19, 76-30, 76-31, 76-34, 76-51, 76-60, 76-64, 76-74, 76-80, 76-82, 76-93, 76-97, 76-101, 77-13, 77-33, 77-51, 77-57, 77-60, 77-62, 77-66, 77-68, 77-75, 77-83, 77-112, 78-21, 78-28, 78-32, 78-46, 78-52, 78-70, 78-93, 78-97, 78-140, 78-158, 78-181, 78-186, 79-87, 79-94, 79-118, 80-173; supply of plants, material, equipment, etc., 66-99, 68-68, 68-69, 69-55, 70-75, 70-89, 71-23, 71-24,

73-11, 77-67, 75-57, 76-100,
78-7, 79-99, 79-105, 79-133,
79-136, 80-154

Arrangements (see under subject
matter and party)

Articles of Agreement, M-42,
M-43, M-45

Aviation, civil; communications,
66-55; cooperation, 72-114;
Convention on International
Civil Aviation, M-15, M-16,
M-17, M-18, M-19, M-20,
M-21, M-47; general (transport, air service), 66-23, 66-
24, 66-54, 66-108, 69-47, 71-
50, 72-33, 72-36, 72-42, 72-
82, 72-85, 72-99, 72-115, 72-
137, 73-2, 73-56, 73-57, 73-
63, 73-69, 73-76, 73-124, 73-
125, 74-29, 74-44, 74-57, 74-
105, 75-3, 75-37, 75-91, 75-
106, 75-116, 78-85, 78-92,
78-96, 78-123, 78-176, 79-11,
79-44, 79-62, 79-78, 80-18,
80-66, 80-67, 80-113, 80-
130, 80-138; membership in
ICAO Council, M-15; miscellaneous, 72-60, 74-59, 77-
34, 77-65, 79-62; opening
flight routes, 73-126, 77-72,
77-76, 78-16, 78-147, 79-62;
safety, M-48, M-49; technical
service, 66-85, 73-76, 75-2

Bank, International; World Bank,
M-43

Banking (see also Payments;
Currency; Trade), 73-16,
70-45, 79-54, 80-116, 80-168

Boat-building (see Navigation)

Boundaries and border (see also
Trade; Navigation; Railway);
inspection, 67-59, 78-76, 78-
128, 79-26, 79-98, 79-122;
landmark, 72-93; use of boundary waters, river transport,
70-34, 71-21, 72-83, 73-91,
74-114, 76-5, 77-15, 77-41,
78-13, 79-23, 79-34, 80-17,
80-72

Certificate of job completion
(see Aid)

Charter of the United Nations,
M-1

Claims settlement, 79-50

Collaboration (see Scientific and
technical cooperation)

Commerce (see Trade)

Constitution, M-2, M-4, M-9,
M-13, M-27

Consular, 71-37, 75-67, 78-66,
78-129, M-35

Constructions; factory, 79-99;
headquarters of Revolutionary
Party, 80-37; hotel, 79-79;
nuclear power station, 80-157

Contracts (see under subject
matter and party)

Convention, Multilateral, M-3,
M-5, M-6, M-11, M-12,
M-14, M-23, M-24, M-25,
M-26, M-29, M-30, M-34,
M-35, M-36, M-37, M-40,
M-41, M-47, M-48, M-49

Cooperation (see Friendship;
Cultural cooperation; Scien-
tific and technical cooperation;
Aid, economic and technical)

Copyright (see Cultural cooperation)

Credit (see Aid)

Cultural organizations (see
cultural cooperation)

Cultural cooperation/ general
exchange; cultural, 66-94,
67-8, 75-82, 78-133, 78-161,
79-16, 79-40, 79-76, 79-97,
79-112, 79-121, 80-29, 80-
47, 80-58, 80-65, 80-79,

80-88, 80-92, 80-101, 80-
104, 80-119, 80-120, 80-126,
80-137, 80-142, 80-161, 80-
181; cultural and economic,
72-87, 79-15; cultural and
education, 78-187, 80-125;
cultural and scientific, 68-
17, 70-60, 73-52, 79-18, 79-
108
Cultural cooperation/exchange
by specific forms, problems;
copyright, 79-92; corre-
spondents, 69-10, 80-148;
cultural life, 80-148; exhibition, trade fair, 73-36, 73-
84, 73-117, 73-121, 73-138,
74-22, 76-8, 76-47, 76-53,
76-54, 76-59, 79-48, 80-69;
information, materials, 79-
92, 79-106, 80-21, 80-81;
music, 80-148; news agen-
cies, 66-58, 68-21, 68-44,
74-85, 75-100, 78-159, 79-
90, 79-93, 79-106, 79-123,
80-144, 80-148; news cooperation (general), 72-45, 72-
56, 74-100, 78-30, 78-60,
78-88, 78-152, 80-52, 80-
148; news items, 80-52, 80-
148; news device, 79-90;
personal exchange, specialists, (in general), 79-15, 80-
81; photo album compiling,
80-64; radio and television,
66-61, 66-127, 68-35, 71-
102, 72-17, 74-88, 75-86,
78-29, 78-125, 78-148, 79-
67, 79-68, 79-123, 80-118,
80-171, 80-189; sending
teachers, 72-58
Cultural cooperation/ plans for
exchange, etc. , Communist
partners, 66-7, 66-10, 66-
43, 66-52, 66-70, 66-71,
66-73, 66-83, 66-97, 67-15,

67-17, 79-67; non-communist
Afro-Asian partners, 66-27,
66-30, 66-34, 66-40, 66-41,
66-44, 66-47, 66-48, 66-57,
66-60, 66-65, 67-39, 67-42,
78-11, 80-135, 80-165, 80-
170; others, 66-35, 78-149;
cultural and economic, 66-32;
cultural and scientific, 66-21
Currency; payments, 67-18, 67-
24, 70-37, 71-44, 71-53;
trade, 71-29

Diplomatic Relations, Vienna
Convention, M-26 (see also
Friendship)
Dispatch of medical teams (see
Medical aid)

Economic Aid (see Aid, economic and technical)
Economic council, 80-4
Economic cooperation; economic,
79-30, 79-39, 79-111, 80-85,
80-86; economic and technical,
79-33, 79-59, 79-61, 79-82,
79-100, 79-127, 80-5, 80-
50, 80-51, 80-71, 80-78, 80-
95, 80-102, 80-105, 80-115,
80-117, 80-133, 80-162;
economic, technical, and industrial, 79-15, 79-72, 80-
145, 80-164, 80-76; economic,
technical, and scientific, 79-
29; economic, technical, scientific, and industrial, 79-
63, 79-71; economic and
trade, 80-10
Educational cooperation, 79-19
Exchange of goods (see Trade)
Exemption of taxes (see Tax
exemptions)
Exhibition (see Cultural cooperation)
Export credit (see Trade)

Fair (see Cultural cooperation; Trade)

Fisheries and marine; bilateral, 70-39, 70-109, 70-110, 72-35, 72-155, 73-81, 75-72, 79-47; others, 75-78, 79-8

Food and Agricultural Organization, M-9

Friendship, etc.; communiqués (lower-level talks), 71-143, 72-40, 73-44; diplomatic relations, 66-3, 71-101, 72-16, 72-55, 72-139, 75-64; M-26, M-35; embassies and consulates, 72-20, 75-12, 78-129, 79-21, 79-113, 80-22, 80-124, 80-139, 80-158; establishment of diplomatic relations, 70-70, 70-71, 70-92, 70-98, 70-103, 71-10, 71-22, 71-26, 71-38, 71-47, 71-71, 71-82, 71-89, 71-106, 71-114, 71-115, 71-116, 71-138, 71-139, 71-141, 72-6, 72-12, 72-13, 72-29, 72-43, 72-63, 72-71, 72-102, 72-106, 72-112, 72-116, 72-128, 72-133, 72-141, 72-146, 72-157, 72-159, 72-166, 73-99, 74-21, 74-28, 74-42, 74-46, 74-47, 74-52, 74-56, 74-106, 75-1, 75-48, 75-53, 75-65, 75-92, 75-110, 75-113, 75-118, 76-26, 76-36, 76-58, 76-71, 76-79, 77-16, 77-38, 77-58, 78-72, 78-104, 78-185, 79-1, 79-21, 79-24, 79-70, 79-135, 80-26, 80-55, 80-98; formal treaties [peace and friendship], 78-108; friendly cities, friendly relations, friendly cooperation, 79-32, 79-117, 79-126, 80-91, 80-94, 80-96, 80-156; friendship association, 80-35; joint communiqués (high-level talks on general policy alignment, closer cooperation, etc.), [Communist partners, 66-42, 66-71, 67-48, 68-58, 69-42, 69-46, 70-21, 70-61, 71-19, 71-56, 71-58, 71-77, 71-109, 71-127, 72-79, 72-162, 73-1, 73-17, 73-65, 73-78, 74-19, 74-71, 74-91, 74-95, 75-14, 75-38, 75-93], [Arab countries, 72-82], [other Asian countries, 66-22, 66-25, 66-28, 67-57, 68-9, 68-42, 70-24, 70-25, 70-90, 70-93, 71-63, 71-96, 71-103, 71-125, 72-7, 72-77, 73-126, 73-139, 74-37, 74-41, 75-43, 75-74, 75-120, 76-37, 77-3], [other African countries, 66-93, 67-9, 67-28, 67-53, 68-39, 71-73, 73-12, 73-42, 74-39, 74-61, 75-17, 76-88, 79-1; others, 72-15, 73-21, 73-53, 73-96, 73-114, 73-123, 75-119, 78-98, 79-24, 79-70, 79-135]; miscellaneous, 66-80, 66-101, 78-140; office of diplomatic representative, 79-15; official links of friendship, 79-125; sister-cities, 80-20, 80-30, 80-31, 80-45, 80-160; strengthen friendly relations, 80-142, 80-160; specialized agencies, M-37; table tennis friendship tournament, 71-111, 71-113, 71-117, 72-25, 72-26, 72-49, 72-94, 72-95; talks, 68-26, 71-7, 71-16, 71-58, 72-31

Gifts, Grants (see Aid)

Government officials conference, 80-178

Health (see Scientific and technical cooperation; Medical aid)
Highways (see also Construction—road), 66-72, 67-23, 67-65, 68-61, 70-4, 71-18

Information exchange (see Scientific and technical cooperation; Cultural cooperation)
Insect pests (see Scientific and technical cooperation)
Instruments (see Trade)
Insurance, 73-52, 80-163
Intellectual Property, M-41
Intergovernmental Maritime Consultative Organization, M-7, M-23, M-36, M-38
International Bank for Reconstruction and Development (World Bank), M-43
International Development Association, M-44
International Finance Corporation, M-45
International Monetary Fund, M-42

Joint communiqués (see under subject matter and party)
Joint press communiqués (see under subject matter and party)
Joint statements (see under subject and matter and party)
Joint stock companies; coal, 80-132; elevator, 80-42; jewelry, 80-99; shipping/ maritime transport, 66-31, 66-82, 67-22, 68-43; 69-29, 70-22, 72-37, 72-117, 74-34, 76-91, 77-35, 78-51, 79-91, 80-43
Joint venture construction, 79-107, 79-134

Labor power, 80-150
Land reclamation, 80-8
Loan Lines (see Navigation)
Loans (see Aid, economic and technical)

Mail (see Postal services and telecommunications)
Maritime trade (see Trade)
Maritime transport (see Navigation)
Medical aid, 67-56, 67-64, 67-66, 68-34, 69-55, 70-11, 70-13, 70-47, 70-102, 72-91, 72-101, 72-108, 73-45, 73-67, 73-72, 73-112, 73-134, 74-102, 74-103, 74-112, 75-27, 75-39, 75-79, 76-22, 76-33, 76-61, 76-70, 77-37, 77-52, 77-59, 77-63, 78-42, 78-53, 78-57, 79-102, 79-115, 80-90, 80-110
Metrology, 79-41, 79-46, 79-116, M-13, M-29, M-30
Military (see Aid, economic and technical)
Miscellaneous, 79-15, 79-84, 80-81, 80-107

Navigation; boat-building, 80-1; boundary waters, 69-36, 70-4, 70-48, 70-104, 71-123, 73-10, 73-27, 73-147, 74-23, 74-113, 77-5, 77-90, 78-13, 79-23, 79-34; joint stock companies, 66-31, 68-4, 69-29, 70-22, 72-37, 72-117, 74-34, 76-88, 77-35, 78-51; maritime transport, 66-4, 66-104, 72-109, 73-15, 73-62, 74-27, 74-45, 74-55, 74-75, 74-93, 75-7, 75-31, 75-67, 75-71, 75-77, 75-90, 75-105, 75-114, 76-17, 76-25, 77-7, 78-79, 78-

80, 78-177, 78-182, 79-60, 80-167; shipping (general), 66-38, 72-46, 72-48, 73-96, 80-147; miscellaneous, 75-32, 76-72; technical services, 80-107

News agencies (see Cultural cooperation)

News cooperation (see Cultural cooperation)

Nuclear Weapons, M-10, M-22

Parcels (see Postal services and telecommunications [postal])

Payments (see also Trade); general, 66-74, 66-98, 68-3, 68-49, 68-50, 70-2, 70-85, 71-40, 71-79, 73-47, 76-45, 77-30, 79-57, 80-187; noncommercial, 66-124; trade payments, 78-10

Peaceful use of atomic energy (see Scientific and technical cooperation)

Photo album (see Cultural cooperation)

Plans (see under subject matter and party)

Planes, helicopters (see Trade)

Plant diseases (see Scientific and technical cooperation)

Pollution, M-40

Postal services and telecommunications; express mail, 80-151; general, 74-74, 75-47, 76-3, 78-173; postal, 71-146, 71-147, 80-152; telecommunications, 71-90, M-5, M-28, M-32, M-33; Universal Postal Convention, M-6

Program (see under subject matter and party)

Protocols (see under subject matter and party)

Press communiqué (see under subject matter and party)

Radio and television (see Cultural cooperation)

Railways; bilateral and trilateral, 67-41, 68-13, 68-38, 69-49, 70-51, 71-143, 76-2, 76-49, 76-63, 77-69, 78-90, 78-92, 79-22, 80-127; border, 66-14, 70-84, 71-130, 72-104, 72-105, 73-97, 73-109, 73-119, 74-32, 74-77, 74-84, 75-35, 75-94, 75-108, 76-68, 77-81, 77-82, 78-48, 78-177, 79-97, 79-103; others, 68-22, 68-23, 68-30, 69-50, 69-51, 70-50, 75-84, 76-62, 78-101

Refugees, 79-118

Rescue at sea, 71-64

River transport (see Navigation; Boundaries)

Safety of life at sea, M-11, M-24

Satellite ground station, 80-16

Scientific cooperation, 71-76, 73-40, 73-131, 73-132, 75-28, 75-54, 75-130, 78-127, 78-130, 79-53, 79-131

Scientific and technical cooperation (see headnote); academies of sciences, etc. [agreements, 79-53, 80-172, 80-183]; [plans, etc., for cooperation] (Communist partners, 66-49, 66-51, 66-88, 66-92, 67-63, 70-79, 71-31, 72-134, 73-140, 74-87, 76-99, 78-162, 80-174); (non-communist partners, 78-155, 78-157, 78-168, 79-65, 79-101, 80-15, 80-24, 80-153, 80-176); agriculture, 74-96, 74-116, 74-117, 75-80, 75-83, 79-

18, 79-19, 79-104, 80-14,
80-143, 80-169; animal diseases (see veterinary); atmospheric, 79-45; atomic energy
(peaceful use), 80-63, 80-74,
80-75; cultural, scientific,
and technical (see also Cultural cooperation), 70-60,
79-108; earthquake studies,
80-12; earth science, 80-11;
electronics research and production, 80-89; electrical
engineering, 80-68; fishery
and marine, 79-47; general
cooperation agreement [Com-
munist partners, 66-81, 67-
43, 75-129, 77-61, 78-65,
78-112, 79-27], non-communist partners, 75-81, 76-38,
76-96, 78-9, 78-33, 78-41,
78-106, 78-150, 78-153, 78-
170, 78-179, 79-5, 79-17,
79-63, 79-120, 80-77, 80-87];
geological, 79-37, 79-66, 79-
130; health, 80-39, 80-74,
80-166; high energy physics,
79-18, 79-20, 80-108, 80-111;
hydroelectric power, 79-95,
80-41, 80-154; information,
79-43, 80-81; insect pests
and plant diseases, 72-149,
78-119, 78-165, 80-84; med-
icine, 79-69, 80-39, 80-90;
management, 79-43; mineral
resources, 79-37, 79-54, 79-
99; miscellaneous projects,
71-108, 71-121, 72-155, 73-
60, 73-95, 75-52, 76-92, 77-
49, 78-49, 78-113, 78-119,
78-180; petroleum, oil, 78-
90, 78-125, 80-38; plans,
protocols, etc. , for cooperation (general), [Communist
partners, 66-32, 66-53, 66-
67, 66-76, 66-79, 66-89, 66-

90, 66-106, 66-107, 66-109,
66-122, 67-10, 67-34, 67-
50, 67-52, 67-58, 68-6, 70-
1, 70-12, 70-83, 70-101, 71-
75, 71-105, 71-145, 72-24,
72-53, 72-107, 72-160, 72-
161, 73-48, 73-49, 73-68,
78-70, 73-106, 73-120, 73-
132, 74-22, 74-63, 74-65,
74-83, 74-89, 74-92, 74-111,
75-95, 75-96, 75-99, 75-100,
75-112, 75-123, 75-124, 76-
27, 76-81, 76-87, 76-89, 77-
14, 77-97, 77-102, 77-103,
78-83, 78-141, 78-169, 78-
171, 78-172, 79-25, 79-29,
79-119, 79-132, 80-56, 80-
128, 80-136, 80-170; [non-
communist partners, 75-115,
76-90, 77-8, 77-107, 78-154,
78-156, 78-164, 79-18, 79-
35, 79-41, 79-43, 79-64,
79-71, 79-73, 79-110, 79-
128, 79-129, 80-13, 80-70,
80-73, 80-134, 80-175, 80-
188]; public health work, 66-
100, 67-67, 72-150, 73-73,
74-9, 74-78, 75-138, 77-23,
77-47, 78-145; seabed cable,
73-55; space, 79-18, 79-19;
subsoil exploration (see geological); veterinary science,
66-56, 78-116, 79-28; water
conservation, 76-60, 77-13,
77-66, 79-95; Yalu River
power plant, 70-34, 71-21,
72-83, 73-91, 74-114, 76-5,
77-15, 77-41, 78-13

Ship inspection, 77-32, 77-44,
77-104, 78-144, 80-123
Shipment (see Trade)
Shipping, 73-96, 75-98, 75-104,
76-28, 76-32, 77-115, 78-
74, 78-118, 78-139 (see also

Navigation)
Ship registration, 73-107
Sister-cities (see Friendship)
Sports, 73-6, 73-7, 73-43, 78-
    26, 78-56, 78-84
Standardization cooperation,
    79-46, 79-80, 79-81

Tax exemptions, 77-64
Teachers (see Cultural
    cooperation)
Technical aid (see Aid, eco-
    nomic and technical)
Technical cooperation, 79-22,
    79-49, 79-116, 80-1, 80-
    106, 80-107, 80-122
Telecommunications (see Postal
    services and telecommunica-
    tions)
Television and radio (see Cul-
    tural cooperation)
Textile (see Trade)
Tibet, 66-3, 66-37
Tourism, 76-78, 78-94, 78-
    115, 78-162, 78-167, 79-
    79, 80-21
Trade; barter, 66-77, 70-2;
    border trade, 67-51, 68-64,
    70-29, 71-49, 72-50, 73-59,
    75-50, 76-29, 76-48, 77-79,
    78-86; commodity transac-
    tions (rice, meat, steel,
    papers, fertilizer, etc.),
    [Communist partners, 75-
    104], [noncommunist part-
    ners, 66-26, 66-121, 66-
    128, 67-1, 67-11, 68-67,
    69-19, 69-21, 69-26, 69-39,
    69-48, 70-9, 70-32, 70-46,
    70-62, 70-64, 71-2, 71-3,
    71-98, 75-78, 78-43, 78-81,
    78-82, 78-121, 78-137, 78-
    146, 79-83, 79-109, 80-6,
    80-150, 80-159]; compensa-
    tion trade agreement, 79-137;

cotton, 80-121; crude oil,
    79-4; establishment of trade
    missions, 73-50, 74-73, 74-
    76, 75-9, 75-107, 78-166,
    80-93; exchange of goods
    (also mutual supply of goods,
    etc.), [Communist partners,
    66-19, 66-29, 66-64, 66-123,
    67-33, 67-40, 68-36, 68-57,
    69-3, 70-10, 70-52, 70-81,
    70-82, 70-85, 70-108, 71-12,
    71-54, 71-91, 71-148, 72-51,
    72-153, 73-24, 73-93, 74-33,
    74-110, 75-34, 75-121, 76-
    11, 76-83, 77-70, 78-25, 78-
    61, 78-190, 79-89, 80-40,
    80-54, 80-81], [noncommunist
    Afro-Asian partners, 66-120,
    66-126, 67-55, 69-1, 69-4,
    69-44, 71-1, 72-34, 72-159,
    73-13, 73-145, 74-30, 75-
    42, 76-41, 77-39, 77-94, 78-
    38, 78-188, 79-8]; exchange
    (mutual supply, etc.) of goods
    and payments, [Communist
    partners, 66-6, 66-8, 66-13,
    66-15, 66-17, 66-96, 66-114,
    66-117, 67-3, 67-4, 67-14,
    67-26, 67-29, 67-44, 67-61,
    67-68, 68-8, 68-18, 68-20,
    68-25, 68-31, 68-33, 68-45,
    68-62, 68-72, 69-28, 69-33,
    69-34, 69-45, 69-52, 70-36,
    70-42, 70-43, 70-53, 70-65,
    70-74, 70-78, 79-96, 71-13,
    71-28, 71-33, 71-43, 71-45,
    71-51, 71-84, 71-128, 71-
    133, 72-10, 72-21, 72-27,
    72-44, 72-47, 72-68, 72-131,
    72-144, 72-165, 73-26, 73-
    28, 73-30, 73-34, 73-92, 73-
    113, 73-135, 73-144, 74-5,
    74-12, 74-16, 74-20, 74-25,
    74-37, 74-66, 74-79, 74-104,
    74-107, 75-8, 75-18, 75-19,

75-22, 75-56, 75-69, 75-103, 75-126, 75-133, 76-1, 76-4, 76-7, 76-9, 76-15, 76-35, 77-6, 77-10, 77-26, 77-28, 77-45, 77-50, 77-55, 77-56, 77-78, 77-113, 78-3, 78-4, 78-6, 78-14, 78-23, 78-54, 79-2, 79-3, 79-7, 79-12, 79-14, 79-86, 80-32, 80-44, 80-46, 80-48, 80-49, 80-53], [noncommunist Afro-Asian partners, 67-31, 68-1, 80-33, 80-57, 80-59]; exchange of goods by local state-owned trading companies in border areas, 66-1, 66-118, 67-46, 68-63; export credit, 80-19; general conditions for delivery of goods (see also shipment), [Communist partners, 66-9, 66-16, 66-18, 66-20, 67-5, 67-25, 67-30, 68-26, 68-32, 68-52, 69-23, 69-24, 69-32, 69-35, 70-19, 70-44, 70-54, 79-97, 71-34, 75-51, 72-22, 72-28, 72-132, 72-145, 73-35, 73-133], [noncommunist partners, 79-83]; import and export, 71-118, 72-127, 73-116, 75-101, 78-165, 79-54, 79-109, 80-114; long-term trade, 79-4, 79-36, 79-58, 79-76, 80-33, 80-34; labor-power, 80-150; maritime trade, 80-141; miscellaneous, 68-14, 69-14, 72-146, 75-64, 75-119, 78-73, 78-109, 78-175, 80-150; machinery, 80-7; most-favored-nation status, 79-138, 80-23, 80-103; Olympic coins, 80-28; miscellaneous, 68-14, 69-14, 72-146, 75-64, 75-119, 78-73, 78-109, 78-175; promotion of trade

relations, 66-4, 68-15, 71-119, 72-64, 75-59, 75-107, 76-23; plans, helicopters, 80-3; shipment, 79-83; small scale trading in border areas, 66-2, 66-119, 67-45, 68-64, 69-53; talks, 66-45, 68-66, 69-16, 71-36, 71-46, 71-59, 71-62, 71-92, 71-120, 72-120, 72-125, 72-136, 73-58, 73-123, 74-15, 76-50, 78-64; textile, 79-136, 80-114, 80-140; trade (general), [Communist partners, 66-50, 67-12, 68-52, 68-60, 69-5, 69-22, 69-27, 70-41, 71-29, 71-39, 71-41, 72-19, 73-19, 73-32, 74-48, 75-40, 76-13, 76-21, 76-44, 76-46, 77-24, 77-25, 77-42, 78-35, 78-114, 79-9, 80-36, 80-185, 80-186], [noncommunist Afro-Asian partners, 66-3, 66-5, 66-11, 66-37, 66-46, 66-78, 66-112, 66-116, 67-7, 67-19, 68-10, 68-28, 68-37, 68-40, 68-41, 69-8, 69-17, 70-7, 70-26, 70-27, 70-30, 71-5, 71-9, 71-32, 71-99, 71-107, 71-124, 72-2, 72-9, 72-14, 72-54, 72-59, 72-69, 72-70, 72-90, 72-97, 72-121, 72-124, 72-126, 73-9, 73-18, 73-89, 73-104, 73-110, 73-111, 73-126, 74-1, 74-7, 74-14, 74-54, 74-64, 74-69, 75-13, 75-21, 75-26, 75-45, 75-49, 75-63, 75-97, 75-102, 75-111, 75-135, 76-56, 76-57, 76-85, 77-46, 77-74, 77-77, 77-96, 78-11, 78-20, 78-22, 78-34, 78-40, 78-59, 78-69, 78-107, 78-138, 78-151, 78-183, 79-4, 79-36, 79-55, 79-56, 79-58, 79-76,

79-138, 80-25, 80-27, 80-33,
80-34, 80-57, 80-155, 80-
184, 80-182], [Arab countries
(including Sudan), 66-39, 66-
86, 67-20, 68-46, 68-47, 69-
9, 69-15, 70-14, 71-20, 71-
78, 72-30, 72-62, 72-147,
73-85, 74-51, 74-97, 75-45,
75-122, 76-24, 77-21, 77-29,
77-31, 77-54, 78-39, 78-131,
79-38, 79-51, 79-88, 80-150],
[others, 67-16, 68-2, 69-13,
69-18, 70-8, 71-8, 71-122,
72-67, 72-87, 73-25, 73-51,
74-10, 74-108, 74-109, 75-
125, 76-96, 77-12, 77-100,
78-2, 78-17, 78-45, 78-77,
78-91, 78-137, 78-143, 79-
6, 79-52, 79-75, 79-114, 80-
23, 80-146]; trade and payments, [Communist partners,
69-11, 70-18, 71-13, 74-2,
80-82], [noncommunist partners, 66-12, 67-54, 68-11,
68-48, 70-107, 71-73, 71-
81, 71-95, 71-112, 72-66,
72-96, 72-122, 72-154, 72-
168, 73-41, 73-46, 73-61,
73-86, 73-102, 74-31, 74-43,
75-46, 76-14, 77-2, 77-40,
77-93, 79-57]; trade fair,
79-48, 80-69; trade and economic cooperation, 80-10

Trademark registration, 67-2,
73-3, 73-87, 74-72, 74-90,
75-29, 75-30, 75-31, 75-33,
75-51, 75-66, 75-70, 75-127,
77-4, 77-36, 77-67, 77-89,
78-15, 78-78, 79-85
Transportation (see Aviation,
civil; Railways; Navigation;
Highways)

Understanding between agricul-
tural ministers, 80-129
United Nations Charter, M-1
United Nations Educational,
Scientific, and Cultural
Organization, M-2

Vietnam, M-8
Visas, 73-146

Warsaw Convention (Interna-
tional Air Transportation),
M-25
Water Conservation, 76-60,
77-73, 77-66
Waters (see Boundaries)
Weights and measures (see
Metrology)
Women, M-47
World Health Organization,
M-4, M-13, M-27
World Meteorological Organiza-
tion, M-3

ABOUT THE AUTHOR

HUNGDAH CHIU (S. J. D. , Harvard Law School) is professor of law at the University of Maryland School of Law. He is the author of The Capacity of International Organizations to Conclude Treaties and The People's Republic of China and the Law of Treaties. He is coauthor of People's China and International Law: A Documentary Study, which was awarded a certificate of merit by the American Society of International Law in 1976. He has also edited China and the Question of Taiwan (1973), The Chinese Connection and Normalization (1979), and China and Taiwan Issue (1979), and coedited Agreements of the People's Republic of China, 1949-1967: A Calendar, and Law in Chinese Foreign Policy and contributed to American Journal of International Law, International and Comparative Law Quarterly, China Quarterly, Journal of Asian Studies, Asian Affairs, Journal of Criminal Law and Criminology, OsteuropaRecht, Journal of Ocean Development and International Law, Issues and Studies, and Review of Socialist Law.